Managing People
Sport Organizations

Books in the Sport Management Series

Managing People in Sport Organizations

A strategic human resource management perspective

Tracy Taylor, Alison Doherty and Peter McGraw

AMSTERDAM • BOSTON • HEIDELBERG • LONDON • NEW YORK • OXFORD
PARIS • SAN DIEGO • SAN FRANCISCO • SINGAPORE • SYDNEY • TOKYO

Butterworth-Heinemann is an imprint of Elsevier

Butterworth-Heinemann is an imprint of Elsevier
Linacre House, Jordan Hill, Oxford OX2 8DP, UK
30 Corporate Drive, Suite 400, Burlington, MA 01803, USA

First edition 2008

British Library Cataloguing in Publication Data
A catalogue record for this book is available from the British Library

Library of Congress Cataloging-in-Publication Data
A catalog record for this book is available from the Library of Congress

ISBN: 978-0-7506-8229-9

For information on all Butterworth-Heinemann publications
visit our web site at http://books.elsevier.com

Typeset by Charon Tec Ltd (A Macmillan Company), Chennai, India
www.charontec.com

Transferred to Digital Printing in 2011

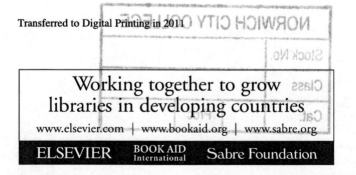

Contents

Contents

Contents

List of Figures

List of Tables

Series Editor

Dr. Russell Hoye is an Associate Professor in the School of Sport, Tourism, and Hospitality Management, La Trobe University, Victoria, Australia. Russell has been involved in sport management education since 1993, working in Australia at La Trobe University, Griffith University, and Victoria University and in China with The University of Hong Kong and Tsinghua University. He is a board member of the Sport Management Association of Australia and New Zealand (SMAANZ). He was the Guest Editor for the inaugural special issue of *Sport Management Review* on professional sport in Australia and New Zealand published in 2005.

Russell's areas of expertise include corporate governance, organizational behaviour, volunteer management and public sector reform within the sport industry. He has acted as a consultant for the Australian Sports Commission, Sport and Recreation Victoria and a number of local government and non-profit organizations. His research interests focus on examining how governance is enacted with sport organizations and how volunteers engage with and are managed by sport organizations. He has published papers on these topics in journals such as *Nonprofit Management and Leadership*, *Sport Management Review*, *European Sport Management Quarterly*, *Society and Leisure*, *International Gambling Studies*, *Third Sector Review*, *Sporting Traditions*, *Managing Leisure*, *Football Studies*, *Annals of Leisure Research*, and the *Australian Journal on Volunteering*.

Sport Management Series Preface

Many millions of people around the globe are employed in sport organizations in areas as diverse as event management, broadcasting, venue management, marketing professional sport, and coaching as well as in allied industries such as sporting equipment manufacturing, sporting footwear and apparel, and retail. At the elite level, sport has moved from being an amateur pastime to a significant industry. The growth and professionalization of sport has driven changes in the consumption and production of sport and in the management of sporting organizations at all levels of sport. Managing sport organizations at the start of the twenty-first century involves the application of techniques and strategies evident in the majority of modern business, government, and non-profit organizations.

The *Sport Management Series* provides a superb range of texts for the common subjects in sport business and management courses. They provide essential resource for academics, students and managers, and are international in scope. Supported by excellent case studies, useful study questions, further reading lists, lists of websites and supplementary online materials such as case study questions and PowerPoint slides, the series represents a consistent, planned, and targeted approach which:

- provides a high-quality, accessible, and affordable portfolio of titles which match management development needs through various stages;
- prioritizes the publication of texts where there are current gaps in the market, or where current provision is unsatisfactory;
- develops a portfolio of both practical and stimulating texts in all areas of sport management.

The *Sport Management Series* is the first of its kind, and as such is recognized as being of consistent high quality and will quickly become the series of first choice for academics, students, and managers.

Preface

The strategic management of human resources in contemporary sport organizations is a challenging task in the context of changing technologies, workforce composition and work patterns, community expectations, employee expectations, employment legislation, and the increasing impact of global competition. This book examines different approaches to strategic human resource management (SHRM) that can help sport organizations respond to these challenges. This book attempts to locate these approaches within various theoretical and regulatory contexts. At the operational level the book explores the day-to-day activities of front line managers and supervisors in hiring, motivating, rewarding, and retaining both employees and volunteers. This book, therefore, is written for students who are planning a career in sport organizations generally rather than in human resource management (HRM) specifically it is also useful resource for sport management practitioners.

SHRM is about the overall process of managing people in organizations, so that they are motivated and able to perform to their potential and thus maximize the overall effectiveness of the organization in meeting its goals. SHRM provides an integrated framework for making decisions about the people in an organization, who to appoint, how to reward good performance, what motivates people to perform to their full capacity, how to determine training and development needs, and when to let people go. This book introduces the basics of SHRM and how the SHRM approach conceptualizes the fundamentals of hiring, performance appraisal, compensation systems, and other HR functions.

This book discusses the contemporary sport organization and how an SHRM perspective can help it to attain its goals. In parallel with this, it considers today's people management challenges and opportunities and the effective management of individuals who come to work and volunteer in sport organizations, by addressing such aspects as their competencies, personality, needs, values, and beliefs. The nature and attributes of workgroups in which individuals find themselves will also be considered as this is a fundamental part of the context of HRM in sport organizations.

Acknowledgements

We would like to acknowledge Francesca Ford for her assistance and encouragement in the preparation of the manuscript and Russ Hoye, the series editor for his support. We would also like to thank those who helped to make the production of this book possible, with particular thanks to Lily Liu, Karina Sherwood and Ruskin Lavy. Finally, we are indebted to the following individuals for providing field examples and cases that have enriched the book:

Julie Kim (Chapter 2, IMG in Korea)

Eric MacIntosh, Doctoral Student, The University of Western Ontario (Chapter 5, GoodLife Fitness Clubs Inc.)

Robert Jefferies, Volunteer Support Officer, British Cycling Manchester (Chapter 6, From the field – Training Officials in British Cycling)

Shannon Hamm, Doctoral Student, The University of Western Ontario (Chapter 8, Royal Canadian Golf Association)

Katie Misener, Doctoral Student, The University of Western Ontario (Chapter 8, Camp Pinnacle)

1 Introduction

Learning objectives

After reading this chapter you will be able to:

- Identify the unique challenge of managing people in sport organizations
- Understand the general concept of human resource management (HRM) and how it has evolved historically from personnel management
- Identify the key human resource (HR) issues that affect sport organizations
- Explain how the HRM perspective affects HR policies and practices
- Describe how effective HRM contributes to the sustainability of sport organizations

In this chapter the concept of HRM will be introduced in the context of a short historical overview of its evolution from personnel management. The case will be made that contemporary HRM techniques are the most effective methods of increasing performance in modern organizations, particularly in the service sector. We will overview some key issues relating to the effective management of both paid staff and volunteers. This chapter concludes with a discussion of various elements of HRM and where these are covered in the remaining chapters of this book.

Managing sport organizations

There has been much written about the unique nature of sport and the organizations associated with its delivery. The premise underpinning the inimitability of sport relates to its ability to engender irrational passions and emotional attachments, despite the often variable quality of the product. This is evidenced in the devoted fans who continue to support their favourite team through product purchases and spectator attendance even though the team is in the bottom half of the competition ladder, the organization is financially mismanaged, or there are questionable ethics employed in player transfers. There is also the example of the wealthy team owner who continues to sustain massive loses year after year, but is alternatively rewarded by the associated status and sense of benevolence of his or her actions in financially propping up the team! This passion for sport may also be reflected in the individuals who choose to work in the sport industry where, besides professional players, salaries and earning potential tend to be below what the same individuals could earn in jobs unrelated to sport (Parks & Parra, 1994). It is also reflected in the thousands of volunteers who congregate to help stage mega-sport events such as the Olympic Games who provide the backbone of coaches, managers, and administrators running community sport clubs and associations (Cuskelly, Hoye & Auld, 2006).

The sport industry's distinctiveness is further exemplified by the features of intangibility, heterogeneity, and inseparability of production and consumption (Buswell, 2004). By way of illustration, a consumer's valuation of, for example, a professional sports match or a personal training session with a coach or fitness consultant cannot be determined until that person has watched the match or engaged in the training session. This underscores the importance, and organizational challenge, of offering what will be seen as a quality product or service. These distinguishing characteristics of sport combine to create a unique management environment for sport organizations, of which the effective management of people who are working and volunteering for the organization is the most critical. In the same way that getting the best out of the players is the hallmark of a good coach, getting the best out of employees and volunteers is the hallmark of a good manager acting within an effective HR system.

As with many industry sectors there is extensive variability in the scope and size of sport organizations. Organizations dealing with sport range from small locally based volunteer run clubs that have no paid employees, to medium-sized organizations with a mixture of paid staff and volunteers, to multinational corporations that are staffed by a large global workforce. In delineating the sport industry, Hoye et al. (2005) classify sport into three sectors: the public sector, the non-profit or voluntary sector, and the professional or commercial sector. Sport organizations in the public sector include the sport and recreation branches of local, state/provincial, and national governments (e.g., city recreation department, and provincial or federal ministry of sport), as well as government-funded specialist agencies that support such areas as elite athlete or coaching development (e.g., national sports institute). The non-profit or voluntary sector includes such organizations as community-based sport clubs (e.g., local swimming or rugby club), regional and national sport governing bodies (e.g., state or national track and field association), and international sport governing bodies (e.g., International Olympic Committee). The professional or commercial sector includes organizations such as professional sport teams and their governing leagues (e.g., Boston Celtics and the National Basketball Association (NBA)), sport apparel and equipment manufacturers and retailers (e.g., Nike, and SportChek, Canada), and sport stadia and facilities (e.g., Rod Laver Arena, Australia; Wembley Stadium, UK; Maracana Stadium, Brazil).

People management issues, processes, and practices are inexorably linked to the orientations of these sport organizations. Some examples of sport organizations, their missions, and their staffing requirements are presented in Figure 1.1 using the Hoye et al. (2005) industry sectors framework.

HRM considerations are shaped by the environment in which the sport organization is located. The environment includes not only the sector but also the geographical location and cultural context. This operating context presents both opportunities and challenges for sport organizations.

In the public sector, government policy and legislation can support, regulate, or dictate activities. At the general level this can impact sport organizations through the financial resources available from government sources for employing staff, to more specific operational implications such as mandatory police checks of all employees and volunteers who work with children under Child Protection Legislation. Non-profit and voluntary organizations inevitably have to grapple with volunteer management challenges. Organizations with a workforce consisting of both paid employees and volunteers require an approach to managing people that recognizes the different perspectives, motivations, and capacity that each group brings to the organization. A volunteer workforce can provide sport organizations with additional resources to perform vital roles as officials, umpires, coaches, team managers, administrators, facility and grounds managers, registration and accreditation officers, fundraisers, and event managers, to name just a few. The challenge is to recruit sufficient volunteers and to retain their services. The importance of volunteers to the sport sector has been well recognized and there are now many well-developed volunteer management programmes and initiatives in countries such as Australia, Canada, New Zealand, the US, and across Europe.

Professional and commercial sport organizations have challenges such as meeting customer expectations and stakeholder demands via an effective workforce. Contemporary sport businesses are now asking questions about where to invest in HR and what types of HR activities will bring a long-term, strategic benefit to the organization. Professional sport organizations have to deal with complex HR matters related to player trades and acquisitions,

Sector	Organization	Mission	Typical staffing profile
Public	National Institute of Sport	To develop elite sport on a national basis with a particular focus on success at the Olympic Games and World Championships	Paid Staff – Head Coach, Executive Director, Technical and administrative support staff, Nutritionist, Sport psychologist Board of Directors – appointed by government
Voluntary	Youth Sport Club	To provide an appropriate supportive environment for youth to enjoy sport in an atmosphere of fun, sportsmanship, democracy, and peace	Volunteers – large numbers in a range of roles. Coach, Manager, Event organizer, Fund raising, Promotion, Maintenance, Legal, Accounting, Risk management Paid administrative staff – limited number (e.g., Executive Director) Volunteer Board of Directors
Non-profit Membership based	Local Golf Club	To be financially self-sustaining while providing an quality experience to members and guests with a commitment to exceptional perceived value through loyalty, growth, leadership and community citizenship	Paid staff – Chief Executive Officer (CEO), Golf Professional, Green Keeper, Catering staff, Administration. Volunteer Board of Directors
Commercial	Sport & Fitness Centre	To inspire our members to achieve their fitness goals with the finest fitness equipment, knowledgeable instructors and a safe, fun, and friendly atmosphere	Paid staff – Administration, Aquatics, Dance & Fitness Instructors, Management, Operations, Personal Training, Reception, Sales
Professional	Sports Franchise	Dedicated to winning Championships, growing new fans, and providing superior entertainment, value and service.	Paid staff – CEO, Vice President, management, Marketing and Broadcasting, Legal & Financial, Administrative and support staff Head Coach, training and sport operations staff Medical Staff Stadium staff Community and event day volunteers Governance – Chair, Board members

4 **Figure 1.1** Sport organization sectors and staffing.

salary caps, and team contract negotiations. In many sport-specific organizations there are also dilemmas about whether to recruit staff for their technical expertise or skills irrespective of their sporting background or their knowledge of the sport.

Regardless of sector or size, successful sport organizations require an approach to managing people, both on and off the field, which ensures that each individual realizes his/her potential and one that leverages capabilities across groups and that provides a rewarding work environment.

Contemporary sport organizations

Increased globalization, commercialization, and accountability in the sports industry over the past few decades have led sport organizations to adopt more sophisticated management systems and become more 'business' oriented. These forces have shaped the scale and delivery of sporting competitions, the ways in which sports are organized, managed and governed, and the multidirectional flow of athletes, coaches, managers, and executives across local, national, and international locations. Significant change can be found in sport organizations in countries where fundamental political and ideological shifts have occurred (e.g., China, Russia) or where government funding in the provision of sport has been tied to restructured sport delivery systems and increased accountability for that funding (e.g., Canada, Australia, New Zealand). We have seen sports assume professional status (e.g., Rugby Union, Triathlon, Snowboarding) and existing professional clubs develop global brand equity (e.g., Manchester United, AC Milan). There has been increasing transnational movement of athletes and coaches in professional sport, and global management of these personnel (e.g., IMG, Octagon). We have seen the growth and increasing sophistication of chain organizations (e.g., Fitness First which operates in 15 countries), and in organizations that deliver major sport events (e.g., Organizing Committees for the Olympic Games, the FIFA World Cup). A vast array of specialist providers associated with sport spectatorship has also emerged (e.g., Global Spectrum – facility management; Nevco – sport scoreboards/displays).

The shift in the way sport has been traditionally organized may be most evident in bodies such as provincial/state and national level representative sport organizations where a growing number of paid staff have been appointed in roles traditionally held by volunteers (Auld, 1997; Kikulis, 2000). The classic example of this is the national sport organization (NSO). These organizations were traditionally managed by former athletes and sport enthusiasts with a passion for the sport and the NSO's measures of success were tied to on-field success and participant numbers rather than operational effectiveness. Changes to the sport environment have meant that increasingly NSO employees are selected for their technical or professional expertise in managing a business irrespective of their knowledge of the sport, and board members are recruited for their business acumen and not their sporting prowess.

As a sport develops, it is important to remain cognizant of how the sport organization has evolved, its cultural context, its origins and core values, who its stakeholders are, and how staffing and HR policies can be used to meet its mission and goals for the future.

The people management challenge in sport organizations

Human resources are of critical importance, alongside other valuable intangibles of a sport organization such as brand value and customer relationships. Attracting, developing, and retaining talented people can provide a sport organization with the resources it needs to prosper, grow, and ultimately, gain competitive advantage. For example, the right coach or manager, a dynamic CEO, or a new key player can transform the fortunes of a sport organization in a short period of time from the bottom of the pile into a league or world champion.

The attraction, retention, and development of high calibre people is a source of competitive advantage for sport organizations. Getting the right people into the organization is a vital step in creating this competitive advantage. This means being able to identify the best mix of technical, team, and leadership skills and abilities required for the organization. The 'best mix' is the combination that will allow the organization to meet its strategic objectives now and into the future. Recruiting the right people into the organization can provide the basis for improved efficiency, increased productivity, and higher morale in the workforce. Such people are likely to be motivated to give their best and will deliver the flexibility and commitment that most sport organizations seek.

Retention of talented employees and volunteers is one of the most important challenges for sport organizations today. Retention is often linked to issues of motivation, satisfaction, positive morale, and appropriate rewards and recognition. Therefore, it is important to find out what creates motivated, committed, and contributing employees and volunteers. Structuring a reward and recognition system that is aligned with the organization's strategic direction can contribute to positive employee and volunteer motivation, morale, and retention. Training and developing employees and volunteers can create a more positive organizational culture by adding value to its key resources, and underpins a commitment to organizational learning and its associated benefits. Training and development of individuals will also assist the sport organization to satisfy current and future HR needs.

Retaining good employees and volunteers also contributes to customer satisfaction and facilitates greater sport consumption. Effective succession planning and talent management will also be of increasing importance, as over the next few years the Baby Boomers (40–58 years old now) will retire, and the much smaller cohort of upcoming Generation Xers (25–34 years old now) will mean that there are significantly fewer people available to work.

How well sport organizations cope with the future challenges facing them will depend to a large degree on how well they can manage people to succeed in new ways of working and how successfull they are at negotiating associated changes. Irrespective of the nature and degree of current and future people management challenges, the importance of attracting, developing, motivating, retaining, rewarding, and managing the 'right' people needed to optimize the sport organization's performance is central to effective human resource management (HRM).

What is HRM?

Human Resource Management is broadly defined as the policies, practices, procedures, and systems that influence the behaviour, attitudes, values, and performance of people who work for the organization. An organization's HRM system at its most basic level administers people management systems which support broader organizational activities. In other words the HRM system follows strategic decisions taken in the mainstream business and ensures that such decisions can be implemented effectively by coordinating the people-related aspects of them. To be effective the HRM system must be both aligned with the strategic direction of the organization and be internally consistent. Strategic HRM takes this idea one step further by integrating HRM decisions into the strategic decision making process so that it no longer just implements strategy, but actually helps to define and enable it in the first instance. The concept of SHRM is discussed in detail in Chapter 2 of this book.

The HRM system within an organization can be shaped by many factors depending on the type of organization (e.g., public or private sector), the external environment in which the organization operates (e.g., the nature of the labour market), and the choices made by the organization about how work is organized (e.g., the extent to which rewards are equally shared within the organization). As a result of these factors and choices there will be different HR configurations within different organizations.

Before we consider a model of HRM it is useful to briefly outline the evolution of the concept from personnel management. This brief history is useful for three reasons. First, it helps us to understand how HRM is conceptually different from personnel management. Second, it helps us to understand how different HR functions have evolved historically at different times and as a result of different external pressures. Third, it helps us to understand that personnel and HR practices have been shaped by key theoretical advances which are to this day important underpinnings of practice and which will be referred to again in the various chapters of this book outlining different HR practices.

7

The evolution of the HRM concept

HRM in practice varies greatly between sport organizations, from those with modern HRM techniques that are integrated, and strategic to others that are still implementing an older style personnel model. In a study of Australian non-profit sport organizations, Taylor and McGraw (2006) found that only a minority had formal HRM systems in place and few organizations took a truly strategic approach. Similarly, at the community sport level, Cuskelly et al. (2006) reported that the use of HRM practices with volunteers varied significantly across community sport organizations. In order to better understand the continuum along which HRM is located the following section will briefly outline the history of the two concepts.

Personnel management has existed in some form or other since large groups of people began to be organized to work for a common purpose. The first formal personnel practices were implemented during the late Victorian period in the UK with the emergence of welfare workers who administered practices such as sick pay schemes, subsidized canteens, and worker education programmes. The earliest innovators in the welfare movement were philanthropists such as Robert Owen, who built a model industrial community at New Lanark. Later innovators were the highly religious Victorian entrepreneurs such as Rowtree, Cadbury, Lever, Salt, and Boot (Watson, 1977). The social reformist orientation of this group was based on a Christian concern for the well-being of the worker coupled with recognition that improved welfare for workers would also enhance the performance of the business. Cadbury explicitly made this connection describing welfare and efficiency as 'two sides of the same coin' (Legge, 1995: 11). These early initiatives led eventually to the establishment in 1913 of the Institute of Welfare Officers in the UK (now the Institute of Personnel and Development) and employee welfare continues to be a part of the HR in contemporary organizations.

New elements were added to the personnel role around the time of the First World War with the widespread introduction of scientific management (Legge, 1995). Scientific management was associated with the ideas of the American Fredrick Taylor whose lifework revolved around scientifically studying the way that work was performed and how it could be made more efficient by finding the 'one best way' to complete a task. Taylor's work led to the advent of highly efficient standardized production techniques into factories with a pronounced division of labour, so that jobs became simple and could be easily learned by relatively unskilled workers. Although Taylor's ideas were widely criticized as leading to 'dehumanization' of work, because jobs became so simple, repetitive, and boring, the efficiency gains from scientific management were so great that it was adopted in industrial countries around the world and laid the foundation for job design for the remainder of the century. Working with the principles of scientific management, personnel specialists became involved with the analysis, design, evaluation, and classification of jobs on the one hand and the use of this information in

8

the administration of wages and salaries, particularly piecework bonus schemes which were also advocated by Taylor, on the other. Involvement with job design and compensation is a major part of the HR role in modern organizations. The application of scientific management to the design of jobs is discussed more fully in Chapter 3 of this book.

Also evident from around the time of the First World War, and the consequent need for greater efficiencies in armament and munitions factories, was a greater focus on environmental factors such as lighting, heating, and ventilation, and their relationship with worker productivity. The focus on these factors and others associated with finding the best match between workers and jobs saw the emergence of the industrial psychology profession and also laid the foundation for the ongoing involvement of HR staff in occupational health and safety matters.

The next major movement to influence the practice of personnel management was the human relations movement which was associated with the motivation theories of the Harvard Professor, Elton Mayo. Human relations focused on the importance of building the social identification of workers with each other and with the organization as a whole as a way of stimulating higher levels of motivation and hence productivity. Human relations work involved initiatives designed to foster better cooperation within and between groups, and stronger identification of employees with the overall goals of the organization. Human relations quickly became popular and a strong influence on the practice of personnel management because it provided a strong counter-force against the alienating side effects of scientific management, and many elements of human relations are still practiced by the HR staff today, particularly those associated with building high performance teams.

The period following the Second World War saw the growth of legal, administrative, and industrial relations components of the personnel function. This occurred in the tight, highly unionized labour markets associated with the long post-war boom which existed in developed countries around the globe. Legge (1995) identified three key developments in the overall role of personnel departments (from the 1960s onwards). First, the emergence of a role concerned with organizational efficiency. The emphasis was on creating clear objectives in jobs and fostering wider organizational commitment. Legge (1995) has suggested that the aim was the development of an open, flexible work culture that could fit more easily with the demands of a changing business environment. Involvement in organizational development and attempts to build cultures high on trust were characteristics of this period.

Second, the emergence of a role dealing with the legalities associated with, increasingly complex, employment law. This has been termed as a 'legal wrangling' role by Torrington (1989). Personnel managers often became experts in interpreting the rights of employers, employees, and trade unions during this era of high union membership and influence. The third role, 'manpower analyst', was concerned with achieving the tightest fit between resources and organizational needs, and encompassed forecasting and implementing plans associated with future needs for manpower (Torrington, 1989).

9

These developments overlapped, and in some cases complemented, the emergence of the HRM movement.

Early approaches to HRM

Increasing levels of global competition in the 1980s focused attention on HRM in North America (Guest, 1987; Legge, 1995). In particular growing competitive pressure from Japan stimulated a response from organizations in the USA (Tichy, Fombrum & Devanna et al., 1982; Fombrum, Tichy & Devanna et al., 1984; Beer, Spector, Lawrence, Quinn & Walton , 1985), which focused on ways of replacing adversarial labour relations with more collaborative relationships. The patterns of collaboration between management and labour developed in Japan were admired by many American managers, at least in terms of outcomes, and inspired in USA a call for improvements in management–union–employee relations. Alongside this change in management thinking was pressure from workers with higher levels of education to be more involved in their organizations (Guest, 1987).

In response to these developments, a new course was developed in HRM at the Harvard Business School. This move reflected the understanding that managers required a new set of skills to cope with future organizational challenges. The authors have described the ideas presented as a 'broad causal mapping of the determinants and consequences of HRM policies' (Beer et al., 1985: 15). The projected outcomes of commitment, competence, congruity, and cost effectiveness at organizational level, it was argued, would generate long-term benefits for individuals, organizations, and society, provided there was wholehearted commitment to the effort (Beer et al., 1985). This theoretical development ushered in the use of the term 'human resources management' which defines the area today as well as a conceptual model which has been highly influential in defining the practice of HRM as something very different to old style personnel management.

The Harvard model of HRM

An important analytical framework for understanding HRM has been developed by the scholars at Harvard University (Beer et al., 1984) and is particularly useful for beginning an analysis of HR in sport organizations. This model is shown in Figure 1.2.

The model notes how HRM policy choices and outcomes are influenced by a variety of stakeholder interests and situational factors. Effective HRM involves managers in an appropriate balancing of the claims of the various interest groups whilst responding to almost constant changes in situational factors. The policy choices are what results from the balancing of these interests and factors. Within this model a balance is struck between business and

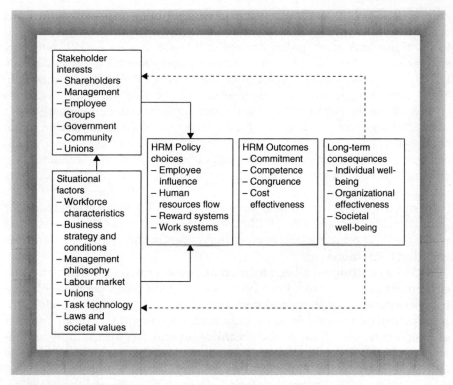

Figure 1.2 The Harvard model (*Source*: Beer et al., 1984).

societal expectations, so whilst organizational strategy has a major influence, other factors such as labour market regulations, community expectations, the characteristics of the workforce and the presence, or absence, of unions are also relevant. The model is dynamic because the balance of interests and factors changes almost constantly.

The model first outlines the various stakeholders of an organization. The influence of respective stakeholders may vary enormously, depending on the type of organization. For example, in community sport organizations, the most important stakeholders are the community sport participants. By contrast, a professional sport franchise has to first and foremost satisfy the interests of shareholders who own the business. In the vast majority of organizations the interests of different stakeholders are contested and subject to subtle shifts which represent a changing point of balance in the interests of the various stakeholders.

The model then focuses on macro-level situational factors influencing the organization, including the workforce characteristics, business strategy and conditions, philosophy of management, the state of the labour market, influence of unions, level of technology employed, and societal laws, norms, and values. These too will change over time and influence a dynamic process of HR change and adaptation to shifts in the external environment. Next, broad HR policy choices are considered. These relate to, for example, the level of

11

employee and volunteer involvement as well as policy choices about reward systems and the way work is structured within the organization. According to the framework these policy choices will result in various HR outcomes such as the level of employee or volunteer commitment, the organization's HR capability, and the overall cost effectiveness of HR within the organization. These outcomes, in turn, have long-term consequences for the individuals who work for the organization, the overall organizational effectiveness and hence its long-term survival, and the contribution of the organization to the community. Finally, a feedback loop is incorporated into the model which can operate both ways. Thus situational factors can not only influence and constrain policy choices but can also be influenced by long-term outputs from the employment process.

In short, the Harvard model provides a useful holistic framework for understanding and analysing HRM within the broad societal context and as well as in relation to specific choices that organization can make about the way that HR is managed.

HRM has traditionally been focused almost exclusively around employees, but has more recently been broadened to include all people who contribute to the work of an organization as reflected in the Harvard model. This is particularly important for sport organizations where a significant number of people who contribute to the organization may be, for example, volunteers or short-term contractors or consultants. Another key feature of HRM is that it incorporates, implicitly or explicitly, the idea that the way that people are managed makes a difference to the bottom line of the organization. In other words organizations that manage their people effectively are more likely to be successful in the marketplace because their HR system confer a competitive advantage. This will lead to superior performance relative to competitor organizations through, for example, faster speed of execution, higher quality of service, and/or more flexibility of response to customer specifications.

The purpose of HRM is to attract the best people to an organization, allocate them to appropriate roles on the basis of their skills and attitudes, manage them so that they can maximize their contribution to the organization, and retain them for an appropriate length of time so as to maximize the contribution from the 'resource'. In this way HRM makes a critical contribution to both the effectiveness and competitiveness of the organization.

It is important to note at the outset that the work of HRM is not undertaken solely by staff employed in the HR department. Much of the management of people in any organization is done on a day-to-day basis by general or line managers. So, for example, whereas HR staff may establish hiring procedures for an organization they should not necessarily be the only ones involved in hiring decisions. Similarly, whereas the performance management system in an organization may be set up and monitored by HR staff, the actual appraisals should be conducted by line managers. In this sense it is useful to view the 'HR function' as a broadly dispersed people management competence in an organization rather than just the activities carried out by specialists in the HR department. It is quite possible to have good HR procedures, but if these are poorly implemented by general managers then the net outcome is poor HRM. When looking at HRM effectiveness in an organization the effectiveness of line managers in managing people must also be considered. This is particularly critical in small organizations where there are limited or no dedicated HR staff.

At its simplest level HRM involves recruiting and selecting the best available staff, getting high productivity from these employees through high commitment management practices, retaining them for longer, maintaining high levels of staff satisfaction and morale through providing them with interesting work, and managing them in a way that generates commitment to the organization and low levels of grievances and associated 'maintenance' costs. Another way of thinking about this is to envisage the most desirable outcomes that organizations want from their staff policies and practices. Effective HRM should produce elicit staff who are creative, loyal to the organization, and committed to its long-term survival, can work independently without extensive supervision and produce high-quality outputs, are flexible in their work practices, and prepared to embrace change.

In synthesizing the work of a number of writers, Guest (1987) summarized the conceptual model of HRM as comprising the following four propositions. First, 'if human resources can be integrated into strategic plans, if HR policies cohere, if line managers have internalized the importance of human resources and this is reflected in their behaviour, and if employees identify with the company then the company's strategic plans are likely to be more successfully implemented' (Guest, 1987: 512). Second, 'organizational commitment, combined with job-related behavioural commitment, will result in high employee satisfaction, high performance longer tenure and a willingness to accept change' (Guest, 1987: 514). Third, 'flexible organization structures together with flexible job content and flexible employees will result in a capacity to respond swiftly and effectively to changes and ensure the continuing high utilization of human and other resources' (Guest, 1987: 515). Finally, 'that the pursuit of policies designed to ensure the recruitment and retention of high-quality staff to undertake demanding jobs, supported by competent management will result in high performance levels' (Guest, 1987: 515).

Effective HRM requires each strand of the suite of HRM policies and practices to work together in an integrative form and to complement and reinforce one another. For example, an effective recruitment and selection system should dovetail with well-developed orientation and training processes to help the employee adjust to and learn organizational systems and procedures, and acquire further skills as necessary.

Overview of book content

The requirement for integration between different elements of HR provides a useful framework for overviewing the contents of this book. The book outlines the different HR activities in a similar sequential order to that taken by an organization looking to build its HR practices from the ground up.

Chapter 2 outlines *the concept of SHRM*, its links to overall business strategy as well as some key strategic planning tools for establishing a broad framework of policies, principles, and practices in a sport organization. The origins of SHRM and the difference between the concept of personnel management, HRM, and SHRM are presented. A model of SHRM and key elements of SHRM good practice are discussed within the context of sport organization performance.

Chapter 3 covers *human resource planning and strategy*, the fundamental building blocks for ensuring that the organization has the right human resources in place to meet the organization's strategic goals. This involves the assessment of the organization's internal and external environment, forecasting a sport organization's future demand and supply for employees and volunteers, based on its organizational requirements, and developing associated strategies. We outline how HR planning is used to identify the organization's HR management goals and expected results, identifying strategies and activities to achieve those goals, and measuring organizational progress towards their achievement. A process for selecting HR management practices that will enable the sport organization to meet its strategic goals is presented.

Recruitment and selection for sport organizations are presented in Chapter 4. Recruiting and selecting the right people for the right job is crucial to an organization's success. The recruitment and selection challenge is to ensure that each individual brought into the organization has the appropriate mix of skills, expertise, and knowledge to assist the organization to meet its goals. Ways to achieve an effective recruitment process that will generate a suitable pool of people from which an appointment can be made are presented, along with elements of a good selection process that can be used to increase the likelihood that the best candidate is appointed for the position.

Chapter 5 covers *orientation and organizational culture*. The stages of organizational socialization are described along with a variety of orientation strategies and practices. The importance and process of orienting sport volunteers and the role of organizational culture and in newcomer orientation are also elaborated upon.

Chapter 6 is about *training and development in sport organizations* and the establishment of training priorities and outcomes that are aligned with strategic objectives. Training and development processes to ensure that the organization's workforce has the skills, knowledge, abilities, and performance to meet current and future needs and objectives are discussed.

Chapter 7 looks at how *performance management* systems can be used as a means to recognize and reward good performance, to manage under-performance and to maintain and improve the performance of individuals, teams, and organizations. Approaches to identify and define the performance expectations for individuals and teams are presented. It should be noted that in sport, 'high performance' is a term used to describe the support given to elite athletes to achieve international success both as individuals and as a team. This could include training programmes, direct athlete support, employment of coaches or associated support staff, talent identification, and support for elite squad members. These types of programmes, while important for athletes, are outside the scope of this book.

Motivation and rewards management in sport organizations are outlined in Chapter 8. This includes the role of rewards in employee and volunteer motivation, different types of intrinsic and extrinsic rewards, and components of a financial compensation plan. The importance of volunteer recognition is also highlighted in this chapter.

Sport organizations and employee relations are covered in Chapter 9. What employee relations means in sport organizations? The role of the psychological contract in employee–management relations and different forms of organizational justice in the workplace, the bases and process of workplace grievance are presented. The concept of trade unions and the collective bargaining process is outlined. The nature of volunteer relations in sport organizations is also discussed.

Chapter 10 presents *succession and talent management* systems and the initiatives that target those with the potential to reach the top. This chapter provides the basics for developing an understanding of the principles of effective succession management and how to implement a successful succession and talent management programme within a SHRM approach.

Diversity management is covered in Chapter 11. People differ in many ways and this has implications for workplace interactions. Diversity management refers to the management of differences to capitalize on the benefits of diversity and to minimize its potentially negative consequences. Sport organizations can use diversity management to enhance their competitive edge and deliver increased value for stakeholders. Diversity management also addresses demands for equity, equality, and fairness in an era of growing demographic diversification.

Evaluating and improving HRM are presented in Chapter 12. How evaluation assists sport organizations to assess the financial costs and benefits of HR plans and polices and identifies which of these are meeting their objectives or need to be revised or replaced in a process of continuous improvement is outlined. A range of techniques for calculating return on investment in HR initiatives and human capital cost benefit analysis of HR initiatives, and measuring how HR can contribute to achieving organizations goals and objectives are presented.

Lastly, *managing change and future challenges* are presented in Chapter 13. It is a major HRM challenge to successfully plan, implement, and communicate organizational change. As discussed earlier in this chapter the sport industry has undergone dramatic changes over the past 20 or so years. Change in sport organizations has been needed to deal with a range of issues including: problems with board governance, tension between paid staff and volunteers, movement from amateur to professional status, declines in skilled and committed volunteers, and demand for greater accountability, higher performance and quality programmes and services from a whole range of stakeholders. Effective change management processes and future challenges are reviewed in Chapter 13.

Summary

This chapter has identified the key challenges of managing people in sport organizations. The chapter has also described the nature of contemporary sport organizations. The general concepts of HRM and SHRM have been introduced and explained, and the ideal outcomes of an effective HR system have been outlined. Finally, the key areas of HRM have been overviewed as they relate to sport organizations and the case has been argued that effective HRM is essential to the sustainability of sport organizations.

Discussion questions

1. Describe the different categories of individuals that typically work in sport organizations and outline some of the challenges of managing them side by side.
2. Name three key theoretical developments in the evolution of personnel management.
3. What are the key conceptual features of HRM?
4. Think of a sport organization that you are familiar with. Is it practicing HRM or personnel management? Think of examples to justify your answer.
5. Identify three examples of challenges facing sport organization in different areas of HR practice.

2 Strategic human resource management

Learning objectives

After reading this chapter you will be able to:

- Identify the origins of strategic human resource management (SHRM) and how it relates to broader developments in the practice of management
- Understand the difference between the concept of personnel management, human resource management (HRM), and SHRM
- Understand the developments in theories of strategy and how these emphasize the importance of efficient internal processes such as SHRM within sport organizations
- Describe a model of SHRM and identify the key elements of SHRM's good practice
- Outline the key theoretical approaches linking SHRM and sport organization performance

Chapter overview

The main elements of HRM were described in Chapter 1 using the Harvard model which emphasizes the importance of integration between different elements of HR practice; overall alignment of the organization's HR system with the external environment; the importance of building a positive organizational culture; and an alignment between the behaviour of all employees and volunteers and the overall strategic direction of the organization.

SHRM takes this approach further by mandating an explicit strategy to use the human resources of an organization to gain competitive advantage over other sport organizations in the industry through better use of its human capital. Thus rather than seeing HR from a follower perspective vis-à-vis the strategic direction of the organization and implementing effective HR systems accordingly, the SHRM views stresses that HRM can be a shaper of and contributor to strategy and can have an active role in defining as well as implementing strategic decisions.

In order to properly understand the SHRM we need first to appreciate some of the main theories and techniques of strategic management which SHRM draws upon. The first section of this chapter therefore outlines the key approaches to business strategy focusing in particular on the resource-based view (RBV) of the organization this view provides a strong rationale for regarding the management of HRM as strategic. Fundamental tools for conducting a strategic analysis will also be described. Following this a model of SHRM will be outlined and discussed. This chapter concludes with a discussion of the key approaches to linking SHRM and sport organization performance.

Theories of strategy

The classic view of strategic management presents the 'process' as involving six steps. These are as follows:

1. Clarification of corporate mission, goals, and values.
2. Analysis of the organization's external competitive environment to identify strengths, weaknesses, opportunities, and threats (a SWOT analysis – described in detail below).
3. Analysis of the organization's internal operating environment to identify strengths and weaknesses (again using a SWOT analysis).
4. Selection of strategies that build on the organization's strengths and correct weaknesses, to take advantage of external opportunities and counter-external threats.
5. Strategy implementation.
6. Strategy evaluation with corrective feedback to the implementation phase.

A SWOT analysis as depicted in Figure 2.1 is a simple tool for analysing the strategic position of an organization, or part of an organization, by identifying strengths, weaknesses, opportunities, and threats. In a SWOT analysis internal factors are typically identified as strengths or weaknesses whilst external factors are identified as threats or opportunities. Typical factors that can be considered in both categories are included in Figure 2.1 depicted by an example of what issues may be covered as provided by NSW Sport and Recreation with reference to running Sporting Clubs (NSW Department of Sport and Recreation, 2007). A typical use for a SWOT analysis in HR is described in Chapter 3 in relation to HR planning.

An alternative to conducting a SWOT analysis in relation to external factors is to use a PEST analysis. PEST refers to political, economic, social, and technological and is a more wide-ranging analysis of the macro-external variables that may be impacting upon an organization. In sport organizations some typical examples of factors that might be considered in a PEST are as follows:

- *Political*
  - Government commitment to increasing participation in sport: for example, current concerns about obesity have led to governments increasing spending on children's and youth sporting programmes in many countries.
  - Government targeting of certain ethnic/age or gender groups for increased participation.
  - Government funding for sport infrastructure: for example, the Olympic games in Sydney generated many improvements in local sports facilities which greatly assisted many sports federations in their development.
- *Economic*
  - The potential of sport to create employment.
  - The potential to use sport as an adjunct to promoting tourism: for example, Golf in Ireland, Surfing in Hawaii.
- *Social*
  - Aging populations, health issues, diversity agendas, population growth, etc.
  - Urban/rural growth and decline and the need to rebalance sporting infrastructure in changing communities, for example the decline of small rural towns in many countries which leads to the loss of players for town sporting clubs.
- *Technological*
  - Competition from computer games vis-à-vis children's sport.
  - Use of the Internet to better promote sport: for example, advertise and sell tickets online.
  - Alternative technologies: for example, online sports betting or virtual football.

Conducting SWOT and/or PEST analyses as part of a strategic planning process such as that referred to above is consistent with the most influential theoretical work on strategy undertaken by Michael Porter. Porter (1979)

Internal factors

Company culture
Organization structure
Key staff
Resource access
Experience
Operational capacity
Operational efficiency
Financial resources
Patents
Customer knowledge and contacts

External factors

Customers
Competitors
Intensity of competition in market
Suppliers
Partnerships and alliances
Change
New technology
Economic environment
Political issues

Strengths

■ Strong financial base
■ Growth area for your product
■ Group of skilled volunteers
■ Support from local businesses
■ Support from local politicians
■ Support from local service organizations
■ Well-equipped club house
■ Well-structured committee
■ Enthusiastic and capable committee

Oportunities

■ Promotion of sport by government authorities (e.g., renewed 'Life in it' campaign)
■ New population of potential users moving into the area, housing estates with children
■ Grants by local authorities to encourage sport
■ Grants by state authorities to encourage sport
■ Grants by federal authorities to encourage sport
■ Organizations looking to sponsor local activities
■ Seasonal interest in particular sports, cricket in summer, football in winter
■ International or national interests in sports (e.g., Commonwealth or Olympic Games)
■ Promotion of sport to different age group (e.g., lawn bowls to teenagers)
■ Promotion of sport to different gender (e.g., football – all codes – to girls)

Weaknesses

■ Weak financial base
■ Diminishing need or desire for your product
■ Few volunteers
■ No support from local businesses
■ No support from local politicians
■ No support from local service organizations
■ Out of date ill-equipped club house
■ Poor committee structure
■ Overworked and tired committee
■ Fewer new members
■ Lack of interest in your sport

Threats

Organizations giving up sports to sponsor to concentrate on other areas

■ Seasonal interest in particular sports which is in direct competition with your own sport (e.g., competing code of football)
■ Promotion of sport to different gender which competes with your sports interest (e.g., netball and soccer for girls)
■ Other interests including hobby groups, television, video games, school activities, part-time work for teenagers and so on
■ Time-related issues, for example, competition for volunteers time, longer working hours, both parents working – children unable to attend, limited available free time for both children and parents
■ Other organizations with better facilities
■ Lack of knowledge and interest in your product

Figure 2.1 Example of a SWOT analysis (*Source:* Adapted from NSW Department of Sport and Recreation, 2007).

developed a tool for analysing an organization's competitive position within an industry which is generally referred to as the five forces model. This analysis is performed as a preparatory exercise to assist an organization with the identification of its correct strategic direction. The five forces are as follows:

1. *Overall industry rivalry*: This identifies the intensity and patterns of competition. This is not only influenced by the other four factors but also by separate factors such as industry growth, the level of product differentiation, and barriers to exiting the industry: for example, competition for members between golf clubs in the same geographical catchment area.
2. *Barriers to entry*: The obstacles to entering the industry presented by: for example, the need for economies of scale, access to scarce resources, or the need for large amount of capital: for example, limits on numbers of franchise teams in a league.
3. *Buyer power*: The level of choice available to customers: for example, there may be several fitness centres to choose from in a particular geographical area.
4. *Supplier power*: This is dependent on factors such as the number of suppliers in the industry: for example, being the only tennis centre in town.
5. *Threat of substitutes*: The number of alternatives available to consumers and the switching costs associated with consuming an alternative product: for example, fans switching from baseball to soccer.

Porter suggests that when positioning itself relative to competitors in an industry, an organization can only outperform its rivals in two fundamental ways: by operational effectiveness or strategic positioning.

The first concept, operational effectiveness, means performing similar activities better than rivals perform them. Whilst this can be a source of competitive advantage, few organizations have competed successfully on operational effectiveness alone for an extended period of time. Easily imitable areas such as technologies and input improvements do not typically provide organizations with long-term advantage because they are quickly copied by competitors. Therefore, a fitness centre's purchase of the latest fitness equipment might provide a short-term advantage, but this position could quickly erode as competitors buy in similar or even newer machines.

The second concept, strategic positioning, on the other hand refers to performing different activities from rivals or performing similar activities in different ways. Thus the fitness centre mentioned above might not only have the latest in equipment but might also offer a range of exercise programmes that are unique to that centre. According to Porter the two fundamental sources of sustainable competitive advantage lie in either cost leadership or product/service differentiation relative to competitors. A third possibility is for an organization to focus on a particular segment or niche rather than compete across the board in a given market, but even then, according to Porter, a focused strategy requires a competitive position based on cost leadership or differentiation. In this case the fitness centre could be exclusively for women.

Although positioning within an industry is an important element of strategy it is not sufficient to give a complete explanation of the success of some sport organizations in relation to their competitors. In fact some studies suggest that industry structure accounts for as little as 8–15 per cent of the variance in an organization's performance (Black & Boal, 1994). This is because industry structural factors impact upon the entire industry and do not adequately explain the sustained competitive performance of some firms but not others. Critics of the industry structure model therefore argue that a significant component of strategic success must be explained by factors within the organization.

An alternative view of strategy is provided by the resource based view (RBV) of the firm (Barney, 1991). This theory argues that the source of an organization's competitive advantage lies in its internal resources such as patents, copyrights, proprietary technologies as well as human and intellectual capital, and its ability to manage these resources strategically. From this perspective, a sport organization's resources are viewed more widely than can be understood in the formal accounting sense. Instead resources include any aspect of the sport organization with value-creating capabilities including those that are intangible such as the 'culture' of the organization and its ability to convey a certain image or embody a set of ideals. Examples of resource-based analysis of sport organizations can be found in the work of Amis, Pant and Slack (1997) in relation to successful and unsuccessful company sponsorship arrangements and Gerrard's (2005) analysis of English professional soccer.

Amis et al. (1997) used RBV to assess what allows a sport sponsorship relationship between a sport organization and sponsoring company to provide sustainable competitive advantage. They concluded that a sponsoring organization should invest in athletes, team, or events when the sport organization they are sponsoring satisfies the requirements of heterogeneity, imperfect mobility, imperfect imitability, and up front limits to competition. Using the example of Owens Corning sponsorship of the Canadian freestyle skiing team, they showed that this deal was heterogeneous due to the length of the arrangement and its symbiotic relationship (both represent symbols of winter, innovation, and excitement). Imperfect mobility was satisfied via the long-term contract and the name association that developed between the two parties over this time. As the contract was non-tradable, and the Canadian freestyle team was committed to the relationship, the criterion of imperfect mobility was met. And finally, Owens Corning's decision to get involved with freestyle skiing before it became an Olympic event and experienced huge growth provided the sponsorship relationship with limits to competition.

Employing an RBV analysis of professional soccer teams, Gerrard (2005) explained how sustainable competitive advantage and sporting and financial success can be related to ownership status and the way in which professional sports teams use their resources (athletes) and allegiance (their fans). The increased financial efficiency of stock market listed teams provided the basis for improved financial performance and did not have any significant negative impact on the teams playing talent and sporting performance. While it is widely acknowledged that allegiance resources (i.e., team market size), athletic resources, and coaching resources are major contributors to organizational performance; the efficiency gains linked to organizational changes of business structures, governance processes, and managerial recruitment were also critical. Shareholders in listed teams can monitor and assess organizational performance and, as a consequence, provide stronger incentives for management to maximize organizational efficiency. 'This, in turn, is likely to lead to listed teams assigning greater status and financial rewards to commercial management functions resulting in a greater propensity to recruit specialists with business experience outside the professional teamsports industry (i.e., the "suits"). In contrast, non-listed teams face less pressure from investors to transform traditional organizational structures in which commercial management plays a subordinate role to the sporting functions managed by former players (i.e., the "shirts")' (Gerrard, 2005: 167).

An example of how this theory applies in the HRM area is given by Lado and Wilson (1994) who argue that HRM systems can facilitate the development of competencies that are specific to the organization in the sense that they are contained in social relations which are embedded in an organization's history and culture. These competencies generate tacit organizational knowledge which allows for efficient execution of tasks in the same way that tacit knowledge in a mature sporting team allows players to 'know' what other players are about to do and coordinate their own movements accordingly. From this perspective an HRM system can be unique in two senses. First, because the outputs of the system, that is the employee actions resulting from it, are unique. Second, because the system itself is a source of competence as it: for example, attracts employees to work for the organization. It is therefore useful to define HRM competence as tangible (HR performance, planning, training, selection systems, etc.) and intangible (shared mindsets, team synergies, accumulated operational experience in creativity and problem solving, etc.).

At the heart of the RBV of the firm is the argument that the intangibility of such resources gives the organization holding them a competitive edge because it means that they cannot be easily replicated by competitors. Implicit in this view is the idea that such resources can sustain an organization's competitive advantage over a long period so long as such resources are valuable, rare, imperfectly imitable, and non-substitutable. An example of such a set of resources in professional sport might be found in a successful team's scouting network, which brings talented young players into a junior academy. Such networks are often established in longstanding relationship with key scouts or feeder clubs who are generally loyal to one senior club. The scouting network is reinforced by other intangibles such as a club's playing history, traditions and its glamour, its reputation for looking after young players, and its ability to provide opportunities for player development not offered by other clubs.

The first attribute is that a resource must be valuable, in that it has the capability to exploit opportunities and/or neutralize threats in the organization's environment. Resources can be considered valuable when they provide the organization with the ability to conceive or implement strategies that improve its efficiency effectiveness. An organization's reputation and image are a valuable resource, consider how Nike built its reputation as the athlete's choice for footwear. The second attribute requires that a resource must be rare among an organization's current and potential competition. Resources that are readily available to competitors cannot provide a source of sustained competitive advantage. In Nike's case its acquisition of Michael Jordan as its iconic athlete representative left its competition floundering for alternatives.

The third attribute is that these resources must be non substitutable i.e., there cannot be strategically equivalent substitutes for this resource that are valuable but neither rare nor imperfectly imitable. When the governing body for football in Australia was radically restructured into the Football Federation of Australia (FFA) in 2005 the organization was completely re-staffed and the initial acquisition of a respected, wealthy, influential businessman Frank Lowry into the role of Chairman was critical to its capacity to obtain critical human resources. Lowry was able to spearhead a campaign to acquire John O'Neill as CEO of the FFA; O'Neill had previously headed the successful Australian Rugby Union and he brought with him a significant number of senior managers from rugby across to the FFA. The transition to the new governance structure and the subsequent success of the FFA and its new league competition have been attributed to the 'resources' of Lowry and O'Neill (Lock, Taylor & Darcy, 2007).

The fourth attribute demands that it must be imperfectly imitable. The term 'imperfectly imitable' refers to the difficulty that competitors may face in imitating or substituting an identified resource that confers value in a successful organization. Professional football (soccer) in the UK provides several examples of unique managers who by the force of their personality have transformed the long-term fortunes of the football clubs that they managed. Jock Stein with Glasgow Celtic, Bill Shankly with Liverpool, and Sir Matt Busby and Sir Alex Ferguson with Manchester United all provide perfect examples of this, managers who have provided sustained competitive advantage for their clubs.

Valuable and rare resources can only be sources of competitive advantage if the organizations that do not currently possess these resources cannot obtain or imitate them. Organization resources can potentially be imperfectly imitable for three reasons. First, because obtaining the resource is dependent upon unique historical conditions. Second, because the relationship between the resource possessed and the organization's sustained competitive advantage is causally ambiguous. Third, because it is socially complex in nature (Barney, 1991). A study using the RBV theory of strategy to assess the sustainable competitive advantage of Pennsylvania State University's football programme found that the programme's competitive advantage is located in its 'history, relationships, trust, and culture that have developed within the programme's coaching staff over many years. Such complex and interdependent organizational resources tend not to be subject to imitation' (Smart & Wolfe, 2000: 144).

As implied in the discussion of the conditions of inimitability, proponents of the RBV argue that in most cases, competitive advantage cannot be traced to a single or isolated component, but instead is derived from an effectively executed combination of human capital elements such as the development of skill stocks, the encouragement via effective performance management systems of strategically relevant behaviours, and generally supportive people management systems. Such intangible assets, it is argued, confer upon the holder the ability to implement strategy more effectively than competitors and thereby provide a strong basis for a potential source of competitive advantage.

The growth in popularity of the RBV of the organization has focused the attention of both practicing managers and academics on the internal configuration of resources in the organization and led to many initiatives in areas such as learning systems, knowledge management, intellectual capital, organizational culture, and above all strategic human resource management.

The SHRM process

Strategic human resource management builds on the insight provided by the RBV of the organization because it emphasizes the importance of an organization's internal resources and capabilities in helping it achieve its strategic objectives rather than merely its strategic positioning within an industry which was the focus of earlier theorizing. In other words, it is the extent to which a sport organization can quickly and efficiently implement its strategy that differentiates it from its competitors and not just the formulation of its strategic position in the sport industry. This is particularly the case in service industries, such as sports, where customer interactions are crucial in determining the 'value' of the transaction for the customer (as opposed to just the price of a particular service). Perhaps the most critical internal capability or resource that an organization has from this perspective is its people and the internal HR systems and processes that lead to a unique culture and performance in a business that is not easily copied by competitors.

Wright and McMahon (1992: 298) define SHRM as, 'the pattern of planned human resource deployments and activities intended to enable an organization to achieve its goals'. For example, a sport consultancy organization will generally seek to employ only the most intelligent candidates with sophisticated interpersonal skills because they recognize that the calibre of their consultants confers a competitive advantage. Similarly, a sport organization that recognizes its dependence on volunteers may seek ways to 'retain' volunteers through matching them to the task via appropriate managerial action (Kim, Chelladurai & Trail, 2007).

The essential idea of SHRM is to treat employees and volunteers as investment assets, who through a series of organizational practices develop a strong psychological commitment to the organization and unique ways of working together that delivers superior performance levels. From this perspective, sport organizations can attain a strategic advantage over their rivals because, unlike other assets such as technology, human assets are inimitable in the short run.

Key features of organizational practice associated with SHRM are not only 'pure' HR techniques such as rigorous selection systems, but also a range of associated management practices related to high-commitment work systems, employment models, leadership philosophy, and style.

Figure 2.2 illustrates the factors to be considered in the SHRM process. The model contains two processes: strategy formulation and strategy implementation. Two advantages apply when considering strategy from these two

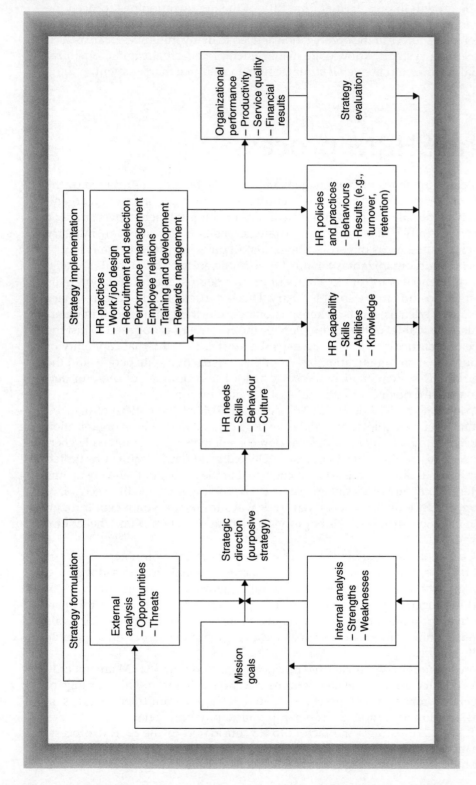

Figure 2.2 The SHRM process (*Source:* Adapted from De Cieri et al. 2003: 50).

perspectives. First, the two processes reflect recent theorizing whereby strategy is not always seen as purposive and top down but also 'emergent' (Mintzberg, 1990) in the sense of incorporating flexible responses to unforeseen environmental turbulence. Second, from this perspective strategy is viewed as potentially problematic in terms of execution which was problem often overlooked by earlier thinking about strategy.

The implication of this perspective is that the choice of strategy is not only limited by the existing capabilities possessed by an organization, such as how intelligent its staff are, but also by deficiencies in organizational capability to implement strategy effectively, such as the ability of staff and volunteers to work together effectively at the necessary pace. Recently deficiencies in execution competencies have been claimed to have more potential to derail competitive positioning than choice of the wrong strategy in the first instance (Beer & Eisenstat, 2000). Almost inevitably strategic decision making involves people-related issues; therefore, a logical corollary to this is that HR implications should be considered when strategic decisions are made.

Another argument for SHRM is that in the last two decades there has been a growing recognition amongst theorists and practitioners alike that traditional sources of competitive advantage such as technology, product innovation, or location are being eroded more quickly due to fiercer, globalized competition, and a more rapid pace of diffusion and that a committed, skilled, and flexible workforce can confer a long-term advantage for an organization which is inimitable by competitors. From this perspective the essence of competitiveness lies in better business processes or higher levels of 'core competence' and 'core capabilities' (Prahalad & Hamel, 1990) rather than just specific technologies or products. The key to better processes often lies in the HR domain, for example hiring the right kind of employees, retaining volunteers, or stimulating more effective teamwork to allow different sections of an organization to work together more efficiently.

Referring again to Figure 2.2 we can see that the strategy formulation role involves consideration of the organization's overall mission as well as a SWOT analysis. Using the output of a SWOT analysis, an organization will typically consider three critical strategic questions:

1. Where will we compete? (In what areas and/or using what products?)
2. How will we compete? (On the basis of cost, differentiation, focus? What is our customer value proposition?)
3. With what will we compete? (How do we acquire/develop and deploy our resources in order to compete?)

HR implications can emerge from each of these strategic questions, but it is in relation to the 'with what will we compete' question that HR has the most obvious involvement in formulating strategy. Take for instance a community-based sport association that is dependent on a large volume of volunteers to run the organization, coach the children, manage squads, and act as officials. In order to attract and retain an adequate pool of quality volunteers, Australian Little Athletics highlights its vision of developing children of all abilities by promoting positive attitudes and a healthy lifestyle through family and community involvement in athletics activities. The emphasis of positive family and community involvement provides fundamental strength for the organization as participants' parents and community members can be targeted as volunteers. In terms of 'with what will we compete' Australian Little Athletics can refer to its Officials Scheme which provides training for volunteer judges, time keepers, umpires, and recorders. This comprehensive training offers four levels of official gradings commencing at the local level with D Grade, progressing through to C Grade for Zone level and B & A Grades for State and National level officials. Rewards and recognition are given via badges to qualified officials, and there is an excellent support network with newsletters and other publications that acknowledge volunteer contributions. Intangible benefits such as being out on the field where it is all happening, having fun, and gaining an increased appreciation of their child's activities are also critical. This example illustrates the importance of ensuring that the sport organization's HR planning, policies, and activities for volunteers build on its strengths to strategically build its resource base.

Another example is a commercially oriented sport organization expanding operations beyond its domestic borders for the first time. They may face critical questions relating to staffing. How will we get properly trained staff in our new market? Should we send domestic staff as expatriates or hire locally? Are the staffing problems in relation to the overseas branch so great that we should reconsider our original decision to enter this new market? This problem was exactly what confronted many overseas organizations when they first entered the Japanese market because typically the best Japanese employees preferred to work for Japanese and not for foreign organizations. In fact many western organizations were eventually forced to withdraw from the Japanese market because the staffing problems were too great. This is a vivid example of unforeseen HR problems derailing a strategy.

IMG in Korea

IMG is a diversified global business with two major business segments: IMG Sports & Entertainment, and IMG Media. IMG employs over 2300 people in 30 countries. Forstmann Little & Co. purchased IMG in 2004. IMG Sports & Entertainment includes: consulting services; event ownership and management; fashion events and models representation; licensing; golf course design; client representation in golf, tennis, broadcasting, European football, rugby, cricket, motorsports, coaching, Olympic sports, and action sports. In addition, IMG Academies are the world's largest and most advanced, state-of-the-art, multi-sport training, and educational facility, delivering world-class sports training experiences to over 12,000 junior, collegiate, adult, and professional athletes each year.

IMG only runs a worldwide website and recruitment notices are put on the website. This includes jobs, required conditions of applicants, and benefits for employees. The IMG worldwide website indicates jobs in the US and UK only and the HR departments are located in New York and Cleveland (head office). For the Korea office, there is no HR manager. When a vacancy arises, the managing director and administration manager ask other employees for recommendations. At the same time, the job opening notice will be announced on online recruitment websites. In some cases, a recruitment headhunter will be used.

IMG believes that it is only as strong as the individuals they employ, IMG provides competitive compensation and comprehensive benefits to keep employees happy, including medical, dental, prescription drug programme; optional vacation purchase programme; paid sick and bereavement time; medical expense reimbursement programme; parking and transit assistance programme; and accidental death and dismemberment insurance. These are for US employees. For the Korea office, there is 'generous paid holiday and floating holiday time'.

IMG recruits for the most skilled personnel in sales, law, marketing, client and event management, licensing, television production, graphic design, multi-media and website development, corporate tax, corporate finance, promotions, account management, administrative support, and customer service. For the Korea office, there is only one manager in each division. When a vacancy occurs, most candidates are recommended by internal employees. If this is not successful, the position will be open on the public through recruitment websites and recruitment headhunters. The resume review and interview is done by the Managing Director and the final selection is made by the line manager.

Discussion question
1. Discuss the application of the 'industry positioning' and 'RBV' of the firm perspective to the IMG case.
2. Is there any evidence that IMG Korea is following a SHRM approach?

Case supplied by Julie Kim.

Clearly HR needs to be involved in strategic decisions, although the actual degree of integration of HR with strategy formulation may vary from organization to organization depending on the philosophy of the company. At the most basic level HR has to implement the people-related aspects of any strategy. Therefore, the most primitive type of involvement is for HR to be engaged in strategy in the role of an administrative adjunct or in other words a receiver of strategy. A second and more sophisticated level of involvement is where HR issues are considered at the same time as strategy through a process of consultation whereby HR is informed of and asked to comment on HR aspects of a strategic plan drawn up by a strategy team such as an Executive Committee. Finally, at the highest level of integration, HR may be fully involved in all aspects of strategic decision making. This is often facilitated by appointing the most senior HR person onto the sport organization's Executive Committee so as to be involved in all aspects of strategic decision making and to comment specifically on the organization's internal capabilities. The latter position is consistent with the logic of the RBV of the organization since HR is a key source of internal resources.

After a sport organization has completed its strategic analysis and formulated a strategy, it must then effectively execute the agreed strategy. As noted earlier, implementation has recently come to be seen as the most important component of all the steps in overall strategic management. Becker, Huselid and Ulrich (2001) suggest that organizations, in general, do a reasonably good job of formulating the right strategy, to the point where it can no longer be seen as a source of differentiation. By way of illustration, in a US survey where subjects were asked to rate the 'suitability' of their strategy and how well their strategy had been implemented, analysis showed that the capacity to execute well had a 10 times greater effect on the organization's financial performance than did the strategic choice (Becker et al., 2001).

General organizational issues to be considered when implementing strategy typically concern the following:

- The allocation of sufficient resources (financial, time, technology, and support).
- Setting up an organizational hierarchy and chain of command or some alternative structure (such as cross-functional teams).
- Delegating responsibility of tasks or processes to individuals or groups.
- Managing the process. This includes monitoring results, comparing against benchmarks or good practices, evaluating the effectiveness and efficiency of the process, and making adjustments to the process as necessary.

When implementing more specific programmes, implementation may also involve acquiring the requisite resources, developing the process, training, process testing, documentation, and integration with (and/or conversion from) existing processes.

Effective implementation of strategy requires not only decisions in relation to all of the above but also the coordination of a number of HR practices as detailed in Figure 2.2. As noted in Chapter 1, these HR practices are discussed more fully in Chapters 3–12 of this book. The correct choice of practices will result in the sport organization developing the required HR capability in terms of skills, ability, and knowledge as well as the right behaviours.

The final component of the strategic management process is that of evaluation. Evaluation involves measuring progress against agreed objectives and taking corrective action as necessary. Sometimes this corrective action can be so fundamental as to lead to a new strategic direction being taken. This is referred to as an emergent, as opposed to fully pre-planned, strategy and is an increasingly important component of the overall strategy process given the turbulent environment within which most sport organizations operate today.

Historically, evaluation was done using mainly financial measures and ratios but more recently there have been attempts to measure progress using wider organizational measures. Notable amongst these innovations has been the Balanced Scorecard (Kaplan & Norton, 1996b) which measures organization progress against four criteria: financial, customer, learning and growth, and internal business process improvement. This framework is discussed further in Chapter 12.

In the academic literature on SHRM there are three main schools of thought concerning the link between HRM practices and organizational performance. First, there is the so-called 'best practice' approach that is associated with the work of researchers such as Pfeffer (1998a). This approach can be seen as directly in the tradition of the Harvard approach, discussed in Chapter 1, as it advocates what is essentially a normative approach to HRM. Based on extensive research of successful organizations, Pfeffer identified seven HRM practices that closely correlated with exceptionally high performing and profitable organizations. In combination these practices led to high-performance work systems that added value to the organizations' overall performance, including financial, in ways consistent with the RBV of the organization. Moreover, the top performing organizations in Pfeffer's study were in industries which were characterized by intense competitive rivalry. These high-performance work systems involve sophisticated HRM practices aimed at:

1. selective recruitment;
2. developing a decentralized organization which supports self-managed teams;
3. providing employment security;
4. providing high rewards relative to other organizations, but based on performance;
5. extensive training;
6. sharing information;
7. reducing status differentials in the workplace.

Essentially the 'best practice' approach argues that a well-executed investment strategy in people will always pay dividends irrespective of industry. This view has been criticized primarily for underestimating the importance of external factors which may limit the opportunity to invest in people. Thus, a national sporting organization might devise an HR policy which emphasizes competitive recruitment for all positions, accompanied by an attractive reward package, access to regular training and development and a collegiate team-based work environment. However, a change in government funding, a change in personnel and power structures on the Board of Directors, or loss of a major sponsorship or media deal might compromise the delivery of these practices. Cuts to funding and revenue streams may require that training and remuneration is cut back and changes to the Board may result in the senior management team being replaced by personnel that have close connections to the new board members.

The second approach is best described as a 'contingency' approach and addresses the key limitation of the best practice approach. This approach argues that HR practices should be closely integrated with organizational strategy and structure, and recognizes that different behaviours may be required from individuals in order to enact different competitive strategies. For example, a sport organization following a cost minimization strategy will have a different HR imperative than a sport organization seeking to innovate. Thus, a sport and recreation centre following cost minimization may seek to retain its current staffing profile, provide basic training and development, and have a traditional performance management and reward system. On the other hand a sport centre intent on pursuing an innovation strategy may seek to hire individuals with higher qualifications, establish training and development initiatives that promote creativity and innovation, and use reward incentives that recognize employee innovation and risk taking.

Researchers such as Jackson and Schuler (1999) have emphasized the importance of identifying the behaviours required by staff to achieve the organization's goals and ensuring that these are consistent with the overall business activities of the organization. The term 'integration' is used to refer to the need for internal consistency, so that HR practices do not contradict one another. Criticisms of the contingency approach have been directed at the underestimation of the influence of external stakeholders such as trade unions who are largely excluded from the analysis. Moreover, the focus of this approach on strategy formulation has meant that there is often an under-emphasis of the importance of strategy implementation. These limitations provided the basis for the emergence of the configurational approach which has a much greater emphasis on flexible implementation.

The third approach which is known as the 'configurational' approach suggests that HR practices need to fit with each other as well as broad organizational strategy, but this fit should involve 'bundles' of HR practices which can be mixed and matched in contrast to the more programmatic approaches of the good practice and contingency schools. To put this another way, the primary emphasis of this approach is on internal fit between groups of HRM practices which operate to create a synergistic focus of organizational effort. Thus MacDuffie (1995) demonstrated how good HRM practices were associated with high productivity in the car industry and how productivity increased to higher levels in organizations which combined good HRM with flexible work systems, quality discussion groups, and job rotation practices. In a larger study of nearly 1000 organizations Huselid (1995) found that combinations of high-performance work practices had a statistically significant positive impact not only on intermediate employee outcomes such as productivity and turnover, but also on long-term corporate financial performance. Moreover, strategy implementation had a far greater impact than strategy content on shareholder value, and effective HR practices ('human capital architecture') were found to be critical to strategy implementation. According to Huselid (1995) the most important of these HR practices are selective hiring, performance-based reward systems geared to organizational strategy, and sophisticated training and performance management systems.

An example of the configurational approach is found in the UK-based Royal Yachting Association's (RYA) recently advertised Onboard Development Officer[1] job. Candidates for this position required 'a passionate and dynamic approach to sailing' along with technical knowledge and skills appropriate for the job. As the job involved working with volunteers the duties for this position also incorporated further development and encouragement of more volunteers into the sport. This approach is aligned with the RYA's view that volunteers should be integrated into the organizational structure and the expectation that staff at all levels will work positively with volunteers and will actively seek to involve them in the work of the club or organization. Additionally, consistent with the RYA's mission of developing young people through sailing, the RYA recruits staff with a 'real desire to achieve professional personal development'.

In summary, the recent research on SHRM, irrespective of the approach, provides a body of evidence which establishes a link between good HRM practices in the areas of selection, training, performance management and reward, and higher levels of organizational performance. There is also evidence of this link from research in the UK by Patterson, West, Lawthorn and Nickell (1997) where data from a 10-year study on more than 100 manufacturing organizations has shown strong positive relationships between employee attitudes, organizational culture, HRM practices, and organizational performance. However, whilst this research is emphatic in its conclusion that good people management is more highly correlated with organizational performance than quality systems, technology, or competitive strategy, it does not emphasize HR practices to the exclusion of broader managerial practices which also impact upon employee motivation. Instead, it is argued that 'good people management' involves all areas that can contribute to employee satisfaction and motivation including supervision style, relationships with colleagues and balance between work and home life as well as traditional HR practices.

Overall, this research suggests that whilst there is no specific normative list of HR practices that will lead to good organizational performance outcomes in all circumstances, there are certain bundles of key practices which, if used in the right combination for a particular sport organization, will stimulate good performance outcomes. Moreover, some of these bundles appear to be more important across a range of organizational contingencies such as selective hiring practices. According to configurational approaches internal fit between HR practices, strategy, structure, and other organization is more important than any external fit with a normative HRM model which might be suggested by the best practice approach. Thus even in organizations with 'good HRM' practices some variation should be expected depending on how these HRM practices are geared with the organization's overall strategy as well as its culture. Moreover, it is clear from the research that not all organizations practice 'good HRM'. Variations in the type of demands posed by the

---

[1] http://www.rva.org.uk/AboutRYA/jobvacancies/onboarddevelopmentofficer.htm accessed 29 April 2007.

business environment have resulted in a number of very different, often concurrent roles for those involved in personnel or HRM.

Summary

This chapter has identified the origins of the SHRM approach within the broader strategy literature and identified it specifically with the RBV of strategy. A model of SHRM was presented which makes an explicit link between the goals of the organization and the need for congruence in the HR system. The model serves as a useful guide for both strategy planning and strategy implementation in relation to various HR activities. Finally, this chapter has outlined three competing theories: best practice, contingency, and configuration explaining the links between SHRM and organizational performance and concluded that configurational theory offers the most comprehensive and compelling explanation of the link between SHRM and organizational performance.

Discussion questions

1. Exercise: Conduct a SWOT or PEST analysis for a sport organization that you know well. Take the perspective of a CEO planning the organization's strategy for the next 3 years.
2. Use the four attributes of the RBV to analyse a sport organization that you think has a competitive edge in the marketplace. How does HR fit into this analysis?
3. Using the same sport organization discussed in question 2 reviews the organizations HR practices and discusses the level of fit with Pfeffer's seven best practices.

3 Human resource planning and strategy

Learning objectives

After reading this chapter you will be able to:

- Explain the process of human resource (HR) planning for future organizational requirements
- Describe the process of job analysis
- Outline the key components of job description
- Explain different approaches to job design
- Describe how effective HR planning can enable the strategic achievement of organizational goals

Chapter overview

Strategic HR planning refers to the development of policies and procedures to ensure the acquisition, development, retention, and effective deployment of a workforce that will allow the organization to meet its mission and goals now and in the future.

The dynamic external environments that sport organizations operate in create an imperative to plan for current and future workforce demands.

Effective planning requires that the organization has a clear picture of their current workforce, its strengths, weaknesses, and potential. The assessment of the current state of play is conducted within the context of the organization's ability to achieve its goals and objectives. The next step in planning is to examine future directions, requirements, and capabilities to ascertain how the current workforce will meet future needs and then determine what plans need to be put in place to address any gaps or concerns.

This chapter presents a model of HR planning and discusses dimensions of development and implementation. It then provides an overview of workforce planning, and job analysis and design within the context of delivering organizational goals through HR and discusses the option of outsourcing HR functions.

A strategic approach to human resource management planning

The planning of HR is an integral part of how an organization is going to achieve its mission, by ensuring that the right people, with the right skills and knowledge are in the right positions to deliver on the organization's mission. Strategic human resource management (SHRM) planning is located within the organization's overall strategic planning process. Overarching organizational goals determine the content of Human Resource Management (HRM) policy, strategies, goals, and measures to achieve what is most important to the organization and address the challenges it will face in the forthcoming years.

The HR plan generally takes one of two forms, as a component of a general strategic plan or as a separate HR strategic plan. In both cases the plans developed would form the basis for implementation of actions to achieve set goals, strategies, and measures on issues such as recruitment, retention, employee development, and succession. Just as the form of HR planning varies, so does the approach to planning. Typically, large multifaceted organizations with greater and more complex HR issues to manage will have formal strategic planning processes in place, while smaller organizations may be less formal and more flexible in their HR planning. For example, a fitness centre that identifies expansion into new locations as part of its overall strategic plan would require a formal and detailed HR plan for staffing its new centres. On the less formal side, a regional basketball association may take the opportunity, when presented, to bring in an internship student to develop a membership benefits package, even though the association had not previously identified this position or job task as a priority.

Effective HR planning serves many purposes. It allows an organization to deploy its people to meet its strategies and goals, assists with cost reduction by anticipating and dealing with labour shortages or surpluses in a timely manner, ensures optimum use of each individual's skills and knowledge, and capitalizes on the talents of a diverse workforce (Kane, 1997). The challenges to HR planning largely centre on the rapidly changing internal and external environments of sport organizations. These factors include changes to the way in which the sport is organized and delivered; increased competition for staff, volunteers, participants, and clients; an aging population; the need for a workforce skilled in new technologies and other specialized areas; and workforce diversity. Such challenges increase the importance of effective HR planning in the strategic planning process of sport organizations.

The HR planning process

HR planning is a dynamic process that involves analysing an organization's HR requirements necessary to achieve its mission, strategies, goals, and objectives within a continuously changing environmental context. Planning aims to achieve the desirable workforce balance and mix through integrated HR practices such as job analysis and design, staffing, learning and development, and evaluation. An overview of the HR planning process, as a system of demand and supply forecasting, goal setting and strategic planning, identification of gaps between current and forecast requirements, development and implementation of HR programmes and evaluation, is presented in Figure 3.1.

The planning process is a complex combination of assessment of the organization's internal and external environment and mapping of the HR requirements to meet current needs and future projections. If the assessment determines that there is a gap between demand and supply the development of an HR plan to narrow the disparity would result. The assessment takes into account the current knowledge, skills, attitudes, attributes, and capabilities of the workforce, and establishes whether or not these are sufficient to meet the organization's strategic goals and priorities. A strengths, weaknesses, opportunities, and threats (SWOT) analysis, described in Chapter 2, is a useful framework for the assessment of internal strengths and weaknesses, and external opportunities and threats and its results would feed into the HR planning process.

The internal analysis phase can be conducted at the broad macro-level or the more precise micro-level. A macro-level examination takes into account the organization's structure, core values, culture, that is its shared values, norms, and expectations that guide the organization's members in terms of

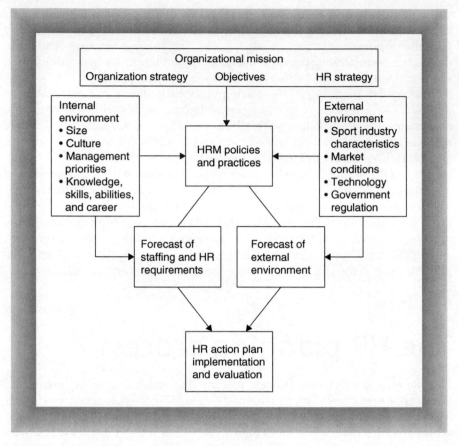

Figure 3.1 HR planning process (*Source*: Adapted from Kane, 1997).

how to approach their work and deal with each other and customers/clients. Information about aspects such as culture or climate can be obtained via a cyclical survey process (i.e., every 2–3 years) or external review (often out-sourced to a specialist management consultancy firm). Instruments used to assess culture, such as culture inventories, range from generic question-naires to diagnostic tools which are custom designed for the organization. A micro-level analysis assesses the number of employees or volunteers, their skills, abilities and knowledge, qualifications, demographics (e.g., age, sex, etc.), level of payment, leave entitlements, and records of performance appraisals. Some larger organizations use in-house HR information systems to collect, store, and manage such data.

The analysis of the external environment entails ascertaining emerging issues and trends significant for the organization and determining if these will impact on HR strategies. Considerations include government policy, administrative/legal, economy, technology, social and culture, and stake-holder environments. The PEST framework, as described in Chapter 2, is commonly used for analysis whereby all the relevant external forces are listed under the four headings: Political, Economic, Sociological, and Technological. Another popular reference framework is Michael Porter's (1980) 'five-forces' model. This model identifies five competitive forces that shape industry's profit potential (as measured by the long-term return on investment): (1) the bargaining power of suppliers, (2) the threat of new entrants, (3) the threat of product substitutes, (4) the bargaining power of buyers, and (5) the intensity of rivalry among established organizations within an industry (see Chapter 2 for further detail).

An example of how HR planning works in practice illustrates this process. A sport facility company with a strategy of growing its market share through the use of cutting-edge technologies identifies a trend towards greater flexibility and functionality in online customer services. An internal skills audit of current staff finds that few employees are technologically savvy and determines that current selection, performance management, and training policies favour face-to-face customer interaction skills and current career paths are oriented around success on this dimension of the job. In response, the company develops an HR plan to emphasize greater technology-oriented customer focus and uses this for recruitment, selection, training and development, and career management.

HR planning is about translating strategic objectives into action plans that will deliver on key performance indicators (both qualitative and quantitative). Although dynamic in nature, formal planning is typically undertaken on an annual basis. As a manager you will need to be able to use systematic analyses to determine if current knowledge, skills, and abilities found within the organization are adequate to achieve its strategic goals. Therefore, the need for accurate and reliable data and information on which assessments and forecasts can be made is critical.

Forecasting

Forecasting demand involves estimating the size and composition of the workforce required to meet the organization's objectives. Forecasting techniques may be quantitative or qualitative, and include the use of predictions of experts within and outside the organization, benchmarking estimates based on similar organizations, and scenario planning several potential outcomes. Each of these techniques can assist the HR planning process by identifying how many and what kind of employees may be needed.

Demand forecasting techniques fall into five major categories: direct managerial input, best guess, historical ratios, other statistical methods, and scenario analysis (Ward, 1996), and overviews of each are provided here.

Direct managerial input is typically done via a directive that the number of people in the organization or the workforce budget will adhere to a specific number. For example, the budget of a state sport organization is set at $1.5 million per annum for staff and in consequence the organization either appoints new staff or reduces current staffing levels to meet this ceiling. This technique, while easy to calculate is not linked to actual workload requirements and does not distinguish between critical and non-critical skills. From a strategic planning point of view the weakness of this approach is that analysis of the human resources required to best meet organizational objectives is often not undertaken.

Best Guess is when the managerial judgement process is formalized into a demand forecast. Data on the demand for employees and/or skill and knowledge requirements is collected from each section manager, this could include marketing, accounts, community development, etc., and is collated for an overall projection. Each manager estimates the impact of anticipated productivity and technology and business changes. Assessment of the current staffing profile alongside the anticipated positive and negative changes provides the future estimate. While this approach provides a great deal of flexibility, it assumes that all managers have the time and ability to produce an accurate forecast.

Historical ratios capture historical trends in the organization's demand for human resources. Overall requirements for staff can usually be strongly correlated with other factors such as the number of programmes delivered, size of membership, or number of competitions held. Let us look at an example using simple ratio analysis. In this case, a sport company has identified that it takes 10 employees to produce 100 tennis racquets a day. A recent sponsorship signing of a Top 10 men's tennis player, a crowd favourite, has led the company to forecast an increase in demand to 150 tennis racquets a day, thus, five more employees will need to be hired to meet production demand.

The major strength of this approach is that it is simple and easily developed with simple methodologies such as Excel spreadsheets. As the mixture of regular employees, casual workers, volunteers, and outsourced contractors changes, these historical ratios can also change dramatically. Its weakness is that it requires adjustments for a rapidly changing sport environment and the ability to make adaptations may be beyond the skills of the individuals developing the projections. For instance, quick adjustments may be needed for unexpected weather conditions that result in lower than anticipated snowfall for a ski resort, as the resulting poor ski conditions correlate with lower customer demand and consequently impact staffing requirements.

Other *Statistical methods* include regression, linear programming, simulations, and demand flow models. The simplest version of these is a linear regression model in which time is used as the independent variable and headcount is the dependent variable. A more common variation is the use of multiple regression techniques in which variables used in the historical ratio approach are used as independent variables. A regression model is able to incorporate a rate of change based on the historical productivity improvement trends, whereas this would require additional data manipulation for the historical ratio approach. There are also sophisticated modelling programmes available that provide simulation capabilities that can be used to project the future movement of employees within the organization (see Ward, Bechet & Tripp, 1994 for a fuller review of methods).

The major drawback associated with these models is that they typically require a large sample size and its complexity is difficult to master. Software packages such as SAP® and Peoplesoft® incorporate forecasting tools to assist with this process, but these are generally only used in larger organizations and require specialized HR planning skills.

Statistical approaches to forecasting have an inherent bias in favour of the past, as the assumption underlying such analyses is that past trends will continue into the future. A weakness of this method is that the assumption that the past predicts the future does not always hold true. For example, contracts could be lost or gained depending on the team's win/loss performance. Significant changes in government funding of a particular sport could likewise create new opportunities or restrict growth. Therefore, purely statistical analyses should be used with full knowledge of their limitations.

Scenario analysis uses workforce environmental scanning data to develop alternative workforce scenarios through brainstorming sessions. This approach encourages blue sky outside the square thinking, and can be done within the organization or developed with the use of experts. One method, the Delphi technique involves getting a group of experts to provide individual forecasts, which are in turn collated and then sent back to each individual, usually presented anonymously, for another round of forecasting, the process continuing until a consensus is reached by the experts. For example, the South African Football Association could use this method to forecast the growth of local football in the wake of hosting the 2010 FIFA World Cup. Experts in the impact of hosting mega-events and modelling post-competition changes, football experts and individuals with detailed knowledge of the South African environment and economy, and other relevant experts could form the basis of the Delphi group. Each expert would be asked to map out their predictions and rationale, all the individual responses are then anonymously distributed, each expert would take these into consideration and develop replies, with the distribution of responses continuing until a general consensus is reached.

The Delphi method is generally economical and avoids groupthink and conflict problems that arise in face-to-face group meetings. A weakness is its ability to deal with complex forecasts and with multiple factors, and, as forecasting contains a large amount of uncertainty, a high degree of error is possible.

Scenario planning is another form of analysis. Scenario planning is a forward-looking process of creating possible future stories and considers the unthinkable. The steps are firstly to develop credible scenarios; secondly, list key success factors and HR requirements for the organization to deal with each scenario; and thirdly, to focus resources on initiatives that promote these requirements. The benefits are building into HR strategy an awareness of impending changes and forward planning for these changing conditions. The most commonly cited example of successful scenario planning is Royal Dutch Shell's creation of one simple scenario: What if oil prices dropped dramatically? (Wright, 2000). When oil prices were cut in half, the company avoided catastrophe and grew from 11th to the 4th largest oil company by virtue of 'thinking ahead' and using scenario planning to build HR competencies. However, in general terms it seems that strategic HR planning has not fully embraced scenario planning in the development of individuals and organizations and its potential remains unexploited (Chermack, 2004).

Collaborative forecasting at Brooks Sports

Brooks Sports designs and develops high-performance running footwear, apparel, and accessories which are sold worldwide. In 2001, when the company shifted from a broad product line to focus on high-performance products targeted at serious runners, a new forecasting process was needed to support the strategic direction of the company. The existing forecasting process, based entirely on the judgement of the sales team, was limiting the company's ability to grow.

Challenges

The strategy shift created a number of forecasting challenges for Brooks including the following:

- Inconsistent growth: new products experience growth anywhere from 0 to 50 per cent annually.
- Long production planning horizon coupled with short product life.
- No exposure to retail sell-through: the high-performance products are sold primarily through independent speciality stores who do not have the capability to share sales data with vendors.

Solution

Brooks completely revamped its forecasting process. An independent forecasting group was established to coordinate input from various groups – sales, marketing, product development, and production – and to remove bias from the forecasting process.

The forecasting group established a collaborative forecasting process with three primary steps:

Step 1: Produce monthly statistical forecasts to capture level, trend, seasonality, and the impact of events based on historical data.

Step 2: Sales management and sales representatives to forecast sales for a 12-month horizon, focusing on major accounts.

Step 3: Compare the statistical and judgmental forecasts, and make adjustments to create the final monthly forecast. Ninety per cent of the final forecasts are the same as the statistical forecasts – changes are most commonly made to the forecasts for new styles where the sales organization has important knowledge to add.

Results

Forecast accuracy has improved on an average by 40 per cent, and the improved forecasting has also helped to smooth out production, resulting in lowered costs and better margins.

Class discussion: How can the forecasting undertaken by Brooks be used in HR planning?

(*Source*: Adapted from ForecastPro© March 2006, ©Copyright 2006, Business Forecast Systems, Inc.)

Research suggests that most workforce changes that will occur over the next 3 to 5 years are already well in progress and can be anticipated with a reasonable range of parameters (Ward, 1996). HR planning processes for forecasting should recognize change drivers and the associated HR implications and choose workforce planning tools, techniques, and models that suit the sport organization and will help deliver its strategic goals.

Determining HR supply

Having determined and forecast HR demand, the next step is to assess the internal and external sources of supply. *Internal analysis* takes into account the likelihood of retirements, turnover, potential training needs of current employees, and future staffing requirements. Skills inventories are a common method used to collect data on current employees and volunteers. An individual will complete the inventory form on an annual basis and include information such as age, work/volunteer experience, job classification, qualifications, training, areas of expertise, and professional association memberships.

Organizations are increasingly incorporating inventory data and workforce profiles as part of online HR systems, which allow managers access to the data for planning and performance management tasks. These systems track the numbers of new recruitments, transfers, and promotions, along with retirements, voluntary departures, and redundancies.

External analysis looks at the demographic, occupational qualifications, eligibility, and skill availability composition of the workforce in the relevant labour market. Environmental factors that affect the available labour market include the aging of labour force, immigration patterns, occupation-related supply, and economic conditions.

The demand analysis forecast is then matched with the supply analysis. Any gaps indicate either a projected unmet need or a surplus, either of which presents a challenge. It is then necessary to develop action plans to close the demand–supply gap, outlining objectives, specific activities, recruitment and selection, training and development, outsourcing and contingency staffing, performance indicators, rewards, and evaluation methods.

Some challenges

Despite its acclaimed benefits, many organizations do not engage in strategic HR planning. The inherent complexity associated with efforts to model HR systems is a drawback, especially when this is combined with uncertainty of HR needs in the future and an assumption that there will always be sufficient time to ascertain and then meet those needs. However, in many sectors of the sport industry recruitment lead times have become more of an issue in recent years because of the need for more highly skilled and specialized managerial and professional staff, and volunteers. Thus HR planning is increasingly important for good strategic decision making within sport organizations.

Job analysis and design

Once sufficient HR planning has been undertaken, an articulation of the activities required to meet the organization's strategic goals and a determination of the positions that are needed to fulfil these tasks is completed. This involves undertaking a job analysis and then using this information in job design.

Job analysis is a systematic analysis of the tasks and responsibilities of a given job, along with the skills, knowledge, and experience needed to perform the job. Systematic identification of the duties to be performed in any given role provides the basis for effective HR planning. What a 'sports development officer', a 'competition coordinator', or a 'membership liaison manager' does may vary from organization to organization. Therefore, a shared understanding of the expectations of the position within the specific sport organization is essential. Analysis is an ongoing process within the organization as the tasks comprising most jobs will change over time owing to technological innovations or other reasons. Up-to-date job analysis may provide an indication of when jobs need redesigning because of task content changes.

For example, a competition coordinator for a state sport organization may have been hired when the organization was relatively small and mainly used manual systems for record keeping and communication. Subsequent changes may have included the introduction of online customer relationship management programmes and databases, along with a growing membership with higher expectations of service from the state body. Ongoing job analysis would identify and document the new duties, providing a better understanding of the current responsibilities of the competition coordinator. If the incumbent competition coordinator left the organization then the position description for the replacement competition coordinator should consequently reflect the job at that time rather than when the position was originally filled. Thus the new competition coordinator would need to have relevant online + customer skills.

Accurate job analysis is required for an effective recruitment and selection process. Job analysis produces a job description and a job specification. Job analysis provides data for performance appraisal that can be used to compare an individual's actual performance with the specified job expectations. It is also the basis for wage and salary determination and can be used to evaluate and compare jobs for wage and salary purposes. In addition, job analysis data should feeds into the organization's training and development strategy.

Job analysis has become increasingly important as it forms a component of legal requirements for hiring, promotional, wage and salary, and other personnel practices. Legal regulations vary from country to country and it is important that all sport organizations are aware of any relevant government requirements in this regard. In the US, Federal regulations provide that each employment practice of the Federal Government, and of individual organizations, use a job analysis to identify:

- basic duties and responsibilities;
- knowledge, skills, and abilities required to perform the duties and responsibilities;
- factors that are important in evaluating candidates.

Additionally, the US Federal Guidelines for job analysis and *Equal Employment Opportunity Commission's Uniform Guidelines for Employee Selection Procedures, 29 C.F.R. Part 1607[1]* provides a framework to help assure that hiring, evaluation, or promotion processes are employed in a non-discriminatory manner. Furthermore, it states that a thorough job analysis is needed for supporting a selection procedure. This may have implications for proving or disproving that discrimination has taken place. For example, a job description may be tendered in laying charges of discrimination against an organization charged with paying a female less than a male in the organization, even though the woman is performing what is essentially the same job as her male counterpart.

Job analysis data

The most frequently used technique for collecting information for a job analysis is the *interview*. It is used to collect data from the employee who is performing the job or the job incumbent's manager. Critical incident interviews, where the individual or manager describes incidents where underperformance or success has eventuated, are used to identify vital skills and abilities required to perform the job. A weakness of this approach is its subjectivity. Employees may overstate the duties they perform or they may neglect to mention certain responsibilities which are infrequent but critical. On the other hand, the manager may speculate about what they think the employee is doing rather than the tasks that are actually being performed.

Structured questionnaires, completed by the employee or manager and others who have some relationship to the job, are also commonly used. To avoid problems of respondent bias many organizations use some form of 360 degree feedback where the job holder, peers, direct reports, and managers all answer questions about the one job. The data is then collated to provide a 'rounded' perspective on the job.

Direct observation of the individual performing a job, with a record taken of the observations, is used where work behaviours are observable. The subjectivity of other methods such as interviews or self-complete questionnaires is removed, but there is a danger that the employee may change his or her behaviours if they know they are being observed. *Diaries or logs* in which employees record their daily activities and tasks can also be used to record what the job entails.

Combinations of the four methods outlined above will usually provide better results than just using one method on its own. Regardless of the method used, the information collected should be comprehensive and align with an organization's vision and strategic goals.

Job descriptions and specifications

Two primary outcomes of job analysis are the provision of information for job descriptions and specifications. Where the job description outlines the duties and responsibilities attached to a position, the specification delineates the qualifications and skills required. While in practice aspects of the specification are likely to be embedded in the job description, it is a useful exercise to conceptually differentiate between the two as each has a different purpose. The job specification and description act as a guide for recruiting the right person into a job that the sport organization needs performed. The description also provides the basis for determinations of the level of remuneration and is used in performance management.

A job description should be concise, accurate, and contain achievable tasks. The job is identified with a title (e.g., Sport and Recreation Officer), location of the job within the organization (e.g., programmes division), and the reporting relationship of the job (e.g., to the Executive Officer). The job's definition is contained in a summary statement that includes the purpose of the job, its function, and its relationship to the organization's strategy. The job delineation includes the duties, responsibilities, reporting relationships, and other tasks or functions and is the lengthiest part of the description. In general, job descriptions tend to be less specific at higher levels within the organization such as for senior managers or executives than for lower level positions.

The *job specification* outlines the minimum qualifications required to perform the job. This would typically include education, experience, or skills. Determining the base-level qualifications for a job requires a thorough job analysis and a good understanding of the skills needed to perform the work effectively. For example, in the case of the competition coordinator, knowledge of appropriate competition software packages and the ability to operate website software systems would be included in the job specification. This job specification would enable the organization to engage in targeted recruitment and selection procedures.

A Sport and Recreation Officer example is presented below.

Position Description – Sport and Recreation Officer

1. Position Details

Position: Sport and Recreation Officer
Classification: Level (EBA) 4 $40,344–$44,951 +
                   11% superannuation.
Location: 3N 121
Job status: Full time
Reports to: Executive Officer

2. Job Summary

To provide students and staff, and the wider community with the opportunity to participate in a wide range of sport and physical recreation activities and programmes. To achieve this requires application in the areas of planning, promotion, implementation, and evaluation, which are to be accomplished both as an individual and as part of a team.

3. Duties and responsibilities

Representation

- Attend and report at staff meetings.
- Attend and assist with the running of Sport and Recreation Collective meetings.
- Be a representative on any other appropriate committees and at relevant conferences.

Programmes

- Orientation: contribute to the running of the Orientation programme by providing activities and promoting sport & recreation programmes.
- Social sport: plan, promote, and implement a social sports programme.
- Trips and tours: plan, promote, and implement a trips and tours programme.
- Come and try activities: plan, promote, and implement a range of 'come and try' activities.

Administration

- Follow all policies and procedures. Review and make recommendations on policies and procedures.
- Assist with the planning and preparation of the Sport and Recreation budget and ensure that the budgetary constraints are met for all activities/programmes.

47

- Follow the correct procedures for purchasing equipment or services from external providers.
- Manage individual and/or team registrations and organize appropriate payment systems.
- Maintain records of all equipment borrowed.

4. Relationships

This position reports directly to the Executive Officer. A close working relationship with the Sport and Recreation Director and other relevant staff is essential. Positive working relationships with the other departments and community organizations should be developed and maintained.

5. Qualifications

Qualifications deemed appropriate for this position would be the successful completion of a relevant tertiary course or degree such as Sport and Event Management or Physical Education.

6. Knowledge base

- Successful completion of a relevant tertiary qualification.
- A high-level understanding of planning and budgeting, experience in assessing needs and programming, a broad knowledge of the rules and regulations governing sport and recreation.
- A good understanding of the sport and recreation needs and requirements of the client body.
- Sound computer skills in using email, Internet and programmes such as Word and Excel.
- Qualified in Level 2 First Aid.

7. Authority

This position is responsible for an annual budgeted expenditure of approximately $100,000, maximizing sources and levels of income from Sport and Recreation activities/events, signing off on Sports and Recreation Purchase and organizing casual staffing as appropriate. They will operate within a team environment, however is expected to demonstrate initiative, sound judgement, decision making, and problem-solving skills. This position requires the incumbent to have the ability to be self-motivated and work with minimal supervision, be able to build relationships, and have excellent oral and communication skills.

8. Accountability

The Sport and Recreation Officer is responsible for the provision of sports and recreation programmes in a polite, courteous, well-organized, and efficient manner to the community. The Sports and Recreation Officer is responsible for ensuring all logistical considerations are met in carrying out sport and recreation programmes and ensuring all sports and recreation equipment is kept in good order and maintaining strict confidentiality and privacy when handling personal or commercial information.

Selection Criteria – Sport & Recreation Officer

Applicants must address each of the following selection criteria:

1. Tertiary qualifications in a related area and previous experience in the sector.
2. An understanding of and a commitment to the values of the organization.
3. An ability to plan, promote, implement, and evaluate a sport or recreation programme.
4. An ability to assess, manage, and prevent potential risks associated with a sport or recreation programme.
5. An ability to frame and manage an annual budget.
6. An ability to manage and/or work with volunteers.
7. An ability to deliver a high level of customer service.
8. An ability to work well under pressure and meet deadlines, whilst maintaining attention to detail.
9. An ability to not only work independently, but also, to contribute effectively as part of a larger team.
10. An ability to advise and provide administrative support to committee structures and student groups.
11. Previous experience working in or with sporting organizations, clubs, teams, or athletes and a broad understanding of a range of sports.
12. Excellent interpersonal and written communication skills.
13. A sound and competent level of computer skills.
14. Other associated qualifications, such as level 2 first aid, drivers licence, bus license, and safe food handling.

As jobs change over time, and the incumbents in an existing job may modify their approach to performing the jobs to deal with such changes, the job analysis process is vulnerable to potential inaccuracies. While it is not realistic to expect that the job descriptions are continuously updated with every change, there is a need for a systematic review process. Responsiveness to change in this regard needs to be balanced with the legal requirements for documentation. Flexibility can also be maintained through an active job-design approach.

Job design

Job design is the process of outlining the way work is performed and the required tasks, using job analysis and contextualizing this information by locating the job within the work group. Job design takes into account the needs of both the work group and the organization in the design of the job. De Cieri, Kramar, Noe, Hollenbeck, Gerhart and Wright (2005) note that research has identified four basic approaches to job design: 1. motivational, 2. mechanistic, 3. biological and 4. perceptual-motor, and each approach has implications associated with its use.

The *motivational* approach acknowledges the psychological needs of employees and how the fulfilment of these, when built into job design, can lead to increased job satisfaction, motivation, performance, and involvement. Typical motivational components considered are as follows:

- Autonomy – level of independence in carrying out job duties.
- Intrinsic job feedback – the work in itself is motivating.
- Extrinsic job feedback – external sources of feedback are provided.
- Social interaction – avenues for team and collegiate work.
- Task/goal clarity – job requirements are clearly delineated.
- Task variety – the job involves engaging in different activities.
- Task identity – a complete, indefinable piece of work is produced.
- Ability/skill level requirements – the knowledge level required is high.
- Ability/skill variety – use of different skills and knowledge.
- Task significance – the job is interconnected and important to other jobs.
- Growth/learning – opportunities for learning are provided.
- Promotion – the job has career pathways.
- Communication – receiving and disseminating information.
- Recognition – scope for reward and acknowledgement of good work.

The use of motivational approaches to job design such as job enrichment (providing more decision making responsibility), job enlargement (widening the scope of tasks), job rotation (moving employees around a range of jobs), flexible work practices, and self-managing teams, all focus on increasing the potential of the job to motivate. A well-designed job based on this approach will typically result in an increase in number and level of skills required. Research shows that motivational techniques, while increasing satisfaction, do not necessarily lead to better performance quality. Motivation of employees and volunteers is discussed further in Chapter 8.

The *mechanistic* approach was dominant throughout the 20th century and is underpinned by principles of scientific management, time and motion studies, and work simplification. The premise of this approach is that there was one best way to do a job, and by analysing workers movements the most effective way to perform a job could be designed. The key components considered in this approach are as follows:

- Job specialization – the degree to which specialization of tasks is possible.
- Specialization of tools and procedures – the degree of special purpose use of tools and procedures.

- Single activities – can the job be done one task at a time?
- Skill simplification – the basic skill and training required.
- Repetition – the repetitiveness of the tasks.
- Spare time (decrease) – the time between tasks is minimized.
- Automation – what tasks can be automated?

The mechanistic approach is oriented towards HR efficiency and flexibility outcomes such as staffing ease and low training times. As such, it suggests designing jobs with reduced mental demands. The benefits of this work design approach are decreased costs of training, lower staffing difficulties, fewer errors, decreased mental overload, and fatigue. The disadvantages are that the mechanistic approach is associated with increased absenteeism and boredom, together with decreases in job satisfaction and motivation (Das, 1999). Its task focus suggests a 'dehumanization' of work.

The *biological* approach (Campion, 1988) is based on the human factors related to work design, and is also referred to as the *ergonomic* approach. It is based on the science of biomechanics, or the study of body movements, and is concerned with the design of jobs and physical environments to match the physiological capabilities and limitations of people. This approach analyses the physiological needs and physical conditions under which work is undertaken, considering elements such as the following:

- Physical size – aspects such as the need to be of certain height or weight.
- Strength – requirements of lifting or muscular endurance.
- Agility – ability to carry out work that requires physical manipulations.

The aim of a thorough ergonomic analysis and subsequent job design is the reduction in workplace illness and injuries, and fostering of good employee health. Jobs designed using this approach 'have more comfortable employees who report less physical effort and fatigue, fewer aches and pains, and fewer actual health complaints' (Campion, 1989).

The *perceptual-motor* approach also has its roots in the human-factors literature. The focus is on human mental capabilities and limitations. The aim is to design jobs in a way that ensures that they do not exceed the mental capabilities of the job holder primarily by striving to reduce the attention and concentration requirements of jobs, while improving reliability, safety, and user reactions. This approach emphasizes:

- Facilities – adequacy of lighting, workplace layout, and design.
- Equipment – ease of use of equipment.
- Materials – access to manuals, information used in performing the job.
- Information – considerations of the information input required and processing to do the job and information required to be produced by the job.

The benefits of this approach are related to lower error rates, fewer accidents, and reduced training requirements, however, its use has not been found to increase job satisfaction or motivation.

In assessing the four approaches, Campion and Berger (1990) found that jobs designed around the motivational approach had higher pay and job evaluation measures (the determination of the level of the job) reflecting higher skill requirements. Jobs based on the mechanistic and perceptual-motor approaches had lower pay and evaluation measures reflecting lower skill requirements, and jobs using the biological approach and to some degree the perceptual-motor approach, had lower job evaluation measures reflecting lower physical requirements.

Cleave's (1993) study of the appropriateness of Hackman and Oldman's job characteristics model is one of the few studies of job characteristics of sport administrators. The model suggests that workers 'respond more positively to their jobs when they feel that their jobs are valuable and worthwhile, that they are accountable for their work performance, and that they know how well they are performing' (Cleave, 1993: 229). Job dimensions were measured on the relationship of skill variety, task identity, task significance to experienced meaningfulness; autonomy to experienced responsibly; and feedback from the job to knowledge of results. The role of psychological states and the relationship between job dimensions and affective responses of internal work motivation, general job satisfaction, and growth satisfaction was also investigated. This study of administrators of physical education, recreation, and intercollegiate athletic programmes found significant positive relationships between job dimensions, psychological states, and affective responses. The proposed relationships were generally established, but there were some results that were not consistent with the model, specifically the predication that each psychological state is influenced by specific job dimensions. This led to the conclusion that while 'theoretical models developed in other fields can provide useful frameworks for understanding the phenomena in sport management' (Cleave, 1993: 241), such models should be tested in the sport organization and not just simply applied without context.

As can be seen from the above discussion there are trade-off between the various approaches, and this represents a challenge to job design that is simultaneously effective, efficient, and satisfying. On the one hand are the potential organizational costs associated with high mental ability requirements (motivational approach) such as increased training and development, error likelihoods, and compensation requirements. On the other hand are the potential individual costs associated with low mental ability requirements (mechanistic and perceptual/motor approaches) of decreased satisfaction, motivation, and compensation.

Taking these challenges into account Campion, Mumford, Morgeson and Nahrgang (2005) suggest that there are eight obstacles to work redesign. These obstacles are outlined in Table 3.1 along with suggested management responses.

The aforementioned theories of job design are largely based on a traditional workforce and workplace. The increasing use of alternative forms of job design such as high performing teams, virtual locations, and other flexible formations are a reflection of the demands that contemporary sport organizations face and must be responsive to if they are to ensure organizational sustainability. Changing employee, volunteer, and customer expectations requires continuous change, improvement, and responsiveness. Together with this is the changing workforce that includes an increased proportion of

Table 3.1 Work Redesign: Eight obstacles and opportunities

Obstacle to work redesign	Suggested approach
1. Job design influences multiple outcomes	Choose a job-design approach that is appropriate for the HR strategy of the organization.
2. Trade-offs between different design approaches	(a) Minimize inherent trade-offs. (b) Specify the desired outcomes of the redesign process. (c) Consider a variety of approaches to work design in order to reduce needed trade-offs.
3. Difficulty in choosing an appropriate unit of analysis	Use four levels of analysis: (a) Jobs represent the highest level of analysis and can be defined as a group of duties performed by a single individual. (b) Duties are composed of multiple tasks that form a major portion of the work performed. (c) Tasks are typically discrete work activities. (d) Task cluster is an intermediary level between tasks and duties.
4. It is difficult to predict the nature of a job before it exists	(a) Take into account both the motivational value and the interdependencies of tasks. (b) Once the job is designed, it must be viewed in its entirety to fully understand the nature of the job being created.
5. Individual differences complicate job redesign	(a) When designing jobs for multiple employees, the role of individual differences should be considered, but not viewed as a major obstacle. (b) Examine the preferences of large groups of employees (e.g., in a specific occupation) rather than the preferences of particular individuals.
6. Job enlargement can occur without job enrichment	Implement work designs that involve decision making influence and control rather than simply increasing the number of tasks. This may lead to desired outcomes such as employees carrying out more proactive, integrative, and interpersonal tasks.
7. New jobs need to be created as part of growth or downsizing	(a) Establish clear roles and responsibilities for employees and inform and involve employees in the change. (b) Enhance levels of control over the timing and methods of work.

(Continued)

Table 3.1 (Continued)

	(c) Give attention to the design of work and the wider organizational context in order to enhance an organization's ability to achieve contraction without incurring long-term negative consequences.
8. Long-term effects may differ from short-term effects	From the planning stages of the job-design intervention, consider the long-term and short-term effects of job design.

Source: Adapted from Campion et al. (2005).

women, more dual working couples, more cultural diversity, higher-educated employees, and an aging workforce. Workplace tenure changes mean that employees now expect to change organizations several times during their career and the extent to which existing approaches can respond to these changing environments will be a increasingly paramount issue.

Outsourcing HR

For many smaller sport organizations that do not have the staff, expertise, or volume of work to justify the operation of a separate HR function within the organization an option is to outsource some aspects of HR. Outsourcing involves entering into contractual arrangements with external service providers to deliver a product or service to the organization. Considerations in decisions to outsource usually revolve around more effective provision of the service, cost and quality wise; or the need for expertise, knowledge, or skills that are not present in the organization. Typically, outsource providers are specialists able to provide a central product or extensive service across a range of organizations and thus gain economies of scale. The outsourcing arrangement should be assessed in terms of organizational effectiveness and its impact on the internal workforce. For example, a relatively small sport organization might outsource a straightforward transactional activity such as payroll. The outsourcing of this function might then allow the staff member currently undertaking the activity to work on other HR activities that are more developmental.

Within outsourcing it is common to develop a service level agreement (SLA). SLAs are contracts between service providers and sport organizations that define the services provided, the metrics associated with these services, acceptable and unacceptable service levels, liabilities on the part of the service provider and the customer, and actions to be taken in specific circumstances. An example of an SLA for HR services is provided below.

SLAs – HR outsourcing will

1. Recruitment and selection

Pre-advertisement

Advise on recruitment policy.
Assist in job/role design.
Undertake job analysis/evaluation and compliance matters as necessary.
Campaign planning.

Advertising

Agree advertisement text with organization representative.
Liaise with advertising agency and place advertisement in agreed media. The organization representative will respond to requests for approval.

Preparation of documentation

Prepare and agree electronic and hard copy job packs for candidates.
Collate all job applications and enter all applicants onto database.
The organization representative will carry out short listing exercise and decide candidates to be interviewed.

Interview

Advise on interview arrangements.
Obtain references.
The organization representative will:
   Invite candidates to interview.
   Organize interview venue.
   Organize selection arrangements.
   Organize panel and interview pack for panel members.
   Make verbal conditional offer to successful candidate, including negotiation of salary.

Appointment offers

Issue conditional offer letter and contract including relevant Terms and Conditions organize medical clearances. Notify unsuccessful applicants.

Another form of outsourcing in HR relates to contracting another body to deliver a specific service or product and have HR built into the arrangement. For example, the SLA presented below is a contract for programme delivery but as part of the arrangement the contracted body is responsible for staff training.

Sheffield City Council, Activity Sheffield – SLA for Activity Provision

Sheffield City Council Activity Sheffield and Partner/commissioning organization

Introduction

This agreement is intended to clarify the responsibilities of Activity Sheffield as the service provider. The description, 'Activity leaders' will include sports coaches, casual play workers, Area Workers, and other employees of Sheffield City Council Activity Sheffield. Partner/commissioning organizations include schools, other local authority and statutory service providers, clubs and community organizations, and privately managed service providers.

Activity Sheffield – Our responsibilities

- We will ensure that the Activity leaders are trained and familiar with current practices in the activity they are to lead.
- We will ensure that activity leaders working with children and vulnerable adults have attended an Activity Sheffield induction session including the section's own child protection policy and have been CRB checked.
- We will carry out a prior risk assessment at the chosen site, in conjunction with the coordinating body.
- We will work with a ratio of participants appropriate to the activity involved, in accordance with play and sports governing body guidelines, but never more than a maximum ratio of 30 per session leader.
- We will arrive in good time to complete necessary preparations and commence at the agreed time, except in the event of, and where possible by prior notification of exceptional circumstances.
- We will conduct the session with due regard to the enjoyment, safety, fair, and equitable inclusion of all participants.
- We will ensure that dress, appearance, and personal conduct of the activity leader will be appropriate to the needs of the participants, the requirements of the activity, and in accordance with Activity Sheffield standards.
- We will insist that the activity leader is always accompanied by a responsible person from the coordinating organization during activity sessions.
- We will use equipment that is appropriate, sufficient, and safe for the requirements of the activity and participants.

- We will actively discourage any inappropriate behaviour by participants, but it will be the responsibility of the on-site coordinating body to respond to any request to exclude an individual in order to permit the continuation of safe and enjoyable activity.
- We will promptly report and record any accidents, inappropriate behaviour, or language involving participants, to the on-site representative from the coordinating body.
- We will act on any issues arising from an apparent breach of this agreement, in accordance with existing City Council policies and practices.

(*Source*: https://www.sheffild.gov.uk/EasySite/lib/serveDocument.asp)

In this case the SLA in turn acts as the framework for evaluating the outsourced HR activity.

Summary

Strategic HR planning provides a framework for sport organizations to assess where they are, where they want to go, and how they plan to get there. Strategic implementation of HRM means performing activities that support the organization's mission accomplishment and measuring how well those activities contribute to achieving strategic goals. The critical aspect of HR planning is that the organization engages in efforts to anticipate and take actions to ensure that the organization will have the requisite human resources in place to meet its goals.

The HR planning process examines the organization's internal and external environment and uses this information to determine HR requirements required by the organization to meet its goals. Five major categories of demand forecasting techniques were presented in this chapter: direct managerial input, best guess, historical ratios, other statistical methods, and scenario analysis. The internal supply analysis uses skills inventories and workforce profiles to classify current employees and determine the required number of new recruitments and departures. The external analysis considers demographics type and the composition of the workforce in the relevant labour market. When demand and supply are not aligned a plan is put in place to address and close the identified gap.

Job analysis and design are key activities in the planning process. Job analysis is an examination of the tasks and sequences of tasks necessary to perform a job. Job descriptions are a product of job analysis and list the tasks, or functions, and responsibilities of a position which include reporting relationships and specifications such as the qualifications required. Job design is the process of outlining the way work is performed and the required tasks using the job analysis and contextualizing this work within the work group. The challenge for job design is to acknowledge the trade-offs that have to be made between using the different approaches to job design and structure jobs that will be able to meet future challenges and create a motivating and satisfying workplace.

Discussion questions

1. What does HR planning involve?
2. What is job analysis and what is it used for?
3. How does job analysis support SHRM?
4. What is typically included in a job description?
5. What are the advantages and disadvantages in outsourcing all or part of the HR function?

Case Study: HR Planning for the 2002 Salt Lake City Olympic Games

In major events such as the Olympic Games HRM is consolidated and an intensive accelerated programme of planning and activity. The following overview of the planning required (adapted from the *Official Report of the XIX Olympic Winter Games – Salt Lake City 2002*) provides a snapshot of this overall process.

Human resources function at a Glance

- Formed: September 1998
- Ended: April 2002

Programme deliverables

- Develop the overall staffing plan for the Games.
- Recruit qualified staff to fill approved positions.
- Manage the consolidated labour and benefits budget.

Budget

- Total: $226 million (Training, Team 2002 Retention, Staffing, HR).

Pre-games staffing

- One year out (February 2001): 47 (plus 15 for training) – December 2001: 65.

Games – time staffing

- Paid Staff: 110 (total includes 60 paid temporary workers) – Volunteers: 435

Key challenges

- Ensuring broad participation of diverse communities.
- Raising a temporary workforce without the assistance of a temporary employment agency.
- Rejecting surplus volunteer candidates.

Key milestones

- November 1998: Pre-Games volunteer recruitment campaign launch.
- March 2000: Games volunteer recruitment campaign launch.
- July 2000: Volunteer interview launch.
- March 2001: Temporary employee recruitment launch.
- September 2001: Offers to volunteers sent.
- 2001–2002: Training volunteers, including those from out-of-town, and staff members.

Human Resources

Human Resources was formed in 1997 and supported more than 28,000 staff, contractors, and volunteers during the Games. Staff planning and recruitment were consolidated under staffing, using a variety of methods to recruit individuals and provide a training and retention programme. The function comprised five elements: human resources and International Entry, HR Planning and Operations, Retention, Staffing, and Training. These five departments oversaw the entire life cycle of Salt Lake Organizing Committee's (SLOC) employment services from recruitment, compensation and benefits to training, evaluation, and outplacement. To streamline training and Games-time operations, HR combined volunteers and paid staff into one entity: Team 2002.

Planning and Operations

Planning and operations was responsible during the Games for staff check-in, staff break and meal management, staff relations, staff training, scheduling support, uniform distribution, headquarters operations (i.e., payroll, benefits, out processing), incident reporting, and staff communications.

HR planning and operations maintained two significant roles during the Games. First, the function managed the Team 2002 Processing Center, which involved distribution of uniforms, credentials, and retention items to the 26,000 members of Team 2002. Second, the function continued to manage the operational components of the function, including tracking SLOCs attrition and no-shows, scheduling support, meal programme administration, and overseeing HR operations at the venues.

Staffing

HR staffing was responsible for developing the overall staffing and training plan for the Games, recruiting qualified staff members and managing the consolidated labour, and benefits budget. Its mission was to assess, integrate, standardize, and streamline staffing requirements.

Staff Planning

By the end of 1998, HR staffing had surveyed SLOC functions to identify what positions were needed for the pre-Games and Games-time periods and used this data to build the position management reporting system database – designed to manage the labour and benefits budget as well as recruitment. SLOC functions created job descriptions for each position and refined staffing projections and positions needed to stage test events from January through March 1999.

By the end of 1999, HR staffing began a series of reviews to refine SLOCs Games-time head-count projection and standardize Games-time titles and the organizational structure at the venues. Title standardization significantly reduced more than 1000 titles that had been created. It also revealed overlaps in planning, in which more than one function had planned to assign staff members to the same duties.

HR staffing produced the official Head-Count Report for functions such as Food Services, Transportation, human resources, Planning and Operations, and Team 2002 Retention. Functions used this report to plan for meals, transportation, uniforms, and retention items for staff and volunteers before and during the Games. Staffing also created venue-based function organizational charts to reinforce the standard organizational structure that had been established.

Recruitment

Staffing created an in-house team of recruiters (staffing specialists) to partner with each functional area to recruit paid staff members (regular employees, loaned employees, consultants, and temporary employees), volunteers, and interns. Staffing specialists worked within two central recruitment groups, volunteer staffing and Games-time employment (GTE), to fill volunteer or temporary employee positions.

Volunteers

As a function of staffing, an SLOC employee managed the growing number of relocations for regular, full-time employees. SLOC relocated more than 400 team members from 1997 to 2001.

Training

The successful performance of Team 2002 was based on the training of volunteers, with a focus on excellent customer service, professionalism and a positive attitude. *Further details of this training are included in Chapter 6.*

Temporary employees (GTE)

In mid-2000, HR staffing created its GTE team to lead its recruiting and selection of the thousands of employees working 6 months or less who were necessary to stage the Games.

Games-time assignment and redeployment

To increase retention rates of temporary workers, SLOC created a Job Completion Pay programme. Temporary employees who completed their assignment became eligible to receive $1 per hour for every hour worked if he or she completed his or her assignment.

Consolidated labour and benefits budget

HR planning and operations created a daily newsletter at each venue, and provided critical information to staff and volunteers each morning. SLOC consolidated its labour and benefits budgets under staffing to ensure this large budget item was well managed and to provide consistent salary and wage administration throughout the organization.

Evaluation

Some key HR planning recommendations made after the event:

- Consolidate staff planning and all recruitment under staffing to reduce competition for candidates and confusion within the organization regarding who is responsible for what.
- Planning and operations recommends moving job-specific training as close as possible to the start of a volunteer's shift in order to help with the retention of information.
- Support as many HR business processes with one system. Most delays and data integrity issues occur in the interfaces between systems.

Discussion questions:

1. Using Figure 3.1 as a framework outline the key steps the Salt Lake City planning team took to ensure they met their 'programme deliverables'.
2. Discuss the implications of using each approach to job design (motivational, mechanistic, biological, and perceptual-motor) for the volunteer positions. What might be some of the trade-off's between approaches?

4 Recruitment and selection for sport organizations

Chapter overview

Recruitment and selection are terms that are often used as synonyms. In fact they are separate but linked processes. Recruitment refers to the activities and processes undertaken by an organization in order to define its employee or volunteer needs and generate a suitably qualified pool of candidates for various positions. Selection refers to the techniques and methods of choosing the best candidate from the pool that has been generated by recruitment.

This chapter begins by establishing the reasons why recruitment and selection are such important human resource (HR) activities and then describes a sequential process of managing both activities from the beginning to the end. Various alternatives are outlined in relation to each activity and the advantages and disadvantages associated with these alternatives are outlined.

An overview of recruitment and selection

Chapter 3 introduced the concept of strategic human resource planning and the associated techniques. This chapter should be read in conjunction with Chapter 3 because the HR activities of attracting and selecting employees are closely connected with workforce planning and job design, which are covered there. HR planning provides forecasts of future staffing needs so that the organization has the necessary human resources in order to properly implement its strategy. Job analysis along with the job descriptions and specifications, which are derived from job analysis, are the foundations for recruitment and selection in that they specify the knowledge, skills, and abilities required by new staff and volunteers, and outline how these are translated into discrete jobs.

Attracting and selecting the right individuals for the organization is a critical strategic human resources management (SHRM) decision. In the words of the former Chief Executive Officer (CEO) of General Electric, Jack Welch, 'strategy begins with the people that you hire'. In Chapter 2 on SHRM hiring the right person was consistently cited as a key activity in ensuring that an organization meets its goals and this approach is mirrored in the recruitment and selection policies of a large number of best practice organizations (Pfeffer, 1998a). There are a number of reasons for this emphasis on selecting the right persons for your organization.

First, people are at the centre of all organizational processes and the amount of discretionary effort that they put in can vary enormously. Getting the right people can literally mean the difference between success and failure in an organization. Fredrick Taylor, the so-called father of scientific management, whose work is discussed in Chapters 1 and 3 was a fervent advocate of careful selection having observed first hand how much productivity varied between workers even in simple manual labouring jobs in controlled environments. More recent research studies also strongly support this argument. Studies on the productivity of workers in self-paced jobs have found that the gap between the best and the worst performers varies on average by a factor of two or more (Schmidt & Hunter, 1983; Goleman, 1998). In another study, high-performing employees were found to outperform a control group by 129 per cent on average (Boyatzis, 1999). Such findings indicate that attracting and selecting the right people is perhaps the single most important part of the entire HRM process. This is reflected in the often cited aphorism amongst employers that it is better to hire for attitude and train for skills rather than hire for skills and try to train the attitude. An example from an organization providing summer camps is found in its criteria for hiring camp counsellors. Genuine enjoyment of working with or around children, an outgoing, cheerful, adaptable, flexible and diligent nature, and the ability to live in a cabin or a platform tent with children or co-workers for 9 to 11 weeks are highly valued. In a job like this these attributes are often more important than technical competence or relevant knowledge as having the right attitude is critical to success.

Second, people can make a large difference to the culture of an organization and the culture of an organization can in turn be a powerful influence on recruitment. Using a sport analogy, the introduction of a new player into a team or the appointment of a new coach can galvanize performance and provide the impetus for a team to improve their performance and increase success. When power forward Alana Beard joined the Washington Mystics of the Women's National Basketball Association in 2006 the coach Ritchie Adubato noted that her contribution made a massive difference to the team's success. A teammate, Mystics forward DeLisha Milton-Jones added 'Having her on this team is invaluable ... she's a great luxury because she can do so many things' (Gallo, 2006: 6). The Mystics went onto make the 2006 playoffs after having missed out in the previous season.

The culture of an organization is both influenced by selection decisions, that is whether new people will fit in, and the attractiveness of the organization to potential new employees, that is whether good people will want to join. The latter point is confirmed in research by Judge and Cable (1997) who showed that potential employees seek to match their values with the reputation of an organization's culture. This has also been reinforced in surveys of the best organizations to work for such as those conducted by Fortune Magazine (2007) and Hewitt and Associates (2007). In such studies, CEOs often cite the culture of the organization as one of the keys to attracting and retaining the most talented employees. Conversely, it has also been found that the inclusiveness of the sport organization's culture can effect the recruitment and involvement of women and individuals from diverse ethnic groups (Thomas & Dyall, 1999). Thus, an organization's culture can potentially encourage or exclude good candidates from joining and is thus an important force in recruitment.

Third, consistent with the resource-based view (RBV) of the organization that was outlined in Chapter 2, organizations today are more reliant on internal transformation processes that build, for example, speed and efficiency, than on traditional sources of competitive advantages such as location and technology. Therefore, attracting the right talent (i.e., people) becomes a key strategic process in ensuring the future viability of the organization.

Fourth, looking at the direct and indirect costs associated with sub-optimal hiring decisions also provides compelling reasons to recruit and select carefully. Selecting the wrong candidate can result in disruption to an organization because of reduced productivity, poor interpersonal relationships and team morale, reduced customer service levels, and high-associated costs. In direct monetary terms alone, an incorrect hiring decision has been estimated to cost between 40 and 60 per cent of the total annual compensation for a given position (Byham, 2001). An extreme example of the cost of a wrong hire is illustrated by events that happened at Nike. In 2004, Bill Perez was handpicked to be Nike's new CEO by Nike co-founder Phil Knight. However, Knight forced him out of Nike after just 13 months, noting that Perez just didn't understand what Nike was about and that there was too much for an outsider to learn. It is estimated that Perez received a severance package, coupled with salary and bonus that totalled $19.4 million. This was a very costly mistake in hiring.

In most large organizations the recruitment and selection process is managed by the HR department in conjunction with line managers. In a small- to medium-sized organization, such as many sport organizations, recruitment and hiring decisions tend to devolve to line managers alone. Figure 4.1

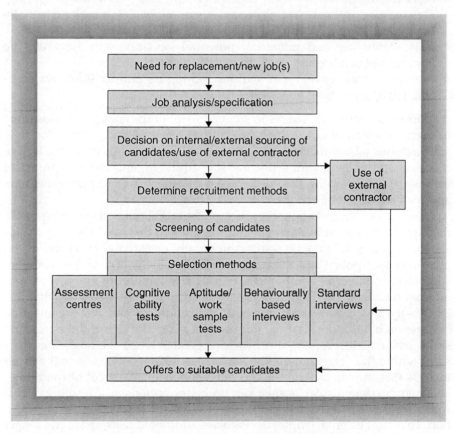

Figure 4.1 An overview of the recruitment and selection process.

represents an overview of the recruitment process showing the various stages and options. The remainder of this chapter will discuss each of the major components and the options which are available to managers in working through the recruitment and selection process from the beginning to the end.

Recruitment

As noted at the start of this chapter, the overall purpose of recruitment is to generate a pool of qualified candidates in the right areas sufficient for the sport organization to meet its strategic goals. More specifically, the purposes of recruitment are to:

- determine the present and future recruitment needs of the organization in conjunction with the HR planning and the job analysis processes;
- source a pool of appropriately qualified job applicants at minimum cost who are likely to stay with the organization if hired;
- meet the organization's legal and social obligations in terms of staffing, for example, by not excluding certain ethnic minorities or seeking to make the organization more attractive to women with children;
- start identifying and preparing potential job applicants who will be appropriate candidates;
- evaluate the effectiveness of various techniques and locations for sourcing job applicants.

A sport organization that seeks to succeed in all of the above activities must be well-informed about upcoming internal demand and supply for new staff; external labour market conditions for different groups of staff; effective channels and materials for attracting staff to the organization; appropriate techniques for assessing the effectiveness of different recruitment methods and relevant legal obligations.

The actual process of obtaining job applicants is about both reaching qualified applicants and stimulating enough interest so that candidates apply for the job. Candidates may be sourced internally or externally depending on organizational policy and the nature of the positions. Internal recruitment sources include current employees, friends and families of employees, and internal transfers. The main advantages of recruiting internally are that it is less costly and reduces risks for both the candidate and the organization because each has more accurate information about the role and the required skills. Internal recruitment also provides greater scope for career development within the organization. The major disadvantage with internal recruitment is that the organization is choosing from a smaller pool of candidates and may become insular or miss out on better options as a result. External recruitment is when the new employee is sought from outside the organization. To recruit external employees involves additional costs, risks, and longer training and adjustment periods than internal recruitment, but recruiting externally means that you can access a wider pool of potential talent. Most organizations will employ a mix of external and internal recruitment for different positions.

Recruitment methods

With reference to Figure 4.1, once an organization has determined a job specification it must then make a decision about whether to recruit internally, externally, or through an external contractor. Internal recruitment methods tend to be simple and often revolve around the efficient dissemination of job information. Thus in national sport association office the recruitment of an internal person into a newly created volunteer management role might involve the executive director and senior managers notifying or speaking with the current staff members, who they feel have the right qualities and competencies for the position. Intranet bulletin boards which advertise positions may also be used. However, many organizations will employ more sophisticated approaches by searching the HR information system for qualified candidates or using succession management techniques, such as those discussed in Chapter 12, for senior jobs. An example of the latter was when, after a major corporate restructure, Octagon Worldwide appointed Rick Dudley as its new President and CEO. Dudley had formerly been President of Octagon North America and had a long and successful track record in sports marketing.

With regard to external recruitment, the need to be more attractive to employees has led many organizations to try to build an employment 'brand' by becoming an 'employer of choice'. To become viewed as an 'employer of choice' sport organizations will commit themselves to offering reward packages, fringe benefits, or job opportunities that make them stand out. Organizations may promote such benefits in their direct advertising and/or seek to become recognized as a 'best employer' by an independent external body. There are a variety of competitions that seek to identify the best organizations to work for including the examples mentioned earlier of Fortune Magazine's 100 Best Companies To Work For (2007), the Hewitt Best Employers in Asia 2007 Awards (Hewitt & Associates, 2007), or the Employer of Choice for Women Award conducted by the Equal Employment for Women in the Workplace Agency in Australia (EOWA, 2007). However, organizations that promote themselves as employers of choice should be mindful that they need to live up to the designation on an ongoing basis and some employee surveys indicate a growing level of cynicism relating to this practice.

External recruitment methods include traditional methods such as advertisements in newspapers or trade journals, the use of public employment agencies, internships and recruitment of graduates direct from universities. More recently *e-recruitment* has become a substantial component of the recruitment strategy for a wide range of sport organizations and an increasingly popular method for job seekers in searching and applying for jobs. These include the UK-based The Sports Recruitment Company, the Australian-based

Sportspeople, Cosmos Sports Jobs in Canada and SportsJobsUsa.com in the United States. The latter not only lists current positions vacant but also provides a database of professional sports team contacts, a sports internship database for entry-level candidates, and a resume writing service.

The Internet can also be used to facilitate any or all of the main processes of attraction (advertising/recruiting), selection, and assessment (screening and testing). In addition, e-recruitment systems can be used, in parallel, to support applicant tracking and workflow systems. Advantages of e-recruitment relates to ease of use; amount of coverage, both geographical (worldwide) and in terms of target audience (all candidates looking for jobs in certain fields can be automatically notified of vacancies); reduced costs per hire when compared with traditional methods; shorter hiring cycles; improved quality and frequency of candidate responses; and recruitment can be tailored more precisely to the required job/candidate profiles.

Let us look at how this might work in practice. The national peak body for golf has just approved funding for an exciting and innovative project with the objective of increasing female participation into the game. A women's golf development officer job description is then written and posted on an Internet recruitment site. This is complemented by advertisements placed in professional golf magazines and in regional and national newspapers as well as the organization's own website. All applicants are requested to access an online application form, complete this form, and submit their applications online. Job seekers that have signed up with the Internet agency and that fit the profile of the candidates being sought will be notified of this vacancy. The Internet recruitment agency will also provide the golf association with data relating to remuneration practices to assist with setting an appropriate reward package for the position. When the applications are received the agency will assess each applicant and determine those who meet the key selection criteria. The list of potential interviewees will then be forwarded to the golf association for approval and the agency will notify unsuccessful candidates. The agency may then exit from the process at this stage, or they may undertake the full selection process and recommend the appointment of the best applicant to the golf association.

However, Internet-based recruitment does come with a major disadvantage, in that the front-end efficiencies can often be counteracted by inefficiencies at the back end related to having to filter good applications from the hundreds or thousands of inappropriate or irrelevant ones. This highlights the need to use effective filtering software or services which can be sensitive to well-defined criteria relating to candidates who may fit the job profile. Other challenges encountered by organizations in implementing e-recruitment include problems with technology and difficulties in tailoring e-recruitment systems to meet specific needs in a recruitment process. Some organizations also encounter problems in simultaneously operating both online and paper-based systems, and fail to integrate e-recruitment systems with existing HR systems. Some of the earlier concerns about excluding potential applicants have diminished with the growth in the use of the Internet and there are now indications that the Internet is the preferred application method for a large majority of candidates.

A common practice if the organization is handling large numbers of candidates is to outsource the recruitment and screening to a professional employment organization as represented in Figure 4.1. Professional employment organizations come in two main forms. First, there are full service recruitment consultants who will help the client organization to define position requirements, advertise, interview, and provide a shortlist of candidates, some of whom will be on the consultant's placement books. In this sense, some consultants act as brokers or agents for prospective staff as well as organizations seeking staff.

The second type of professional employment organizations are *executive search firms* who specialize in finding staff for very senior jobs. Unlike regular consultants, these firms do not find positions for job seekers but seek out candidates who fit the specific requirements of a particular job. These firms tend not to advertise but rely instead on their own research and databases to find candidates. Typically, these 'head hunters' (as executive search firms are colloquially known) are expensive and can charge up to 50 per cent of the first year's salary for a successful placement.

Another recent trend in recruitment is the increased use of referrals and networking where staff from within the organization recruit people via their personal and professional networks. This involves a more or less constant search for top quality candidates and involves existing organizational staff spreading information about available positions. Organizations may also target trade shows, customer contacts, academic connections, alumni networks, and professional associations. Specific initiatives might be to send current staff members to industry professional associations and conferences where they are likely to meet potential candidates and the use of professional association websites and magazines to advertise for professional staff.

The choice of recruitment method will vary depending on the type of sport organization, the state of the labour market, and the type of position being filled. For example, a small community sport organization might recruit using local networks and partnerships whereas a global company such as IMG might use recruitment consultants for senior positions.

If the recruitment exercise generates a large number of applicants then the next step is for the sport organization to undertake some preliminary selection activities and screen the candidates. This process will leave only those who are most likely to have the best fit for the job in terms of qualifications, skills, experience, etc. The process of selecting new employees from a pool of job applicants is analogous to a filtering process where at the end only the most qualified candidates remain.

For many voluntary positions in sport organizations the recruitment process is somewhat different. Recruiting is typically informal, and attracting a sufficient number of qualified applicants can be difficult. In some other non-profit sport voluntary positions such as board members may be elected or appointed on an exofficio basis. In the latter situation recruitment is by nomination and selection is via election.

The most common pathway for involvement in voluntary work in a sport organization is through friends, family, or individuals already involved in the organization or via a 'tap on the shoulder'. Therefore, asking people to volunteer is the best way to recruit volunteers into your sport organization. In the early stages of the recruitment process the potential volunteer should be given a realistic overview of what the role entails before they are asked to commit their time and energy to a position. This should include a job description with meeting times, major tasks, and average weekly or monthly time commitment. Benefits and conditions need to be clearly specified so that applicants are in a position to make an informed decision about whether a job might suit their skills, experience, and availability (Cuskelly & Auld, 2000).

Relatively, few community sport volunteers are recruited through advertising or the media (Cuskelly et al., 2006). An exception is the large-scale mega-sport events such as the Olympic Games, World Championships, and the like. These massive events recruit via advertisements, announcements, partnerships, and target volunteering associations, sporting organizations, professional groups, multicultural groups, educational institutions, and sponsors. Various volunteer positions will be needed and will range from specialist volunteers (e.g., a technical knowledge of the field of play of a particular sport) to general volunteers (e.g., spectator services, transport, community information). The scope of recruitment for such events is extensive, for example the 2008 Beijing Olympics estimates around 70,000 volunteers, the 2006 Commonwealth Games Melbourne and 2006 Asian Games in Doha each had approximately 15,000, and the 2007 International Cricket Council's Cricket World Cup reported 3500 volunteers.

When recruiting volunteers it is important to emphasize the benefits for volunteers rather than the needs of the organization (Australian Sports Commission, 2000). Volunteers should be valued by the sport organization and not feel as though they are being recruited to fill a position that no one else wanted or that they are not being paid just to save the organization's money.

Selection methods

Once the organization has screened out unsuitable candidates, a number of selection options are available. Some of the more commonly used methods are presented in Table 4.1, together with indicators of the cost and validity associated with each technique. When discussing selection techniques, account should be taken of the reliability and validity of each method.

In relation to selection, reliability refers to the extent to which a selection technique is free from random error or, put it in another way, the technique produces a consistent result with repeated use. Research on selection methods reveals that easily observable characteristics, such as verbal fluency, can be more reliably measured using an interview than, for example, leadership ability, which is far more complex and deeply embedded in the individual's personality and therefore not easily assessable during a selection interview.

Validity refers to how well a measure on a selection technique relates to the individual's actual performance in a job. This means the extent to which a selection measure is a predictor of job performance. So whilst verbal

Table 4.1 Common selection methods, cost, and validities

Selection technique	Cost	Validity	Reliability
Behaviourally based interview	Low	Very good	High
Assessment centre	High	Very good	High
Cognitive ability test	Medium–low	Very good	Medium
Work sample test	Low	Good	High
Aptitude test	Medium–low	Good	High
Standard interview	Low	Poor	Low
Personality inventories	High	Poor–medium	Variable but average overall

fluency may be measured reasonably reliably in an interview, it does not necessarily mean that verbal fluency is a good predictor of performance for a given job. On the other hand, a word processing test used in a selection technique for an administrative position is likely to have a high validity since it directly measures a significant job component. When selecting individuals for a job the selection process may require different techniques to be used for reasons of validity, even if the actual technique has a lower reliability score. Perhaps the best example of this is the traditional interview, which according to HR research has a low reliability score, but it is considered essential in most selection procedures because of the need to judge a candidate's sociability and other attributes that can be reliably observed in an interview situation and which have a high validity in relation to the ability of a candidate to 'fit in' with an organization's culture and values.

As can be seen in Table 4.1, some techniques have more validity than others, and choosing the right technique or combination of techniques varies according to each selection scenario. The advantages and disadvantages associated with each of these techniques, and the situations in which each one is most appropriate, are discussed in the following section.

Cognitive ability tests

Cognitive ability tests differentiate people on their mental capacity and can involve tests of verbal comprehension, numerical ability, abstract reasoning, inductive reasoning, pattern recognition, and memory. These tests are often used to evaluate more complex jobs and have been used since the early 1900s. Cognitive ability tests are reliable and have good validity. They are typically used for middle – to senior-level positions and are often used as part of the 'multiple hurdles' approach. That is to say, passing such a test does not qualify a candidate for the job, but failing it may legitimately be used as a basis for eliminating a candidate from further selection procedures. For example, a professional sport organization is recruiting a business administration trainee in the corporate partnerships section. The position requires research, communication, and investigation skills. Therefore, a standard cognitive ability test that measures verbal reasoning and numerical tests would be appropriate as such tests have shown high validity for jobs requiring these abilities.

Work sample tests

Work sample or job performance tests attempt to simulate a job in the controlled conditions of a selection process or require candidates to provide samples of their actual work, such as a portfolio. Candidates tested via a simulation are asked to complete verbal or physical activities that closely mirror real work tasks. For example, a potential manager of an aquatic and recreation complex might be asked to do an 'in basket' exercise in which the candidate is given a hypothetical case company and a range of memos asking for managerial type decisions to be made on a range of issues in a short time frame. Such tests usually require the candidate to evaluate and prioritize the multiple requests outlined in the memos and emails and devise a plan of action to address the issues in the most logical way. Thus the exercises given to the candidate for the aquatic and recreation complex position might include being asked to respond to a customer service complaint, a notice of non-compliance of safety equipment operation, a sudden resignation of her head lifeguard, and a last minute request for additional lifeguards for a school swimming event to be held later in the day. As a result of the close association with real jobs, work sample tests have a high reliability and validity. The major problem associated with these tests is the possibility of less than optimum performance due to anxiety in the testing environment.

Aptitude tests

Aptitude tests attempt to simulate work sampling tests in situations where the candidate has not previously worked in the job for which she/he is being recruited. The key issue with these tests is the validation of the test as a good predictor of success in relation to the actual job. Tests can be used to cover a range of areas, with the most common relating to clerical and numerical aptitude and mechanical or physical dexterity tests. For example, applicants for a computing position in a sport information company that provides sports statistics and information services online could be assessed using a programming aptitude test. Some of these will use 'pseudocode', flowcharting, or assembly language.

Cognitive ability, work sample, and aptitude tests can sometimes be purchased from HR consultancy firms or can be obtained directly from organizations such as the Australian Council for Educational Research. Various versions of these tests are also found on the Internet and are relatively inexpensive. Research suggests that generic tests are equally good predictors of job success as specially tailored tests.

Personality inventories

Personality inventories are intended to measure an individual's personality traits or characteristics and are generally used to guage the likelihood of someone fitting into a particular job or organization or the likelihood that they will perform well in a job. These inventories are usually comprised of statements or questions relating to behaviours, attitudes, or beliefs for which the subjects are asked to agree or disagree with by choosing from a number of alternatives. Personality inventories attempt to measure the major psychological characteristics of a person using standard personality constructs such as the so-called 'Big Five' dimensions of personality. These characteristics are listed below along with a list of adjectives that describe their sub-scales:

- Extraversion (social, gregarious, assertive, talkative, expressive).
- Adjustment (emotionally stable, non-depressed, secure, content).
- Agreeableness (courteous, trusting, good-natured, tolerant, cooperative, forgiving).
- Conscientiousness (dependable, organized, persevering, thorough, achievement oriented).
- Inquisitiveness (curious, imaginative, artistically sensitive, broad minded, playful).

There are numerous commercially available psychological inventories but they can be expensive and there is considerable debate about their usefulness in assessment with many questions about their reliability and validity. In a meta-analysis of the 'Big Five' only conscientiousness displayed any real validity across a range of job categories (Barrick & Mount, 1991).

Assessment centres

Assessment centres employ a comprehensive approach to selection, and are usually used for management candidates, often at entry to mid-manager level where the organization is trying to assess potential beyond the immediate position. Assessment centres incorporate a range of techniques typically based on behaviour assessment. Some very large organizations run their own assessment centres, but it is more common for smaller organizations to use the assessment centre services of HR consulting firms. Candidates in an assessment centre will undertake a range of observed group-based and individual problem-solving exercises that simulate actual managerial tasks. Assessment candidates may also be required to complete psychological and cognitive ability tests, work sample tests, and interviews. The components of assessment centre activities are usually evaluated by multiple, professionally trained raters. Performance of candidates is typically measured using competencies profiles such as those discussed in Chapter 3. Assessment of values can also be covered by assessment centres, which can provide good opportunities for determining whether or not a candidate will fit in with the prevailing culture of an organization (motivational fit).

As an example, a state governing body of rowing is looking to appoint a state development coordinator. The position will be generally responsible for the overall management, promotion and development of the sport and its affiliated rowing clubs and competitive and recreational members throughout the state. Specifically, the development coordinator will run rowing campaigns focusing on underage athlete and coach pathways and the development of underage activities for beginner to elite. An assessment centre approach could be used to assess potential candidates, whereby each person would be required to complete a series of activities and tests to assess the candidate's interpersonal skills, and their demonstrated ability to inspire and elicit cooperation of people across a wide range of organizations, including teenagers, volunteers, rowing clubs, and secondary schools. Organizational skills and their ability to set priorities, plan work programmes, and meet deadlines could also be assessed. The assessment centre programme might include aptitude and cognitive ability tests, 'in basket' exercises, scenario simulations, a presentation to the 'board of directors', and a group exercise involving teenagers and volunteers. Personal data could be collected via a CV to determine if candidates had relevant experience and sufficient rowing knowledge including national rowing coach accreditation.

Overall, assessment centres provide a well-rounded measure of a candidate's abilities and potential and have a high level of reliability and a high validity for managerial jobs and executive appointments, particularly those with complex competency profiles. The major disadvantage of assessment centres is the cost and time involved in putting candidates through the centre and completing the assessments.

Standard interviews

While the standard or traditional interview is the most commonly used selection technique it is also the method that is most susceptible to error in its use because of its inherent subjectivity. The poor reliability and validity of the interview relates to faulty processing of interview data, or poor judgements about appropriate questions and responses which are often the result of poorly developed interview skills. Some of the common subjectivity problems that can occur with interviews are 'halo' and 'horn' effects, where interviewers either like or dislike one characteristic of a candidate and this biases all other judgments. For example, an interviewer might dislike to the dress sense, hair style, or jewellery worn by a younger person. At a more subtle level, the effect might manifest itself in stereotypical labels being applied such as 'typical accountant/IT person/jock'. Other subjectivity problems might arise through 'contrast effects', where very good or bad candidates can affect the judgments made about others or 'leniency/strictness' effects, where different interviewers employ varying standards to judge candidates.

Research on 'best practice' relating to interviews (McDaniel, Whetzel, Schmidt & Maurer, 1994) suggests that bias in interviews can be minimized by keeping interviews standardized, structured, and by having multiple, well-trained staff for each interview. Further, it is suggested that interviewers should only rate easily observable dimensions such as interpersonal style or verbal fluency using simple scales. Other recommendations from this research revolve around using the interview to ascertain how a candidate deals with certain situations based on actual experience of real events (McDaniel et al., 1994). Such interviews are known as behaviourally based interviews.

Behaviourally based interviewing

Behaviourally based interviewing is predicated on the idea that past behaviour and performance are the best predictor of future performance, and that past behaviour can be closely examined via a structured interviews based on:

- questions built around job-related information;
- questions aimed at revealing in some detail how candidates have handled situations and tasks involving similar competencies to those of the job in question, and the results of those actions;
- questions that unearth the true nature of the candidate's knowledge, behaviours, motivation, and values.

As reported by Pulakos and Schmitt (1995) interviews based on behavioural rather than situational criteria – that is to say on what candidates really did in past situations rather than what they might do in hypothetical future situations – elicit higher levels of predictive validity.

The process of conducting behavioural interviews begins with the construction of a list of competencies which are specific to the job in question. Within the competency framework for the job, the interviewers will question the candidates about their qualifications and skills, about specific experiences where they have used the skills and the results of this usage, and about the underlying motivations behind their actions and behaviours. For example, if a sport travel company is looking to select a new sales person and one of the key dimensions is persuasiveness. The behaviourally based interview should be built around getting the candidates to talk about situations where they were required to be persuasive in previous jobs. Questions might follow a sequence similar to that set out below, where each question probes further into the detailed actions, consequences, and underlying motivations of the candidate.

- Describe a situation where you had to overcome extreme buyer resistance to get a sale.
- What was different about this situation?
- What objections did the client raise?
- How did you answer them?
- How did you feel in response to the client's negativity?
- What did you say next?
- How did you close the sale?
- What was the result of your action?
- How did you feel at the close and why?

By probing for such detail about real events, the behavioural interview almost becomes a re-enactment of the candidate dealing with previous work situation. In this way, 'real' behaviours can be observed and any pretence on the part of the candidate can be brought to the surface.

The selection process for volunteers should be quite intensive and can involve a number of steps which may mirror those taken when hiring a paid employee. However, few community-based sport organizations are in a position to conduct a formal volunteer selection process, and often the number of vacant positions is greater than the number of people prepared to volunteer.

Considerations in volunteer selection can include appropriate accreditation or preparedness to undertake a relevant course (e.g., coaching certification), experience in working with teams, good communication skills, specialist skills needed (e.g., an accountant to look after the organization's finances), and reliability and trustworthiness. Reference checks are advisable when appointing individuals to a position that involves close contact with children and in many countries criminal history checks are a legal requirement if the volunteer is working with under 18-year old children. A positive outcome of such policies is that people are less suspicious of coaches and officials. An example of volunteer recruitment can be found in the following textbox. This is the notice that the Beijing Organizing Committee for the Olympic Games broadcast on their website to solicit volunteer applications. It also outlines the criteria to be applied in selecting volunteers.

One World One Dream!

In hosting the Olympics the Games organizing committee (BOCOG) embarked on a massive recruitment of volunteers from China and around the world. BOCOG's General Policy for Volunteers for the 2008 Beijing Olympic and Paralympic Games:

Volunteers for the Beijing Olympic and Paralympic Games are accredited personnel recruited and managed by BOCOG, who take proper responsibilities, work at the time and in the position designated by BOCOG in service to the Beijing Olympic and Paralympic Games without payment.

Basic requirements

1. Voluntary to serve the Beijing Olympic and Paralympic games.
2. Born prior to (and on) 30 June 1990, and in good health.
3. Abide by China's laws and regulations.
4. Able to participate in the pre-Games trainings and related activities.
5. Able to serve consecutively for more than seven days during the Olympic and Paralympic Games.
6. Native Chinese speakers should be able to communicate in essential foreign language(s), and applicants whose first

language is not Chinese should be able to engage in conversations in elementary Chinese.
7. Possess professional knowledge and skills necessary for the posts.

Rights and obligations

Rights

1. To be aware of the Games-time volunteer policies.
2. To express position preference before they are assigned to a job.
3. To be entitled to necessary working conditions.
4. To safeguard their lawful rights.
5. To be entitled to participate in evaluation and honoring of the Games-time service of the volunteers.
6. To give suggestions and advices for the volunteers' work.
7. To withdraw from the volunteers' services.

Obligations

1. To abide by the Olympic Charter, Paralympic Charter, and promote Olympic spirit.
2. To comply with BOCOG's policies and regulations.
3. To observe volunteers' commitment.
4. To complete related trainings.
5. To be in deference to the BOCOG assignment.
6. To be in deference to BOCOG's management and sincerely perform the tasks.
7. To obey the rules of the volunteers' team during the service.

Recruitment

Volunteers for the Olympic and Paralympic Games will mainly be recruited in Beijing area with college students as the principal source. Meanwhile, a fraction will be recruited from among mainland residents of outside Beijing, from compatriots of Hong Kong, Macao, and Taiwan, as well as from overseas Chinese and foreigners.

Application channels

BOCOG or the organizations designated by BOCOG are responsible for receiving applications.

Application period

Applicants may submit their applications from August 2006 to March 2008.

Source: http://en.beijing2008.com/83/67/column211716783.shtml

At the conclusion of the selection process a hiring organization must make decisions about who to hire. It is at this point that organizations will often check candidate references if this has not been done earlier. Written references generally have a low validity so it is advisable to exercise caution at this point. In fact several large organizations now refuse to provide written references because of the potential for legal action from disaffected former employees and will instead provide only a letter confirming the dates between which a person was employed. 'Off the record' telephone interviews are more likely to generate a candid and truthful response from former employers but these too should be used with caution. A final check that the organization should make relates to the qualifications the candidates claim to hold. Surveys by recruiting companies have revealed a high level of false claims about qualifications from job applicants. After making the necessary checks, the organization is then in a position to make offers. A common practice in many organizations is to rank candidates by order of preference and make offers accordingly. In this way organizations have alternative candidates should offers to candidates be declined. Another common approach is to deem candidates 'employable' or 'not employable' and work through the employable list in order of preference.

Summary

Recruitment and selection, and judicious hiring are critical to a sport organization's success. This chapter has established the links between recruitment and selection and other HRM activities and described different sources and methods for generating a pool of job applicants as well as recent trends. This chapter has also reviewed a variety of selection techniques and outlined the advantages and disadvantages of each as well as issues relating to reliability and validity. No one method will be right for all situations and, thus, the choice of technique should be considered in relation to the circumstances of each selection decision. Sources of bias and subjectivity in selection decision making have been canvassed, particularly as they apply in standard selection interviews. An improved method of interviewing based on behavioural attributes has been outlined and recommended. Equally, no single technique is without the possibility of error, although some are clearly better than others. Uncertainty in selection can best be reduced by the use of multiple techniques provided the time and resources are available.

Discussion questions

1. What are the key reasons for claiming that recruitment and selection are *the* most important of all *HR* processes?

2. Identify the sources of bias in relation to interviews. How can bias be minimized?

3. Using the Job Advertisement in Appendix 1, outline three different recruitment methods you could use for the position. What would be the advantages and disadvantages of each?
4. Using the Job Advertisement in Appendix 1, construct an interview schedule using the behaviourally based interviewing method described at the end of this chapter. Focus on the two essential competencies:
   - Experience in the delivery of innovative sport and recreation programmes, events, and initiatives for people with a disability.
   - High level of organizational, interpersonal and presentation skills.

(Optional role play: In pairs practice interviewing each other using the behavioural method to probe the experience of the other person for each of these competencies.)

Appendix 1: Sample job advertisement

Programme coordinator – disability sport

Position description

- Plan, develop, and facilitate the implementation of programmes and events to enhance opportunities for people with a disability in sport and recreation.
- Liaise with ACT and national sport and recreation agencies and other relevant groups on issues related to participation in sport and recreation by people with a disability.
- Manage a budget and develop strategic and operational plans for the delivery of sport and recreation to people with a disability.
- Develop partnerships with organizations and individuals involved in the development of sport and recreation for people with a disability.
- Professionally represent the ACT to the executive of a variety of National Sporting Organizations for people with a disability.
- Coordinate and deliver disability awareness courses, workshops, and services for the ACT community.
- Provide coordination and secretariat support to the Disability Sport Education Programme (DSEP) Steering Committee.
- Prepare reports, briefs, grant applications, sponsorship proposals, and other correspondence.
- Selection criteria.

Essential

- Contemporary knowledge about sport for people with a disability.
- Experience in the delivery of innovative sport and recreation programmes, events, and initiatives for people with a disability.

- A demonstrated ability to meet strategic and financial outcomes.
- High level of organizational, interpersonal, and presentation skills.
- Well-developed written and oral communication skills.

Desirable

Relevant tertiary qualifications in sports administration, business, and/or disability studies would be an advantage.

Source: http:www.sportspeople.com.au/sp/position/getfile.asp%3FFileID%3D1353+ position+description+sports+organization&hl=en&ct= lnk&cd=1 &gl=au23/4/07

5 Orientation and organizational culture

Learning objectives

After reading this chapter you will be able to:

- Explain the importance of orientation in sport organizations
- Describe the stages of organizational socialization
- Describe a variety of orientation strategies and practices
- Understand the importance and process of orienting sport volunteers
- Describe organizational culture and its role in newcomer orientation

Chapter overview

Orientation may be viewed as the final step in the recruitment and selection process, or as the first phase in a staff member or volunteer's involvement in an organization. Either way, it is a critical part of effective strategic human resource management (SHRM). This chapter examines how orientation can make a difference to a new-comer's successful transition to a new job, role, and workgroup, and to the organization as a whole. It is important to recognize that there are many different types of newcomers, from novices in the workforce to veterans in the industry. Yet all experience the three basic stages of socialization to an organization which coincide with pre-entry, entry, and adaptation to the organization. For those with previous experience, orientation is more of a process of resocialization from one organizational environment to another. Orientation, in the form of resocialization, must also occur when a current staff member or volunteer within an organization moves to a new position, perhaps with a new workgroup, a new workplace, or new responsibilities.

The purpose of orientation is to socialize newcomers to their new work environment. This process also gives them a chance to align, or realign, their preconceived expectations about the organization. The notion of an individual's psychological contract is introduced here as the orientation process can play an important role in ensuring that a newcomer's understanding of the mutual expectations between him or herself and the organization are aligned. Orientation also provides a chance for an individual to judge his or her degree of personal fit with the organization. It is important that newcomers receive, or at least have access to, accurate information that represents the reality of the workplace and organizational expectations. This process will increase the likelihood of newcomers' role clarity, workgroup integration, and understanding of the politics of the organization; aspects that are ultimately factors in their job satisfaction, commitment, and retention. Likewise, orientation can serve as a probationary period during which the organization is able to assess the fit of the individual from its perspective. While this particular perspective is not the focus of the chapter, it does highlight another practical component of systematic orientation.

A framework outlining the three stages of organizational socialization is presented, along with strategies and further orientation practices that can be engaged for effective socialization at each stage. One of the key aspects to which newcomers must be socialized is the culture of the organization. Organizational culture is the values, beliefs, and assumptions that underlie how things are done within an organization. It is critical for newcomers to get a handle on this as quickly as possible as culture serves as an important guiding force for members. The last part of the chapter focuses on the meaning and role of organizational culture in the workplace, and its place in newcomer orientation.

The importance of orientation in sport organizations

Orientation or 'induction' may be seen as the final stage of the recruitment and selection process (Booth, Fosters, Robson & Welham, 2004) and a critical aspect of successful human resource management (HRM). Substantial time and resources may have been put into looking for, screening, and ultimately hiring new staff and volunteers who are expected to make a meaningful contribution to the sport organization. To ensure that the newcomers to the organization hit the ground running, do the work that is expected of them, and stay with the organization, it is essential that they have an appropriate introduction to their new work environment. It is contended that the 'period of early entry is one of the most critical phases of organizational life' (Kammeyer-Mueller & Wanberg, 2003: 779). Newcomers' initial work attitudes are strong indicators of attitudes and behaviour several months down the road, including the likelihood that they will stay or leave (Kammeyer-Mueller & Wanberg, 2003). Early socialization is critical to getting newcomers started on the right foot, and keeping them there. Effective orientation can help new staff and volunteers adjust to their job, workgroup, and workplace. This, in turn, will contribute to their job satisfaction and commitment to the organization (Kammeyer-Mueller & Wanberg, 2003), and reduce the stress and anxiety that is commonly associated with facing an unfamiliar situation (Saks & Ashforth, 1997).

Figure 5.1 depicts the organizational adjustment process for newcomers. It highlights the short-term or proximal outcomes and longer-term or distal

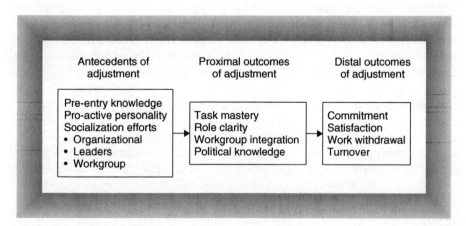

Figure 5.1 A model of newcomers' organizational adjustment. Kammeyer-Mueller, J.D. and Wanberg, C.R. (2003). Unwrapping the organizational entry process: Disentangling multiple antecedents and their pathways to adjustment. *Journal of Applied Psychology*, **88**, 779–794. Published by the American Psychological Association. Adapted with permission.

outcomes that are the objective of systematic orientation. Task mastery (skill and confidence), role clarity (direction and purpose), workgroup integration (perceived approval and inclusion), and political knowledge (understanding of the informal power relationships) are 'direct representations of the quality of a newcomer's adjustment, indicating both the acquisition of requisite knowledge and skill for the organizational role as well as the development of social relationships that will help to bind the newcomer to the organization and its goals' (Kammeyer-Mueller & Wanberg, 2003: 781). In combination, these factors have been shown to have a direct impact on organizational commitment, job satisfaction, work withdrawal, and turnover (Kammeyer-Mueller & Wanberg, 2003). Commitment to systematic orientation in the organization will stem from recognition of both the short-term objectives and longer-term impact of this process. Figure 5.1 also outlines the factors that contribute to newcomers' adjustment; namely, pre-entry knowledge about the organization, newcomers' proactive personality which determines the individual's propensity to seek out information, and external socialization influences by the organization, its leaders, and co-workers and the workgroup. These factors in the newcomer adjustment process are examined below.

New staff and volunteers may have acquired some degree of familiarity or pre-entry knowledge about the organization and their particular role there as part of the recruitment and selection process. Well-prepared candidates for a job can be expected to have familiarized themselves with the mission, mandate, products, services, programmes, and structure of the organization, at least before applying for the job, and certainly before being interviewed for a position. Candidates may have gained further insight by walking around and talking with current staff during the interview process. This is, of course, important for them to get a sense of whether the organization is, in fact, a place they would like to work. For example, a potential board member for a community sport club would likely ask questions before agreeing to stand for a position; 'What would I do?' and 'How often are meetings?' would be typical questions of someone considering volunteering their time to help out. A prospective collegiate basketball coach would likely ask questions about the team's budget and would want to check out the facilities as part of the recruitment and selection process. She might want to know upfront about other expectations with regard to contributing to the work of the athletic department. As these examples illustrate, some preliminary orientation to an organization may have taken place during the recruitment and selection process; however, it is critical that newcomers have a formal orientation to their new work environment upon entry. As we shall see below, pre-entry knowledge can sometimes be inaccurate and insufficient.

Without formal orientation, a new hire can be expected to take longer to get up to speed on the organization's expectations and ways of doing things. He or she can be expected to experience some degree of stress and reduced performance because of having to figure it out 'on the go'. The often challenging process of recruitment and selection would not be complete without further orientation of new staff and volunteers.

Organizational socialization

Orientation is essentially familiarizing oneself with something new. This corresponds with the process of socialization, whereby 'a person learns and acquires the values, attitudes and beliefs, and accepted behaviours of a culture, society, organization, or group' (Tosi, Mero & Rizzo, 2000: 35). We are socialized whenever we become involved in a new situation – when we're born, when we first go to school, when we go to (new) work, and when we move to a different country or culture. Socialization is the process of orienting oneself to the customs, language, expectations, and so on, of the new environment. One may be socialized into several different environments at the same stage of life; for example, a new job and a new city. It is important to become familiar with the new setting, to learn what is expected and accepted there, so that one can fit in more quickly and effectively.

While an individual inherently wants to be comfortable in a new situation as quickly as possible, a sport organization also wants its new hires or volunteers to fit in right away, so that they can begin contributing to the organization. *Organizational* socialization is defined as 'the process by which a person learns the values, norms and required behaviours which permit him to participate as a member of the organization' (Van Maanen, 1976: 67). This is still a broad definition; to what, exactly, is the newcomer being oriented? Aspects of the organization with which a newcomer needs to become familiar in order to develop task mastery, role clarity, workgroup integration, and political knowledge include the following:

- Formal work-related aspects of the organization (e.g., mission and goals, rules and regulations, organizational structure and chain of command, reporting relationships, the evaluation and reward system, health and safety standards, disciplinary and grievance procedures).
- Formal personnel-related policies and procedures (e.g., pay, employee benefits).
- Role and assigned tasks, including the skills required, and specific reporting requirements.
- Workgroup, including supervisor(s) (e.g., individual personalities, group norms and expectations).
- Physical layout of the workplace.

One additional aspect with which the newcomer should become familiar is the culture of the organization.

Organizational culture is the core values, beliefs, and assumptions about how things are done within the organization. It is represented by visual artefacts, such as logos, displayed pictures and awards, as well as stories, myths, rituals, and styles of dress. These things reflect what the organization is all about and what is valued there. Values, beliefs, and assumptions about the organization are also manifested in organizational processes, such as communication (formal and informal lines), decision making (who gets to be involved), and rewards (as an indicator of what is valued). To the extent that organizational culture reflects a shared understanding, it serves as a control mechanism such that members understand 'how things are done around here.' For example, there may be an unspoken rule that you 'arrive before, and leave after, the boss'; or it is understood that the best, or most important, work is really done over coffee, or on the golf course. Organizational culture is important to maintaining strategic direction, because of the coordinating effect it has on members. Thus it is important that an organization's culture – what is valued and understood to be 'the way of life' (Johns & Saks, 2001: 256) – is aligned with the organization's corporate strategy (McKenna & Beech, 2002). Much insight into organizational culture can be picked up from newcomers' orientation to artefacts and organizational processes. Organizational culture is reviewed in more detail below.

Newcomers

As mentioned earlier, it is important to recognize that there are several types of newcomers in an organization: (1) those who are new to the organization and the workplace in general, (2) those who are veterans of the workplace but new to the organization, and (3) those who are veterans of the organization but new to a different part of the organization. As indicated in the chapter overview, individuals require at least some orientation to new situations, whether that new situation is by virtue of joining an organization for the first time, or moving to a new job, department, or location within the organization. Not all newcomers have the same background experience, which may be an important consideration in the orientation they require.

'Neophytes' or novices (i.e., recent graduates and those with little or no work experience) are new to the organization and to the type of job, and may be new to the industry and the full-time working world as well (e.g., Carr, Pearson, Vest & Boyar, 2006). These recruits may fill entry-level jobs, where relatively basic skills are required and the organization has an opportunity to groom them for further roles; for example sales associates with a sporting goods retailer or a sport event facility. Organizations also recruit and select veteran staff and volunteers with prior experience in the organization, in the industry, or in a particular type of job (e.g., Carr et al., 2006). For example, sales staff are moved up to management positions, or a media relations person is hired from the collegiate sport environment to work in a professional sports franchise. These individuals are moved up or hired on because of their previous experience, and the knowledge and skill sets they can offer to the organization. The focus of their orientation is really resocialization to a new organizational environment. Resocialization may also be required when existing staff or volunteers are faced with major changes to the organization (Rousseau, 2001).

Stages of socialization

It is helpful to think of orientation to a new job or organization as occurring in stages, as an individual transitions from 'newcomer' to 'insider' (Wanous & Colella, 1989). There are three basic stages in the work socialization process

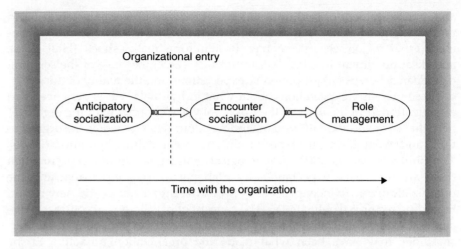

Figure 5.2 The stages of organizational socialization (Feldman, 1976).

(Feldman, 1976): (1) anticipatory socialization, (2) encounter socialization, and (3) role management. Instead of focusing exclusively on orientation that begins when an individual first enters the organization as a member, and ends once they have met everyone and read all the organizational manuals, this framework acknowledges that a newcomer's understanding about an organization begins before they even enter the workplace, and continues as they adapt to their role. The three stages are depicted in Figure 5.2.

The first stage of the organizational socialization process occurs before entry to the organization (Feldman, 1976). As a result of anticipatory socialization, most newcomers have some preconceived ideas or expectations about what it means to work in a particular segment of the sport industry, in a particular role, or in the new organization itself. These pre-entry ideas, expectations, and knowledge may be formed as part of the individual's formal education, previous work or volunteer experiences, and through other sources of information (e.g., friends, family, fans, media). Sport management students often declare that they want to work for a particular (perhaps their favourite?) professional sports team. While this may be a worthy career goal, there may be gaps between what an individual thinks it will be like to work for a given team or organization, and what it is really like. According to Hofacre and Branvold (1995: 174), 'the potential for a discrepancy between expectation and reality seems especially high in careers … in professional sports.' A job in pro sport may be perceived to be glamorous, where employees get to rub shoulders with sports stars. Yet, the reality is more likely long hours, low pay, and little glamour (Hofacre & Branvold, 1995). In a study of the expectations and realities of a front office career in minor league baseball, Hofacre and Branvold found that 'job seekers' differed from front office personnel in this sector in terms of the perceptions of important skills and job characteristics. They found that job seekers rated having knowledge of baseball and sports in general as significantly more important to a successful career in minor league baseball than did current staff. Job seekers also had unrealistically high expectations about advancement opportunities, decision making power, job stability, and receiving a good salary in a career in professional baseball. The authors concluded that the job seekers may have been in for a 'reality shock' (Hall, 1976), and disappointment in a baseball front office career, because of the seeming discrepancy between their pre-entry expectations and the reality of the job.

These pre-entry expectations about what individuals will experience in an organization form the basis of their psychological contract with the organization; that is, an individual's understanding about what they owe the organization, and what they can expect from the organization in return (Lewis, Thornhill & Saunders, 2003). Psychological contract violations can occur when there are unrealistic expectations by both parties (the individual and the organization) due to incongruence between the organization and new recruit regarding reciprocal obligations. (The concept of psychological contract is discussed in more detail below.) Many of these pre-entry experiences and understandings may have been what made the organization attractive to the individual and the individual attractive to the organization. However, it is important to recognize that anticipatory or pre-entry socialization contributes to newcomers' ideas and expectations which may be at odds with what the organization or job is really like; these expectations may differ from the values, norms, and behaviours considered important and required for effective contribution to the organization. According to Kammeyer-Mueller and Wanberg (2003: 782), 'those who have accurate information about all aspects of the job will be better able to assess the extent to which they will "fit" in their new positions and will be in situations that better match their abilities and preferences.' Research supports this contention such that newcomers with more accurate pre-entry knowledge about their job report better adjustment (see Kammeyer-Mueller & Wanberg, 2003 for a review). At the least, it is critical to recognize that newcomers do not enter the organization as empty slates, but will have varying degrees of pre-entry knowledge about the job and the organization, which will have implications for their further socialization there. Beyer and Hannah (2002) found that veteran newcomers tend to use past experiences, which have shaped their 'personal identities' about who they are as workers and their place in the work environment, to adjust to a new workplace. They are likely to draw extensively on these cognitions and so 'past work experiences are likely to have especially strong effects on socialization to new work roles and settings' (Beyer & Hannah, 2002: 641). Any difference or disparities will become evident during the second stage of encounter socialization. Orientation is important to help newcomers develop accurate perceptions about the organization and their obligations.

The second stage of encounter or accommodation socialization takes place at or immediately following entry to the organization or new job. At this point the individual experiences the organization 'for the first time as one of its members' rather than as someone who is just trying to get in (Tosi et al., 2000: 102). This is when the individual begins to gain deeper insight into the reality of the organization, and his or her identity in the organization begins to form (Beyer & Hannah, 2002). The newcomer is formally introduced to his or her task, and is initiated into the group. According to Johns and Saks (2001: 245), 'if accommodation is reached, the recruit will have complied with critical organizational norms and should begin to identify with experienced organizational members.' Johns and Saks (2001: 247) suggest that the socialization challenge is to sufficiently orient new staff and volunteers to the organization 'without frustrating them or stifling their uniqueness.'

An organization's commitment to orientation will help to ensure that the newcomers will have the formal opportunity to learn what they want and need to know about their new work environment. This may be particularly important with veteran newcomers, who have more extensive anticipatory socialization and thus pre-entry knowledge. Research suggests that veterans are more likely to be effectively resocialized when they are oriented as if they were novices (Rousseau, 2001); that is, they are given opportunities and encouragement to gather information, discuss, and negotiate its meaning, and make sense of their new environment, rather than assuming that they 'know the ropes'. Through a strategically designed orientation process, the organization can take advantage of the formal opportunity to communicate what it wants neophyte and veteran newcomers to know.

The third stage – role management – is a process of adaptation socialization that involves fine tuning one's expectations about the organization, and understanding reciprocal obligations, after some time in the organization. This stage may not be clearly defined in terms of start and end points as the first two stages. It is more likely defined by the new member than by the organization, as the individual comes to terms with the final stage of adjustment to task mastery, role clarity, workgroup integration, and political knowledge. Nonetheless, it is important to recognize that orientation to the organization does not necessarily end for newcomers after the, perhaps more formal, entry stage of encounter socialization.

(Re)aligning expectations

Anticipatory socialization suggests that individuals are likely to enter the workplace with preconceived ideas about their new job, the organization, the sport, and the industry. These pre-entry expectations form the initial basis of a psychological contract that new staff and volunteers develop with a particular organization. The psychological contract is an unwritten agreement that represents shared expectations between an individual and the organization. It is a pattern of rights, privileges, and obligations that is established during orientation, yet it is continuously negotiated throughout one's career or time with an organization (Tosi et al., 2000). As noted earlier, during orientation an individual may find inconsistencies in what he or she understands about and expects from an organization; for example, the working conditions, co-workers, opportunities for advancement, and so on. Thus, it is an important stage during which one's psychological contract will undergo some meaningful development.

During the orientation process, newcomer staff or volunteers may also experience for the first time an awareness of the alignment between their own values and beliefs and those of the organization. This will give them a

89

further sense of what is known as person-organization fit, or 'congruence between organizational values and [one's] own individual values' (Tosi et al., 2000: 102), than what they may have felt during the recruitment and selection process. Research indicates that accuracy of expectations and perceived person-organization (P-O) fit have direct implications for newcomers' short-term job satisfaction and retention (Tosi et al., 2000).

The psychological contract

The employment relationship is a social exchange or transaction where member effort and loyalty is given in return for fair rewards. Beyond the formal agreement which forms the basis of that relationship is an individual's psychological contract with his or her organization. The psychological contract comprises an employee's or volunteer's beliefs about what they can expect to receive from the organization in return for their work, effort, performance, and commitment. Perhaps most importantly, the psychological contract is based on the individual's belief that it is a mutual agreement between themselves and the organization; that is, both parties understand their respective obligations. What employees expect to receive in return for their effort, loyalty, and commitment may vary from one person to another, and from one organization to another. However, expectations generally include fair compensation, guaranteed work of a minimum specified duration, a safe work environment, socio-emotional security, training and development as required, and a sense of community (Taylor, Darcy, Hoye & Cuskelly, 2006).

Volunteers, by definition, will not have any expectations for financial compensation, however their psychological contract may comprise expectations that their needs and motives for volunteering will be met; for example, that there will be an opportunity to make a difference and to connect with others through sport volunteering (Cuskelly, Hoye & Auld, 2006). In a study of the psychological contracts of community rugby volunteers in Australia, Taylor et al. (2006) found that the participants were in fact most focused on the intrinsic characteristics of their volunteer role; specifically their expectation for rewarding work, social environment and networking opportunities, and recognition and appreciation for their contributions. Their next greatest focus was working conditions; specifically, expectations about the number of volunteers to do the work and support from the club.

The psychological contract is essentially a member's way of compartmentalizing his or her expectations of the organization, and the organization's expectations in return. The contract is violated when an individual's expectations are not met by the organization, or that person does not meet the expectations of the organization. For example, a manager of merchandise for a professional sports franchise finds out that she does not actually have as much decision making discretion as she thought she was going to have with regard to selecting new products. The fallout may be frustration, dissatisfaction, or disillusionment on the part of the member, with further implications for the individual's work behaviour (Johns & Saks, 2001). The likelihood of a perceived violation or breach of the psychological contract is increased when an individual has an inaccurate understanding of the mutual obligations between himself and the organization. In their study of community rugby volunteers, Taylor et al. (2006) further found that club administrators had different expectations than the volunteers, focusing particularly on transactional elements such as volunteer recruitment and turnover rather than intrinsic volunteer role characteristics and working conditions. The authors concluded that there is a distinct possibility of psychological breach in the community rugby club setting because of the discrepant expectations and obligations.

Unrealistic expectations about the job or organization likely develop during anticipatory socialization. It may be the fault of the organization itself if it portrays an inaccurate image of the reality of the workplace and the organization's expectations during the recruitment and selection process. The discrepancy may become apparent over time as an employee or volunteer comes to realize that what was expected from the organization is not being offered. It can also happen in the short term as newcomers learn, as part of their orientation, that what may have been expected will not be realized. This 'reality shock' can have important implications for reduced obligations on the part of the newcomer, as well as lowered satisfaction and increased stress from realizing expectations will not be fulfilled.

The psychological contract is of concern to systematic orientation because it is important for the newcomers and the organization to develop a mutual understanding that is based on realistic expectations about the reciprocal relationship. 'It is important that newcomers develop accurate perceptions in the formation of a psychological contract' (Johns & Saks, 2001: 246), many of the terms of which are established during the anticipatory socialization phase of orientation.

Person-organization fit

According to Cable and Parsons (2001: 1), 'person-organization (P-O) fit, or the compatibility between people and the organizations in which they work, is a key to maintaining a flexible and committed workforce that is necessary in a competitive business environment and a tight labour market.' Research consistently suggests that 'operating in an environment consistent with one's values is a more positive experience on many levels' (Meglino & Ravlin, 1998: 380). Right from the start, newcomers will likely ask themselves whether and how they fit in with the organization. If they perceive that their values do not match those of the organization, they will deal with this dissonance by either changing their perceptions (i.e., their personal values), or leaving the organization (Cable & Parsons, 2001).

Organizational values are highlighted and clarified through the orientation process and thus newcomers can quickly begin to determine whether they fit in. Socialization can be a significant force in aligning newcomers' values with organizational values. For example, a new coach may become more comfortable and feel a greater sense of fit in his new work environment after meeting with other coaches and gaining an understanding of formal and informal practices in the organization. Cable and Parsons (2001) found that certain orientation or socialization strategies were significantly associated with P-O fit; namely, sequential, fixed, serial, and investiture approaches, which are discussed below. We can expect veteran newcomers to have a more positive perception of P-O fit as they are likely to seek out and join a new organization where they perceive they fit (Cable & Parsons, 2001).

Orientation strategies

Individuals tend to be active participants in their own socialization, in terms of seeking out information they need to help understand their new environment (Allen, 2006). They also have a tendency to build supportive relationships and attempt to put a positive frame around the new situation (Ashford & Black, 1996). In order to gain a sense of personal control in a new situation, newcomers will undertake some self-management activities to ensure that they gain adequate information about their new environment.

The extent to which newcomers engage in this proactive socialization can be expected to vary. For example, individuals can be expected to differ in the degree to which they feel the need for personal control in a new situation. Ashford and Black (1996) found this to be a factor in the extent to which newcomers used a variety of proactive tactics. Proactive socialization will also be more likely with veteran newcomers, who may be more comfortable in the work environment in general, and in the organization itself if they are moving within, as they will have more confidence and awareness regarding what they need to know. Finally, the degree of proactive socialization can also be expected to vary depending on the extent to which the organization engages in systematic orientation of its newcomers. Given the importance of orientating newcomers to the organization, and likely variations in the extent to which newcomers will be proactive in their own socialization to the new setting, organizations should not leave it to newcomers to find their own way. Rather, various strategies and practices may be used as part of a systematic orientation process, and are presented here.

Van Maanen and Schein (1979) proposed a framework that describes different types of orientation strategies that may be utilized in an organization. The six strategies are arranged as dimensions representing contrasting approaches:

1. Collective vs. individual
2. Formal vs. informal
3. Sequential vs. random
4. Fixed vs. variable
5. Serial vs. disjunctive
6. Investiture vs. divestiture

With the collective approach, a sport organization may provide orientation to several newcomers as a group. One advantage with this approach is that the organization can orient several members at once rather than individually. Another advantage is that the group of newcomers has an opportunity to learn about the organization together, helping each other to understand, and sharing individual perspectives. Social interaction during the learning process is recognized as an important part of successful socialization (Ostroff & Kozlowski, 1992). The group is given standardized or common information about the organization, which can help to reduce uncertainty and contribute to a sense of shared values as individuals know they are learning what others are learning (Allen, 2006). The collective approach is favoured when there are several newcomers commencing at the same time and all require orientation to the same information. This might be the case with new sales staff at a fitness club, or venue staff at a stadium. It would also be favoured for more routine and more technical jobs where newcomers need to know the rules and procedures in order to do their job effectively; for example, locker room attendants, or sales or venue staff. It is possible that a collective approach would be used on an individual basis, when standardized information is the focus yet only one newcomer is coming on board. In contrast, an individual approach focuses on orientation that is tailored to each new member. This approach is most appropriate when standard information about the organization and job is seen as less valuable than on-the-job training as a means of organizational socialization. This might be the case with less routine jobs; for example, a head coach or marketing director position.

Formal strategies involve a planned approach to orientation where the information to be shared is strategically selected and the means to impart the information is carefully designed. Informal strategies are the opposite, where orientation is essentially unplanned and impromptu. It is more likely to be on an ad hoc or 'as need' basis, and involves on-the-job learning rather than formal sessions. As such, formal strategies tend to present a more consistent message, whereas information imparted through informal strategies may be more varied, from one individual or group to another, or from one job to another.

Sequential orientation strategies rely on a step-by-step formula that has been determined to provide appropriate stages in learning about the organization. For example, a newly hired swimming instructor, who has the required qualifications, may be expected to be oriented through a sequence of formal learning about the facility, programmes, and specific safety and risk management measures (either through an interactive orientation session, or reading a manual), followed by observing or shadowing a current instructor, and finally teaching a class himself while being observed by a supervisor. In contrast, a random approach is less of a staged process. Orientation to the job and workplace tends to be arbitrary, or 'figuring it out as you go.' A sequential approach may be expected to reduce a newcomer's uncertainty or anxiety about whether there will be a thorough orientation when it is seen as an organized process (Allen, 2006).

Another dimension of orientation strategies is whether the approach is fixed or variable. A fixed approach refers to orientation that occurs within a set timeframe (e.g., 3 days, 1 week, or 3 months). A variable timeframe means that there is no specific end to the orientation; rather, it may be assumed to continue until the newcomer has adjusted (i.e., achieved task mastery, role clarity, workgroup integration, and political knowledge). Fixed orientation can be suited to newcomers' needs and learning curves (e.g., novices may require more time than veterans). This approach can also ensure that there is an opportunity to develop and test competence on the job (Allen, 2006). Variable orientation is more open-ended and flexible, allowing for individual differences along the way.

Another orientation strategy dimension – serial vs. disjunctive – refers to whether regular members are directly involved in the orientation of newcomers. The serial approach involves current members directly in newcomers' socialization; for example, through formal mentoring or the use of role models, and hosting orientation sessions. This may be the case when new lifeguards are hired and oriented to the facility by a more senior guard. The orientation may involve formal information sessions, on-the-job shadowing by the new guard, and finally monitoring and evaluation by the senior guard. Disjunctive orientation, on the other hand, does not formally involve regular members in newcomers' socialization. Rather, they tend to be left to their own devices, to figure it out on their own. The major benefit of the former approach is integrating newcomers with regular members for social learning. Another benefit is the opportunity for informal socialization that can take place in this shared environment; that is, learning about the organization and its people beyond the planned or required information sharing. Organizational culture can be transmitted through stories and myths that are passed along to new members, and from informally observing member behaviour.

The final dimension of orientation strategies is the investiture vs. divestiture approach. The former involves inducting the newcomer into the organization by focusing on what positive and unique attributes they have to contribute to the organization. This can help the individuals to understand how they fit in, and begin to build a positive personal identity in the workplace. Investiture provides 'positive social support from experienced organizational members' (Allen, 2006: 240). In contrast, divestiture involves inducting the newcomer to the ways of the organization through breaking down any misconceptions they may have about the organization upon entry. Divestiture often involves debasement or humiliation through one or more 'tests' that are intended to show the newcomer that they do not, in fact, really know what goes on in the organization. Divestiture is essentially 'negative social feedback [about preconceptions] until newcomers adapt' (Allen, 2006: 240). This approach is most common in the military and on sports teams, and is consistent with the notion of hazing – tearing new members down in order to build them back up. Once the newcomer's preconceptions have been rescinded, orientation focuses on socializing the individual to the desired ways of the organization. This approach is more likely to occur in entry-level jobs where the organization wants to start with a clean slate.

Consider the following example of staff orientation at GoodLife Fitness Clubs Inc.:

New staff orientation at GoodLife Fitness Clubs Inc.

GoodLife Fitness Clubs Inc. is a recognized leader in the fitness industry with clubs located across Canada. At GoodLife, understanding the culture is of paramount importance to the organization's leaders. For this reason, the company promotes their core values during 'on-boarding' of new 'associates' (staff) through a series of orientation days and specific training modules with the intent of indoctrinating the new employees to the organization and their job.

New associates attend the 'GoodLife Base Camp,' which is a two or three day (depending on the position) orientation and training seminar aimed at introducing them to the company and their specific job (e.g., customer service representative). Base Camp is run periodically by the human resource department out of a central location (e.g., Home Office in London, Ontario) and new staff from clubs in that region or from across the province attend, at the organization's expense. Prior to attending Base Camp, all new associates are given two books that relate to the company's history, core values, and culture, a training manual that outlines policies, procedures, and responsibilities, and a 'Base Camp Success Package' that includes pre-training activities to set them up for success during the training sessions. The first day of Base Camp consists of various interactive activities where new associates learn more about the organization and its mission and vision. The second and/or third day is more specific to the job position where the new associate will learn his or her appropriate scripts (e.g., fielding incoming calls, sales pitch), and get hands on learning about other operational procedures. During Base Camp, new associates are also tested on their knowledge of the core values, job-specific scripts, pricing of memberships, and other areas of operations. Most new associates attend Base Camp within their first month on the job.

Back at the club, new associates also participate in job shadowing, which pairs them with a more experienced person in that role and allows them to learn more about the job through observation, practice, and feedback on their performance. Role playing at weekly team meetings, as well as at less frequent club-wide meetings, is another method of orientation where new associates practice their scripts in a group setting, and get feedback on their performance. During these meetings, staff also learn about the job responsibilities and experiences of their colleagues in similar and other positions in the club. The weekly team meetings are an important mechanism for helping to orient new associates to how things are done at GoodLife.

Each new associate is subject to a job evaluation at the 3-month mark, and provided with feedback on their performance by their General Manager. GoodLife also provides each General Manager with a series of interactive activities designed specifically for on-boarding new associates. These activities help the new associate learn more about their manager, colleagues, and the company, as well as helping the manager to learn more about the new associate.

The company holds a separate orientation for the General Manager position which is the 'GoodLife Boot Camp'. These sessions are also centralized, and new General Managers travel from across the country to participate as a group. There are two levels to Boot Camp: Level One occurs during the person's second or third month with the organization; Level Two occurs around the 6th month. At Boot Camp, General Managers learn about such things as client retention, employee engagement, employment law, and company operations. Senior executives attend these sessions and present information on their respective departments and how they function (e.g., Human Resources, Group Fitness, Sales, Marketing). At the club, typically incoming General Managers will not have any one to shadow for their particular job as they have either replaced the former leader or assumed that role in a new club. Instead, the regional manager orients a new General Manager to the club and that particular role on site. As well, a new General Manager is expected to 'try out' or at least observe each staff position in the club (e.g., customer service, personal training, sales, instruction) to become familiar with club operations.

At GoodLife Fitness Clubs Inc. orienting new associates to the organization's culture through various documents, formal and on-the-job training, and constant feedback helps indoctrinate the core values for new employees. These procedures have contributed to the organization being repeatedly recognized as one of Canada's 50 Best Managed Companies.

Prepared by Eric MacIntosh with information from GoodLife Fitness Clubs Inc.

Discussion questions

1. With reference to Van Maanen and Schein's (1979) framework, what type of orientation strategies does GoodLife Fitness Clubs use for its new associates? What strategies does it use for its new General Managers?
2. Do you think these are the best strategies for the different positions? If not, what could be done differently?

Research has shown that the six socialization approaches outlined by Van Maanen and Schein (1979) can be grouped into two patterns of socialization (cf. Johns & Saks, 2001). *Institutionalized socialization* is described by collective, formal, sequential, fixed, serial, and investiture strategies. It reflects a more structured process of socialization which has been shown to promote newcomer loyalty, commitment, and consequently reduced turnover (Ashforth & Saks, 1996; Cable & Parson, 2001; Griffeth & Hom, 2001). Allen

(2006) found that collective, fixed, and investiture tactics in particular had the greatest effect on newcomer commitment or embeddedness in the organization. That is, orientation in the group setting, for a set period of time, that focuses on what the newcomers bring to the organization and where they will fit in, will be most effective.

In contrast, *individualized socialization* is described by individual, informal, random, variable, disjunctive, and divestiture strategies. It reflects a relatively less-structured approach to newcomer socialization, and parts of it are consistent with leaving newcomers somewhat to their own devices, to engage in proactive socialization. In related research, Ashford and Black (1996) concluded that obtaining information from written materials was associated with job performance and satisfaction, yet not to the same extent as relationship building. Taken together, implications from the research direct organizations to provide institutionalized socialization wherever possible, and at least provide opportunities for social learning through interaction with others (newcomers, but preferably regular members and one's supervisor) in addition to written materials. Reconsider the orientation process at GoodLife Fitness Clubs Inc. in terms of whether that organization uses more of an institutionalized or individualized socialization process.

Orientation practices

In addition to general orientation strategies, there are specific practices that are consistent with the adoption of one or more of these strategies. A number of orientation practices have been mentioned throughout the discussion thus far, including organizational literature and document review, formal orientation sessions, and job shadowing. We focus here on the job preview and mentoring, which correspond to newcomers' pre-entry, and entry and adaptation to the organization, respectively.

Reflect back on the stage of anticipatory socialization discussed earlier and the potential impact of newcomers' pre-entry expectations for their psychological contract, short-term job satisfaction, and retention. It is important to consider sources of anticipatory socialization that are under the control of the organization itself. The job preview is an orientation practice that is used to give candidates a greater sense of the job and the organization (Johns & Saks, 2001). Rather than focusing on the positive aspects alone to entice a candidate to view the organization favourably, the job preview should be used to present a realistic and balanced picture of the organization during the recruitment and selection process (O'Nell, Larson, Hewitt & Sauer, 2001). When a candidate is presented with realistic work expectations (including both positive and negative aspects of the organization and job), he or she is better able to determine whether a job will be attractive according to whether it coincides with his or her needs and values. If the individual accepts a job offer based on a more accurate picture of the organization, the actual workplace experience is more likely to be aligned with his or her pre-entry expectations. Consequently, there is a greater chance of effective adjustment in the short and longer term (see Figure 5.1).

There is a range of possible mechanisms for ensuring a realistic job preview. At the least, interviewers should present an accurate picture of the workplace, the organization's expectations, and the nature of the job; revealing the more negative aspects along with the positive features. While this may be difficult to do when trying to attract a top candidate, the payoff in the long run will be a more quickly and better-adjusted employee who entered the organization with more realistic expectations. Another means to present an accurate picture of the organization during the job preview is to collect the views of experienced employees about positive and negative aspects of the job and workplace, and present these through a booklet or videotape presentation. Alternatively, a candidate could spend a day or more in the workplace, either meeting with different groups of employees, or job shadowing with an experienced staff member.

The job preview may be particularly important for jobs where candidates may not have a lot of information about the actual tasks and responsibilities involved in a particular organization (O'Nell et al., 2001). For example, it may be useful for a candidate being interviewed for an intercollegiate sports information director position to have a realistic job preview that provides an opportunity to gain a balanced perspective on the organization. The job preview might involve spending a day on campus, with some time in the intercollegiate athletics office, as well as meeting with coaches, athletes, and other intercollegiate athletic department personnel. This would give the candidate a better feel for the sports information director's role, who he or she would be working with, and what it would be like to work in the campus environment.

Once the newcomer has entered the organization, mentoring is an increasingly popular practice that may be used to facilitate successful orientation and socialization. The notion of mentoring is consistent with the importance of social learning, and the opportunity to directly observe, interact with, and learn from another member of the organization. A mentor is typically a more senior person who gives a junior person advice and assists them during the early stages of their career, including entry socialization. Mentoring is introduced briefly here because of its potential role in newcomer orientation, and is covered in more detail in the discussion of training and development in Chapter 6.

The organization may have a formal mentoring programme, or it may be based on informal, even spontaneous relationships that develop. Research suggests that both forms are effective, and more beneficial than no mentor at all (Noe, 1988; Chao, Walz & Gardner, 1992). A newcomer to a sport organization, for example in a sport marketing agency, may be set up with a mentor that can help orient the person to formal work-related aspects of the organization, such as rules and regulations, reporting relationships, and the evaluation and reward system. A mentor can facilitate relationship building by introducing the newcomer to colleagues in his own department (e.g., event management) and other departments (e.g., accounting). Through job shadowing, a mentor can help orient the newcomer to a particular role; for example, demonstrating the preferred process of pursuing and then following up with event management clients, and managing expense accounts.

In the organizational entry stage, one of the most important differences between a mentor and a colleague who helps show the newcomer what to do may be the psychosocial support the former provides (Johns & Saks, 2001). A mentor can help a newcomer build self-confidence, a sense of identity, and the ability to cope with any distress that may be experienced during the early stages. This can be done through modelling acceptable behaviour for the newcomer to imitate, providing encouragement and confirmation, and offering counselling and advice for the newcomer regarding any anxieties or personal concerns he or she may have about the workplace (Johns & Saks, 2001). Where there is no formal mentoring programme, or as an alternative, a newcomer would benefit from developing a network of close peers that can provide some if not all of the functions served by a formal mentor.

Orienting sport volunteers

References throughout this chapter to the orientation of both employees and volunteers have been intentional. In general, the same stages of socialization (Figure 5.2) and adjustment (Figure 5.1), and the same orientation strategies and practices apply to both groups of personnel. As with paid employees, 'a well designed orientation process reduces stress on new volunteers, makes them feel welcome and may reduce the likelihood of turnover' (Australian Sports Commission [ASC], 2000a: 23). As a start, new volunteers should be provided with a copy of the organization's constitution, introduced to and provided with the names and contact information of key volunteers and any staff, familiarized with the responsibilities and accountabilities of their new role and how their role relates to others in the organization, and familiarized with any facilities, equipment, or resources that are used by the organization on a regular basis (ASC, 2000a). It should not be assumed that new volunteers know what they are supposed to be doing, how, when, and with whom, just because they have offered their free time to help a sport organization. Rather, it is important to effectively orient volunteers, so that they develop a strong, realistic psychological contract with the organization (Taylor et al., 2006).

Turning to sport event volunteers, training is deemed to be a critical component of event volunteer management (Gladden, McDonald & Barr, 1998; Chelladurai & Madella, 2006). Event volunteer training is analogous to orientation as it typically coincides with volunteers' organizational entry, or the first time they experience the organization as one of its members. As with staff and volunteers who are new to an organization, we may expect that volunteers who are new to an event have experienced some anticipatory socialization. For example, citizens of London, Ontario, and communities in the surrounding region were very familiar, through media and word-of-mouth communication, with the fact that an alliance of the communities bid in 1997 to host the quadrennial Canada Summer Games in 2001, and that the Games were successfully awarded to the region later that same year. Following that, local citizens would have been aware of the progress of capital enhancements to the region, in the form of new and upgraded sport facilities, and the need for over 6000 volunteers to stage the event. All of this information and these experiences would have given them some background on the nature of the event, its progress, political issues, and so on. In fact, 'media announcements' was one of the main factors that led citizens to sign up as volunteers (Doherty, 2003). Thus, we can presume that each volunteer became involved with the event organization with some pre-conceived ideas and expectations, although these were not necessarily accurate or complete. For the successful operation of the Games it was important for the host committee to ensure that the 6000 plus volunteers had a common understanding of the vision, mission, and planned legacies of the Games, the management structure and venue management plans, and available positions and responsibilities. This information was shared at several mandatory General Orientation sessions held for registered volunteers 6 months before the Games began.

According to Chelladurai and Madella (2006), this preliminary orientation phase of event volunteer management is critical for sharing with volunteers 'the nature and goals of the event, its functioning, key roles, persons and responsibilities, and role of volunteers and specific human resource policies and procedures applying to them' (2006: 61). It can also be used to 'create a good atmosphere and to develop ownership in the volunteers with respect to the event' (Chelladurai & Madella, 2006: 61). The preliminary orientation phase may be part of, or in addition to, further task-specific training. This was the case with the 2001 Canada Summer Games, where venue orientation sessions took place a few months after the general orientation sessions (and after volunteers had been given their assignments). During these types of task-specific training sessions, newcomers are typically still learning about the organization, its expectations, and adjusting their own expectations about being involved. At the Venue Orientation sessions for the 2001 Canada Summer Games, volunteers were oriented to their specific venue team of volunteers and the various roles involved, and provided detailed written and verbal information about transportation and parking issues, security, accreditation, customer service, conflict resolution, cross-cultural awareness, disabled integration, and dealing with the media. Following the formal information session, volunteers were given a 'venue walk-through' to familiarize themselves with the physical space where they would be working.

The following case of the 2005 Canadian Women's Open LPGA golf event provides an opportunity to consider the importance of effectively orienting personnel to a sport event:

Orientation at the Canadian Women's Open

The Royal Canadian Golf Association (RCGA) is the governing body of golf in Canada. Established in 1895, the RCGA prides itself on preserving its history, while providing leadership for the future of the game. In addition to several national amateur championships, the RCGA conducts the only PGA Tour and LPGA Tour events in Canada.

The organizational culture of the RCGA is very strong, framed by core values of leadership, openness, respect, responsiveness, and relevance. Staff are committed to the traditions and integrity of golf while ensuring that 'our stakeholders can depend on us to knowledgeably, professionally, and proactively build interest in, and excitement around the game in Canada' (RCGA, 2007: 1). When half of the RCGA staff head out of the office during the summer to oversee the many men's and women's golf championships and events which the RCGA coordinates across the country, they carry these values and principles with them.

The Canadian Women's Open is one of these events. The RCGA has overseen the Canadian Women's Open at various locations across Canada since 1973. A non-profit organization, the RCGA, operates these professional sporting events with the help of both paid and volunteer staff. Yearly, the Open brings in over 150 athletes, and relies on approximately 1500 volunteers and nearly 30 paid staff prior to, during, and after championship week. In 2005, the Canadian Women's Open was held in Glen Arbour, Nova Scotia, on Canada's East Coast. Preparation for the event started 2 years prior to the event itself. At this point, a volunteer-organizing committee from the host region was selected to act as a liaison between the RCGA and the host city volunteers and community. The host club, the Glen Arbour Golf Course, selected this committee which consisted of 1 Host Chair and 5 Directors.

In the 2 years prior to the 2005 Open, the RCGA conducted monthly conference call meetings with the Host Organizing Committee to ensure that the planning of the event was running smoothly. Three in-person trips to Nova Scotia were taken by staff during this timeframe. A month before the commencement of the tournament week, three full-time RCGA staff headed to Glen Arbour to oversee volunteer training and the final stages of event planning. When the RCGA staff arrived, more in depth meetings quickly revealed that the Host Committee had not sought approval from the RCGA Board of Governors for several initiatives planned for the event; a practice which is standard within the RCGA. There was also an apparent difference of opinion with regard to the emphasis that the RCGA insisted be placed on sponsor recognition. As it turned out, the Host Committee was never informed about these practices or perspectives, and had been operating with a focus on promoting the local community and the golf club itself.

This led to major difficulties in the final planning stages. It also became a challenge for event volunteer training. Local volunteers had developed certain expectations about the Open prior to becoming involved, as part of the recruitment process, and during a general orientation session conducted by the Host Committee. During the subsequent training sessions, the volunteers began receiving a second, different message from the RCGA representatives, which emphasized the priorities and focus of the RCGA.

The event was a success from an operational point of view; however, many of the Host Committee representatives were dissatisfied with their participation in the Open and remain uncommitted to the RCGA agenda.

Prepared by Shannon Hamm, with information from the RCGA.

Discussion questions

1. How can the RCGA improve its relationship with host organizing committees at future events?

Organizational culture

The concept of organizational culture has its roots in anthropology. Culture refers to the social context in which people live. Just as a group, community, or society has shared meanings and values, so too does an organization. Organizational culture is an underlying system of values, beliefs, and assumptions about how things are done in an organization (Schein, 1985). Just as our individual values and beliefs guide our behaviour, organizational values, and beliefs serve as a guide to individual behaviour in the organization. Thus, organizational culture is a key component of SHRM.

Schein (1985) defined organizational culture as:

> A pattern of basic assumptions – invented, discovered, or developed by a given group as it learns to cope with its problems of external adaptation and internal integration – that has worked well enough to be considered valid and … to be taught to new members as the correct way to perceive, think, and feel in relation to those problems (Schein,1985: 9).

Core values, beliefs, and even further underlying assumptions about 'how things are around here' may be difficult to know directly. Instead, they are manifested or reflected in organizational practices and member behaviour. These are more visible artefacts that represent what is valued in the organization, believed to be important, and assumed to be acceptable. To the extent that these values, beliefs, and assumptions are known, and accepted, by members of an organization, they serve to guide or control organizational behaviour. Therefore, it is to the organization's advantage to ensure newcomers understand and embrace the culture of the organization. Similarly, it is to the newcomers' advantage to understand as quickly as possible how things are done around their new workplace.

Organizational culture has consistently been shown to be associated with staff attitudes and behaviour. The extent to which particular values and beliefs are perceived to be manifested in an organization has been shown to engender workplace satisfaction, organizational commitment, increased effort, and reduced turnover (e.g., Sheridan, 1992; Lok & Crawford, 1999; Adkins & Caldwell, 2004; Silverthorne, 2004; MacIntosh & Doherty, 2005) and further organizational performance in the long term (Carmeli & Tishler, 2004). The positive influence of organizational culture is likely due to a combination of members' understanding of and comfort with how things are done.

A 'strong culture' is one where the values, beliefs, and assumptions about the organization are widely understood and strongly accepted across the organization. It can be expected that a strong culture is more of a guiding force, as members understand and accept how things are done in the organization (McKenna & Beech, 2002). However, a strong culture can be a liability when it is characterized by values, beliefs, and ways of doing things that run counter to an organization's corporate strategy, HR plan, and overall best interests; for example, restricted communication, intolerance of differences, or resistance to change. In contrast, a 'weak culture' is one where the values, beliefs, and assumptions about the organization are not widely known or not strongly accepted. As a result, culture is less of a guiding force for members. Newcomer orientation is an opportunity to strengthen an organization's culture by imparting to the newcomer desired behaviours and the underlying values and beliefs. Additional mechanisms by which a desirable organizational culture can be developed, strengthened and maintained, and a less than desirable culture may be changed, are discussed below.

The discussion thus far has focused on the notion of an overarching culture that is understood and accepted to some extent by staff and volunteers. We can also consider that within an overarching or 'dominant' culture there may be several differentiated subcultures (Martin, 1992). Subcultures are unique sets of values, beliefs, and assumptions that develop over time within an organizational group or unit. Subcultures may form among individuals who work in the same functional area (e.g., marketing, sales, coaching, administration), at the same hierarchical level (e.g., management, staff), or in the same geographical areas (e.g., fitness clubs within a larger parent organization). Subcultures reflect shared values and beliefs based on common or shared experiences of group members. Subcultures may also form among staff or volunteers who have similar socio-demographic characteristics (e.g., women, former athletes). These forms of subcultures are personal rather than work related and may be analogous to 'cliques.' While a clique can provide an important source of support for newcomers and veterans alike, it may be viewed as an exclusionary group. Subcultures that develop based on function can be very positive if they provide members with a more work-specific frame of reference in the workplace. However, culture or subcultures are only positive from the organization's perspective if the values and beliefs they represent, and the further behaviour they engender, align with the strategic focus of the organization.

The notions of a dominant culture and subcultures are not necessarily antithetical, as some might suggest (Martin, 1992). Rather, 'a subculture could consist of the core values of the dominant culture as well as the values of the area to which they relate' (McKenna & Beech, 2002: 93). In a study of the dominant culture and subcultures in a large multi-franchise fitness organization, MacIntosh and Doherty (2005) found that the corporate values of passion, peak attitude, fitness, and organizational performance were perceived to be more prevalent by club staff than head office staff. The authors concluded that the distinct subcultures were likely consistent with the respective functions of the two different groups. For example, it was not surprising that the corporate value of fitness was more pervasive in the club subculture 'given that the mandate of the clubs is to provide quality fitness services to clients. In contrast, head office is responsible for [a myriad of organizational operations] and is not as directly involved in the delivery of fitness services' (MacIntosh & Doherty, 2005: 17). The possible existence of subcultures within a dominant culture means that the newcomer may need to be socialized to the values and beliefs of the group as well as to the broader culture of the organization.

There are many different ways to describe the nature of a particular organization's culture. It is argued that culture is unique from one organization to another, and therefore the only way to know it is to examine the visible manifestations (i.e., organizational practices, member behaviour, symbols, myths), and talk to people about how things are done and why (Sackmann, 2001). This can help to uncover the underlying values and beliefs that are shared in the organization. However, there are also several frameworks and corresponding instruments that comprise what are considered to be sets of key characteristics that organizations value. Robbins (1997: 602) suggests that the following values 'capture the essence of an organization's culture':

- Member identity: The degree to which staff and volunteers identify more with the organization or with their field of expertise.
- Group emphasis: The degree to which work is organized more for individuals or for groups.
- People focus: The degree to which organizational decisions consider the impact on the task or on the people who work there.
- Unit integration: The degree to which work units or groups are encouraged to operate more independently or in a coordinated, interdependent fashion.
- Control: The degree to which the management of staff and volunteers is quite loose or is based on rules, regulations, and direct supervision.
- Risk tolerance: The degree to which staff and volunteers are quite restrained or are encouraged to be creative, innovative, and to take risks.
- Reward criteria: The degree to which rewards are based more on performance or on some other criteria like seniority.
- Conflict tolerance: The degree to which conflict is seen as something negative and to be avoided or is valued and encouraged.
- Means-ends orientation: The degree to which the organization focuses more on the methods and processes to achieve outcomes or on the outcomes themselves.
- Open-system focus: The degree to which the organization focuses more on internal processes of the organization or focuses outwards on the environment and responds to changes there.

These characteristics can be used to describe an organization's culture profile, based on members' perceptions of how things are done there. It is possible to determine whether there is widespread understanding and acceptance of the profile (a strong culture), or whether it is unclear what is going on, what is expected, or why things should be done in a certain way (a weak culture). It is also possible to determine whether subcultures exist within an organization, based on variations in the perception or importance of these characteristics, and perhaps the existence of other important elements. Although these key characteristics are presumed to have universal relevance to organizations of all types, research suggests that organizational culture may be specific to different industries (Lee & Yu, 2004). Smith and Shilbury (2004) found that history and tradition were highly valued elements in voluntary amateur sport organizations, while MacIntosh and Doherty (2007a) uncovered member success and a sense of connectedness within the club as valued aspects in the fitness industry; elements that were not apparent in universal measures of organizational culture.

Organizations should have a thorough understanding of the nature and strength of the core values and beliefs of their dominant culture, as well as the presence of any subcultures, and particularly whether they are consistent with the strategic direction of the firm. With regard to orientation, there are several mechanisms by which newcomers can learn the culture of an organization, and these are discussed below.

Learning organizational culture

Organizational culture is learned as part of the socialization process. A newcomer may develop some sense of the organization's values and beliefs before entering the organization. This may happen as part of the recruitment and selection process, or even prior to that, based on the individual's knowledge of the organization through personal experience or learning about the organization from others. For example, as a former client or member of a sporting goods retail store, fitness club, or local sports club, a new employee or volunteer likely developed perceptions about the organization's culture, or how things are done there, which contributes to his or her image of the organization (Hatch & Schultz, 1997; MacIntosh & Doherty, 2007b). As noted earlier, however, anticipatory socialization may be a source of inaccurate information about an organization. It is important that newcomer staff and volunteers have a clear understanding of organizational reality. As noted earlier, this can be enhanced with an effective, and realistic, job preview, during which a candidate can develop some sense of the organizational culture.

The most meaningful orientation to organizational culture occurs, however, once the newcomer becomes involved in the organization, during entry socialization. At this point, the individual has direct exposure to cultural artefacts that reflect what is valued and considered most important. Newcomers learn about organizational culture through symbols, including such things as office furnishings and decor, and manner of employee dress (e.g., formal or casual office attire; matching uniforms or individualistic dress). These

105

symbols convey to staff and volunteers what is important, accepted, and expected in the organization. Organizational culture is also passed along through stories that 'anchor the present in the past and provide explanations and legitimacy for current practices' (Robbins, 1997: 616). For example, at the University of Western Ontario in London, Ontario, Canada, stories continue to be told about Mr. John 'The Bull' Metras, who was a very successful head coach of the football team from 1939 to 1969, head coach of the basketball team from 1945 to 1964, and served as Athletic Director from 1945 to 1972. These stories highlight the importance of history, tradition, and athletic excellence that continue to be core values at the institution to this day.

Company rituals and ceremonies are another mechanism by which culture is transmitted. A fitness club or sports retailer may have sales performance awards and ceremonies that convey the importance of this form of achievement. The orientation process itself may be seen as a rite of passage (e.g., Base Camp at GoodLife Fitness Clubs), to the extent that it is systematic and thus conveys the importance of learning about how things are done in the organization. Annual staff picnics or bowling tournaments, or entering a team in a charity tournament, are other examples of company rituals that communicate and reinforce certain values in the organization.

Observing the behaviour of others and, perhaps most importantly, seeing what is rewarded (i.e., valued) and what is not tolerated by the organization is a fundamental way to learn about organizational culture; for example, seeing how members act and react in certain situations, observing patterns of formal and informal communication, and realizing the tolerance for ambiguity or conflict in the organization. These visible artefacts and manifestations of organizational culture not only teach, but also reinforce the existing values and beliefs (Johns & Saks, 2001).

Strengthening or changing organizational culture

Given the potential impact of a strong, positive organizational culture – that is, one which is widely shared by members and aligns with the organization's objectives and corporate strategy – it is important to consider how it is possible to strengthen an existing culture (so that it is more widely and deeply embraced). Alternatively, it is important to understand how to change a culture that is either weak and not shared by many, or is not aligned with the intended direction of the organization.

There are several ways to strengthen or change an existing organizational culture. It is widely recognized that the founder of the organization typically sets the path for the organization at the outset (Robbins, 1997). This has been the case with GoodLife Fitness Clubs (David Patchell-Evans) and Nike Corporation (Phil Knight), and of course with McDonald's (Ray Kroc) and Microsoft (Bill Gates). The organization's leaders, which may or may not include the founder, continue to guide, or change, the direction of the culture. It is modelled and reinforced by what they pay attention to in the workplace, their own work behaviour, as well as their reaction to crises or critical incidents. John Stanton 'found' running in 1981, then founded the Running Room in 1984, a sport and exercise retail chain and meeting place for runners, with outlets across Canada and the US. He continues to join staff and clients for Running Room club runs (Running Room, 2007a).

Organizational culture is also strengthened, or changed, through recruitment and selection. Hiring employees or bringing on board volunteers who 'fit' with the current or desired culture can help to perpetuate and reinforce that culture, or help to change culture in the desired direction. Continuing from the example of the Running Room, the sport and exercise retail chain hires only runners to staff its stores:

> Who else but a runner is knowledgeable about the needs of runners, as well as the products that cater to those needs? The Running Room philosophy is that if you're out there running on the same roads as the customers, you can relate to their exact needs. The Running Room is truly a store for runners by runners (Running Room, 2007b: no page).

The socialization of newcomers is another important point at which existing culture can be strengthened, or changed. Desirable culture can be reinforced during either formal or informal orientation, when newcomers learn about the organizational culture; for example, through symbols, stories, rituals, and the behaviour of other staff or volunteers. As may be expected, socializing newcomers to an organization's culture is more difficult to do when the culture is weak to begin with; that is, when the underlying values and beliefs are not widely understood or accepted. Following orientation, culture can be strengthened and maintained by rewarding behaviour that is consistent with desirable values and beliefs in the organization.

Summary

Orientation is the socialization of newcomers to the organization. It is critical that both 'neophyte' and 'veteran' newcomers have a relevant and thorough introduction to the organization so that they are more likely to hit the ground running, do the work that is expected of them, and stay with the organization.

New staff and volunteers ideally adjust to their new working environment as they move through three stages of socialization; anticipatory, encounter, and role management socialization correspond with newcomers' pre-entry, entry, and adaptation to the organization, respectively. The intended outcomes of orientation and socialization are task mastery, role clarity, workgroup integration, and political knowledge. Successful adjustment is characterized by organizational commitment, job satisfaction, and retention.

Orientation is critical for aligning, or realigning, newcomers' expectations about the organization and their role there. An employee or volunteer's psychological or unwritten contract with an organization is based on mutual expectations and obligations, some of which will be established and some of which may need to be aligned with the reality of the organization. A newcomer's perception of P-O fit is important to their successful adjustment to the organization; thus, orientation is critical to create or strengthen one's sense of whether their values are consistent with those of the organization.

107

Newcomers may be proactive in their socialization to the organization, seeking out information they want and feel they need. However, it is important for the organization to implement a well-designed orientation process that lets it control what information newcomers receive and how. A framework of 6 contrasting approaches highlights strategies an organization can use to effectively implement orientation. The job preview and mentoring are 2 specific methods of orientation that correspond to newcomers' pre-entry, and entry and adaptation to the organization, respectively.

The orientation of sport volunteers, including those involved in staging events, should not be taken for granted. Like employees, newcomer volunteers likely have preconceived ideas and expectations about the organization or event that are not necessarily consistent with organizational reality, and are not necessarily complete. The various strategies and practices for orienting and socializing employees are applicable to volunteers as well.

Finally, organizational culture is the values, beliefs, and assumptions that underlie how things are done in an organization. It is reflected in an organization's symbols, stories, rituals, and practices. To the extent that organizational culture is understood and accepted by staff and volunteers, it serves to guide and control behaviour, by letting members know what is expected and how things are done. Thus, it is important that organizational culture is aligned with an organization's corporate strategy, and that newcomers come to understand and embrace that culture as quickly as possible.

Discussion questions

1. Discuss your experience with entering and adjusting to a new organization, or a new job. What socialization strategies and practices were used? Were your values and expectations aligned with the organization? Did you experience any 'reality shock'? What could the organization have done to make your orientation more effective?
2. Describe the psychological contract you have with an organization for which you are employed or volunteer. What are your expectations of the organization, and what do you perceive the organization expects from you? Have you had to adjust your psychological contract during your time with the organization?
3. Using an institutionalized or individualized approach, design an orientation process for each of the following:
   (a) A new college/university athletic director
   (b) New summer sports camp counsellors
   (c) A neophyte volunteer coach
   (d) A veteran newcomer volunteer coach
4. Describe the organizational culture of a sport organization with which you are most familiar (consider visible artefacts such as symbols, stories, rituals, myths, and behaviours, and the core values they represent). How could a newcomer learn the culture of that organization?

108

6

Training and development in sport organizations

Learning objectives

After reading this chapter you will be able to:

- Articulate the significance of training and development in sport organizations
- Understand the aims of employee and volunteer learning
- Explain the training and development model
- Describe how effective training and development contributes to organizational development and enables strategic achievement of organizational goals.

Chapter overview

Training and development are important ingredients of human resource management (HRM) and thus are critical to an organization's success. Broadly, training and development are used to build the skills and capabilities of the organization to meet its strategic

109

challenges. More specifically, training and development are used to close the gap identified, either implicitly or explicitly, in the actual vs. desired performance of the employee or volunteer at an individual, group/team, or organizational level.

The contribution this HRM function can make to a sport organization's effectiveness, competitiveness, and to employee and volunteer satisfaction is outlined in this chapter. Training and development processes and activities are discussed from the perspective of a systemic and integrated (i.e., strategic) approach to planning can be applied to any employee group (senior executives, line managers, operational staff, volunteers). Underpinning this approach is the premise that sport organizations should ensure that their training and development initiatives are aligned with the strategic objectives and mission of the organization. The notion of the learning organization, or viewing the organization as a total learning system that has core competencies which can be addressed via 'collective learning' (Prahalad & Hamel, 1990), is also discussed in this chapter.

The significance of training and development in sport organizations

Sport organizations that have well-managed training and development programmes can more easily retain employees and volunteers, ensure that their human resources have the capability to deliver on the organization's strategy, and provide future leaders for the organization. Organizational investment in employees has been positively associated with creating higher levels of employee loyalty (Mowday, 1999) and facilitating a sense of obligation to give something back to the organization (Meyer, Allen & Smith, 1993). Research has also found that training and development can positively impact overall organizational performance, product quality, market share, workplace relationships and lead to higher profits, and lower absentee rates (for an overview of related research findings see Boselie, Paauwe & Jansen, 2001).

The rationale for strategic training and development in sport organizations includes the following:

- Increased job satisfaction and morale among employees and volunteers.
- Reduced turnover of employees and volunteers.
- Increased employee and volunteer motivation.
- Improved efficiencies in processes and procedures.

- Enhanced capacity to adopt new technologies and methods.
- Risk management in terms of better knowledge of compliance requirements.

Training and development is equally applicable to paid staff and volunteers. Effective training and development of volunteers is fundamental for the continued existence of many community sport organizations, as these organizations rely on developing and retaining such personnel to deliver their core services. The Australian Sports Commission's *Volunteer Management Program*, Sport England's *Volunteer Investment Program*, and Sport and Recreation New Zealand's *Running Sport Program*, just to name a few, all emphasize the importance of training practices in the management of volunteers. A study of community sport volunteers in Australia, (Cuskelly et al., 2006) found that the retention of volunteer committee and board members was positively related to training and support practices.

Training and development involves an alignment of the strategic objectives of an organization with the capability of those involved in the organization to achieve these objectives. For example, a community fitness centre with a mission to be the first choice for fitness services of its local citizens might develop a specific training programme focused on customer care and relationship management issues to ensure that its employees understand how to deliver customer satisfaction, ensure customer retention and develop customer loyalty. In a study of fitness centre employees, Makover (2003: 91) found that 'specific training and mentoring programmes can help elevate employees' awareness, efficacy, commitment and satisfaction, and as a result ... improved quality of the service that they provide to customers'.

The purpose of training and development is to ensure that employees and volunteers are provided with opportunities to learn new skills, knowledge, and attitudes that will allow them to deal with the demands of the sport organization in which they work and volunteer. Training and development can be initiated for a variety of reasons for either individuals or groups of employees or volunteers. Some common reasons for engaging in specific programmes of training and development are as follows:

- To train about a specific topic or skill.
- As a component of an individual's overall professional development programme.
- When a performance appraisal indicates that performance improvement is required.
- As part of a succession management or a strategic talent management process.
- As a way of developing a common and shared mindset and approach to decision making amongst managers.

Typically, 'training' refers to the development and enhancement of technical, job-related skills and abilities, either on-the-job or off-the-job. 'Development' is more concerned with changing attitudes and behaviours as well as skill building, and aims to improve the interpersonal capabilities of the person. In recent years there has been an increasing focus on moving beyond the confines of these conceptions of training and development and creating 'learning organizations' that integrate work and learning in all aspects of organizational life. Such a holistic approach requires the support of the organization's senior management and an accommodating organizational culture.

Bratton and Gold (2003) identify two premises that underpin the learning organization approach. Firstly, learning is viewed as an expected and embedded activity. The latter infers that learning is integrated into the day-to-day operations of the organization.

When a person is recruited it should be not only for his/her ability to perform a current work role but he/she should also demonstrate the potential to learn and change as the role evolves. Secondly, informal learning is considered as a part of the job and is the responsibility of all managers and supervisors. This means that job performance, appraisal, and development are undertaken by managers and supervisors in the course of their work, and as a result they are continuously assessing the need for job improvement and career development. Understanding the role of learning in this process is essential.

Employee and volunteers learning

The basic premise of learning, acquiring new skills, knowledge, attitudes, and behaviours as a result of interactions with one's environment underpins the concept of training and development. Learning occurs in context, and it can be achieved through active, social, and reflective means (Driscoll, 1994). Learning is individualistic and people have different preferences. Some people learn best when the learning takes place within certain environment (context), others prefer to be mentally active (active) to make connections between the new knowledge and existing knowledge and then construct meaning from their experiences, some like to work collaboratively in groups and gaining from different perspectives (social), and others learn best when given the opportunity to critically think about their actions and outcomes (reflective).

There are three distinctive theories about how learning occurs that managers should understand and apply to maximize the success of training and development. These are *behavioural*, cognitive, and constructive learning orientations. The behavioural approach focuses on changing observable behaviour through either positive or negative reinforcement and the learner engages in the behaviour in order to learn. For example, a fitness centre manager might train a new instructor by complementing her/him on actions which are generally desirable, but then as the instructor gains these competencies the manager would gradually move to only praise those precise behaviours that are considered essential for the job. This type of learning can produce a relatively permanent change in behaviour due to the learners' experience (Ormrod, 1999).

Cognitivism focuses on mental processes and suggests that learning occurs when information is mentally processed and the result is a change in the structure of learner's knowledge. The cognitive orientation to learning considers how people perceive, interpret, and think about the environmental events they experience in a way that enables them to modify their behaviour fairly rapidly (Gagne & Driscoll, 1988). Continuing the example above, the manager would provide cognitive feedback to the fitness instructor, that is, specific information about performance and his/her success or failure in delivering key aspects of his/her job.

The *constructive* orientation to learning contends that a person's knowledge, together with the learning process itself, is constructed by the learners' interpretation of their experience. Learning is taken to be a relatively permanent change in a person's knowledge or behaviour. This premise consists of three components: (1) the duration of the change is long term; (2) the change involves the content and structure of knowledge in memory or the behaviour of the learner; and (3) the cause of the change is the learner's experience in the environment (Mayer, 1982). Constructivism suggests that learning is an intentional, conscious activity on the part of the learner. In this approach our fitness instructor would actively and consciously engage with learning the practice required for the job through action and then reflect on the activities.

Constructed learning is a shared responsibility of the sport organization and of employees, volunteers, managers, and supervisors at all levels. Employees should pursue learning that is aligned with organizational priorities and which prepares them to do their job into the future through the acquisition and maintenance of knowledge, skills, and competencies related to their level and function. Managers and supervisors are responsible for enabling training that supports organizational objectives. Organizations can provide opportunities for continuous learning in order to optimise organizational learning. Sport organizations that explicitly encourage and support this learning process from a strategic perspective are called 'learning organizations'.

The learning organization

The 'learning organization' (Senge, 1990), 'knowledge creation' (Nonaka & Takeuchi, 1995), and knowledge management (Drucker, 1995), all represent frameworks designed to improve organizational capacity for learning. A learning organization incorporates the development of organizational level, collective intelligence, and acknowledges the importance of knowledge, and in particular, tacit knowledge. To this end training-based development fosters learning in different ways (learning networks, communities of practice) than might be traditionally found in HR training and development.

The concept of organizational learning refers to the development of skills, knowledge, and associations between past actions, the effectiveness of those actions, and future actions (Fiol & Lyles, 1985). The knowledge generated through such learning enables an organization to understand the consequences of past actions and respond to environmental stimuli. This approach suggests that effective learning leads to an enhancement of an organization's skills and capabilities (Levinthal, 1991).

A learning organization is where 'members are continuously deliberately learning new things. They apply what they learn to improve the product or service quality, the processes involved in making the product or providing the service, the quality of the environment in which employees work and the performance of members of the organization' (Honold, 1991: 56). The key driver to becoming a learning organization is the desire to be more client centred through continuous improvement and innovation. In learning organizations managers, supervisors, employees, and volunteers are active partners in supporting learning. Each person plays a role in identifying learning needs, stimulating and supporting informal learning, and ensuring the continuous learning of themselves and others.

In the learning organization employees and volunteers are encouraged to learn, acquire new knowledge and skills, and disseminate this knowledge to others within the organization to improve or renew existing work practices, products or services, or to initiate innovation. Learning is regarded as a normal part of everyday work and working is seen as a context for learning (McGill & Slocum, 1994). Training and development activities are structured to enhance the learning capacities of employees and volunteers and are delivered within an environment favourable for learning. This might include using job rotation, mentoring, self-directed study, or task simulations in a stimulating work environment. In this organizational context, training and development are a form of learning and there is a strong link between learning and working. Strategic viability of all organizations is tied to the continuous training and development of employees and volunteers.

A training and development process

The basic components of training and development are represented in Figure 6.1 and may encompass collective or individual training processes. The typical first step in an systematic approach to training and development is the implementation of a thorough *training needs analysis*. This is followed by the development of *training goals*, which in turn inform the *design* of the training or development intervention. *Implementation* of the selected initiatives is accompanied by an *evaluation* of the training and development programme.

Step 1: Training needs analysis

The objective of undertaking a thorough training needs analysis to collect information that will assist in the development of training strategies and objectives. The process typically involves a three-level approach. First, an organizational level analysis is used to examine how a training and

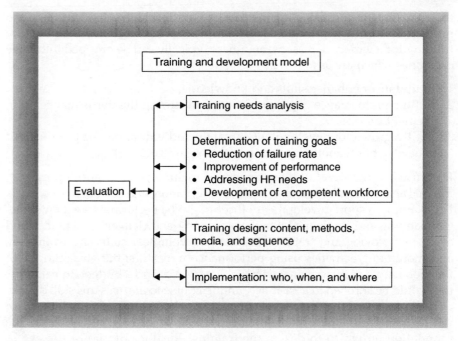

Figure 6.1 Training and development model (*Source*: Baumgarten, 1995: 209).

development programme can support the strategic direction of the organization and be aligned with organizational goals. The question asked is, where is training needed and which organizational goals can be achieved via training? For example, a golf club identifies a performance gap shown by a declining number of membership renewals and low member satisfaction with service. Data used in the analysis might include the golf club's strategic goals, culture, quality assurance processes, and employee turnover and absenteeism rates. As a result of the analysis, the training requirements needed to address this issue would be identified.

At the next level of assessment, an operational task analysis is performed to identify the nature of job tasks and the knowledge, skills, and abilities required to perform the job effectively. The question asked here is, what needs to be learned to do the job effectively? Data used in this level of analysis might include position descriptions, performance criteria, and market research about the requirements of similar positions in other organizations. For example, after researching the training needs of officials, British Cycling developed a standardized programme for training cycling officials, with a standardized format for all disciplines comprising training and hands-on experience gained over the course of six races and including child protection, communication, administration, technical, and competition (see Note – From the Field at the end of this chapter).

Finally, an individual level analysis is carried out to see how well a person performs a job. This is undertaken to ascertain which individual should be trained and the type of training that they require based on an assessment of

115

their current performance against desired performance. It identifies who needs training at the individual level. Employees and volunteers can require training for a variety of reasons, and these typically can be grouped into three categories which are as follows:

1. To update or enhance skills and knowledge.
2. To fill a performance gap that is identified during the performance management process.
3. To fill a growth or development gap, if the individual is to be promoted or to be able to fill another position in the organization.

Data used in this level of analysis would include performance appraisals, internal and external customer feedback, observation, and 360 degree feedback. For example, a sport development officer might be performing well on strategic planning and implementation; coordinating and delivering activities and events; employing and training coaches and volunteer staff; and evaluating and monitoring activities using performance indicators; but struggling with their job requirement to manage financial resources and a budget. In response, they could be enrolled in a basic accounting course to address this skill deficit.

Taken together, the three levels of analysis should provide the basis with which to identify the organization's training objectives and provide the foundation on which to design the training. Ideally, criteria for the evaluation of the training initiatives are also established during this phase to measure success on achieving the training objectives.

Not all organizations have procedures for systematically determining training and development needs. Those who do engage in this process are usually organizations with HR professionals on staff and organizations, such as government departments, that are required to do so for funding or accreditation purposes. The needs analysis in small or non-profit sport organizations is generally done on a more broader level. An example would be to operationally identify deficiencies, such as the necessity for higher order financial skills to manage budget submissions, or required compliance standards, such as legislated risk management documentation. An example of broadly identifying volunteer satisfaction as a key training and development need is provided below in the 'Snapshot of an AFL Club'.

Snapshot of an AFL club

The Australian Glenelg Football Club has a very well run and successful volunteer management programme. With approximately 130 volunteers, the club has identified a systematic and committed approach to developing a team environment which optimizes job satisfaction. The process the club went through to establish the programme is as follows:

■ A coordinator for the Tiger Volunteer Programme was appointed.

- The coordinator reviewed training requirements, and identified a need for key volunteer personnel to get immediate training in administration, first aid and medicine, and volunteer management issues.
- All existing and new volunteers are required to complete an application form and are presented with a copy of the club's volunteer policy.
- All new volunteers are placed under a mentor scheme.
- All training staff have upgraded first aid and sports trainers' qualifications.
- Club paid staff have attended Office for Recreation and Sport Volunteer Management forums.
- Team managers have attended South Australian National Football League Tribunal Procedures training workshops.

Source: Australian Football League (2004).

Step 2: Setting training and learning goals

The goals developed for training and development should state what will be accomplished as a result of the training and should be specified in light of the needs identified. These will arise out of gaps and deficiencies identified in the preceding needs analysis. Training goals and objectives indicate the organization's expectation of the employee or volunteer in relation to their understanding of relevant concepts (e.g., privacy requirements), ability to perform a skill (e.g., public speaking), or demonstrate a change in behaviour (e.g., improved decision making). Common training programmes for the employees and volunteers in sport organizations include: communication, negotiation, customer service, developing codes of conduct, issues of conflict of interest and corporate social responsibility, good corporate governance, diversity issues, volunteer management, and coaching and officiating. The latter training is usually located within a state or national accreditation framework.

All training should consist of observable and measurable learning objectives so that everyone are involved in the process, this means that the trainee, trainer, manager, and any other relevant party will have clarity on the expected outcomes. To take an example, a basic level training programme on diversity objectives might include the following:

- Demonstrate an understanding of the value, importance, and impact on for your organization of managing diversity and inclusion.
- Recognize and encourage behaviours that value diversity in the workplace.
- Develop strategies that will enhance the organization's capability by capitalizing on differences and improving workplace harmony.

Once the training and development objectives are determined then the next step is to design relevant programmes and ensure infrastructure support.

Step 3: Designing training and development

As noted previously, the training goals and objectives will influence design. The determination of the way in which the training will be delivered also relates to the content, method of instruction, material, exercises, and sequencing. The content of the training course should link directly with the areas that were identified in the needs assessment and align with the training goals. The design of training is a highly specialized area and it is not the intention of this book to provide precise guidelines on designing organizational training programmes. However, there are some guiding principles that should be considered in assessing the appropriateness of the training design and methods.

A wide range of skills and tasks categorizations exist, but basically these aspects can be grouped into three general categories: cognitive, interpersonal, and psychomotor (Goldstein & Ford, 2002). Cognitive skills and development are related to problem solving, understanding, and knowledge requirements. Interpersonal aspects are to do with interactions with others, including colleagues, volunteers, and stakeholders. This covers a very wide array of skills such as leadership, communication, negotiation, conflict resolution, and team building. Psychomotor skills are related to manual or physical activities that require specific movements.

Training methods

There are a range of methods that can be used to deliver the required outcomes of skill, knowledge, attitudinal, or task development. The method is chosen to match the skill or task required. Training may include formal, structured learning experiences such as classroom, seminar, or conference-based training or the use of online training packages. Table 6.1 outlines some common off-the-job training methods.

Volunteers may need to receive specific on-the-job training to provide the information and skills necessary to effectively perform the volunteer role. Unlike most paid positions, many volunteer roles will be filled by individuals who do not have prerequisite skills or expertise in the job they will perform. Given that: (a) skills and abilities are not the basis for a volunteer's recruitment; (b) several volunteers may share or rotate in a task; and (c) volunteer work is often undertaken with little supervision; effective volunteer training has been found as a critical component for good volunteer management, and sport organization effectiveness (Kim, 2004). For example, a volunteer may be recruited as a duty manager based on her knowledge of a particular sport rather than her experience as a manager. Once fully skilled, the volunteer will then be in a position to further develop her skills and knowledge or acquire further knowledge through engagement in developmental initiatives.

Table 6.1 Common off-the-job training methods

Lecture	Mostly an oral presentation, but may be supplemented with visual aids or handouts; the technique is generally confined to presenting only the expert's point of view; often used because it is easier to organize and a great deal of information can be presented in a short period of time.
	Useful when there are a large group of trainees.
Lecture/discussion	Variation of the lecture where the trainer increases trainee participation through facilitation of discussion at set times during the session; discussion is often initiated through the use of questions; trainer must plan the discussion and carefully choose the questions to lead the discussion.
Demonstration	Oral explanations combined with visual activities; method demonstrations show processes, concepts, and facts and are especially effective in teaching a skill that can be observed.
	A result demonstration shows the outcome of some practice or innovation.
Group discussion	Trainer leads the trainees as a group through a discussion of a given topic; may or may not be preceded by a short explanatory lecture.
Symposium	A series of lectures presided over by a moderator; allows for the presentation of several points of view or several-related topics.
Panel	A dialogue among several experts sitting in front of the room.
	A moderator coordinates the discussion.
	Differs from a symposium because panel members have an opportunity to discuss and interact with each other's ideas and views.
Forum	Following one or more presentations, the audience interacts and discusses the topic(s), bringing up a wider range of views.
	Discussion groups encourage/allow everyone to participate, even if the audience is large.
Case studies	Information is given to the trainees detailing a specific situation or problem and the trainees are assigned (as individuals or discussion groups) the task of making recommendations for the most appropriate action to solve the problem.
	Introduces a practical aspect to the training environment and creates a problem-solving situation similar to that many trainees may face after returning to work.

119

(Continued)

Table 6.1 (Continued)

Simulations and games	Ranges from simple individual or small group problem-solving experiential exercises to complex multi-dimensional business simulations.
	Contains a planned sequence of developmental activities; simulations allow the participant to observe the impact of their choices without the outcomes having any impact on the real organization.

Source: Adapted from Carey (1999).

The motivation of volunteers to undertake training may vary from that of paid employees, and it is highly contextual. In a province-wide study of sports, culture, and recreation organizations in Saskatchewan, Canada Dorsch, Riemer, Sluth, Paskevich & Chelladurai (2002) found that volunteer commitment was linked to satisfaction with organizational performance; organizational identity; the safety of the psychological climate; role identity; and role acceptance. The authors of the study recommended that sport volunteers are provided with opportunities for relevant training and development to increase the volunteer's identification with the organization, which will in turn lead to increased satisfaction and commitment.

In her study of training and volunteers in the American Youth Soccer Organization, Kim (2004) found that a volunteer's commitment to the organization was strongly related to their willingness to be trained. Learning orientation (the belief that making an effort to learn leads to an improvement in outcome) and understanding (opportunities for learning and the exercise of knowledge, skills, and abilities that might not be used elsewhere) were also significant factors in a volunteer's willingness to engage in training.

As the Australian Sports Commission (2000) notes in their volunteer training modules, many volunteers will actively seek out and engage in training but others will feel as though training is not the best use of their time. Additionally, 'the issue of who should pay for training (individual volunteers, the organization, or some combination of the two) needs to be considered particularly when training is considered to be a compulsory requirement (e.g., officiating)' (Australian Sports Commission, 2000: 7).

The advent of easy to access Internet training has spawned a range of online manuals, support materials, and training courses, developed by government, national, and state sporting bodies, and non-government organizations (NGO), that can be accessed free of charge and at convenient times. Such courses are relevant for both volunteers and paid staff working in community sport. An example of one such on-line training intiative is provided below.

Online training – Play by the Rules programme

Play by the Rules is a free, online training course for coaches, administrators, umpires and referees, participants and volunteers. The courses are short (up to 2 hours), may be done in part or all at once, and make extensive use of case studies.

Play by the Rules has three main aims which are as follows:

1. *Information*: it provides information exploring discrimination, harassment and child protection.
2. *Rights*: to explore rights, and how the law protects these rights to participate in sport and recreation activities and not be unfairly discriminated against.
3. *Responsibilities*: responsibilities under the law.

The courses provide up-to-date information on rules, legislation, and examples of best practice. There is an online quiz at the end of each module. An official certificate is provided on successful completion of the course.

For more information: see www.playbytherules.net.au. Link active as of March 2007. Play by the Rules is supported by the Australian and State and Territory Governments.

Employee and volunteer development

Development of individuals within the organization focuses on improving organizational performance through enhancement of the employee's or volunteer's abilities. Developmental interactions have the potential to enhance not only personal growth, through increased knowledge and career advancement, but also organizational goals, through enhanced performance and increased employee retention. There are various forms of development-oriented activities, such as: trainee positions, job rotation, leadership and management development programmes, mentoring, and coaching; an array of topics of developmental interactions such as: career advice and work life support and balance; and numerous factors that may contribute to development (Higgins & Kram, 2001).

Trainee positions provide an individual with specific responsibilities beyond their normal duties and/or a senior person to work with and learn from. Job rotation involves providing the individual with the opportunity to perform a number of jobs, each chosen to build their skills, knowledge, and expertise across a range of the organization's activities. Orientation processes and programmes are also fundamental for achieving employee and volunteer development. The place of orientation and its use in development is discussed in further detail in Chapter 5.

121

Table 6.2 Differences between mentoring and coaching

	Mentor	Coach
Focus	Individual	Enhance performance
Role	Facilitator with no agenda	Specific agenda
Relationship	Self-selecting	Assigned
Source of influence	Perceived value	Position
Personal returns	Affirmation/learning	Teamwork/performance
Arena	Life	Task related

Development-focused initiatives such as *mentoring* programmes and *coaching* assignments have substantively gained in popularity (Eddy, D'Abate, Tannenbaum, Givens-Skeaton & Robinson, 2006). One of the reasons for the surge in the use of mentoring and coaching is the mounting evidence of the positive contributions that mentors can make to career success, and the use of these methods to achieve competitive advantage through people (Veale & Watchel, 1996). Coaching and mentoring programmes may reside either on or off the job, depending if the coach or mentor is located within the organization or is external. While the terms coach and mentor are sometimes used interchangeably there are differences in the role each plays and these are outlined in Table 6.2.

Mentors, whether it is in a formal mentoring programme or in an informal relationship, focus on the person, their career and support for individual's growth, while the coach is more job focused and performance oriented. The coach aims to assist the individual by increasing their capabilities through clear goals, techniques, practice, and feedback, not unlike a sport coach. Coaches may be peers or hold a more senior role than the person being coached.

Mentoring

Mentoring is about relationship building. The mentor is usually a person who holds a more senior role than the 'mentee' and is able to impart his/her knowledge about career development. Mentoring is a formal relationship structured around developmental needs. A mentor can share wisdom and experience, and provide support, advice, and counsel to enable a mentee to grow and develop. Mentors can make important contributions to understanding how to get things done, ethical decision making, understanding of other people and their viewpoints, and accessing networks and identifying beneficial individuals. The relationship is mutually beneficial with mentors often profiting from communication and feedback from their mentees. Both parties need to work at building and maintaining the mentoring connection, and deal with issues such as power, diversity, resistance to change, learning styles, and how to successfully end the relationship (Shea, 1999).

Most facilitated mentoring programmes have a formal process which defines each step and monitors the ongoing success of the programme. Although programmes will differ, generally, mentoring can be classified into an eight-step process as follows:

1. *Choosing the mentee*: this may be done via a specific job or general area that needs attention and may be through a self or manager nomination process.
2. *Identifying developmental needs*: areas for improvement or further development are determined via self or managerial assessment.
3. *Choosing potential mentors*: a mentor's capability and willingness to undertake the role is assessed.
4. *Pairing the mentor and mentee*: the skills and knowledge needed by the mentee and the ability of the mentor to provide practice or guidance in those areas are assessed for fit.
5. *Orientation for mentors and mentees*: outlines expectations about time commitments, interactions, reporting requirements development-related responsibilities.
6. *Drawing up the contract*: includes the development plan, confidentiality arrangements, the length of the relationship, frequency of meetings, and the role of both the mentor and mentee.
7. *Implementation and reporting*: carrying out the contract with regular reporting on the relationship and progress towards the development goals.
8. *Evaluation and follow-up*: an assessment is undertaken.

Mentoring requires commitment from both parties, a common issue arising in mentoring programmes relates to finding an appropriate mentor who can provide both the professional (career) and personal (psychosocial) dimensions for the mentee. Weaver and Chelladurai (2002: 98) note that successful mentoring can result in 'positive outcomes for the protégé (advancement, growth, and satisfaction), for the mentor (intrinsic satisfaction, status, respect, and power) and for the organization (reduced turnover and development of management potential).' Their study of intercollegiate athletic administrators found that mentored staff were more satisfied with the organizational supervision and respect they received, the people they work with, and their extrinsic rewards, than their non-mentored colleagues (Weaver & Chelladurai, 2002).

Developing and implementing mentoring schemes is also a strategy advocated to address problems in the development and retention of sports officials, coaches, and volunteers. In an Australian study of recruitment and retention of sport officials Cuskelly and Hoye (2004: 30) reported that national and state sport organizations felt 'the focus of training should shift from a culture of "testing" to one of mentoring and updating.'

Additionally, mentoring has been identified as a way to support and encourage more women to become leaders in sport organizations (Sisley, 1990; Abney, 1991; Lough, 1998;). Abney (1991: 50) suggested that 'the mere existence of women as role models and mentors is a motivating factor for other women'. In complement, in her study of women involved in athletic leadership

Kelly (2004), concluded that the task of searching out an appropriate mentor, and being an appropriate mentor, was paramount to the experience of successful leaders. Kelly also noted that professional training for women in athletic leadership was limited, and recommended more research into the establishment of a developmental process to introduce women to the demands of interscholastic and intercollegiate coaching environments. A research study with female employees and elected representatives in the Norwegian Olympic Committee and Confederation of Sports on gender difference perspectives on women leadership (Rimeslåtten, 2004) found that women without formal sports education considered mentoring somewhat more important than those with formal sports education. This suggests that the use of mentoring as a development activity needs to be assessed on a individual basis.

Coaching

There are numerous models of performance coaching but essentially coaching involves one person supporting and directing another person (the client) through encouragement, questioning, and support. The client agrees to a plan of action, and the coach will help to motivate and guide them to complete their plan. The coach–client relationship is designed and defined in a relationship agreement based on the client's expressed interests, goals, and desired outcomes.

Coaching is different from mentoring, as a coach will seldom offer advice. Coaches typically use questioning, reflection, and discussion to get the client to identify their career or development goals, develop options, strategies, and action plans to achieve the desired outcomes. Clients are responsible for their own achievements and success, and a coach does not expect that a client will take any specific action or attain specific goals. A coach monitors the client's progress towards the achievement of his or her action plan. A coach does not provide counselling or therapy.

As the use of coaching as a development option grows, so do the range and complexity of models, frameworks, and theories on coaching. The GROW model (Whitmore, 2004) is a commonly used coaching framework. The basis of this model is that you need to know where you are going (the Goal), where you are (current Reality), and the possible ways of achieving your goal (Options) before you can choose the best path. The final ingredient is the motivation or 'Will' to undergo change and commit to action. The four key components of the model GROW can be used to structure a total coaching programme or a single session.

Transformational coaching (Hargrove, 2002) takes coaching beyond a single-loop learning model such as GROW by seeking to identify the source of an individual's behaviour and frames of reference (double-loop learning) and facilitate the client to look at different ways of being (triple-loop learning). This transformational model involves coaching the client to continuously improve their current practices or do what they are already doing better, enabling them to fundamentally reshape their patterns of thinking with the intent of helping them break through impasses and learn to do different

124

things, and then to move to the triple-loop aspect of empowering the client to create a shift in their context or point of view so that they can learn to open up new possibilities and support them in fulfilling their potential. This approach uses the constructive orientation to learning that was discussed earlier in this chapter.

Similar to mentoring, coaching can provide training and development outcomes to both the coach and the client. The coach may develop additional skills and techniques related to coaching, while the client is supported in reaching their desired goals. Research has clearly shown that learning is much more likely to translate into on-the-job behaviours or performance change if the social context of the organization is receptive and favourable post-training conditions exist. If the client does not have the opportunity or support to demonstrate or use the learned skills and behaviours then the coaching, however good, will be redundant (Arthur, Bennett, Edens & Bell, 2003).

Leadership development

Management and leadership development, along with team-building programmes and initiatives are important developmental areas. Included are on-the-job training, external short courses, special projects, residential courses, and executive development courses (such as a company specific MBA). These development programmes are delivered either through internal processes or externally by training companies, government bodies, or universities. External programmes can be designed specifically for the sport organization and its personnel, or the employee/volunteer may be integrated into 'open' programmes that comprise participants from a range of organizations, such as, the Canadian Association for the Advancement of Women and Sport programme outlined below. Assessing the requirements of training and development of leaders and managers involves the complex task of identifying the competencies relevant to any given job and there are many instruments which aim to measure managerial and leadership behaviours and skills. As with all forms of training and development, programmes which develop management, leadership, and team capabilities should be

Leadership development for women in sport

The Canadian Association for the Advancement of Women and Sport and Physical Activity's Women and Leadership Program consists of a series of professional development sessions that have been designed for women, by women to prepare them for leadership roles in sport and active living communities.

Development sessions blend theory with practical applications and provide an opportunity for women working or volunteering in sport to share experiences, reflect on ideas and apply specific techniques. The sessions also allow for networking opportunities among participants.

- *Effective communication*
  - Practice effective self-introductions
  - Discuss passive, aggressive, and assertive communication styles
  - Practice using assertive communication in sport-related scenarios
- *Conflict resolution*
  - Identify sources of conflict
  - Learn tips for successful problem solving
  - Identify the best approach for a number of scenarios
- *Influencing change*
  - Discuss how to be a successful advocate
  - Identify the factors that influence decision makers
  - Suggest ways to make meaningful change in sport
- *Creating work life balance*
  - Explore the need for balance in your life
  - Examine 10 key solutions to help you find and maintain balance
  - Share hot tips and success stories
- *Effective networking*
  - Explore the value of personal and professional networks
  - Identify strategies to build and maintain your network
  - Rehearse networking scenarios

Source: http://www.caaws.ca/e/leadership/programme/

entered into with due consideration about how this development will enhance the organization's ability to meet its strategic objectives.

Career planning and development

'Effective career planning and development involves the alignment of individual employee development needs with the strategic capability requirement of an organization' (Watt, Bennett & Taylor, 2004: 372). Career development is a combination of career planning, which is the individual's responsibility, and career management, which relates to the organization's training and development requirements and initiatives. Career planning is the process that the individual undertakes to assess their strengths and development opportunities relative to the job they are currently performing and the future career that they aspire to. Career management refers to the support an organization affords an individual, through training and development and performance feedback, to assist in the implementation of the individual's career plan.

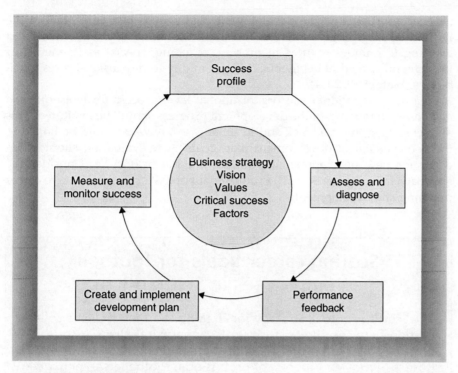

Figure 6.2 Development cycle (*Source*: © Development Dimensions International Inc., MMI. All rights reserved).

A supportive organizational infrastructure and culture can greatly facilitate effective career development. This includes devising processes to diagnose development needs, provision of the time and space to engage in development opportunities, monitoring and feedback systems, mentoring and coaching, and establishing a culture that values learning. The development process can be illustrated as a cyclical process as seen in Figure 6.2.

The first step in this process is the development of a *success profile* of competencies categorized under domains such as interpersonal, management, or leadership skills. These are the competencies required to achieve individual and organizational goals and might include competencies such as decision making, negotiation, and creativity. The success profile will change in response to demands of both the internal and external environment.

The next step is an *assessment* of the individual's current level of capability against the success profile. A wide range of assessment techniques exist, and include testing, competency-based performance evaluations, and multi-rater surveys. Once assessed, *feedback* of the assessment results is provided to the individual. This should include provision of specific examples of the individual's behaviours that can be used to illustrate both his/her strengths and his/her areas for development.

Following the feedback session the individual should create a *development plan*, determine priorities and target two or three key areas to concentrate his/her efforts upon. The development plan should take into account the individual's learning preferences and should combine a variety of tools and learning techniques such as mentoring, coaching, special assignments, or implementing tactical behaviour changes in day-to-day tasks and responsibilities (Watt et al., 2004).

Finally, an individual and organizational level process for *measuring and monitoring* the success of the development progress should be instituted. This allows for periodic feedback and in some cases, rewards could be linked to the achievement of development plan goals. A re-evaluation should then occur for new developmental priorities for the next cycle. Consider the approach taken by the Scottish Professional Footballers Association to career planning and development.

Scoring career goals for football employees in Scotland

The Scottish Football Strategy for Lifelong Learning (SLL) is a collaboration between the Scottish Professional Footballer's Association and key agencies in football, education, and employment. The purpose is to provide support for professional footballers to engage in learning, career planning, and development.

Objectives

- To appoint a coordinator to establish a learning representative network to support lifelong learning in the industry.
- To pilot a programme of learning representative training and development with clubs.
- To establish collaborative relationships with Careers Scotland; the enterprise networks, and other key stakeholders.
- To secure the cooperation of and joint working with Scottish Football Association, Scottish Premier League and Scottish Football League on career transition planning and lifelong learning for all employees in the industry.
- To investigate with Careers Scotland and the University of Paisley the feasibility of providing a web-enabled information, advice and guidance service for members and other employees.
- To establish in the longer-term working relations with the emerging Football Academies and where possible seek to extend their role to encompass provision of lifelong learning services to older footballers and other football employees.
- To research the learning needs of players and other employees including literacy, numeracy, core skills and information technology and identify means of meeting these needs perhaps through online learning and shared learning facilities for clubs.

- To develop and deliver programmes consistent with the objectives and goals set out in the Scottish Executive Strategy Report
  'Adult Literacy and Numeracy in Scotland'.
- To disseminate information about the project and raise awareness so that more clubs and individual employees take up guidance and learning opportunities.
- To work with relevant education providers and training organizations in Scotland to remove barriers to learning and enhance
  the potential for growing the learning market within the football sector.

Source: Adapted from McGillivray, 2006 – see his article for a detailed theoretical assessment of the programme.

Step 4: Training and development evaluation

The evaluation of training and development activities should occur before,
during, and after implementation. The evaluation process has been described
as having four different levels, commonly referred to as the Kirkpatrick levels
(outlined in Table 6.3). In relation to effectiveness, the goals and objectives of
the training and development programme determine the most appropriate
criteria for assessment. Evaluations should be valid, accurate and reliable,
practical and relevant.

Learning criteria are designed to objectively measure the learning outcomes of the training on skill type tests, such as an ability to produce a financial plan, while behavioural criteria measure on-the-job performance.
Reaction measures are widely used to evaluate training programmes, despite
the lack of any relationship between reaction measures and the other three
criterias (Arthur et al., 2003). Results and effectiveness criteria of the learning
and behaviour are measured by the impact of the training on organizational
performance. Increases in efficiency or customer satisfaction would be
examples of a positive return on investment. The evaluation undertaken
should relate to the strategic goals of the organization. The choice of evaluation strategy will depend on the purpose of the evaluation.

Evaluation can occur prior to implementation of the training or development programme through the assessment of the adequacy, scope, and coverage of the proposed programme. The aim is to assess any deficiencies and
allow for corrective steps at an early stage, in other words is there evidence
that the selected training and development methods will result in the knowledge and skills acquisition needed to complete the job task or role? During
the course of the programme the recipient may be asked about their perspective about the programme as a form of evaluation.

Assessments conducted both prior and post the training and development
can be used to measure the results of the intervention. Post-programme surveys or interviews with participants are useful to gauge perceived outcomes

Table 6.3 Evaluation criteria

Level		Assessment measurement
1. Reaction	What does the participant feel about the training?	Self-reporting of affective and attitudinal responses to the training
2. Learning	What facts, knowledge, and understandings were gained?	Performance tests
3. Behaviours	What skills were developed?	Supervisor rating
4. Results or effectiveness	What results occurred?	Utility analyses

Source: Adapted from Kirkpatrick (1976).

and satisfaction with the programme. Post-programme monitoring of task and role performance will also assist with the evaluation process. The effectiveness of the training is best assessed after allowing sufficient time for participants to incorporate the developments into their job.

The trainer, coach, or mentor should also be asked about the receptiveness of the participants and their developmental progress/outcomes. For training and development to be successful the employee or volunteer's motivation is critical. Research has shown that learning is at a maximum when people are motivated to learn (Knowles, Holton & Swanson, 1998). However, it is not just openness to learning which is important for effective training and development. The training and development programme and activities should be firmly positioned within the organization's strategic framework, be supported by top management, and be delivered with full awareness of cultural and situational contexts for maximum impact.

Limitations and constraints to training and development

While the strategic human resource management (SHRM) literature expounds the virtues of strategic implementation of a systematic training and development process, and the benefits of creating a culture that characterises a learning organization, the reality of practice tells us a somewhat different story. Exemplary businesses exist, as evidenced in the proliferation of awards for being an 'Employer of Choice' for training support, but research suggests that a large number of organizations are less than strategic in the way they train and develop their staff (McGraw, 2002; Gratton & Truss, 2003).

Sport organizations have been found to have widely variable approaches to training and development, ranging from highly planned and strategic to completely ad hoc and reactionary (De Knop, Van Hoecke & De Bosscher, 2004; Taylor & Ho, 2005; Taylor & McGraw, 2006). In a study of 1657 Flemish sport clubs, De Knop et al. (2004) noted that there was an inherent weakness in the strategic planning process of clubs, and training opportunities of administrators was limited. Taylor and McGraw (2006) concluded that within national and state sport organizations in Australia, the facilitation of employee development is not widely supported via formal systems of training. Koustelios (2001: 160), in commenting on the poor effectiveness of Greek sport centres, noted that a key reason was the lack of specialized sport centre managers and trained staff, and the fact that 'after their initial appointment in the sport centre, employees have limited training in new technologies relevant to their jobs'. In consequence, he called for the implementation of better training programmes to address the low level of employee's personal accomplishment.

A further limitation to effective training and development relates to competing expectations of the various stakeholder groups. For example, Cuskelly, Taylor, Hoye & Darcy (2006: 158) found that management preferred highly formalized HRM practices, including training, do not always necessarily fit comfortably with the expectation of volunteers, 'viewing sport volunteers as an human resource tends to overlook the complexity of relationships between volunteers and CSOs'. In a similar vein, Papadimitriou and Taylor (2000) concluded that it is not uncommon for Hellenic national sport organizations to forfeit training of administrative staff and neglect activity evaluation and proper planning in order to generate sufficient resources for rewarding outstanding sports performance. These examples of competing expectations are derived from the different perspectives of different constituencies. Therefore, the challenge for sport organizations is to provide training and development programmes that facilitate positive and motivating environments and do not unnecessarily compromise the mission and integrity of the organization, its employees, and/or volunteers.

Summary

Training and development are critical dimensions of a strategic approach to HRM. Attending to the learning requirements of employees and volunteers provides appropriately skilled and knowledgeable human capital that can effectively contribute to the attainment of organizational objectives. A supportive learning environment together with relevant training and development can lead to improved employee satisfaction, retention, and motivation which in turn can create enhanced organization performance.

Training refers to the acquisition of knowledge, skills, and competencies as related to specific job or task requirements. Development is learning new attitudes and behaviours that will result in personal growth. Underpinning the concept of training and development is the premise of learning. The three key learning orientations, behavioural, cognitive, and constructive, provide the basis on which to structure training and development initiatives. In the 'learning organization' training and development are strategically incorporated into the organization's culture as a form of learning. Employees and volunteers are encouraged and supported to learn, acquire new knowledge and skills, and disseminate this knowledge to others within the organization.

In this chapter the five steps to implementing a systematic training and development process were presented: (1) a training needs analysis is undertaken and from this analysis training goals are established (2) which are then used to inform the design of training or development programmes (3) these are consequently implemented (4) and routinely evaluated (5) Numerous training and development methods can be used to attain the organization's training goals and the employee or volunteers' career planning objectives. Effective training and development benefits the individual, other employees and volunteers and aligns with strategic directions of the organization.

Discussion questions

▥ What are the three orientations to learning discussed in this chapter? Discuss the implications of each for designing training programmes.
▥ What is the difference between training and development? Discuss how these activities are viewed in a learning organization.
▥ Describe each step in the training and development process.

From the field – Training Officials in British Cycling

British Cycling identified the need to more systematically train officials (known as commissaires) and organizers who would are or would like to become involved with the promotion and management of British Cycling events. The aim of this training is to encourage more people to organize races and become event officials. As an NGO British Cycling also wanted to be confident about consistency of officiating and offer a clear entry point for potential officials. The training is aligned with an overall strategy to increase standards.

British Cycling also identified that the government was taking more of an interest in sports volunteering as a whole and would like to ensure that people involved have undergone certain checks.

As a sport that takes place on public roads and other places British Cycling are also increasingly under pressure from government sources (and the police and local authorities) and the training programme aims to increase the confidence from these bodies as well.

The training is of benefit to the volunteers in terms of clarifying that the standard British Cycling are aspiring to for events, and for British Cycling as better organized events should mean that they are more effectively protected (from a litigation point of view) as the volunteers would learn about correct operational procedures to follow in the training.

The organizer training is aimed at the organizers of small grass-roots events (events where most of the budget comes from entry fees and the organizer is a volunteer). In these events the roles of organizer and chief official have become somewhat confused. British Cycling had limited resources available for organizers and little more than the rule book available for officials. So in order to start the volunteer Support Officer from British Cycling had to assess and diagnose the responsibilities of the organizer, chief official, and the competitor. In broad terms the responsibilities were divided into three types of task: administration, technical, and competition.

The administration, technical, and competition responsibility of each group were defined as follows:

Organizer: takes the entries, sets up (and removes) the course, maintains the course during the event.

Officials check validity of entries, competitors bikes, and clothing, manages the race on the day, validates the result.

Competitors: enter correctly, bring equipment within the regulations and fit for purpose, compete fairly.

This standard format could be applied to any type of cycle race and therefore all British Cycling training could be taught in a similar way. British Cycling has now written training using the same module titles to introduce officials to road racing, track racing, BMX, and cycle speedway.

The training for officials covers five modules taught over 1 day plus an introduction and conclusion, and then candidates have to attend at least six competitions as an Assistant Commissaire before they can become a Chief Commissaire. The modules are as follows:

1. *Introduction*: to introduce the tutors, candidates, and to outline the aims of the day.

2. *Child protection (good practice)*: to give officials an idea of best practice when dealing with young and vulnerable persons.
3. *Communication*: working as part of a team and being an authority figure during an event.
4. *Administration*: necessary paperwork that a Commissaire will need to complete before, during, and after an event.
5. *Technical*: issues related to the competitors bike and clothing.
6. *Competition*: discipline (sanctions there and who can issue them) using the road and race simulation.
7. *Conclusion*: evaluation of the course and what candidates will need to do next in order to qualify as a regional (chief) Commissaire.

The course was well received and attracts both new and existing officials. It has also gone someway to reassuring officials what their roles and responsibilities are. The post-qualification assessment has also started a useful process of post-course formative assessment leading to the summative assessment when they have gained enough experience to go up to the next rung of the ladder. Again this should ensure that standards should rise over the next few years.

Discussion questions

1. Outline the steps which British Cycling undertook in this training programme – as per the training and development process.
2. Discuss the aspects that you would include in an evaluation of this training programme.
3. How might you incorporate a mentoring scheme or other development initiatives into British Cycling?

Prepared with information provided by Robert Jefferies, Volunteer Support Officer, British Cycling Manchester.

7 Performance management

Chapter overview

The contemporary sport organization, like many other organizations, faces some major challenges in managing the performance of its staff and volunteers. In order to understand how best to manage performance we first need to take a holistic view of the factors that impact upon it. We start by defining and outlining an approach to performance management that includes consideration of many parts of an organization's human resource (HR) system. Performance appraisal, a vital element of an overall performance management system, is also defined. Performance appraisal refers to the formal system that operates to set goals, monitor performance, and establish consequences and improvement actions for organizational staff. The many benefits associated with effective performance management are described as well as some of the common systemic and operational problems that can occur. A sequential model of performance management is presented introducing key research findings relating to the effective management of both paid staff and volunteers in sport.

Performance management and performance appraisal

The performance management system in any organization comprises a series of linked processes designed to elicit the highest levels of employee performance. Taking a holistic view, the process of performance management can be seen as involving a number of components including work and job design, reward structures, the selection of people to do the work, the training and development of those people as well as the system of assessment, and policies for rewarding and improving performance. From a strategic perspective the performance management system in an organization should stimulate the employees to produce high levels of discretionary effort as well as attain basic task accomplishment and provide the linkage which translates the organization's broad goals into superior individual performance. In this way the performance management system in an organization is an essential component of the strategic human resource management (SHRM) approach discussed in Chapter 2 of this book and has elements of many other HR processes contained within it or linked to it.

As an example a holistic performance management discussion might commence with a manager and staff member discussing performance improvements in the context of how work is structured and allocated between different members of a workgroup. The discussion may not only lead to further clarification of job roles for the staff member at an individual level but could also include issues around how the staff member interacts with other team members and how the team as a whole approaches their work. This in turn may lead on to the diagnosis of, say, the need for training for the whole team and perhaps changes to the reward structure to reflect a more team-based approach to working. In this way a performance management process can lead to changes in individual jobs, interactions, and relationships with other team members, training initiatives and the structure of rewards.

An illustration of this holistic approach is provided in the article 'Scouting for the best athletes (or analysts): character vs. performance', in Figure 7.1.

When the Philadelphia Eagles, a perennial contender in pro-football, are checking out young prospects in advance of the annual NFL draft, they certainly look at the player's time in the 40-yard dash and contact his college coach – but the team is just as likely to talk to the guidance counsellor or even the janitor at the young man's high school to see how he treated other people in his life.

That is according to Eagles owner Jeffrey Lurie, who said during a recent Wharton discussion on 'Leadership Lessons Learned from Sports' that character and on-the-field leadership qualities count for more than raw athleticism in putting together the Eagles roster. The Eagles, in building a team that has been to the playoffs six of the last seven seasons as well as the 2005 Super Bowl, use a battery of tests and evaluations in judging future draft choices that is more extensive than most Fortune 500 companies use when hiring MBAs.

The Eagles owner was joined on the panel – sponsored by the Wharton Sports Business Initiative as part of the recent 2007 Wharton Economic Summit – by several other team owners or executives with a background in sports, including Robert Castellini, CEO of the Cincinnati Reds baseball franchise. Although the wide-ranging panel touched on a number of topics, one central theme was this: What are the qualities that make someone a sports leader, especially on the playing field, and can the successful qualities of a winner in athletics be applied to the world of business?

In introducing the panel, Kenneth Shropshire, director of the Wharton Sports Business Initiative, invoked the increasingly popular science of analysing the habits of highly successful coaches to see which of their leadership skills are useful away from the playing field. For example, championship basketball coaches Phil Jackson, Pat Riley, and Mike Krzyzewski have all written books on leadership, while there is a cottage industry studying the wisdom of late football coach Vince Lombardi.

The panellists have hired or worked with some of the most accomplished names in sports, including Eagles coach Andy Reid and baseball manager Lou Piniella, now with the Cubs but a long-time friend of Castellini. Both Lurie and Castellini, in particular, described a similar model for constructing a sports team: Start with a foundation of players with personal character and a winning attitude, then hire coaches with the right kind of intelligence and the motivational skills to get the most out of them.

Lurie, in particular, quoted former Dallas Cowboy coach Jimmy Johnson, now a TV analyst, who said a successful player personnel director in the NFL is essentially 'a chemist.... Football is such a team game, and so you need a mix of leaders, followers, people who will react well under stress'.

'The chemistry dynamic is very important', agreed Gary Lieberman, president of West Side Advisors and part-owner of the New Jersey Nets basketball franchise. 'We try to think that if someone is a good guy in the locker room, so to speak, then he will do what's right for the team.'

If the general manager is a chemist, the head coach is the catalyst who makes the team perform well on the field. Lurie said that his 1999 hiring of

Figure 7.1 Scouting for the best athletes (or analysts): character vs. performance.

Reid – a quarterback coach who lacked experience as a top assistant coach – was borne out of his desire to find a head coach who thought outside the traditional box and who would be an on-field innovator.

Lieberman agreed with the point. 'I was really surprised at the level of intellect' in the New Jersey Nets coaching staff, he said, adding that he expected them to be motivational 'rah-rah' guys or strict disciplinarians, but not as cerebral as they actually are. 'I would welcome the opportunity to work with them' – his coaching staff – 'in a different situation.'

Lieberman noted that the Nets have been under media and fan pressure this season to replace the current coach, Lawrence Frank, but that the owners believe the team's sometimes spotty performance has been, in part, the result of injuries and not due to a problem with Frank. 'He continues to be well prepared, and he continues to motivate the players', he said.

The Reds' Castellini added an important caveat to the discussion. 'Tommy Lasorda [the longtime Dodgers' manager] told me that while it's important to have chemistry in the clubhouse, if you don't have the talent, you don't win.' He also said a good manager helps to nurture two or three star players, such as a starting pitcher, as clubhouse leaders and role models. 'You pick people out to be leaders so that they can help you manage those 25 very individualistic people', the ones who, 'let's just say, have a high opinion of themselves.'

Point guards, centerfielders

Several panellists said that while sports leadership skills are not easily learned, they can be transferred quite successfully to the business world.

Mark Fisher, founder of MBF Clearing Corporation, the largest clearing firm on the New York Mercantile Exchange commodities exchange (NYMEX), told the panel that a disproportionately large number of the traders that he has hired for his firm have a background in college or professional sports. 'As a trader, I have found that the qualities that made the best traders are the ones that make the best athletes.' One reason is that athletes may have a losing day on the field just as a trader will make a bad trade, but the successful ones have the ability to move on.

A competitive nature is important, noted Fisher, who is a major supporter of youth basketball on Long Island. 'At the end of the day, you know how you did .... There is no bureaucracy.' When hiring, he tends to focus on people who were in key on-the-field leadership positions – point guards in basketball or baseball centerfielders.

While there may be a lot of accountability on the playing field, there is less in the front office than one might expect. Castellini said he was surprised by the lack of any kind of evaluation system, similar to what might be found in the more traditional business world. He noted that when he arrived at the Reds' organization several years ago, the team was 29th out of 30 major league franchises in developing players through its own farm system, and that no one was deemed responsible for that failure. 'You might be paying a $4 million bonus to sign a high school player, and so you had better be right', Castellini said. 'And if you're not right, you ought to be held accountable.'

But that is only internally. Several of the attendees noted that the media attention a sports owner or general manager receives is comparable to just a few top superstar CEOs in other types of business. Castellini – who continues to

Figure 7.1 (Continued)

manage Castellini Companies, a fruit and vegetable wholesaler, in addition to the Reds – said that he went to a kind of 'charm school' to learn how to deal with reporters. 'One little slip of the lip, and you are in trouble', Castellini warned. What's more, both fans and journalists tend to have longer memories in sports than people do in the business world. One former sports owner who could attest to that is President George W. Bush, who, even after six years in the White House, still hears about the time his Texas Rangers traded away slugger Sammy Sosa back in 1989.

'Every decision that you make is really scrutinized, not just in the moment but for years to come', noted Lieberman.

There is one other important issue that arises in professional sports as well as in business: finding a balance between the need to make a profit and the need to put a winning team on the field. As team executives such as Lurie and Castellini explained it, there is constant pressure and intense scrutiny – from both the fan base and from the hometown media – to win now and to make short-term moves that might prove counterproductive in the long run.

'The fans want you to win, but you can't engage in a popularity contest or you will be in last place every year', said the Eagles owner, who insisted that the best moves have tended to be the ones that were not popular with the fans. Although he did not mention this at the Wharton event, Lurie may have been thinking of his 2004 signing of flamboyant wide receiver Terrell Owens, who was applauded in Philadelphia initially but who ripped the team apart with his antics a year later.

Owens may have been on the mind of one audience member who asked why more players did not negotiate contacts with performance incentives, as is common with top executives in other businesses. Again, the answer was that such incentives did not gybe with the type of winning, high-character athlete that these sports executives wanted. Said Lieberman: 'Fundamentally, players have to be motivated by more than money.'

Figure 7.1 (Continued)

The situation described here reflects a number of aspects concerning the complex nature of stimulating performance in professional football clubs in the USA. First, the importance of selecting the right people in key roles is emphasized, a point discussed at length in Chapter 4. In particular, the importance of 'character' and 'winning attitudes' of players is stressed, and by implication fit with other team members. Second, the critical role of the coach in working as a catalyst for team performance and getting the best performances from individual players is pointed out. Third, the importance of developing on-field leaders amongst the senior players is stressed. Fourth, we see the need for the managers of the clubs to manage the sometimes contradictory pressures of on-field success with shorter-term financial health of the club. Finally, the importance of intrinsic rewards as a motivational element in player performance is illustrated.

In contrast to performance management, performance appraisal, which is sometimes used as an inaccurate synonym, consists of only a narrow subsection of the overall performance management system described above.

139

Performance appraisal is a formal system for setting goals, assessing perform-ance, and rewarding the level of achievement. When employees and man-agers talk about performance management they are often referring to the appraisal system. Unfortunately, the performance appraisal system, as will be discussed in more detail later in this chapter, can elicit a negative result and thus the perception of the whole performance management process and effec-tive performance management is compromised. One way of thinking about the outcome of a performance appraisal discussion is to regard it as similar to a contract where the staff member and manager enter into a series of under-standings about what each party is giving and what each is getting from the relationship. This involves both tangible aspects of the working relationship such as not only the level of performance and reward but also important ele-ments of the 'psychological contract' (referred to in Chapters 5 and 8). Consequently, a sport organization needs to carefully balance the control and motivational elements in its performance system and manage the operation of the system to ensure that it is producing positive and not negative outcomes.

What are the benefits of performance management?

Performance management systems can be used to achieve a number of bene-ficial outcomes for organizations. When managed well, a good performance management system should be as follows:

- Align people's behaviour to achieving the organization's strategic vision and mission by translating the high-level strategic goals of the sport organ-ization into individual objectives and job performance. This is often achieved by the 'cascading of objectives' down the organization from top to bottom with all managers translating and interpreting their personal goals into meaningful goals for their staff. A good example of this can be found in the use of 'the balanced scorecard' methodology discussed in Chapter 12. In a performance discussion about multiple objectives a man-ager may help a staff member by clarifying expectations about which objectives should be given priority and by coaching the staff member in the areas of performance that need further development (see Chapter 6 on training and development).
- Align organizational and individual values by establishing clear behav-ioural norms for employees and volunteers. For example, a sport club which is based in the local community may promote values associated with respect for all community members. This may translate into codes of conduct for players concerning matters such as alcohol consumption in public places, dress codes on match days, racial vilification, and devoting a certain percentage of time to charitable work in the community.
- Provide a fair and objective basis for rewarding the relative contributions of different staff to the organization. Thus the performance appraisal

mechanism should link to the reward system and provide financial incentives for employees to contribute high levels of discretionary effort (for more detail see Chapter 8 on rewards).

■ Provide a basis for discussing the longer-term career development of staff. The performance management system also provides a framework for talented employees to be developed by identifying and preparing individuals for increased responsibilities (this is further elaborated upon in Chapter 10 on succession and talent management).

■ Provide information which helps to evaluate the effectiveness of HR processes such as recruitment, induction, training, and reward management. For example, in relation to training and development, performance review data might bring to light the fact that the organization is not using effective training methods (see Chapter 12 re-evaluation).

■ Provide an opportunity for the manager to better understand the personal goals and concerns of staff members and volunteers.

■ Provide a system of employee information so that an organization can meet minimum legal obligations concerning unfair dismissal and equal opportunities (this is addressed in further detail in Chapter 9 on employee relations).

This extensive list of potential benefits provided by performance management systems has led to a wide diversity of performance management practices and it is common for organizations to try to achieve multiple objectives with the use of one system (Armstrong & Baron, 1998). Looking at the list above, three broad objectives are in evidence. First, performance management can be a control and judgement system through which decisions are made about job responsibilities, pay, and career progression. Second, performance management can be a developmental system through which decisions about training and development are taken. Third, performance management can be an information system which collects data on employee performance. Whilst the broad nature of performance systems is a potential virtue, it can also lead to tension, particularly between judgement and development processes. The sport organization needs to think carefully about the primary goal of the system and potential unintended consequences from operating a system which tries to achieve too much. These potential problems will be discussed in a later section in this chapter.

A model of performance management

A flow model of the performance management process is presented in Figure 7.2.

Stage 1

The first part of the model involves defining and agreeing on performance standards with the employee. Clearly the criteria for evaluation must first be

Stage 1

■ Prepare/Revise individual job goals, accountabilities and relationships.
■ Agree with staff member on measures of performance for each accountability area (e.g., key performance indicators). Clarify values related to the job
and behavioural dimensions of performance. Clarify reward expectations.

Stage 2

■ Remove barriers to job performance.

Stage 3

■ Ongoing assessment of job performance; provision of feedback.

Stage 4

■ Formal review of action on previous appraisal recommendations;
appraisal of performance against goals.

Stage 5

■ Establish new goals; identify performance improvement action.

Stage 6

■ Assess future career potential; plan next career steps, individual training,
and development needs.
■ Implement performance improvement and career development strategies.

Stage 7

■ Recommend merit-based adjustments to remuneration.

Figure 7.2 The performance management process.

established if these are to form the basis for the later discussion on actual performance. This part of the process can involve revisiting, and if necessary,
amending the job description and defining agreed levels of performance
outcomes. Many basic jobs have clearly defined task outputs and can be managed with rudimentary performance management systems as it is clear what
has to be done and whether or not it is being done. For example, an office assistant in a state tennis association may be required to record, collect and dispatch
mail, receipt all income, complete photocopying and printing as directed, and
maintain office stationery. It is relatively straightforward to monitor the completion of these duties. In jobs where successful outcomes are more ambiguous
and where employees have more discretion, outcomes cannot simply be listed
as completion of a series of tasks and performance management becomes a
more complex and important process. For example, the position description for
a chief executive officer (CEO) of a peak national sporting organization desig-
nates the person in this role as responsible for the overall efficiency and effectiveness of all the organization's operations, including the management and
development of all stakeholder and member relationships, and supervision of

the strategic planning and marketing activities necessary to meet the organization's objectives. The position description also contains a section setting out the requirement for regular performance appraisals, against mutually established performance objectives, at agreed intervals. As the measurement of effective performance of these responsibilities is not necessarily obvious it is critical that the objective setting exercise is undertaken when the position is first filled, and then on a regular basis, so that the CEO is clear about the measurements that will be used to judge his/her performance.

A common technique used with more complex jobs such as the CEO position noted above is to define job performance by the extent to which goals or key performance indicators are met. Developing criteria for performance appraisal and determining which aspects of a job are the most appropriate to use in measuring performance can be approached in a variety of ways. For example, research on how to measure the performance of sports coaches (MacLean, 2001) has defined performance in terms of behaviours (process and product) and designated categories relative to assessment. In this approach behavioural process factors are evidenced in job behaviours, including task- and maintenance-related factors. Behavioural product factors are the result of the process factors and are often quantifiable aspects measured by key performance indicators. MacLean and Chelladurai (1995) identified six categories of coaching performance related to behavioural product and process factors. This scheme is outlined in Table 7.1.

Table 7.1 Measuring coaching performance

Behavioural product factors	Team or athlete outcome measures	Personal outcome measures
	Number of competitions won	Receipt of coaching awards
	Improvement in placing over previous attempt	Upgrading of coaching qualifications
	Improvement in skill levels	Advice sought by other coaches
Behavioural process factors – task related	Direct task	Indirect task
	Application of strategies to enhance performance	Recruiting talented players
	Applying coaching knowledge	Maintaining and applying relevant statistics
	Effective communication	
Behavioural process factors – maintenance related	Administrative	Public relations
	Adherence to policies and procedures	Relationship with stakeholders
	Effective financial management	Liaison with community groups

Source: Adapted from MacLean & Chelladurai, 1995; MacLean, 2001.

In applying this framework to a golf club operations manager, we could designate task-related behavioural factors to a job-specific requirement to schedule and run club competitions, and maintenance-related process factors to issues such as liaising with corporate clients and other club personnel. The behavioural product factors for the golf operations manager may relate to the number of players entered in competitions over a period of time or the amount of corporate sponsorship funding that the manager is able to secure for club competitions. Each of these factors could be assessed when undertaking a review of the golf operations manager's performance.

Defining complex, high-discretion jobs in terms of outcomes is entirely consistent with both the nature of the role and the fact that individual employees will have different approaches to achievement of set goals. Furthermore, clear and well-communicated goals provide direction to staff, encourage above the norm levels of effort, and serve as a basis for appraisal feedback later in the process. The basis for effective goal setting is that goals should be specific, measurable, achievable, realistic, and time bound or SMART. The more specific the goals, generally the higher the performance level, provided that the goals set are not only difficult and challenging, but also realistic. Participation in goal setting also enhances performance in that it generates increased understanding of goals, increases the likelihood of goal acceptance and increases commitment (Armstrong, 2006).

Also of relevance at this stage might be clarification of values that are important to the organization and the communication of clear expectations about these. Such values can be crucial to the identity of a sport organization and might include, for example, a commitment to a certain philosophy such as playing a sport in a particular way. To take an example from professional football in Europe, teams such as Manchester United, Real Madrid, and AC Milan have been associated throughout their history not only with winning tournaments, but also with playing an attractive, adventurous, and attacking style of football which have won them legions of fans around the world. Clearly part of the expectation of the coaching staff in such organizations is that they will continue in the club traditions which would form a component of their performance management. Many sport organizations seek to develop and maintain a high-performance culture and thus may expect employees to have a personal commitment to unconditional excellence.

Finally, during this stage there needs to be some discussion of the rewards that are to be forthcoming for performance at the desired level, especially if this is not already clear (rewards is discussed in more detail in Chapter 8). A sport organization's rewards management system must outline the basis, level or rate, and types of rewards available, including financial and non-financial extrinsic rewards. In general, individuals are motivated to perform to the extent that rewards are available that meet their personal needs.

Stage 2

The second stage in managing performance is to remove any barriers that may be inhibiting the performance. This may mean providing appropriate levels of resources for a position or simply providing adequate tools. In circumstances where adequate resources are not provided, employees have been found to become quickly frustrated and demotivated (Cascio, 1996). Take the case of the national programme director of high-performance sport who is expected to create a world class performance environment, embracing, and supporting technical staff and personal coaches. If the director is not given the discretion to select appropriate technical staff or a sufficient budget to reward talented coaches the director may not be able to achieve the organization's goal of world class ranking.

Stage 3

The third stage in managing performance is to revisit performance on a regular basis and provide corrective feedback as required. Studies of coaching and provision of channels of feedback have conclusively shown that the feedback keeps goal-directed behaviour on course and influences future performance goals by creating objectives for achieving higher levels of performance in the future (London, 2003). Providing corrective feedback is a vital stage in the development of performance. Giving feedback is an important managerial competency and the skilful manager knows how to blend positive and corrective (constructively critical) feedback, so that the outcome of the discussion remains positive and constructive.

However, the value of feedback is influenced by factors other than the skill of the manager. Two important moderators of feedback in performance management have been identified by London (2003). First, there is the individual's overall receptivity to receiving feedback. Important factors influencing receptivity are comfort with feedback, propensity to seek feedback, mindfulness with which feedback is processed, and sense of accountability to act on feedback. Second, there is the organization's feedback culture which will impact the quality of the feedback provided, the overall importance attributed to feedback by an individual, and the support available for processing feedback such as provision of coaching services.

It is important to note here that the feedback which is perceived as negative criticism has been found to have a demotivating effect on employees. In a seminal study at General Electric in the US (Meyer, Kay & French, 1965) it was found that

- criticism had a negative effect on motivation and goal achievement;
- praise had little effect one way or the other;
- the average employee reacts defensively to criticism during the appraisal interview;
- defensiveness resulting from critical appraisal produced inferior performance;
- participation of employees in goal setting produced superior results;
- coaching by managers was most effective when done regularly.

There are two main approaches to overcoming the problems associated with the demotivating effect of negative feedback. The first involves getting feedback from multiple sources where feedback is more likely to be seen as objective and thus less of a personal attack. A version of this type of appraisal, 360-degree feedback, is discussed later in this chapter. A second approach involves giving feedback in a way which is less likely to generate a negative reaction. Research findings on the best way to give feedback are best discussed in relation to stage four of the model – the appraisal interview.

Stage 4

Stage 4 in the performance management process involves a formal review of the performance during the interval since the goal setting meeting. At the heart of this review is a conversation or appraisal interview during which the manager and employee discuss performance achieved relative to objectives. There are a number of key recommendations concerning how such interviews should be conducted, which are as follows:

1. Use a style of interview that encourages joint problem solving between the manager and staff member. This type of interview has the advantage of allowing opinions to be expressed which are less likely to be seen as judgements and is more likely to produce a mutually agreed outcome to which both parties are committed.
2. Encourage staff members to evaluate their own performance as a starting point and to find out as much as possible about how they see the situation. Research has shown that self-evaluation has the overwhelming advantage of getting staff to think about their performance and any shortcomings, which in turn leads to higher commitment to agreed improvement outcomes (Steel & Ovalle, 1984).
3. Focus on factual data wherever possible and use specific examples to illustrate optimal and sub-optimal performance. By focusing on objective data the manager can avoid being seen to make personal judgements about the character of the staff member and avoid defensive reactions to criticism of the type referred to above.
4. Use inclusive language wherever possible to depersonalize the discussion and reduce defensive behaviour (e.g., 'what are we going to do about this' not 'what are you going to do about this').
5. Finally, it is recommended to hold the interviews in a private and neutral setting and allow enough time to properly deal with all the issues.

Stages 5 and 6

Stages 5 and 6 of the performance management process also, usually, occur during the performance appraisal interview. Stage 5 involves reaching consensus on any performance improvement actions that result from the review and setting new goals for the next performance period. Stage 6 involves a discussion about career planning and training stemming from Stage 5. Together these stages consist of the formal developmental component of the performance management process and are essential elements of an organization's SHRM strategy. A fuller discussion of training and development and its relationship to performance management can be found in Chapter 6.

Stage 7

The final stage of the performance management process is to determine and provide appropriate merit pay, financial bonuses, or non-financial rewards, based on the formal review of performance. Rewards may be provided on a continuous (e.g., commission) or graduated (levels) scale, for individual performance, or unit or organizational results. Performance-based rewards systems are described in more detail in Chapter 8.

Potential problems with performance appraisal

As performance appraisal systems have the potential to achieve so many things, they are sometimes seen as a panacea for organizational problems that really should be resolved elsewhere. For example, in some sport organizations the performance appraisal system is used primarily to provide corrective discipline and collect data about employees that can be used to justify corrective or punitive action. The term 'performance-manage someone out of the organization' is indicative of this. Whilst collecting data on inadequate performance is a legitimate use of a performance management system, a narrowly focused performance appraisal system used primarily for this purpose may not uncover the root of the problem or help identify its solution and may also generate negative assessments of the appraisal system. Therefore, when addressing problems with employee performance managers should think beyond the narrow approach that is possible within the boundaries of the appraisal system. In order to improve their performance the staff may need (instead of more intensive performance appraisal) as given below:

- Better tools, equipment, and work methods.
- More cooperation and support from co-workers or managers.
- Opportunities to demonstrate improvements.
- A better understanding of their job-accountabilities, goals, priorities, and performance measures.
- New knowledge and skills (and opportunities to learn).
- Incentives to improve.
- A different job.

The above list of considerations illustrates the point made at the beginning of this chapter that performance management systems need to be broadly based within the sport organization, and able to diagnose fundamental causes of underperformance rather than provide mere evidence of such performance, which may be all that is captured in the appraisal process. Theoretically, performance appraisal is one of the most powerful tools that managers have to influence staff behaviour since it is the mechanism through which organizational rewards are administered. In practice, however, it can be disliked by both

147

employees and managers equally and has the capacity to turn manager and employee into adversaries. The next section explores some of the reasons why performance appraisal can produce negative assessments and outcomes.

The first set of potential problems of poorly designed and executed performance appraisal processes can be termed systemic. As noted earlier, many appraisal systems attempt to achieve too much. There is an inherent underlying conflict between the judgemental and developmental components in the appraisal process for both managers and employees. First, managers have been found to dislike playing 'god' (McGregor, 1957) and often experience guilt about making negative judgements about others. Second, employees are unlikely to be completely open about their need for development when, as part of the same process, managers have to make judgements about their pay and promotion prospects. In order to overcome systemic conflicts such as those discussed above some sport organizations operate the judgemental and developmental components of appraisal as separate processes at different times of the year. An alternative and more radical way to overcome this problem is to use performance appraisal for only one purpose, either as a development process and part of the training and development system, or, as a judgement process and part of the pay and rewards system, not both. It is also advisable to keep disciplinary and grievance issues separate from the performance management process wherever possible.

A second systemic problem might occur when there is poor integration between organizational strategy and the type of appraisal system used. For example, a sport organization might be trying to encourage team-based operating systems, but continue to evaluate and reward individual performance merit increases. Thus, football teams that reward individual players for the number of goals scored in a season need to be careful to also reward assists and other aspects of team play so as not to provide an incentive for players to pursue self-interest before that of the team. The well-known adage that 'what gets measured in an organization, gets done' also needs to be considered. If the performance system is used to determine rewards it must try to fully capture all elements of performance if it is to avoid encouraging behaviour only in the particular direction that is assessed.

Further systemic problems can occur if performance appraisal systems are not fully integrated into other HR systems. A common example of this concerns rewards where at the end of a complex appraisal system overall pay is capped within a narrow band due to wider cost containment initiatives in the organization. Such circumstances often lead to disaffection as the system is seen as lacking credibility by the staff and generating irrelevant workload by managers. Take for example, the Head Coach of national volleyball association who has to manage day-to-day operation of the office, coordinate the development and maintenance of processes and procedures that ensure effective and efficient office administration, accept irregular and long working hours, and travel domestically and overseas for extended periods in return. Managing daily office operations and being away from the office for long periods of time may mean that achieving high performance across these two sometimes juxtaposed requirements may be difficult. Even if the coach is able to perform effectively government funding limitations might mean that they receive a minimal pay increase. Therefore, in this instance the performance appraisal process should be flexible enough to deal with the issues identified above and align rewards with appropriate objectives for the coach. Additionally, there should be a clear indication of the range of salary increases, or alternative rewards, that can be provided and the level of performance required to attain these.

At the individual level between managers and employees the appraisal process may suffer from some of the same problems of subjectivity that were discussed in relation to the selection process in Chapter 4. These may include:

- 'Halo' and 'horn' effects where managers are either positively or negatively over influenced by one staff member characteristic.
- Leniency/strictness effects – where different managers rate staff using varying standards.
- Recency effects whereby managers pay too much attention to a recent event rather than considering all events from the whole rating period.
- Central tendency whereby, when using a scale, managers will tend to mark towards the middle so as to avoid controversial decisions.

In order to minimize bias at an individual level it is recommended that managers:

- relate performance dimensions to a single activity (not groups of activities);
- avoid overall ratings;
- observe job behaviour regularly;
- avoid ambiguous terms which can be liable to different individual interpretations (e.g., average);
- are trained to share a common frame of reference.

Notwithstanding any of these problems, performance appraisal remains not only an important part of an overall performance management system, but also a system which most modern sport organization simply must have. Formal appraisal of performance provides the only rational basis for controlling behaviour and distributing rewards and remains, when used well, a potent tool for creating meaning and higher levels of motivation for employees.

Performance appraisal methods

There are a range of performance appraisal methods and criteria which a sport organization can use. First, staff may be compared with each other or compared to some absolute standard. Second, performance can be measured on staff member attributes, behaviours, or results. Third, staff may be measured by managers, themselves or a wider group of respondents. Different appraisal techniques combine elements of each of these approaches. Some of the more common ones are discussed in this section.

Comparative approaches vs. absolute standards

The simplest form of comparative approach uses a ranking methodology whereby staff members are numerically ranked from best to worst in relation to performance. Ranking has become popular again with many large corporate organizations adopting a forced distribution approach where employees are ranked in percentile groups around a standard statistical distribution. This technique has been widely adopted by organizations such as GE, where it is known as the 'vitality curve', in order to overcome the problems of managerial leniency and central tendency and literally force managers to make judgements about their best and worst staff. In many cases staff at the bottom end of such statistical distributions are 'managed out' of the organization on a yearly cycle and new staff are brought in to replace them. Whilst this form of ranking has the advantage of providing a clear mechanism for distributing organizational rewards and punishments it often proves unpopular with managers and staff who feel uncomfortable with making the harsh judgements associated with such techniques.

A rating type approach is described by Lewis (2003) in the book, *Moneyball.* The book is a case study of how one baseball team (the Oakland A's) used statistics on individual contributions to performance to build a successful team. Lewis provides some clear examples of how strong pressures on managers to succeed can be leveraged with a clear measure of efficiency (the number of games won divided by the team salary) to develop an effective performance management system.

The Oakland A's statistically based approach to assessing players became an exemplar of innovation and efficiency via good management. The relentless use of performance information and using such data gave the club a competitive advantage with its human capital (Lewis, 2003). Historically baseball's conservative approach to methods of evaluating players' capacities and performance (i.e., using runs batted in [RBI] and slugging percentage) were not good predictors of team performance.

Using on-base percentage data for recruitment and strategy gave the A's a comparative advantage and this alternative criteria was not only better, but the players required to deliver it were also cheaper to bring in (Wolfe, Wright & Smart, 2006). Other teams were not using the right information, prompting Lewis to pen *Moneyball's* first lesson: Data are not created equal.

Human resource management (HRM) must ensure that the categories within which data are collected and employees are evaluated are systematically consistent with corporate objectives. Lewis concludes that the success of performance management requires that managers whose concern for performance or financial necessity outweighs their attachment to traditional norms must overcome the tendency to overgeneralize from their own experience, or analyse recent performance rather than looking at performance in the long term. However, it should be noted here that while it is possible to isolate and measure an individual performance in professional sport, individual productivity is more difficult to isolate and measure in other sport workplaces.

In an absolute standards approach to performance appraisal the performance of an individual staff member is evaluated against specific dimensions

Using the items in the rating scale, indicate your assessment of performance for each dimension by circling the appropriate rating						
Performance item	Rating	Outstanding 5	Above standard 4	At standard 3	Below standard 2	Poor 1
Knowledge						
Communication						
Management skill						
Teamwork						
Initiative						
Interpersonal skill						
Creativity						
Problem solving						
Willingness to accept responsibility						

Figure 7.3 Sample performance ratings scale combining attributes and behaviours.

of performance and these can be either qualitative or quantitative. These may vary from simple narrative reports to more complex rating systems of behavioural, attitudinal- or results-based measures, or some combination of all the three. Rating systems comprise probably the most common types of appraisal and typically use a form in which the rater, usually the immediate manager, responds with a numerical score against a particular item. In this way an overall score can be derived and strengths and weaknesses are highlighted for the performance discussion. Systems using attributes and behaviours commonly measure items such as those illustrated in Figure 7.3.

Who is involved in appraising performance?

Absolute standards-based systems may involve ratings by different people in the sport organization. The traditional method is appraisal by the immediate manager in the organization combined with an element of self-appraisal. Alternative approaches may use other respondents such as team members, peers in other parts of the organization, customers, and sometimes subordinates. The use of multiple respondents from different parts of the organization is referred to as 360-degree feedback and is designed to eliminate subjectivity by aggregating multiple responses. These systems can provide the person being appraised with an authentic and powerful insight into how they are perceived by various organizational stakeholders and can provide a good foundation for development. However, they should be implemented mainly to assist with employee development rather than rewards and should be maintained with appropriate support mechanisms, such as follow-up coaching, for the person being appraised. Further, these assessments should be avoided in environments where they can be abused due to excessive peer rivalry or when radical changes such as downsizing are occurring.

Management by objectives

Most forms of managerial appraisal usually combine some component of management by objectives (MBO) which has existed in some form or other from the 1950s. MBO commences with the formulation of the sport organization's strategic objectives by the most senior managers, usually the Executive Committee. These managers then formulate goals with their direct subordinates and the process is repeated at each successive level down the organization. The MBO system consists of four steps: goal setting, delegating, ongoing feedback and overall evaluation. As strategic goals are cascaded down the organization they are contextualized at each step for individual managers. Although the system is inherently top down in character, MBO emphasises joint determination of actual objectives followed by joint evaluation of performance to allow situational variability and contextual limitations to be built into the system.

Research on the effectiveness of MBO shows that it usually increases productivity (Rodgers & Hunter, 1991), although care must be taken to avoid the occurrence of some well-known problems. First, MBO can lead to breakdowns in interpersonal and inter-group cooperation if groups and individuals set their goals without reference to the goals of others. This problem is often overcome by having liaison meetings between the various parts of the organization that need to coordinate their activities to ensure goal congruence and having high levels of cooperation built into the goals for each section. Second, comparative assessment of different staff can be difficult with MBO since each staff member is working on unique goals. This problem is typically overcome by combining an MBO system with some degree of attribute or behavioural rating in a hybrid system. Such a hybrid also has the benefit of ensuring that the behavioural standards are maintained and MBO systems do not degenerate into systems where goal achievement is the only thing that matters.

From the brief description of common appraisal methods in this section we can see that sport organizations have alternatives from which to choose when building a performance management system. There is no system which is necessarily better than others in all circumstances. The best system at any given time will be contingent on what an organization considers the most important goal to achieve through the operation of the performance management system. Emphasizing different criteria might yield a different system. Is the main focus developmental or evaluative? Should the system be economical to introduce and operate or error free? Is it more important to emphasize strategic goals or behaviour and values? What is the right balance between a simple scheme which has user acceptance and a complex scheme which captures all of the information that the organization requires?

Baruch, Wheeler and Zhao's (2004) research into the Shanghai Sports Technical Institute (SSTI) performance management system provides an interesting case to illustrate some of these contingencies. In 1985 the Chinese government attempted to develop an incentive reward system to motivate professional sports players, resulting in schemes linking pay to performance which have now become widespread in Chinese professional sports. The SSTI developed a scheme that aimed to motivate sports players, deliver a positive message about performance expectations, focus attention, and drive on key performance issues, differentiate rewards to sports players according to their competence and contribution, reinforce a culture of high levels of performance, innovation, quality and teamwork, and link pay to team performance (Baruch et al., 2004).

The researchers found that when pay had high valence, with clearly established links to well-defined goals and objectives, improvements in performance were likely to be the result. Also, clearly established individual performance standards were highly related to improvements in individual performance levels, but negatively related to team performance. Further, clearly defined team performance standards were related to team performance, but not to individual improvements in performance. This indicates that organizations need to determine carefully whether individual or team performance is the most critical, so that the appropriate emphasis on establishing clear individual or team goals can be established.

Interestingly, female athletes perceived the performance-related pay system even more favourably than males (Baruch et al., 2004). Females had significantly higher valence for pay perceived clearer links between performance and pay, perceived clearer individual objectives, higher equity, and higher improvements in individual performance. By establishing clear links between pay and clearly defined objective goals, females saw a higher probability of receiving rewards proportionate to their accomplishments.

For competitive professional sports, core values and objectives relate to the need for continuing short-term individual and team performance. A reward structure that establishes performance goals with clearly communicated links between performance and rewards would be consistent with these core values. The nature of competitive professional sports, with an emphasis on personal abilities, objective measures of performance, and an emphasis on continuing short-term performance, is particularly suited to a performance-related system of rewards (Baruch et al., 2004).

Incentive-based systems have been found to be a useful tool for competitive professional sports in the US (Becker & Huselid, 1992). Becker and Huselid (1992) examined the effects of the tournament system with racing drivers. They found that large prize differentials between those finishing at the top compared to those finishing lower had incentive effects on individual performance. They also reported that such a spread in the size and availability of prizes could encourage dysfunctional behaviour, some of which

153

could be reckless and potentially harmful, in an attempt to claim the prize.

For volunteers in sport organizations, performance management has become an increasingly important area. Research by Cuskelly et al. (2006) in community sport organizations found that formal practices related to the performance management of volunteers were not commonly used. This is not surprising given that these sport organizations are largely run by volunteers. Thus one set of volunteers would need to be monitoring, providing feedback, and addressing the performance problems of other volunteers. Formalizing performance management may also weaken such an organizations' ability to meet the social needs of the volunteers and may increase the level of bureaucracy and perception of compliance control, thus likely detracting from the volunteer experience (Seippel, 2002). By contrast, interviews with community sport volunteers (Taylor, Darcy, Hoye & Cuskelly, 2006) revealed that many volunteers desired feedback on their performance and clearer guidance about the organization's expectations of them. This suggests that while community sport volunteers should not be treated in the same way as employees, many would appreciate relevant performance appraisals.

Notwithstanding the need to build a performance system that relates specifically to the objectives and characteristics of individual organizations, certain key points emerge from studies of effective performance management systems. These include the need for the following:

- Top management commitment to performance management.
- Use of multiple raters to reduce subjectivity.
- A self-assessment component to increase employee engagement.
- Compatibility between job design and appraisal method.
- A system tailored to organizational strategies, culture, tasks, and workforce.
- A structured process of performance appraisal to assist managers.
- Clear performance measures.
- Ongoing feedback during the performance cycle.
- Recognition of organizational obstacles to effective performance.

Summary

This chapter has provided an overview of performance management and performance appraisal. Managing staff for the highest levels of performance requires a broad approach involving concerted action in many HR systems including those relating to recruitment and selection, the analysis and design of jobs, training and development, and rewards. Performance appraisal has been defined an important component of performance management that deals with the formal system of goal setting and review and consequent action to influence behaviour in the desired direction. The benefits of effective performance management have been outlined as well as some of the more common systemic and operational problems. A stage model of performance management has been presented as well as key research findings relating to the effective management of both paid staff and volunteers in sport.

Discussion questions

1. What are some of the key differences between performance management and performance appraisal? Discuss any experiences that you have had of either.
2. What are some of the benefits that can be expected from a well-developed performance management system? How might they help a staff member? A manager? The organization?
3. Explain the terms judgemental and developmental in relation to performance appraisal. Why might these two processes be in tension with each other?
4. Explain some of the things a manager should and should not do when giving feedback to an employee.
5. Think of your favourite sports team. How do they manage the performance of their playing squad? What are the best and worst features of the performance management system? What would you change if you were the manager?

8 Motivation and rewards management in sport organizations

Learning objectives

After reading this chapter you will be able to:

■ Explain the role of rewards in employee and volunteer motivation
■ Describe different types of intrinsic and extrinsic rewards
■ Describe the components of a financial compensation plan
■ Recognize job design as part of a rewards management system
■ Understand the importance of volunteer recognition

Chapter overview

The purpose of rewards management is to attract, motivate, and retain valuable employees and volunteers. Reward strategies should support an organization's corporate agenda and its human resource plan in order to ensure their success. What gets rewarded will be the focus of employees' attention in the workplace, therefore it should be consistent with what an organization is trying to accomplish and how. A basic understanding of human motivation will help in the selection and design of an effective rewards management system. The first part of this chapter reviews several theories that explain human motivation in general and in the workplace in particular. The second part of this chapter looks at rewards management, beginning with a review of the different types of rewards that can be made available. The focus is on more than financial compensation for work, although that is a large and critical part of rewards management. Rather, consideration is given to the place of intrinsic rewards as well as extrinsic financial and non-financial rewards in strategic human resource management. This chapter reviews the components of a compensation plan, including pay structure and benefits, as well as considering job design and volunteer recognition as important elements of a sport organization's overall rewards management system.

Theories of motivation

Motivation is defined as the 'inner desire to make an effort' (Mitchell & Daniels, 2003: 226). It is not the effort or behaviour itself; rather motivation is a psychological state that describes one's drive to engage in a particular behaviour. This inner drive is believed to be critical to individual performance in an organization. It is motivation that may distinguish the behaviour of two individuals who have similar skill sets; for example, given two volunteers with the same abilities, we can expect greater effort from the one who has a stronger inner desire to get involved. Motivation to exert effort is further characterized by the direction of that intended effort (what), the intensity (how hard), and persistence (how long). Given that, it is important to understand what factors affect individual's inner drive. Sport organizations should be concerned with what will motivate someone to accept a job, to exert effort, and to remain with the organization.

People are motivated to fulfill unmet needs. We work because we need money, we enjoy social interaction, we feel good about helping or serving others, or we want to challenge ourselves. If an individual determines that a particular job can help him satisfy any number of needs, he or she will be motivated to apply for that job, and accept the job if it is offered. Furthermore, if the individual perceives that certain behaviours on the job (e.g., doing what is expected, performing quality work, leading a group, going above and beyond what is asked) will result in rewards that will help satisfy certain needs, he or she will be motivated to engage in those behaviours. The strength of an individual's need (e.g., for money, for recognition, personal growth) will determine the strength of his or her desire to exert effort in a given direction for a given period of time. Of course, the desire to exert effort may not be translated into behaviour or performance. Even skilled and motivated workers may encounter conditions beyond their control that will impede their work; for example, budget restrictions that do not permit sport programme ideas to be put into practice, delayed arrival of sports equipment for instructional activities, or the lack of motivation or ability of other workgroup members.

Content theories

It is helpful if an organization can understand what individuals' particular needs are, and thus provide opportunities (rewards) to satisfy those needs so that individuals are motivated to join, work hard for, and remain with the organization. Content theories of motivation attempt to explain *what* motivates individuals. Three classic theories will be examined here: Maslow's hierarchy of needs theory, Herzberg's motivator–hygiene theory, and McClelland's three needs theory.

An early and seminal framework is Abraham Maslow's (1943) hierarchy of needs theory. This theory contends that there are five progressive levels of needs that every human experiences which are as follows:

1. Physiological needs (e.g., food, shelter, clothing).
2. Safety needs (e.g., security, stability, health).
3. Belongingness needs (e.g., affection, acceptance, friendship).
4. Esteem needs (e.g., self-esteem, confidence, respect by others).
5. Self-actualization (e.g., personal growth, morality).

The first three levels comprise lower order or basic human needs; that is, the need for food and water, for health and safety, and for social interaction. The last two levels are regarded as higher order needs that reflect an individual's need for growth beyond those basic needs; that is, the need to feel valued and to develop to one's potential. Maslow's theory contends that a person may have unmet needs at all five levels, however one of the levels will be predominant at a given point of time and will thus determine the primary direction of that person's efforts. For example, if an individual does not have the resources to acquire food and shelter, he or she will be driven to find a job with adequate compensation to satisfy that basic need. The theory also argues that there is a satisfaction-progression process, such that once needs are met at one level, the individual's predominant driving need will then be at the next level. An individual can remain at the top level of self-actualization, unless a lower level need becomes predominant (e.g., because of job loss, personal bankruptcy, some critical incident that has compromised one's self-esteem or confidence). For example, a recent sport management graduate may be motivated to find a decent-paying, secure job where he feels he belongs and will be respected for what he can contribute. Maslow's theory would argue that one of those needs will be predominant, perhaps in this case a need to pay the bills, and will largely dictate the kind of job the individual will look for and ultimately accept. Once the recent graduate has secured a job with adequate compensation and his basic physiological needs are being met, he will likely evaluate whether there is sufficient security in the job to meet his subsequent need for a stable environment. If this need is met, then the individual is likely to stay and consider whether his need for a sense of belongingness can be met, and so on. If the recent graduate determines that there is not sufficient security in his new job to meet his need for stability, then he is likely to try and secure an adequate paying job elsewhere.

Maslow's theory directs our attention to the concept of levels of human needs, and the notion that one level of needs will be predominant and dictate inner drive at a given point in time. However, critics argue that human needs are more dynamic and complex than Maslow's hierarchical levels allow, and that the model is too inflexible to adequately explain motivation, particularly in the workplace (McShane, 1995). Nonetheless, the theory provides a solid foundation for subsequent need theories.

Frederick Herzberg's (1968) motivator–hygiene theory presumes that only higher order needs will be motivating in the workplace, thus inciting effort there. His theory is derived from research on workers who were asked to describe when they were most satisfied (i.e., their needs were being met) and most dissatisfied (i.e., their needs were not being met). Herzberg found that the workers tended to describe aspects of the job itself (work content) when talking about satisfaction; for example, having responsibility on the job, achievement, recognition, and personal growth. He subsequently argued that only those things associated with satisfaction could be motivating and these he called motivators. In contrast, Herzberg found that the workers in his sample tended to describe aspects of the workplace (work context) when talking about dissatisfaction; for example, company policies, relationship with supervisor, and pay. He labelled these hygienes, and argued that individuals will not be motivated by these factors; rather, they are necessary elements in the workplace to keep the organization running and to ensure employees are not dissatisfied. The motivators tend to align with Maslow's higher order needs, while the hygienes tend to align with the lower order needs in his theory.

Herzberg's findings and conclusions were not definitive such that some of the hygiene factors were reported to contribute to satisfaction (e.g., pay) and could therefore presumably be motivating, while some of the motivators were reported to contribute to dissatisfaction (e.g., recognition). Particularly, noteworthy to this chapter is the contention that pay is primarily a hygiene factor and thus, by definition, cannot be motivating. In fact, Herzberg found that pay is a source of satisfaction, and thus motivating, when it is perceived as a form of recognition for achievement (Milkovich & Newman, 1990). The implication of this theory is that management must be concerned with improving hygiene factors in order to avoid employee dissatisfaction; for example, by providing adequate and fair salary and wages, and job security, and ensuring effective supervision. However, to increase motivation management must focus on providing opportunities for employee's achievement, recognition, and growth. These opportunities can be provided through job design that focuses on maximizing the motivating potential of a job (see Chapter 3 and below for a fuller description of job design). As an example, staff at a sport facility may expect to

159

receive decent pay with good benefits, and work in a safe environment. According to Herzberg's theory, these factors alone will not be sufficient to motivate staff to exert extra effort in the workplace (although, according to Maslow's theory, they may attract someone with predominant lower order needs to consider working there). Rather, it is the responsibility in their jobs, the opportunity to achieve something, to be recognized for it, and to develop as a person, that will incite staff to give greater effort. It is the work itself, rather than the workplace, that is the source of motivation.

A final content theory to consider is David McClelland's (1961) three need theory. This theory argues that individuals have secondary needs in addition to their primary or basic needs for such things as shelter and security. These secondary needs are learned and reinforced over time rather than being instinctive. This notion has important implications for organizations to try to cultivate or at least reinforce certain needs in employees that support corporate strategy. McClelland contends that secondary needs for achievement, power, and affiliation can help to explain what motivates employees beyond financial compensation or security in the workplace.

- *Need for achievement*: A desire to accomplish moderately challenging performance goals, be successful in competitive situations, assume personal responsibility for work (rather than delegating it to others), and receive immediate feedback.
- *Need for power*: A desire to control one's environment, including people and material resources. Some people have a high *socialized power* (italics in original) need in which they seek power to help others, such as improving society or increasing organizational effectiveness. Those with a strong *personal power* (italics in original) need to seek power so that they can revel in their power and use it to advance their career and other personal interests.
- *Need for affiliation*: A desire to seek approval from others, conform to their wishes and expectations, and avoid conflict and confrontation. People with a strong affiliation need want to form positive relationships with others, even if this results in lower job performance (McShane, 1995: 74).

McClelland's theory argues that individuals may have some need for achievement, power, and affiliation, however one of these needs will be predominant. Further, an individual will be motivated by the opportunity to satisfy that predominant need; for example, by leading a group (need for socialized or personal power), accomplishing challenging tasks (need for achievement), or developing positive relationships (need for affiliation). Again, it is important for management to try to recognize an individual's predominant need and provide an opportunity for it to be met – by providing leadership opportunities, challenging but attainable goals, or opportunities to work with others – as this is what will motivate an individual in the workplace. It is equally important, though, for management to guide the direction of an individual's efforts; thus, opportunities for achievement, power, or affiliation should be consistent with the organization's overall strategic plan. The strength of a person's need for achievement, power, or affiliation will determine the intensity with which he or she pursues and engages in behaviour that can help to satisfy that need.

Consider the following case of Ellen Anderson and her decision whether to continue volunteering with the local cycling club or take the offer to move to the state cycling association:

Will She Stay or Will She go?

Ellen Anderson was a volunteer with a local competitive cycling club for 8 years. She had served in various positions on the club's board of directors, including Vice President for the last 3 years. The volunteer board of the local cycling club saw itself as a social group as much as a decision making body, and the directors had been friends for many years. This atmosphere certainly contributed to the continuity and cohesion among the directors.

In her role as Vice President, Ellen had responsibility for communicating between the club head coach and the board. This involved keeping the board up to date on what the coach was doing with the training and competition programme, and bringing the coach's budget requests to the board. Ellen had a good rapport with the coach and the board. The board wanted Ellen to move into the President's position for a 3-year term. The President was essentially responsible for chairing meetings and determining the decisions of the board with regard to any issues that arose (e.g., fundraising, budgeting, hiring coaches). While Ellen appreciated the importance of a board whose members got along well, she found it frustrating that they often spent more time chatting than working. She wondered if she could make a difference in the position of club President.

At around the same time, the state cycling association (located in the same city as the local club where Ellen was volunteering) contacted Ellen to invite her to assume a position on its volunteer board of directors. Each director had responsibility for managing a particular portfolio and subcommittee (e.g., marketing, state race series, junior development). Each director was also responsible for overseeing a particular geographic region of the state. The board would meet every 2 months to receive reports from the various directors and their respective subcommittees.

Ellen knew she had to make a decision between staying with the local cycling club, with which she had been involved for some time, or moving to the state cycling association where she felt she could make a real difference in the cycling world.

For discussion

Use McClelland's three need theory to describe Ellen's motivation to remain with the local cycling club vs. her motivation to become involved in the state cycling association. What needs could be met in each organization? Where do you think she ended up, and why?

This discussion of content theories presumes that individuals are motivated by unmet needs. It further describes the kinds of needs that might be met in the workplace, and what rewards an organization might make available to address those unmet needs and, ideally, motivate individuals to join, work hard for, and remain with the organization. Content theories imply that, to increase work motivation, the organization needs to provide a variety of jobs and rewards that can be matched with members' needs (McShane, 1995). While these theories help to explain what motivates individuals, they do not elaborate on the mechanisms by which individuals determine whether to exert effort, in what direction, or for how long. Process theories attempt to provide further insight into these issues.

Process theories

While content theories help to explain *what* motivates individuals, process theories help to explain *how* they are motivated; that is, the cognitive process that individuals go through that explains how a felt need can result in certain behaviour. There are a number of motivation process theories, however this chapter will focus on two classic theories that have direct implications for rewards management: equity theory and expectancy theory.

Equity theory extends the content theories of motivation by proposing that individuals will be motivated, not just by a given reward, but by whether they perceive the reward situation to be equitable and fair. Specifically, equity theory contends that individuals will evaluate a given reward according to whether they feel it is proportionate with their own efforts (Jaques, 1961) and whether it is equitable to the efforts and rewards of others (Adams, 1965). According to Adams' classic model, 'people will evaluate the fairness of their situation in an organization based on a comparison of the ratio of their own inputs and outcomes with some referent's ratio of inputs and outcomes' (Mitchell & Daniels, 2003: 242). When the ratios are unequal then individuals are motivated or driven by a need to rectify the perceived inequity by (a) modifying their own input (effort) to outcome (rewards) ratio, (b) changing their referent other and focusing instead on another person's ratio of inputs and outcomes, (c) distorting their perceptions, or (d) quitting (Mitchell & Daniels, 2003). Research indicates that the effect of lowered effort to correct negative equity (i.e., when an individual feels under-rewarded in comparison to others) is felt more in an organization than any increased effort to correct positive equity (i.e., when an individual feels over-rewarded in comparison to others) (Mitchell & Daniels, 2003). Thus, potentially underrewarding staff and volunteers should be of concern to an organization.

A telling example of equity theory to explain individual behaviour is the situation with professional athletes' salaries. It may be difficult to comprehend why a player (or his agent) will hold out for another 5% of a multimillion dollar contract, particularly if that player has publicly indicated his desire to stay in a particular city and play with the team there (see the example of National Hockey League (NHL) player Ryan Smyth below). Does that individual really have a need for a further 5% in salary? Equity theory may be able to help and explain this situation. The player (or his agent) is likely not willing to 'settle' for less, or even the same, as what is being paid to players he (or his agent) consider to be of equal or lesser ability. The individual will be motivated to reduce any perceived inequity (i.e., under-reward); in this case, moving to a different organization where he perceives he will be rewarded more fairly.

In February 2007, NHL player Ryan Smyth was traded from his beloved Edmonton Oilers to the New York Islanders. 'Captain Canada', as he was known, grew up in Banff, Alberta only a few hours from Edmonton. He was drafted in 1994 and played all 12 years of his professional career to that point with the Edmonton Oilers, a team he had idolized as a child. The Oilers star had reportedly sought a 5-year deal from Edmonton worth $5.5 million US a season, but it could not be arranged. Smyth denied reports that he and the Oilers split because of a mere difference of $100,000 per season. His agent, Don Meehan, claimed that he and the Oilers tried to find some common financial ground but could not make that happen. According to Meehan, 'both sides compromised throughout this process, but not to the degree where we both felt comfortable that we could come to a deal' (cbc.ca/sports). Smyth shed tears during a press conference at the Edmonton airport as he was leaving town to head to New York.

With information from Wikipedia.com, ESPN.com, and cbc.ca/sports, retrieved on 15 March 2007.

On a smaller scale financially, one research study revealed that 90% of administrators in the professional sport, fitness, and parks and recreation sectors used external referents when considering how satisfied they were with their pay (Smucker & Kent, 2004a, b). The majority of those (73%) made comparisons with individuals working in other organizations in the same field, followed by comparisons with others in their own organization (62%), and past jobs (47%). The authors suggested that this 'market' comparison may explain the tendency of employees in the sport industry to be neutral or dissatisfied with their level of pay, particularly when making comparisons with those who are in fact in a more favourable position. Equity theory appears to provide a useful explanation of individual's motivation with regard to given rewards. Sport organizations should recognize that staff and volunteers are likely to rationalize whether the available rewards are worth their perceived effort.

Expectancy theory is another approach that describes the cognitive process individuals go through when determining whether to exert effort. Expectancy theory, which originated with Vroom (1964), assumes that individuals are rational beings who think about possible outcomes before they engage in behaviour: 'Can I do this? And, if I do this, what will I get out of it, and do I care?' Rewards play a key role in the model as they are the potential outcomes of behaviour – 'What will I get out of it?' A key aspect of the model, and a key factor in effort, is the intrinsic value of the reward to the individual. The motivation to exert effort is a function of an individual's perception that, if he or she engages in a particular behaviour (e.g., takes a job, performs one's tasks at a minimum level or beyond) it will be acceptable and rewarded, and that those rewards will be of personal value. The content theories described earlier help explain what may be valued in the organization. If any part of this cognitive process is compromised, then motivation and hence effort will be compromised. For example, if an individual feels she cannot do what is expected in a job and so will not be rewarded, her motivation is diminished; if she feels she can do a job and will be rewarded but does not value the reward, then her motivation is compromised. If an individual feels he can do what is expected in a job but will not be rewarded, then his motivation is diminished; similarly if the individual feels he cannot do what is expected but he will be rewarded anyway, motivation to exert effort is diminished, because he will be rewarded regardless of his performance.

A key tenet of expectancy theory is that rewards must be tied to behaviour or performance for there to be motivation. It assumes that individuals are most motivated if they know they will be rewarded for their work; motivation is unaffected, or is diminished, if the individuals know they will be rewarded just for showing up. Another key tenet is that rewards must be valued. It is unlikely that financial rewards would be seen as anything but positive, however non-financial rewards may have different value to different individuals. For example, the outcome of acceptable task performance by an individual may be a promotion to leader of a workgroup (think back to the example of Ellen Anderson and her involvement in the local cycling club). Even though one has done very well at a given job, he or she may not want to be – in fact may fear being – the leader (although this did not seem to be the case for Ellen). According to expectancy theory, if the outcome of expending effort and doing acceptable work is being asked to take on a leadership role, the individual may be disinclined to expend the effort in the first place and avoid the perceived risk of being seen as a leader. The personal value of a particular outcome or reward is a direct function of an individual's needs. Thus, a person who perceives he can do an acceptable job and receive valued rewards in return (e.g., a commission on sales), will likely have a greater force of effort to engage in the behaviour. An organization can use rewards to strengthen an individual's motivation or force of effort by providing valued rewards in return for acceptable performance that the individual feels he or she can accomplish.

Content and process theories of motivation help to explain what motivates employees and volunteers in the workplace, and the thought process they go through in determining whether to engage in a particular behaviour. Organizational rewards are a critical component of individual motivation as they are a means by which unmet needs can be satisfied, and thus a basis of individual motivation to exert effort. The next section discusses the rewards management system, beginning with a description of different types of rewards in the workplace, followed by a review of the compensation plan, the role of job design in managing rewards, and volunteer recognition and rewards.

Types of rewards

Rewards are the 'return' individuals receive for doing the work of an organization. While rewards tend to have a positive connotation, we cannot assume that various types of rewards an organization offers carry the same value for all staff and volunteers. This in itself may be the most challenging part of rewards management, providing rewards that are valued enough by staff and volunteers that they are attracted to join the organization, motivated to put in a good effort there, and committed to staying. As noted above, rewards are valued to the extent that they help an individual to meet a felt need (e.g., need for financial security, need for social interaction, need for personal challenge), and are seen to be fair (i.e., adequate and equitable compensation for the work that is done). The role of intrinsic as well as extrinsic financial and non-financial rewards in the total rewards management system is considered here.

Individuals may receive both intrinsic and extrinsic rewards in the workplace. Intrinsic rewards are those that an individual receives directly as a result of performing his or her job; for example, a sense of achievement, feeling of competency, or personal growth. Again, these may hold different value to different individuals, depending on their needs. Intrinsic rewards, by definition, are not something that can be given to staff or volunteers. Rather, intrinsic rewards presume that there can be value in the task itself and, thus, the organization can structure the workplace (e.g., job design) so that the individual has a greater chance of experiencing these rewards. Intrinsic rewards are particularly critical for volunteer management, as extrinsic financial rewards are not, by definition, part of the compensation volunteers may expect to receive. The role of rewards in volunteer recognition is discussed below.

Extrinsic rewards can be distinguished as financial or non-financial. Direct financial rewards include salary or wages, incentives or bonuses, and cost-of-living adjustments that the individual can use at his or her discretion. In contrast, indirect financial rewards are employee benefits (e.g., dental plan, pension contributions, life insurance, paid vacation) that have a monetary value that can be accessed only through the use of these benefits. Indirect financial rewards also include benefits in the form of reimbursement for expenses (e.g., car allowance, skills upgrading). Some individuals may see this form of compensation as a perk of the job, and a very attractive component of the compensation package, depending on the value they attach to it. The organization, on the other hand, can use these benefits as a way to facilitate the work it wants to have it done. Although volunteers do not receive direct financial compensation, they too may receive indirect financial rewards in the form of reimbursement for expenses (e.g., travel, telephone) or costs of training courses, conferences, or seminars.

Non-financial rewards are things provided by an organization that do not have specific monetary value to the individual, but may be highly valued nonetheless. Examples range from a pat on the back for a job well done, to new office furniture or a key to the executive washroom, or promotion to group leader (with no additional financial compensation). In the sport setting, it may be common, and fairly easy, to provide benefits such as complementary tickets to sporting events or team merchandise. Non-financial rewards are an important means of recognizing the effort and contributions of volunteers. These can range from an informal or formal thank you, to more material rewards such as team clothing or trips to national and international competitions. Volunteers are unlikely to cite these non-financial rewards as a reason for being involved, however some are likely to value the recognition that accompanies many of these rewards.

It can be expected that the various financial and non-financial rewards that can be made available will have different worth to recipients, and as such it is important for the organization to understand what rewards are valued. Providing rewards that are not valued can be expected to have little impact on motivation. Furthermore, linking valued rewards with effort and performance can be expected to motivate employees to exert effort and perform at a higher level, yet providing rewards that are not commensurate with one's perceived effort can be expected to detract from work motivation.

The financial compensation plan

Financial compensation is one part of the total rewards management system. Direct financial compensation includes the base pay structure, incentives or merit pay, and cost-of-living adjustments. Indirect financial compensation comprises employee services and benefits, such as paid vacation, medical and dental insurance, and pension contributions. In designing a compensation plan, it is important to determine the objectives of that plan; in other words, what does the organization want to pay for? What does it want to reward? This should be consistent with its corporate strategy and human resource plan. For example, the objectives of a sport organization's compensation plan may be to facilitate organizational efficiency and effectiveness by cost effectively attracting and retaining competent employees, as well as rewarding their contributions and performance (Milkovich & Newman, 1990). These objectives have several implications for the basis upon which pay and incentives will be awarded, which are considered below.

Pay structure

Milkovich and Newman (1990: 31) define pay structure as 'the array of pay rates for different work within a single organization. It focuses attention on the levels, differentials, and criteria used to determine those pay rates', three principles guide the establishment of a pay structure: internal equity, the external market, and employee contribution (Milkovich & Newman, 1990). The importance of perceived equity to employee motivation was described earlier. Similarly, internal equity in determining pay structure refers to the principles of (a) comparable pay for comparable content of work, (b) comparable skills that are required, and (c) comparable contribution of the work or skills to the objectives of an organization. Internal equity calls for consistency within the organization.

The external market principle refers to positioning an organization's pay structure, indeed its overall compensation plan, relative to what competitors are paying their staff. For example, pay levels may be set higher in order to attract and retain the best applicants. Alternatively, pay levels may be set lower, however better benefits or greater job security may be offered relative to the competition. Consider the following case of the YMCA (US) which promotes its employee benefits to potential recruits:

YMCA Employee Benefits

Believing that people deserved the best, YMCAs offer competitive wage and benefit packages. Each YMCA is unique in its benefits offered, but most Ys offer all or a combination of the following:

- Health and dental insurance.
- Disability and life insurance.
- Funded retirement plan.
- Flexible work schedule.
- Subsidized child care.
- Free YMCA membership.
- Tuition reimbursement.
- Discounted programme fees.
- Time-off benefits (vacation, sick days, and holidays).

YMCA (2007). Employee benefits, retrieved on 11 April 2007 from http://www.ymca.net/careers/ymca_employee_benefits.html

Where actual pay levels are set will depend on the need to control labour costs, however the external market principle directs management to establish a competitive (and equitable) compensation package in order to attract and retain competent staff.

The principle of employee contribution refers to the relative emphasis in a pay structure on compensation by job level, skills, seniority, or performance, or some combination. Again, it is important to remember that what is rewarded will be the focus of employees' attention. We consider these four bases of financial compensation in more detail below.

167

With a job-based reward system, the pay structure is determined according to the type of work and its value to the organization. Criteria for determining the levels of pay include task difficulty, responsibility for supervising others, and decision making responsibility (McKenna & Beech, 2002). For example, it is likely that, among sport facility staff, the marketing director will be paid more than the sales staff, who will be paid more than the ticket takers at an event. The marketing director's position has more responsibility than staff at the lower levels, and involves more challenging tasks. The same may be said for sales staff in comparison to ticket takers. In a job-based reward system, compensation is for the position rather than the individual and what he accomplishes or his worth to the organization. What is involved in a job can be known from a description of the duties and responsibilities, as determined through job analysis (see Chapter 3). With this type of reward system individuals doing the same type of work with the same requirements, get the same level of pay, regardless of performance. This system is consistent with the principle of internal equity, however, alone it is not likely to foster motivation for employees to work any harder than what is necessary to keep their job, as rewards are linked to the job rather than the individual's behaviour or performance.

With a skills-based reward system, the pay structure is determined according to the skills and qualifications required for the job; for example, a certain level of education, skills, years of experience, or certification (McKenna & Beech, 2002). It is not unusual for job- and skills-based rewards to be closely linked. That is, particular skills are required for a given level of job. However, one purpose of the skills-based system is to encourage employees to upgrade their skills and qualifications, with the assumption that it will pay off for the organization to have more highly skilled workers. This rewards system supports an organization's training and development initiatives (see Chapter 6). Thus, an individual with higher qualifications will get compensated more than someone with lower qualifications. This compensation may be in the form of moving up the pay scale through a merit increase, or from a one-time financial bonus.

Consider an example of a job in the parks and recreation sector where the pay structure may dictate that an individual with a post-secondary degree will get paid more than someone with a high school diploma. The assumption is that the university graduate is more highly qualified and knowledgeable, and therefore is compensated at a higher level. As another example, a collegiate sport coach may receive an increase in base pay for acquiring higher levels of coaching certification, or a financial bonus for taking the time to apprentice with a master coach. A system that rewards skills may be expected to motivate employees to improve themselves or at least demonstrate to the organization that they have the desired skills. This effort can be expected to have a positive effect in the organization.

With a seniority-based reward system, the pay structure reflects longevity in the organization. The assumption is that employees should be rewarded for staying with the organization because they have acquired skills and knowledge over time that are valuable to the organization. For the staff member, there may be motivation to join and stay with an organization with this type of financial security. With this type of system, an employee knows there will be incremental pay increases over time and this kind of security can be very attractive to staff. It is also a relatively easy system for an organization to administer, and labour costs can be forecasted. However, there may be no further motivation to work hard because longevity rather than behaviour or performance is linked to compensation. A simple example of a seniority-based system is found in the pay structure for Game Staff and Minor Officials hired for intercollegiate athletic competitions at one Canadian university. The 2006–2007 pay rates started at \$8.00/hour, and increased by \$0.25/hour for every year that returning staff had been in that position. Thus, individuals in their first year as a Game Staff or Minor Official were paid the basic rate of \$8.00/hour, while those in their third year in one of those positions were paid \$8.75/hour. This presumably provided some incentive for these staff and officials to return to the job each year.

Finally, with a performance-based reward system, the pay structure provides compensation in return for acceptable results or behaviour. Rewards may be provided on a continuous scale where the better one performs the better the rewards, or on a graduated scale where there are set levels an individual must reach in terms of performance before the next level of rewards is provided. Providing rewards for *individual results* is synonymous with a commission system, where compensation is directly linked to the quantity of the employee's output, such as number of units sold. Compensation by results is not uncommon for employees such as sporting goods sales staff or personal trainers at a fitness club. As well, a winning season may be the basis for determining whether a collegiate coach can expect a raise in pay, or a financial bonus, or to keep his job! With this system the employee is presumably motivated to work harder because pay is directly tied to productivity. The rate of compensation based on results is typically established by determining an acceptable level of performance at an expected level of effort, so that compensation is considered fair.

Rewards in a performance-based system may also be given for *unit or organizational results,* which is synonymous with profit sharing. With this type of system employees are presumably motivated to work harder when they know that their efforts may lead to direct compensation in the form of an increase in base pay or a one-time financial bonus. Profit-sharing systems may distribute rewards to employees soon after profits have been determined (e.g., quarterly or annually), rewards may be deferred until retirement, or both strategies may be used (Milkovich & Newman, 1990). Notably, 'the incentive value of profit distribution declines as the time between performance and payoff increases and as the size of the payoff declines relative to previous years' (Milkovich & Newman, 1990: 350). However, deferred payments have tax advantages that make this strategy increasingly desirable. Profit sharing has the potential to increase employee motivation and effort in the workplace, and directly benefit the organization, if rewards are tied to what is considered to be desirable behaviour and performance.

Instead of relying on discrete results, compensation may also be based on *individual behaviour or performance* that has been evaluated through performance appraisal. With this system, an increase in base pay or a financial bonus is linked to an individual's behaviour and accomplishments. For example, if the marketing director of a professional sports team is evaluated positively, on say, his group leadership, ability to deploy personnel in the marketing department, planning and budgeting for the unit, and sponsorship acquisition, he is likely to be rewarded. The presumption is that the marketing director will be motivated to be effective in these areas when compensation is a direct outcome of his behaviour and accomplishments.

A profile of compensation plans in the sport industry is provided by the results of a study of sport marketing professionals in seven different segments of the industry in the US (Barr, McDonald & Sutton, 2000). Table 8.1 presents examples and a cross-industry comparison of starting salaries and benefits in each of the segments, as well as the prevalence of different performance-based reward systems. A description of different types of indirect financial rewards is also provided and discussed further below.

Barr et al. (2000) found that the starting compensation package for sport marketing professionals was essentially the same across the industry, however the average compensation levels varied considerably by segments. This did not appear to be a function of an employee experience, as the respondent's years of experience in the industry was fairly similar (7–10 years) across the segments. There was also some discrepancy in compensation potential where the top level for employees in arenas/sport venues was considerably lower than the other industry segments, and lowest for the college/university athletics setting. This is likely explained in part by the potential for sport marketers in the different segments to increase their compensation through such incentives as bonuses and commissions. The proportion of the total compensation package from these incentives was highest for broadcast/media and sport marketing agencies, which also had the highest average compensation levels. Table 8.1 also reveals the variation across and within the industry segments in the extent to which the bonuses were based on department, company, and individual performance. Barr et al.'s findings reveal that department performance was the primary basis of allocating these rewards in college/university athletics, major league teams, and broadcast/media, while company performance was the primary factor in sport marketing agencies and minor league teams. Therefore, the incentive to perform was based more on department- or company-wide performance than individual performance. Personal or individual performance was the primary basis of allocating bonuses in major league offices and arenas/sport venues.

A sport organization may implement a compensation plan that is based on a mixture of job-based, skill-based, seniority-based, and performance-based reward systems. For example, in a fitness club, instructors' wages may be based on a given dollar amount for the number and level of classes taught (job-based), with an annual percentage increase of a given amount based on cost-of-living increases, as well as a small increase in their base salary for every year they continue to work at the club (seniority-based). The instructors may also have the opportunity to earn a financial bonus each year for outstanding performance as determined through performance appraisal. It is

Table 8.1 Compensation plans for marketing professionals in the sport industry (Barr et al., 2000)

Factors	Major league teams	Major league offices	College/university athletics	Sport marketing agencies	Minor league teams	Arenas/sport venues	Broadcast/media
Average compensation ($US)	$79,560	$77,500	$44,930	$103,077	$50,698	$63,684	$118,269
Range of compensation	$25,000–350,000	$25,000–312,500	$25,000–85,000	$25,000–350,000	$25,000–337,500	$27,500–162,500	$27,500–350,000
Compensation based on bonus/commission (%)	12.3	13.9	2.5	19.7	18.0	4.7	23.5
Bonuses based on department performance (%)	45.7	37.2	58.3	18.5	8.6	37.8	35.6
Bonuses based on company performance (%)	24.0	20.6	16.7	47.2	61.4	23.3	30.6
Bonuses based on individual performance (%)	28.6	42.2	25.0	34.3	30.0	38.9	33.8
Entertainment expense account (%)	54	41	28	58	32	53	77
Pension (%)	56	59	75	33	11	68	54
Company car/auto reimbursement (%)	42	32	61	35	32	37	25
Tuition reimbursement (%)	13	5	64	6	3	3	25
Country club membership (%)	10	0	11	4	12	11	6

Data is based on a survey of 421 sport marketing professionals employed in seven segments of the sport industry in the US. Respondents were predominantly male (81.6%), average age 35.5 years, holding an under-graduate degree (94%), with an average of 8.8 years of experience in the sport industry, and a 57-hour average workweek.

important for an organization to understand the bases of its compensation plan because employees will pay attention to what is rewarded. Consider the following example of a compensation plan for limited hourly employees at a municipal recreation department:

Compensation Plan for Limited Hourly Employees of a Municipal Recreation Department

Definition: A limited hourly employee is one who works full time or part time on a temporary basis, on an on-call basis, or on an hourly basis in a specified seasonal programme, such as summer camps. Limited hourly employees work less than 1000 hours per fiscal year.

Salary and classifications: It is the City's intent to compensate limited hourly employees at a rate of pay similar to that of regular employees performing similar work. Limited hourly employees are to be hired at a level that is closest to a corresponding regular classification in both level of work performed and rate of pay. In the event a limited hourly employee is required to assume duties significantly above or below the level when first hired for a term of more than one pay period, the employee is to be reclassified into a higher or lower level of work and pay rate that most closely corresponds to the new duties.

Special compensation: Limited hourly employees are eligible to receive holiday pay only when they work 80 or more hours during the pay period in which the holiday falls. Limited hourly employees are not eligible for paid leaves beyond those required by law. Limited hourly employees are eligible for overtime pay at time and one-half when required to work more than 40 hours in a week or on an official City holiday.

Salary increases: Limited hourly employees that demonstrate continued development and efficient and effective service reflected in their performance appraisal may receive a salary step increase after 700 hours, or 6 months, whichever occurs first from the date of hire. A limited hourly employee must receive a 'meets requirements' rating in order to be considered for a salary increase. Upon written justification and departmental approval, a limited hourly employee who demonstrates exceptional leadership ability and job performance may be given a merit raise. Such exceptional leadership must be documented on a designated performance appraisal form.

Sample Job Classifications and Salary

Administrative Specialist I: Performs administrative work that requires advanced skills or knowledge in support of a department/division or programme.

Step 1   *Step 2*   *Step 3*   *Step 4*   *Step 5*

$19.06 $20.17 $21.34 $22.57 $23.88 per hour

Administrative specialist II: Performs more complex work that requires advanced skills or knowledge in specialized software programmes and data analysis in specialized areas in support of a department/division or programme. Two years of experience equivalent to that of an Administrative specialist I.

Step 1   *Step 2*   *Step 3*   *Step 4*   *Step 5*

$22.76 $24.08 $25.48 $26.95 $28.52 per hour

Instructor II: Under limited supervision, prepares classes, programmes and camp curriculum, presents classes and field trips and provides assignments to instructor aides and volunteers. Requires previous teaching experience. Requires in-depth knowledge of the disciplines to be taught. Two years of experience equivalent to that of an Instructor I. May require lifting up to 15 pounds.

Step 1   *Step 2*   *Step 3*   *Step 4*   *Step 5*

$21.94 $23.31 $24.56 $25.98 $27.49 per hour

Based on information from the City of Palo Alto Compensation Plan, retrieved March 9, 2007 from www.city.palo-alto.ca.us/hr/documents.

Discussion questions

1. What is the basis, or bases, of the rewards offered in this compensation plan?
2. What effort or behaviour might the City expect from its limited hourly employees as a result of this compensation plan?

Another potentially valued and therefore important component of an organization's compensation plan is indirect financial rewards. In their study of sport marketing professionals, Barr et al. (2000) found that various types of indirect financial rewards were available to different extents across the sport industry in the US (see Table 8.1). For example, over half of sport marketers with major league teams, sport marketing agencies, arenas/sport venues, and broadcast/media organizations received an entertainment expense account, while this was far less common in the other industry segments. Pensions were most common for sport marketers in college/university athletics and arenas/sport venues.

Indirect financial rewards like pensions, or life or medical insurance plans, are available as employee services or benefits. These may take a variety of forms, and have different value to different employees depending on whether they address important needs. Employee benefits may be particularly important to an organization's reward management system if they make up for relatively lower financial compensation for employees. Consequently, a 'cafeteria style' or flexible benefits system may be most attractive to employees and recruits. A flexible system lets an employee, or group of employees, pick and choose which benefits are most needed (up to a maximum value that is the same for everyone), and as such optimizes the compensation received. In other words, employees are not receiving rewards that they are not likely to use and which have little value or attraction (e.g., child care when one has no dependents, life insurance when one is already covered through a spouse's plan). In some instances, additional salary may be taken in place of the value of certain benefits. Benefits can be an important part of a total compensation plan that helps to attract and retain valued staff.

To conclude, consider the following example of how rewards are managed at Camp Pinnacle, including the compensation plan, extrinsic non-financial rewards that are available, and intrinsic rewards that may be experienced:

Motivation and Rewards Management at Camp Pinnacle

Canadian families have a host of options when it comes to summer opportunities for children and youth. Residential (overnight) camps are only one of the activity possibilities for children. Camp Pinnacle, a summer sports camp, experiences substantial competition not only for customers (campers), but for staff as well. Camp Pinnacle uses a finely tuned system to motivate staff and create incentives for high performance.

Motivating employees begins in the recruiting process, when potential staff members are introduced to Pinnacle's purpose, expectations, and culture. Like many residential camps, Pinnacle is a non-profit organization whose mission – creating a superior sports camp experience for underprivileged youth – is a unifying and motivating factor for staff. The Camp believes that serving the mission of the camp will be a source of intrinsic motivation for staff.

The Camp has a graduated pay structure in which all summer employees earn the same base salary, with increases awarded to returning staff members for each year of experience. In addition to their base salary, all staff receive a stipend of $40/week for 'living expenses' (i.e., laundry, sundries, a treat in town on their day off). Staff are also eligible to be reimbursed for the cost of upgrading their qualifications in Camp Pinnacle's instructional areas; for example, staff can get back up to 100% of the costs of advanced training in kayak or high-ropes instruction certification, and lifeguards can be reimbursed for up to 50% of certification costs per year.

While Camp Pinnacle is focused on motivating staff through rewards, like many summer camps it has limited financial resources to compensate staff. Thus, the organization invests creatively in other! non-financial reward systems. At the end of each 2-week camper session, there is a gathering of all staff. At this time the senior management team recognizes one member of the seasonal staff team from each camper age group and activities area (e.g., water sports, land sports) with a 'Reaching for the Pinnacle' award for exceptional job performance. The selection is based on performance appraisal of each seasonal staff member by the section head for each age group and activities area. Though there is no financial component to these awards, they are highly regarded by staff members, who wear their special edition 'Reaching the Pinnacle' T-shirts with pride.

Another rewards strategy utilized by Camp Pinnacle is job scheduling. Senior management must schedule staff for days off as well as special assignments throughout the season. They recognize that different members of staff may perceive a certain cabin assignment, a particular day off, or a specific out-trip responsibility to be a meaningful perk. To capitalize on these preferences, Camp Pinnacle has created the 'Excelections' system. Staff member submit their preferences for assignments, housing, or days off to their supervisor, who then does the scheduling giving priority to those employees with the highest performance appraisal scores from the previous camp session.

Discussion questions

1. What is the basis, or bases, of rewards at Camp Pinnacle?
2. What other rewards (intrinsic or extrinsic) could Camp Pinnacle use to attract, motivate, and retain staff?
3. Based on your understanding of motivation theory, what factors might staff take into account in their decision whether to return the following summer?

Prepared by Katie Misener based on information about Camp Pinnacle.

Job design

This chapter discusses in further detail the motivational approach to job design that was outlined in Chapter 3. According to De Cieri, Kramar, Noe, Hollenbeck, Gerhart and Wright (2005), the opportunity to fulfill individual needs can be built into the design of a job, and thus increase its potential to motivate employees and volunteers in the workplace. As indicated earlier, typical motivating elements of a job are autonomy (level of independence in carrying out job duties), intrinsic job feedback (from the work itself), extrinsic job feedback (from others), social interaction (through group work and customer-service), task variety, task identity (involvement in a complete or identifiable piece of work), skill/knowledge requirements (level of challenge in the task), task significance (interconnected with other work, impacts others inside and outside the organization), growth/learning (challenging work, support is provided), and recognition (acknowledgement of good work). A job can be designed to increase the likelihood that an employee or volunteer will experience one or more of these rewards, and will thus be motivated by such a job to the extent that the rewards are of personal value.

The work of Hackman and Oldham (1980) supports the notion of job design (or redesign) on the basis of the task itself being intrinsically rewarding. Their job characteristics model of motivation is consistent with Herzberg's (1968) contention that it is the aspects of the work content (i.e., the job itself) that will be motivating. According to Hackman and Oldham's model, five core job characteristics – skill variety, task identity, task significance, task autonomy, and job feedback – contribute to employees' sense of the meaningfulness of their work, responsibility for the outcomes of their work, and knowledge of the results of their work. These three 'critical psychological states' are the intrinsic rewards for doing one's job, and thus are instrumental to one's motivation in the workplace. An organization can manipulate, through job design, the variety of skills and activities required in one's job, the extent to which a job involves a whole, identifiable piece of work (e.g., a project or major piece of project from start to finish), and the importance of the particular job to the organization (or its clients). These three job characteristics are proposed to impact directly on an employee's experienced meaningfulness of the work. Further, an organization is able to increase the autonomy or decision making discretion one has in a job, thus enhancing his or her sense of responsibility. And an organization is able to design a job so that an employee receives feedback directly from the job itself on how he or she is performing, thus increasing the direct knowledge of results.

There are four important considerations for enhancing the meaningfulness, responsibility, and direct feedback in one's work through job design. First, the employee himself must perceive there to be sufficiently high levels of the core job characteristics for there to be an adequate sense of meaningfulness, responsibility, and knowledge of results for the job to be motivating. Second, an individual must be willing to accept a job that has been designed to be more motivating; in other words, these intrinsic rewards must have personal value to the jobholder. Third, designing, and particularly redesigning, a job so that intrinsic rewards are more available may impact on the design of someone else's job. For example, to increase skill variety and task identity in one person's job may mean reducing skill variety and task identity in someone else's job. This can reduce the motivating effect of that individual's job. Fourth, a redesigned job that has, say, increased skill requirements and autonomy, may dictate moving the job to a higher level on the pay scale with financial implications for the organization. Thus, the effect of job design may be felt beyond its potential to increase employee motivation, and not necessarily in positive ways.

Job design as a strategy to create (more) motivating positions is not limited to the paid staff; it applies equally well to volunteers, particularly given sport organizations' heavy reliance on intrinsic rewards as the basis of volunteers' motivation for being involved. Nevertheless, intrinsic benefits are not the only means by which volunteers are rewarded. We turn now to a consideration of the use of rewards for recognizing volunteers.

Volunteer recognition and rewards

Intrinsic and non-financial rewards are the types of incentives that sport organizations have to entice individuals to volunteer. Sport organizations rely heavily on volunteers' attraction to helping out in sport because of a desire to help others, the social benefits of interacting with others, and the personal rewards of contributing one's skills and making a difference (Cuskelly, Hoye & Auld, 2006). These may be classified as (a) normative incentives, where the sport volunteer is motivated by the opportunity to help a cause such as a sport programme which he or she may feel is important for children and for a community as a whole, (b) affective incentives, where the sport volunteer is motivated by the opportunity to work with others, develop friendships, and identify with a group, and (c) utilitarian incentives, where the sport volunteer is motivated by the opportunity to use his or her skills or sport background, to develop new skills and work experience, to network in the community, and to help his or her child participate in sport (Cuskelly et al., 2006). Research further suggests that the importance of these incentives varies by sport volunteers' age (Doherty, 2005a). Older adults (60 +years) are more likely to be motivated by normative incentives and social benefits, younger adults (less than 35-year old) are more likely to be motivated by utilitarian incentives relating to their own personal development, while those in the middle (35–60-year old and most likely to have children participating) are likely to be most motivated by utilitarian incentives followed by social benefits. To attract, motivate, and retain volunteers, sport organizations must ensure that individuals have the opportunity to realize these intrinsic benefits through their involvement in the work of the organization.

Sport organizations also rely fairly heavily on non-financial extrinsic rewards as a form of volunteer recognition and appreciation (Doherty, 2005b). Where extrinsic (direct) financial rewards are not, by definition, provided to volunteers, non-financial rewards can be an important symbolic expression of appreciation for contributions and performance. Perhaps it is the very fact that financial rewards are not handed over that sport organizations are concerned with providing some kind of alternative recognition. It is important to understand that 'recognition stems from genuinely valuing volunteers . . . rewarding volunteers takes recognition a step further, by providing something tangible and extrinsic to the act of volunteering itself'

(Australian Sports Commission [ASC], 2000b: 15). Recognition and rewards for volunteers vary in terms of their formality, cost, individual or group focus, and public or private nature (ASC, 2000b). The following is a list of potential rewards that may be used to recognize volunteers:

Ideas for Recognizing and Rewarding Volunteers

Smiling, saying hello and thank you.

Sending welcome letters when volunteers are first recruited.

Including volunteers on organizational charts.

Offering personal praise to the volunteer while on the job.

Writing letters or postcards of thanks.

Acknowledging, either publicly or privately, volunteers' accomplishments (e.g., a successful season, effective fundraising, or well-organized event).

Giving identification pins, badges, shirts, or caps.

Presenting volunteer awards at the annual general meeting.

Giving complimentary tickets to special events and functions.

Arranging discounts at recreation and sport stores or restaurants.

Awarding life memberships.

Holding social events in honour of volunteers.

Acknowledging efforts during committee meetings.

Listening to volunteers' ideas.

Presenting awards for years of service.

Funding training courses, conferences, and seminars.

With information from ASC (2000b). Volunteer management program – Retaining volunteers. Australian Sports Commission. Copyright Australian Sports Commission.

Discussion questions

1. With reference to the various content theories discussed earlier in this chapter, consider what needs may be met by the different rewards.
2. What can sport organizations do to help ensure that volunteers' higher-order needs (Maslow), motivators (Herzberg), and the needs for power, achievement, and affiliation (McClelland) can be met through volunteering? Give specific examples in addition to those listed above.

Decisions regarding the nature of extrinsic rewards for volunteers should take into consideration what is of value to different volunteers, as well as what the organization is able to spend in terms of time and money. Some volunteer coaches may relish quite public acknowledgements of their involvement or success, while others will shun the limelight and prefer that their athletes receive any accolades that may be due. Some board members may expect team merchandise, while others may prefer the money to be spent on programmes for the participants (Doherty, 2005b). While many volunteers would say they do not expect extrinsic rewards for their efforts, equity theory suggests that individuals will compare the rewards they receive (both intrinsic and extrinsic) with the effort they give, and will further compare that to what other volunteers contribute and receive (ASC, 2000b). If volunteers perceive inequity, then they may be disinclined to continue their involvement. Similarly, if they perceive they are being more than rewarded for their efforts, then they will be more inclined to continue. Along with intrinsic rewards derived from volunteering itself, extrinsic rewards may be a meaningful component of what the volunteer perceives he or she gets back from volunteering, and should be managed carefully.

Summary

Theories of human motivation are fundamental to understanding the impact of rewards systems on individuals' intent to take a job, exert effort, and remain with an organization. Content theories (e.g., Maslow's Hierarchy of Needs Theory, Herzberg's Motivator–Hygiene Theory, McClelland's Three Need Theory) explain what motivates employees and volunteers, while process theories (e.g., equity theory, expectancy theory) explain how they are motivated.

Rewards management systems must include potential for intrinsic rewards from the job itself as well as extrinsic financial and non-financial rewards that are given by the organization. Financial rewards include direct (i.e., pay, bonus, cost-of-living adjustment) and indirect (e.g., reimbursement of expenses) elements. Non-financial rewards are things that have no financial value, yet may be highly valued by an employee or volunteer (e.g., team clothing, national team travel, complementary sport event tickets).

The financial compensation plan is one part of the total rewards management system. The establishment of a pay structure must account for internal equity, external market forces, and employee contributions. The basis of the pay structure may be job level, skills, seniority, individual, group or organization performance, or some combination of these.

Job design is an important element of rewards management. It is a tool that can be used to increase the motivating potential of a job by increasing task variety, task identity, task significance, autonomy, and direct feedback, all of which provide an employee or volunteer with an increased sense of the meaningfulness of their job, responsibility for the outcomes of their work, and knowledge of results of their contributions.

Volunteers by definition do not receive extrinsic (direct) financial compensation, therefore the organization must rely on the intrinsic rewards of the volunteer role itself to ensure their needs are met. Sport organizations also tend to rely on extrinsic non-financial rewards as more tangible tokens of recognition and appreciation. The provision of these rewards requires careful consideration as they can be costly in terms of time and expense wise for the organization.

Discussion questions

1. Consider your most recent job (full-time, part-time, summer employment). What aspects contribute(d) to your satisfaction in the organization? What aspects contribute(d) to your dissatisfaction? Are these things consistent with Herzberg's (1968) motivators (satisfying) and hygiene factors (dissatisfying)? If not, why not? (Consider whether you are/were motivated by higher- or lower-order needs.)

2. List and describe all the intrinsic and extrinsic (including direct and indirect financial, and non-financial) rewards you receive(d) in your most recent job.

3. Consider your most recent job or volunteer experience. Using Hackman and Oldham's job characteristics model, describe whether the five core job characteristics are/were low, medium, or high in that job. Consider how this impacts or impacted your sense of meaningfulness of your work, responsibility for outcomes, and knowledge of results. If several job characteristics were rated low to medium how could the job be redesigned to be more motivating? (Describe how the job characteristics could be improved.) What impact, if any, would this have on others in the organization, including the motivational design of their job?

9 Sport organizations and employee relations

Chapter overview

Employee relations refer to the activities and processes designed to maintain a productive workplace while satisfying the needs and legitimate interests of employees and managing within the law. (Suffield, 2005). This chapter considers employee relations in a broad sense, rather than limiting the presentation to labour relations, which focuses specifically on the union–management relationship. The employee relations approach, with its focus on building a committed and high-performing workforce, is more consistent with strategic human resource management (SHRM) than the traditional industrial relations approach. The latter tends to focus on interactions between management and workers, and there is a connotation of an adversarial (us vs. them) relationship (McKenna & Beech, 2002; Lewis, Thornhill & Saunders, 2003). The basis of effective employee relations is employee involvement, where people have a voice in decisions about their working environment (e.g., pay, workload, task, conditions). The employee's psychological contract, the principle of organizational justice, organizational communication, and employee participation in decision making are the key elements of employee involvement.

Participation through trade unions is one mechanism for employee involvement. The union represents a collective voice for employees in negotiations about labour issues such as pay and workload. The result is a collective bargaining agreement (CBA) that pertains to all employees. This agreement is analogous to an individual employee's contract in a non-union workplace. When an employee, or groups of employees, perceives that the contract or collective agreement has been violated, it becomes grounds for grievance. The formal grievance procedure gives an employee recourse to resolve a formal complaint, and is a critical part of effective employee relations.

Working conditions may be a basis for grievance. In addition to contractual obligations, an employer has a moral and legal obligation to provide a safe and healthy working environment. This chapter examines hazards and risks at work that impact on workplace safety and employee health. Increasingly, organizations are proactive about employee health and wellness, with the intent of supporting a productive work environment and workers. These important elements of employee relations are considered here.

A productive and mutually satisfying relationship between the sport organization and its volunteers is just as, if not more, important than with paid staff. While many of the same principles apply, this chapter examines the specific nature of volunteer relations in the sport organization.

The employee–organization relationship will inevitably end at some point. This chapter closes by considering various forms and bases of termination. Exit interviews to determine reasons for employee resignation are also discussed. Exit interviews, when conducted properly, can be an important feedback mechanism for improving overall human resource management (HRM).

Employee–management relations

The employee relations approach focuses on communication, liaison with individuals, and policies and practices that are directed to the individual in the workplace. This approach does not necessarily replace interactions between management and the group or union with regard to pay systems, or workplace conditions. However, in comparison to traditional industrial relations, 'HRM approaches based on employee relations have sought to broaden the involvement of employees and take a more participative approach to management through increased communication' (McKenna & Beech, 2002: 255).

The relationship between management and employees must be based on exchange (i.e., the organization provides valued rewards in return for staff performance), and the organization's social and moral obligation to treat its workers well (Chelladurai, 2006). The organization must reward its employees fairly, provide a safe and non-threatening working environment, and provide support for them to do the work of the organization. In turn, employees have an implied duty to:

- be ready and willing for work;
- take reasonable care and skill in performing the job;
- obey the employer's lawful orders;
- take care of the employer's property;
- act in good faith (Lewis et al., 2003: 11).

These mutual expectations form the basis of the employee's psychological contract, a concept that was introduced in Chapter 5.

Psychological contract

The psychological contract refers to an unwritten expectations of the employee–management relationship that exist in addition to the formal employment contract (Lewis et al., 2003). It is an important tool to understand

and manage employee relations (Guest & Conway, 2002), and is an important component of the SHRM approach which focuses on generating higher levels of commitment among employees. Although not formally documented, the psychological contract is based on an employee's perceptions that may, in fact, be stronger than the reality of a formal, written contract. For example, a coach will have a certain understanding of what he is expected to do in and for the organization, whether he is employed in a community sport club, in an intercollegiate athletic department, or at a national team training centre. Part of this understanding will be based on the formal details of his job description and contract, but a larger part of it may be based on what he knows about coaching and how to run a team, the culture of the organization or the shared understanding of how things are really done there, and any information and feedback he receives regarding how he is doing on the job. The coach will also have expectations regarding what the organization will provide in return. Guest and Conway (1999) examined the relative influence of HRM policies and practices such as training and promotion, as well as trade union membership, and psychological contract on employee satisfaction. They found that the psychological contract between the employee and management, characterized by expected 'fairness of treatment, delivery of promises on issues such as pay, promotion and workload, and trust that these will be delivered in the future' (Guest & Conway, 1999: 382), was the strongest predictor of employee satisfaction.

Our review of the psychological contract in Chapter 5 addressed the importance of ensuring employees have a realistic and accurate understanding of what to expect, and what is expected of them, in the organization. It was also noted that these expectations may be formed before even becoming involved with the organization (based on pre-entry socialization) and may need to be realigned upon entry (encounter socialization). In fact, there is a continual process of explicit and implicit bargaining over and adjusting the content of the psychological contract in the workplace (Mullins, 1996).

Organizational justice

The notion of organizational justice is a key principle underlying employee relations. Organizational justice may be defined as the perception of fairness in all decisions and practices (Greenberg, 1987). From an SHRM perspective this also includes the processes of recruitment and selection, staffing and task assignment, training and development, performance appraisal, and rewards management. Organizational justice is a reflection of the organization's social and moral obligation to fairness. According to Chelladurai (2006: 122), 'managers should realize that they themselves are the guardians of justice within their organization'. There are also economic and legal rationales for ensuring justice in the organization, given the potential economic fallout of unjust practices from customer boycotts and employee withdrawal of services, and the notion that 'justice in the workplace is fast becoming an arena for legal actions' (Chelladurai, 2006: 123). Most importantly, it is the employees' *perception* of justice that is critical to the role of organizational justice in maintaining a productive workplace while satisfying the needs of employees (Lewis et al., 2003; Suffield, 2005).

There are three basic forms of organizational justice – distributive, procedural, and interactional – each with implications for managing employee relations. Distributive justice refers to the fair and just allocation of resources and rewards in the organization to people and to programmes or units. For example, lifeguard staff at an aquatics facility may question the fairness of pay increases to management, when the guards are the front line workers who have the responsibility of serving the public directly. As another example, coaches of what may be described as lower profile intercollegiate sport teams (e.g., gymnastics, wrestling, and field hockey) may wonder about budget cuts to their programmes while higher profile sports get an even bigger piece of the pie. These employees may perceive that an injustice has been done, which can ultimately affect their attitude towards the organization. Distributive justice is not limited to economic goods such as pay to individuals or budget allotments to groups. It also concerns the fair and just distribution of conditions and goods that affect psychological, physical, economic, and social well-being (Kabanoff, 1991: 417). You may recall the importance of different types of intrinsic and extrinsic rewards in the workplace presented in Chapter 8. The distribution of any type of reward, condition, or good is subject to perceptions of justice and injustice.

There are three bases of distributive justice: (1) equity, which is distribution based on members' contribution to the organization (recall the equity theory of motivation presented in Chapter 8); (2) equality, which is equal distribution to all members, regardless of contribution; and (3) need, which is distribution based on identified individual or group needs (Chelladurai, 2006). Any one of these bases of distribution may be used by the organization, as deemed appropriate to the decision and the situation. Again, the critical implication for employee relations is whether employees perceive the decision as fair and just. For example, if the lifeguards noted earlier recognize that management has taken on additional responsibilities with the recent expansion of programmes or personnel, the decision to increase their pay may be deemed to be equitable, and just and fair. Or, if the lifeguards learn that management has not had a pay increase in 10 years, and that the organization risks losing some outstanding leaders, they may acknowledge the need to provide better compensation to those individuals. In the example of intercollegiate coaches given above, these employees may perceive an injustice in the unequal distribution of resources to higher profile sport teams. The outcome of distributive injustice may be reduced job performance, reduced cooperation, or withdrawal behaviour. Not all employees will agree with the basis of a decision all the time, and perceived distributive injustice is not uncommon. An understanding of how the decision was made may help to restore employees' sense of fairness in the organization.

Procedural justice refers to fair and just procedures for determining the distribution of resources and rewards. In other words not only making a fair decision, but being seen to make a fair decision through the use of proper procedures. When decisions are based on procedures that are considered to be fair and transparent, they are more likely to be accepted by the individuals or groups they affect, even when those decisions have adverse implications such as increased workload, limited or no pay raise, or even dismissal (Folger & Cropanzano, 1998). Employee involvement in the decision making process is linked to perceptions of fairness (Lewis et al., 2003). Other examples might include the right to a 'fair' hearing and 'right of reply' when allegations of misconduct are made, or the right of appeal in relation to some organizational decisions. For example, if sales staff have at least some input in determining the commission rate in their fitness club or sporting goods store, they are more likely to perceive that the final decision is fair, even if it was not as high a rate as they were hoping for.

Interactional justice refers to the fair and just communication and explanation of distributive and procedural justice; in other words, 'this is the decision, and this is how we made it.' It is based on both interpersonal justice, or whether information was communicated in a respectful way, and informational justice, or whether adequate information was provided to explain and justify the decision (Lewis et al., 2003; Chelladurai, 2006). Interactional justice is an important consideration in managing employee relations, particularly when individuals are not formally involved in decision making. Employees may perceive their lack of opportunity to be involved as a procedural injustice. For example, fitness club staff may feel that they should at least be consulted regarding a new pay structure that includes commission rates. If the club's management is able to clearly explain the basis for the decision on the new pay structure, in a way that demonstrates respect for staff knowledge and expertise in this area, this will increase the chances that staff will perceive they have been treated fairly. Another example is the decision to eliminate programmes or staff, or both, from a public community fitness centre like a YMCA. Staff may feel they should have been consulted in the decision process at least regarding what programmes to reduce or eliminate. Interactional justice can help to re-establish a sense of fairness if staff are fully apprised of the basis for the decisions in a respectful and sensitive manner (Lewis et al., 2003). While interactional justice can be critical to effective employee relations, it should not be a substitute for the opportunity to have employees involved in organizational decisions.

Employee involvement

Employee involvement is the principle of engaging staff in the organization through various processes and mechanisms. From an SHRM perspective, the intent is to foster their understanding and support of, and commitment to, the organization's objectives (Lewis et al., 2003). Employee involvement is also associated with trust in management, increased job performance, job satisfaction, and intent to stay (Cropanzano & Greenberg, 2001). Table 9.1 provides a description of several types of employee involvement based on communication, the task itself, financial rewards, and managerial style. Examples of corresponding methods of involvement and their rationale are

Table 9.1 Categories and forms of employee involvement

Main categories of employee involvement	Examples of related forms	Rationale
Communicative involvement: information provision/downward communication	Team briefing; other briefing groups; corporate newspapers, journals, and reports aimed at employees; videos; audiotapes; email; recorded telephone briefings	To provide information; uniform messages; to be educative or re-educative
Communicative involvement: problem-solving involvement and upward, two-way communication	Briefing groups with feedback and managerial response loops; quality improvement teams; suggestion schemes; employee surveys	Explicit access to employees' experience and skills; gain cooperation and opinions
Communicative involvement: consultation	Joint consultation committees, working parties or groups; staff forums	Providing information and testing reactions
Task involvement at job and work organizational levels	Job redesign: job enlargement, and job enrichment. Work re-organization: (semi) autonomous working groups; problem-solving involvement	To be re-educative; providing greater levels of motivation and satisfaction; empowering
Financial involvement	Employee share ownership plans; profit-related pay; performance-related pay; bonus schemes	To be re-educative; providing incentives and promoting effort
Managerial actions and style of leadership	Participative managerial style; being visible; accessible and informal; creating credibility; ensuring actions in line with key messages	To provide support; encourage positive working relationships and trust; reduce barriers

Lewis et al. (2003). *Employee Relations: Understanding the Employment Relationship,* London: Prentice Hall (p. 262).

included. These types or categories describe employee involvement that is more management directed, where the organization decides how staff are engaged. This is in contrast to employee involvement through participation in trade unions, which is discussed below. We turn now to a discussion of communication and participation in the workplace.

Communication

Employee involvement starts with internal communication. Employees can only be involved in the organization if they are kept informed. Effective communication, where the intended message is received and understood, keeps employees informed about such things as the organization's mission and objectives, organizational and HR policies, expectations for and evaluation of performance, and change in strategic direction (McKenna & Beech, 2002; Booth, Fosters, Robson & Welham, 2004). Two-way communication gives employees the opportunity to communicate with management about such things as the direction of the organization, the best ways to get there, and obstacles to performance and goal achievement. The opportunity for two-way communication is related to the degree of employee participation in organizational decision making.

Participation

Employee participation is a specific form of employee involvement which includes 'direct involvement of individuals in decisions relating to their immediate work organization and ... indirect involvement in decision making, through representatives, in the wider socio-technical and political structures of the firm' (Brannen, 1983: 16). The direct and indirect involvement of employees in organizational decision making, including policy and direction, and such processes as hiring, evaluation and rewards, and working conditions, involves a shift in the 'location and nature of power' in the organization (McKenna & Beech, 2002: 285). Although it may be difficult for management to relinquish control, doing so promotes employee involvement. There is likely some variation in the degree or depth, the scope, level, and the form of that involvement (Lewis et al., 2003).

Degree of participation refers to the extent of employees' influence over a particular decision, ranging on a continuum of no influence to complete control. Figure 9.1 illustrates the possibilities for influence that lie between these two extremes, from the 'right to receive information ... to [making] a decision jointly with management, and exercise sole control over a decision' (Lewis et al., 2003: 252). For example, a media relations officer with a professional sports team or intercollegiate athletics programme may only receive information about organizational strategic planning, or she may be consulted about certain aspects that pertain to her area of expertise (e.g., developing a corporate brand), or she may be involved in making a joint decision with management regarding the direction of the organization. The extent to which an employee has influence in decision making may be a function of the type of decision. In general, the greater the degree of influence, the greater the sense of opportunity for involvement (whether staff take advantage of that opportunity or not).

The scope or types of decisions over which employees have some degree of control is a key indicator of employees' participation in the organization. Decision types can be distinguished as strategic (what the organization is

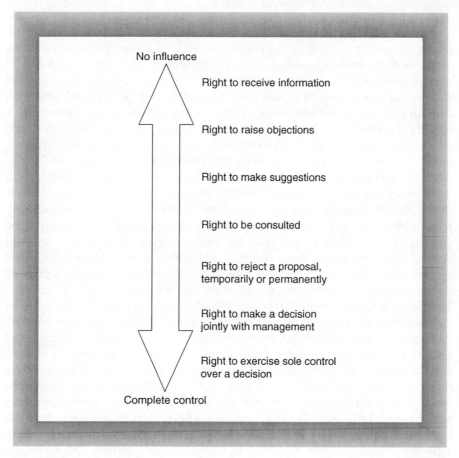

No influence

Right to receive information

Right to raise objections

Right to make suggestions

Right to be consulted

Right to reject a proposal,
temporarily or permanently

Right to make a decision
jointly with management

Right to exercise sole control
over a decision

Complete control

Figure 9.1 A continuum of employee influence over organizational decisions (Lewis et al., 2003).

doing), operational (how it is doing it), and individual task (what each person is doing as part of operations). At the least, staff should have some degree of influence over their own job tasks. Staff may be further involved in operational and even strategic decision making, directly or through a representative. To be able to participate further in operational and strategic decision making can be very rewarding for staff, because of the responsibility, challenge, and even recognition it brings. At the very least, indirect participation through a representative can promote a sense of procedural justice. Using the example of employees at a golf club (e.g., grounds crew, sales staff, 'pro shop' staff), participation can provide at least some influence over decisions regarding their own job, operations in general, and even the strategic direction of the club.

The type of decisions in which employees usually participate depends on the level of the decision and their position within the organization. That is, they are more likely to be involved in decisions that are taken at lower levels

189

of the organization and those that have an immediate impact on their day-to-day work such as individual task decisions. They are less likely to be involved in strategic and even operational decisions that are typically taken at the top management or board level. However, there are a number of exceptions to this that will determine employee involvement. As suggested above, employees may be represented by a delegate to board-level meetings, thus giving them indirect involvement at higher levels. For example, a coach's representative may sit on an intercollegiate athletics advisory council. As well, a macro-approach to strategic and operational decision making entails organization-wide involvement (McKenna & Beech, 2002); for example, a company-wide planning retreat. In smaller organizations, such as an independent fitness club, there may be a monthly or semi-annual meeting of all club staff and management where employees have an opportunity to provide input and vote on organization-level issues. Of course, employee participation in higher level decision making may be restricted to only certain decision areas (e.g., health and safety, workload, performance appraisal policies, and processes), depending on where upper management wants employee input, and where they are willing to concede control. Furthermore, Lewis et al. (2003) note that the participation of employees in decision making at the strategic level tends to be limited in practice because of logistical and attitudinal problems. Specifically, 'greater management familiarity with, and in-depth knowledge of, strategic matters, as well as their control over information, gives them a significant advantage over employee representatives' (Lewis et al., 2003: 254–255). Effective employee involvement through decision making relies on effective communication and shared influence. Finally, typically higher-level decisions may be brought to lower levels with a micro-approach (McKenna & Beech, 2002), whereby decisions are delegated to units or individuals. For example, municipal recreation department staff members responsible for a given sector of the community (e.g., seniors) might be given free reign to design and implement programmes and a marketing strategy for that particular sector.

A fourth consideration in employee participation is the form of that involvement. As already noted, it may be in the manner of direct involvement in decision making, or indirect involvement through an elected or designated representative to formal decision making bodies. The trade union is one form of representation and is discussed in more detail below. The opportunity for indirect employee participation in decision making through a trade union is dependent on the presence and strength of the union in the workplace, and by the scope of decisions on which it is able to negotiate (Lewis et al., 2003). A formal consultation arrangement is an alternative to the trade union. However, with this form of involvement, participation is typically restricted to consultation rather than negotiation where employees actually have control in the decision making process. The lesser influence in a consultation arrangement is likely due to the level of decisions and managerial attitudes towards employee participation in decision making and the associated power sharing that must be realized (Lewis et al., 2003).

Trade unions and collective bargaining

Unions are one-way employees that have formal involvement in the decision making of the organization. A union is defined as 'an organization of employees that has the objective of improving the compensation and working conditions of [unionized and non-union] employees' (Suffield, 2005: 40). In the majority of countries the right of an individual to join a trade union is enshrined in law. The primary function of a trade union is regulating the employment relationship (Lewis et al., 2003). The underlying premise of unionization is that individual employees have little voice or power when dealing with their employer, but they can increase their power as a collective group or union (Suffield, 2005). Consequently, laws such as the National Labour Relations Act in the US give employees the right to self-organization, the right to bargain collectively, and the right to engage in activities for the mutual assistance or protection of employees (including the right to strike) (Gallant, Remick & Resnick, 2005). A union is a formal body established by a vote of organizational members to represent their interests in organizational decision making related to work. Local labour laws dictate the formation and nature of unions, but they are typically potentially powerful forces in an organization, to the extent that members are united in their support of the union which represents them. Union members' involvement, or at least representation, in organizational decision making is mainly through collective bargaining, although unions can also represent individual members in connection with grievances.

There are several notable differences in the employee–management relationship in union and non-union organizations (Suffield, 2005). In a unionized organization, the legal basis for the employment relationship is a collective agreement which has been negotiated by the union. The basic terms of employment are identical for all employees in a given job category that is covered by the collective agreement; for example, the standard players contract in the collective bargaining agreement (CBA) of North America's National Hockey League Players Union (NHLPA, 2005). In a non-union organization, the legal basis for the employment relationship is individual contracts which have been negotiated individually by the employees themselves. The terms of employment may be variable and unique for each employee.

Specific statistics on trade union membership in the sport industry are not available; however, we can consider union density among employed workers in general. For example, in 2006, 12 per cent of wage and salary workers in the US were union members, which represents a drop from 12.5 per cent in 2005, and 20 per cent in 1983 (Finlayson, 2007). There is a much higher union density in Canada where 30 per cent of wage and salary workers were union members in 2006, a rate which has been steady since it dropped from 36 per cent in 1989 (Finlayson, 2007; Morisette, Schellenberg & Johnson, 2005). In Australia, union density was 20 per cent in 2007, which represents a drop from 42 per cent in 1988 (Australian Bureau of Statistics (ABS), 2004b).

In all the three countries union density is higher in the public sector than the private sector. The 36 per cent of salaried public sector workers in the US who were union members in 2006, and the 78 per cent in Canada, were primarily federal and provincial or state employees (Finlayson, 2007). In contrast, less than 8 per cent of private sector employees in the US and approximately 20 per cent in Canada were union members in 2006 (Finlayson, 2007). In Australia, trade union membership rates in the public and private sector in 2007 were 43 and 15 per cent, respectively (ABS, 2007). Statistics also indicate that, in the US, some of the lowest union membership rates are in the 'leisure and hospitality' industry (3.1 per cent; Finlayson, 2007). In Canada union membership in the 'consumer services' sector was only 11 per cent (Morisette et al., 2005), and in Australian the rate was 13 per cent in 'cultural and recreation service' (ABS, 2004b). It is within these sectors that we would expect to find many if not most sport organizations, and thus we can obtain some sense of trade union membership rates in the sport industry.

There are several reasons given for the decline in union density across industries, sectors, and countries. The drop in union membership rate has been attributed to: (1) the macro-economic climate, where high unemployment and real wage growth served to depress union density in the 1980s and 1990s in several countries; (2) the changing composition of jobs and the workforce, for example an increase in women and younger adults in the workforce, both of whom are less likely to be union members; (3) industrial relations laws which restrict the decision making scope and power of unions; (4) the attitude and conduct of employers in their opposition to union organization, or their positive efforts to provide alternatives to employee participation; and (5) the power of unions themselves as their numbers drop off and employees feel that they are being well served by the employer (Lewis et al., 2003; Morisette et al., 2005).

The existence of unions in the sport industry is variable and depends on the segment or the job category. For example, unions are prominent in professional sport leagues, for both players and officials. It is also possible that only certain types of employees within a sport organization will be members of a union; for example, trades people, machine or equipment operators, or concessions staff at sport facilities. Unions are less likely to be found in small sporting good retailers or sport marketing agencies, and in non-profit, voluntary organizations which are prominent in the sport industry (i.e., non-governmental community, state, and national sport organizations). Table 9.2 provides a brief overview of players' unions in the professional sport industry, with the example of the four major sport leagues in North America. There are several similarities and differences between their respective CBAs. For example, the collective agreements in all four players' unions are characterized by a free market system and the certification of player agents. They differ in that two unions have a hard salary cap or limit on total team payroll (NHLPA and NFLPA), while the NBPA has a soft cap with several concessions. The MLBPA has no salary cap; however, it has a payroll threshold beyond which teams must pay a competitive balance tax to lower revenue teams. All four unions have a player compensation floor or minimum salary level, however, the NHLPA also has a compensation ceiling for entry level players, while the NBPA has a ceiling for all players (to try to control what are

Table 9.2 An overview of players' unions in the North American professional sport industry (NBPA, 2005; NHLPA, 2005; NFLPA, 2006; MLBPA, 2007; Gallant et al., 2005).

	National Hockey League (NHL) Players' Association (NHLPA)	National Basketball Association (NBA) Players' Association (NBPA)	Major League Baseball (MLB) Players' Association (MLBPA)	National Football League (NFL) Players' Association (NFLPA)
Year established	1967	1954	1885, 1966	1970
Current CBA	2005–2011	2005–2011	2007–2011	2006–2011
Key features of CBA	Hard salary cap	Soft salary cap (ceiling with several exceptions)	No salary cap	Hard salary cap
	Revenue sharing across lower revenue teams	'Luxury tax' for excess payroll penalty (distributed to teams with lower payrolls)	'Competitive balance tax' for surpassing threshold (to lower revenue teams)	Fines paid to NFL and distributed to NFL-related charities
	Player compensation floor (minimum); Entry level compensation ceiling (maximum)	Player compensation floor and ceiling	Player compensation floor	Player compensation floor
	Free market system, players can move to any team when their contract expires	Free market system	Free market system	Free market system
	Regulation of player agent certification	Regulation of player agent certification	Regulation of player agent certification	Regulation of player agent certification

the highest salaries in professional sports in North America). One thing the four unions have in common is the method of collective bargaining. We turn now to a review of this form of employee involvement.

Collective bargaining

Collective bargaining is a process of negotiating a labour contract that is acceptable to both management and unionized employees. In this process, the trade union negotiates on behalf of its members on issues such as pay, benefits, workload, and working conditions. Local and national labour laws dictate what issues can be addressed through collective bargaining. These can be distinguished as substantive issues (e.g., pay, hours of work, holidays, health and safety, pensions, and training) and procedural issues (e.g., negotiation or bargaining, grievance and arbitration, and disciplinary action) (Lewis et al., 2003). The CBA is the union contract which spells out the details of these issues for a given time period, after which time the contract expires. If the union and management cannot come to a new agreement before the contract expires, employees are said to be 'without a contract,' although the terms of the previous agreement are held over until a new agreement is reached. Nonetheless, being without a contract, or sensing that the collective bargaining process may fail to establish a mutually agreed upon contract, can be the basis for industrial or 'strike' action where workers walk off the job (in essence breaking their contract with the organization). Although there is variation in national and local labour laws, typically union members vote on whether they are willing to go on strike, and ultimately vote (or let their union representatives vote) on strike action.

Collective bargaining between the professional sport leagues and their players' unions presented in Table 9.2 is an interesting case. Within each league, the team owners and management negotiate collectively with the players' union in order to reach a contract agreement. The negotiated agreement applies to each team and all players must abide by the actions of their bargaining unit (Gallant et al., 2005). The collective bargaining process in professional sports tends to be unlike the negotiations that take place in labour industries. Given the relative power of the players' unions in the professional sports industry, collective bargaining 'has been described less as negotiating over working conditions than as "two mega-corporations talking to each other about mergers or splits or sales" (Chass, 1994)' (Kovach, Hamilton & Meserole, 1997: 13).

The context for collective bargaining in professional sport is characterized by a relatively closed and sheltered labour market where only a very small percentage of athletes are likely to make it to 'the big league' (Kovach et al., 1997). Players' unions bargain collectively, but not for union-wide wages like their industry counterparts, although entry level salary floors (NBPA and NFLPA) and ceilings (NHLPA) have been introduced. Rather their focus tends to be on the rules governing the league, such as team salary caps, player-free agency, and salary arbitration (Kovach et al., 1997); that is, procedural vs. substantive issues. The issue of pay is negotiated between the individual (or their agent) and the team. The mutual interest of players' unions and the team owners is to gain what they each see as their share of the revenue pie. It is generally recognized, however, that revenues can only be maintained or increased if there is competitive balance among teams, game outcomes are fairly unpredictable, and hence fan interest continues. The collective bargaining process in professional sports is one of finding a mutually agreeable system of player mobility and salary restrictions, with the intent of balancing teams and limiting spending (Kovach et al., 1997).

Organizations often resist the idea of unionization, because of the inevitable shift in power, and what many deem to be a much more rigid and less managerial decision making structure (Lewis et al., 2003). On the other hand, sometimes organizations embrace unions because they simplify the bargaining process because the workforce speaks with 'one voice' and managers have only one bargaining unit to deal with. Furthermore, to the extent that 'management and unions have learned to cooperate more effectively in the negotiation process, CBAs have become an important tool for ensuring positive relations between employees and the organization, and for making workers and the workplace more productive' (Covell, Walker, Siciliano & Hess, 2003: 335). Also, unions give employees a voice where they otherwise might not have one. Where employees do have a voice, through both macro- and micro-level participation, they may be generally content with the employee–organization relationship and less likely to feel the need for the formal collective voice of a union.

Consider the following case of the evolution of a players union in the Australian Rugby League:

Evolution of a Professional Sport Union: The Case of the Rugby League Professionals Association

The Rugby League Professionals Association (RLPA) represents all players in the National Rugby League (NRL), New South Wales (NSW) Premier League, and Jersey Flegg Competitions. The RLPA is an independent organization governed by a constitution and overseen by a board of directors and a national president. The RLPA appoints two delegates from each NRL club who are invited to meetings and can express comment at any time. There has been an interesting evolution of the representative bodies for professional rugby league players – from a players association to a registered labour union and back to a non-union players association again.

History

In 1979, former rugby league player Arthur Beetson called a meeting to establish the Association of Rugby League Players (Association).

In 1980 the Association was formally registered under the Trade Union Act (1881). Until the mid-1980s, the Association was led by former player and coach, Jack Gibson. In 1985, John Adam, a retired player and qualified solicitor, took on the role of President.

The 1980s saw widely publicized player dissatisfaction over salaries. John Adam was able to use his legal training to help out some players with their contract negotiations. However at this stage, the Association refrained from making any formal or legal representation on behalf of its members. According to former player Steve Rogers, this led to a negative perception of the Association among the players.

'From the talk in the sheds at the time, the union then may have helped one or two guys but any more than that I would doubt it ... they were hardly ever seen around'.[1]

The situation was dramatically reversed in the early 1990s. Kevin Ryan, a former player, and a barrister and State MP, was elected as Association President in 1990. Ryan's first challenge was the highly controversial NSW Rugby League (NSWRL[2]) 'Player draft'.

In 1990, NSWRL proposed a draft system whereby players would simply be assigned to a club, regardless of their individual preferences or where they were living. In a letter to NSWRL, Kevin Ryan made it clear that the players and the Association were 'positively opposed' to the draft and advised them to take heed of this. Despite the Association's opposition to the draft, NSWRL argued that that the system was not an unreasonable restraint of trade or a breach of state or federal legislation and began implementing the draft.

In 1991, the case went to the Federal Court, where Judge Wilcox ruled in favour of the rugby league players (1991:103 ALR 319). This was a crucial victory for both the players and the Association. Association membership rose to around 600, and in 1991 the Association aligned itself with the Labour Council of NSW and changed its name to the Rugby League Players Union (Union). According to former player and former RLPA President Tony Butterfield, the Federal Court victory showed that 'the Union was actually in existence. They really stuck with the challenge and at

[1] Interview by Tilda Khoshaba on 3 March 2003, published in 'The rise and fall of the Rugby League Players' Union: 1979–2000'.
[2] Prior to the introduction of SuperLeague in 1997, NSWRL owned and ran the first grade rugby league competition in Australia. SuperLeague folded in 1999 and the elite competition is now administered by the NRL.

times when the players seemed to lose sight of why we were doing this the Union was there to set us straight.'[3]

In 1994, another rugby league players' union – a part of the sports section of the Media Entertainment Arts Alliance (MEAA) – was established. Over the next 5 years neither of the two unions proved popular or effective.

In 2000, retired player, Tony Butterfield commenced organizing players under the banner of a new organization, separate to the MEAA and the Union, called the RLPA. Around the same time support for the original Union waned, resulting in it being formally deregistered in 2001 for failure to comply with its rules concerning the election of officers and reporting responsibilities under the Industrial Relations Act (1996, NSW). The newly formed RLPA, which functioned as an association, was boosted by the leadership of Butterfield. With his tough and uncompromising personality, Butterfield reignited interest in the RLPA and began to restore its respect and credibility. Slowly, the RLPA gained members and profile.

In April 2002, the NRL hosted a meeting of all team captains and a senior player representative from each club to discuss a new contracting system and a territorial draft. At this meeting, the RLPA presented an agreement to be signed by the NRL that formally recognized the RLPA's role as a truly representative body of the players. The signing of this document signaled the start of negotiations for the first ever CBA for professional rugby league players.

Collective bargaining agreement

During 2002, the RLPA grew increasingly frustrated by the lack of traction on the development of a CBA and were unconvinced of the NRL's commitment to finalizing the agreement. In September 2003, the RLPA gave the NRL a 48-hour deadline to make significant progress on 6 critical issues with the threat of boycotting the Dally M Awards, which could have resulted in the elite players not attending the annual gala event at which the best player in the game is recognized. The progress that the NRL claimed to have made was deemed insufficient by the RLPA and the 2003 Dally M Awards were cancelled. Records show that no awards were made to players for that year.

On 24 February 2004, Butterfield re-aligned the RLPA with the union movement in NSW. The RLPA became the first sporting body in Australia to be registered under the Workplace Relations Act

---

[3] Interview by Tilda Khoshaba on 10 August 2003, published in 'The rise and fall of the Rugby League Players' Union: 1979–2000'.

(1996, C'th). The MEAA did not oppose this registration. Four months later agreement was reached on the new CBA. The Salary Cap for each club was established; $3.3 million in 2005, to be raised 2 per cent the following year. Under this cap, the NRL and the RLPA agreed to a minimum wage of $55,000 for the top 17 players in each club, and $37,500 for the remaining top 25 players. Any player not on a minimum wage would receive a minimum match payment for every first grade appearance and players with jobs outside football now had to be reimbursed for loss of income when required to attend training. Players participating in State of Origin or International matches were awarded a large increase in payments.

The NRL agreed to provide a monthly Club Grant to ensure that player's salaries were paid in case of club default. Contract termination provisions for injured players were extended and the NRL agreed to fund injury remediation for 1 year after the player's last contract. As well, new Education and Welfare provisions were introduced that committed the clubs' and the NRL to investing a total of $1 million per year towards player welfare and educational training.

Despite the fraught and protracted negotiations and planning, the RLPA CBA has since become a model for other Australian sports. Tony Butterfield's role in securing the agreement earned him the NSW Labour Council's 2004 Organizer of the Year Award.

In 2006, the RLPA underwent a restructure to achieve greater involvement from its members. Former player Matt Rodwell was appointed as chief executive officer (CEO), replacing Butterfield and his role of President. Other current players Simon Woolford, Luke Priddis, and Clint Newton were installed as National President, Treasurer, and Vice President, respectively.

Rodwell's first imperative as CEO was to forge closer and friendlier ties with the NRL. In doing so, he agreed (subject to a members, vote) to deregister the RLPA as a union. In return, the NRL pledged $320,000 in annual funding for the RLPA. Rodwell's aim is to re-structure the RLPA along the lines of the Australian Football League Players Association (AFLPA) and the Rugby Union Players Association (RUPA). Both associations are based on an 'independent advocate model', supported by funds from the game as well as memberships and corporate sponsorship.

'We're not coming under the umbrella of the NRL, we'll still be independent,' Rodwell stated.[4]

As the RLPA continues to evolve and assert its position with the game, the next few years will be crucial to its future. 'We are confident of having 100 per cent membership in the 2007 season,' Rodwell claimed.[5] Alongside a large membership drive, arrangements are being concluded for the new 2007–2010 CBA.

Discussion questions

1. What are the advantages and disadvantages of a players union in professional sport? Why might a non-union association be more effective?
2. What are the implications of player unions for employee relations? Can they help or hinder a productive workplace while satisfying the needs of employees?

[4] Sydney Morning Herald, September 27, 2006.
[5] RLPA media release 'RLPA Dismisses Secret Funding Deal Claims', February 2, 2007. www.myfooty.com.au/newsdetail.asp ?News_ID=106

Grievance

Despite an organization's best attempts to provide a workplace that is productive for the organization and rewarding to employees, dissatisfaction is inevitable. This can occur if an individual's needs are not met, their formal or psychological contract is violated, or they have a sense of unfair or ill treatment in the organization. When dissatisfaction is expressed overtly, the organization needs to be prepared to address the employee(s) concerns. Just as providing a positive working environment is critical to employee relations, so too is providing a mechanism for expressing concerns about that environment. At a basic level, a complaint is a 'spoken or written [dissatisfaction] of which supervisors or managers are made aware' (Lewis et al., 2003: 282). Further to that, a grievance is a complaint that is 'presented formally to management or a union official through the use of a recognized procedure' (Lewis et al., 2003: 282). The grievance procedure is reviewed here.

An employee, or group of employees, may have a grievance in relation to (1) the conditions of employment (e.g., pay, physical conditions, job design), (2) ideology in the workplace (e.g., person-organization goal conflict, perceptions of inequity), and (3) relationships (e.g., employee–management, union–management, discrimination, harassment) (Lewis et al., 2003). The latter group constitutes the most common basis of grievance (Lewis et al., 2003).

An organization must have an effective grievance procedure in place so that employees feel they have a viable mechanism for dealing with contract violations and unfair treatment (Booth et al., 2004). A formal grievance procedure is typically built into the CBA of any trade union. However, an organization need not rely on a union to establish a process for dealing with formal complaints in a fair and timely way.

There are several basic steps and elements in any grievance procedure, which are as follows:

1. Attempt informal resolution first. A complaint is more likely to be resolved amicably or in a collegial fashion at an early stage. According to Booth et al. (2004: 102), 'mediating between two aggrieved individuals is often far quicker and easier than immediately suggesting they turn to the [formal] grievance procedure to resolve their differences.' However, a formal process must be available at any point if an employee is not comfortable with an informal discussion, perhaps because of a power differential or the nature of the ill treatment, or feels he or she is not being taken seriously.
2. If informal resolution is unsuccessful or inappropriate, there is a move to formal resolution. This involves the following:
   (a) The complainant or griever provides a written submission to his or her supervisor (or higher if the supervisor is directly involved in the complaint) or union outlining the issue.
   (b) An initial meeting is held, with subsequent meetings as necessary, to investigate the grievance. The complainant is able to be accompanied to any grievance meeting by a colleague or union representative.
   (c) Specific timelines for a decision on the grievance are communicated.
   (d) A decision is rendered by the organization, which may or may not be acceptable to the complainant.
3. If there is no resolution, the grievance may move to arbitration, where an independent body renders a final decision.

In any grievance procedure the following considerations should be taken (Lewis et al., 2003; Booth et al., 2004):

- Attempt to deal with grievances quickly and fairly, 'before they develop into major problems and possibly collective disputes' (Lewis et al., 2003: 286).
- Make all employees and management aware of their right to grieve, and the grievance procedure in the organization. This includes informing the employee of his or her right to appeal the decision, and potential disciplinary action if the grievance is upheld (e.g., formal apology, transfer, termination).
- Maintain written records of all formal interactions during the grievance process, in support of interactional, procedural, and ultimately distributive justice.

Members of a union are bound to a formal grievance procedure for their own protection. If any steps are not followed by either party (employees or management) it amounts to a breach of contract, with further consequences for employees or management. A formal grievance process may be challenging in a small sport organization; for example, a private fitness or sports club where there are relatively few staff and the owner is the supervisor, or there is one manager below the owner. In this case the head of the organization has an obligation to deal with the situation as impartially as possible.

Health, safety, and wellness

Every sport organization has a moral and legal obligation to provide a safe and healthy working environment. We begin this section by considering hazards and risks at work, and conclude with a review of employee assistance and wellness programmes.

Workplace hazards and risks

A safe workplace is one that is relatively free from hazards and risk. A workplace hazard is 'any source of potential damage, harm, or adverse health effects on . . . someone under certain conditions at work' (Canadian Centre for Occupational Health and Safety (CCOHS), 2005: 1). Hazards may be classified as biological (e.g., bacteria, viruses), chemical, ergonomic (e.g., repetitive movements, improper workstation), physical (e.g., radiation, electric shock, lighting, noise, temperature), psychosocial (e.g., harassment, violence), and safety (e.g., slipping, equipment malfunction) (CCOHS, 2005). In the sport organization setting, hazards may include substances or materials such as pool chemicals or cleaning agents, workplace conditions such as wet floors, excessive noise or overcrowding, and certain job practices such as outdoor adventure instruction, race car driving, or fitness class instruction (CCOHS, 2005).

Risk is the 'probability that a person will be harmed or experience an adverse heath effect if exposed to a hazard' (CCOHS, 2005: 1). For example, we can expect that the risk of harm or adverse health effect in the form of fatigue or injury increases in direct relation to the number of fitness classes an instructor teaches back to back, and the level of those classes. The chance of harm to lifeguards is inherently high because of their workplace conditions (i.e., wet floors, proximity to a body of water).

While some hazards cannot be eliminated, the risk of harm or adverse effect can be controlled. It is incumbent on the organization to ensure that the employees are aware of the hazards and risks of a job, and of the procedures the organization has in place to minimize the risk or potentially harmful effect of the hazard. Employees must in turn take some responsibility for being aware of their working environment, and adhering to safety procedures and standards. A job hazard analysis, similar to a job analysis described in Chapter 3, is a systematic way to identify potential accidents or hazards associated with a particular job, and to design appropriate preventative measures (CCOHS, 2005). A sample job hazard analysis worksheet is presented in Figure 9.2. The analysis should be conducted by directly observing the employee doing his or her job, with follow-up discussion to ensure all

Job:		
Analysis by:	Reviewed by:	Approved by:
Date:	Date:	Date:
Sequence of steps	*Potential accidents or hazards*	*Prevention measures*

Figure 9.2 A sample job hazard analysis worksheet (reprinted with permission from the CCOHS, 1998).

steps or activities have been accounted for. For example, a supervisor can analyze the job hazards experienced by a gymnastics coach by observing that person as he or she conducts classes or training sessions. The supervisor can pay attention to what the coach does to prepare him or herself for the physical work involved, the actual tasks involved, time on task, rest periods, and so on. The coach can then discuss what he or she considers to be hazardous and risky activities. The job hazard analysis may be most relevant for employees who do physical work in potentially hazardous conditions. However, workstation design can also be critical to the health and safety of office workers (e.g., gym club receptionist, sports information officer, sports team head office staff).

Hazards and risks can be controlled by (1) elimination of the hazard from the workplace (e.g., removing asbestos, eliminating outdoor adventure classes); (2) engineering controls, which involves re-designing the workplace so that the hazard or risk is reduced (e.g., improved ventilation, reconfiguring equipment or workstations); (3) administrative controls, which involves altering the way the work is done (e.g., shift length, programme scheduling) and work practices standards (e.g., training, personal hygiene); and (4) personal protective equipment worn by employees to reduce the risk of harm (e.g., water shoes for lifeguards, sun hats for camp counsellors) (CCOHS, 2006).

The organization also has an obligation to provide a workplace where employees are not at risk of, and do not suffer from, excessive levels of stress (e.g., Booth et al., 2004). Stress has physical, psychological, and behavioural ramifications, ranging from headaches and sweating to anxiety and job dissatisfaction, to reduced performance and turnover (Robbins & Langdon, 2003). Understanding what contributes to stress in the workplace can help to alleviate or avoid it. Stress is a condition caused by an individual's inability to cope with constraints or demands (Robbins & Langdon, 2003). The more important and uncertain the outcome of a given situation, the more stressful is that situation. For example, a tournament organizer will be more stressed by the demands of getting the event ready to go if she is very committed to the event, but is uncertain whether it will go well. A tournament organizer in a similar situation will be less stressed if he does put a high priority on the event and/or is fairly confident everything will go well.

The hazards and risks presented earlier can be a source of stress in the workplace. Work-related factors that are most likely to lead to stress are 'poor internal communications, lack of resources, and a decrease in staffing resulting in an increase in workload' (Booth et al., 2004: 96). However, stress is not caused by work factors alone. Non-work stress is believed to contribute to an overall level of personal stress that has implications for employee satisfaction and performance at work. Organizations must try to prevent or at least reduce workplace stress by managing the above-noted sources of stress and controlling workplace hazards. In addition, employee assistance programmes (EAPs) exist to help staff deal with stress resulting from various sources (Booth et al., 2004).

Employee assistance and wellness programmes

Employee assistance is a general term that refers to a variety of confidential counselling services that are made available to employees (McKenna & Beech, 2002). EAPs are an employer-sponsored, non-financial extrinsic benefit or reward (see Chapter 8 for a review of rewards). The intent of an EAP is to help an employee whose job performance may be adversely affected by personal problems. Services can include support pertaining to mental health, substance abuse, marital problems, parenting problems, and financial management. Many of the problems that affect an individual's work performance are in fact not work related. However, it is in the organization's best interests to provide support to help its employees deal with any issues that may ultimately impact productivity and employee satisfaction. In-house EAPs, where counselling is provided on-site, tend to be found only in very large corporations. Instead, it is more common to outsource employee assistance services, which also has the advantage of a greater sense of confidentiality and impartiality.

The elements of EAPs tend to be fairly standard across all types of organizations, with some variation in the extent of services supported, and some variation in organization-specific services that may be included. For example, the EAP in several of the CBAs in the professional sports industry reviewed in Table 9.2 focus on support for recreational and performance-enhancing substance abuse.

A more proactive approach to a healthy workforce is the concept of employee wellness programmes. The recent attention to employee wellness in and beyond the workplace is a result of the acknowledged impact that overall physical, mental, and emotional health can have on employee attendance, performance, and retention, with potentially substantial savings to the organization. Thus, the wellness approach to employee health 'focuses on preventing accidents, injuries, or illnesses before they happen' (Covell et al., 2003: 334). This proactive approach encourages employees 'to engage in a range of behaviours and activities associated with better health' (Covell et al., 2003: 334), including regular exercise and better nutrition, regular medical examinations, and financial planning. In-house or outsourced educational seminars on a variety of topics related to a healthy lifestyle complement counselling services offered through an EAP, all in support of a productive workforce. Employee assistance and wellness programmes come at a (sometimes great) cost to an organization. Yet, 'these expenses are generally found to be much lower than the potential productivity gains from a healthy work force' (Covell et al., 2003: 334). In addition, the wellness programme may add to the attractiveness of the organization as a place to work and might be used in recruiting new staff and as a point of differentiation from the benefits offered by competitor organizations.

Volunteer–organization relations

Many of the employee relations principles and practices that have been outlined in this chapter are equally relevant to ensuring a productive and mutually satisfying relationship between the organization and volunteers. The sport organization and its volunteers have reciprocal obligations, which are described below. Like employees, volunteers have a psychological contract with their organization (Taylor, Darcy, Hoye & Cuskelly, 2006), and equally value justice in the organization's practices and processes. Volunteer involvement is critical, as one of the main reasons they contribute their time and effort is to make a difference in the organization (Cuskelly, Hoye & Auld, 2006). Although communication with volunteers may be more challenging than with employees who have a more regular schedule and contractual link with the organization, it is equally important to their involvement in the organization that volunteers are kept informed. Volunteer involvement is also enhanced through participation in decision making, with consideration for the degree and scope of that influence, and level and form of involvement. The health and safety of volunteers is of critical importance to the organization. In addition to the hazards and risks noted earlier, volunteers may be susceptible to liability in certain sport-specific situations, and the organization has an obligation to offer legal protection. For example, the majority of volunteer coaches work with children and youth who are a vulnerable population.

While the sport organization needs to protect its participants, it also needs to protect the volunteers who provide programming and services to those participants.

As with employees, the relationship between the organization and its volunteers must be based on exchange, where volunteers realize valued intrinsic and sometimes non-financial rewards as a result of their involvement and contributions to the organization. The organization also has a social and moral obligation to treat its volunteers well (cf. Chelladurai, 2006). Volunteering Australia (2003: 1) provides a list of volunteer rights, based on moral and legal obligations as follows:

- to work in a healthy and safe environment;
- to be interviewed and engaged in accordance with equal opportunity and anti-discrimination legislation;
- to be adequately covered by insurance;
- to be given accurate information about the organization;
- to be reimbursed for out-of-pocket expenses;
- to be given a copy of the organization's volunteer policy and any other policy that affects one's work;
- not to do the work of paid staff during industrial disputes;
- to have a job description and agreed working hours;
- to have access to a grievance procedure;
- to be provided with orientation to the organization;
- to be provided with sufficient training to do one's job.

In turn, sport volunteers have an obligation to honour their commitment to the organization by undertaking their responsibilities in a timely and conscientious manner, and with respect and integrity (Volunteer Canada, 2006). Again, positive volunteer relations are based on practices and processes that engender a productive working environment that is satisfying to sport volunteers.

Termination of employment

A final consideration in employee relations is the termination of the employment relationship. The employment, or volunteer, relationship ends because of dismissal, resignation, or retirement. When an employee resigns or a volunteer leaves, a sport organization may wish to conduct an exit interview or survey to determine why the individual chose to terminate the relationship.

Dismissal

An employee's employment may be terminated because of dismissal by the employer, defined as an involuntary requirement for the employee to leave the organization. 'Fair' reasons for dismissal include: (1) conclusion of a fixed-term contract, (2) gross misconduct, (3) lack of capability or qualifications for the job, or (4) redundancy through organizational downsizing (Lewis et al., 2003). A volunteer is most likely to be 'dismissed' because he or she has reached the end of a fixed term on a sport organization's board of directors.

Gross misconduct can be distinguished from general and serious misconduct. General misconduct can be characterized by such things as absenteeism or poor performance, while serious misconduct may be characterized by unaccounted absences or a refusal to perform. In contrast, gross misconduct is defined by particularly serious offences such as theft or fraud, violence or abusive behaviour, deliberate damage to company property, significant incapability, or severe insubordination (Lewis et al., 2003). In law, such gross misconduct represents an immediate repudiation of the contract by the employee and usually confers the right on the employer to move to immediate dismissal. Repeated acts of general misconduct may constitute serious misconduct, and repeated acts of serious misconduct may constitute gross misconduct.

Lack of capability or qualifications is a fair grounds for dismissal 'if an employee lacks the skills, aptitude, physical health, or correct qualifications to carry out the duties of the job' (Lewis et al., 2003: 349). This may be due to long-term illness or a series of short-term illnesses, or an inherent inability to do the job (Lewis et al., 2003). The latter may be realized because of ineffective hiring, but it may be more likely to occur when one's job has changed to include tasks that the employee is not capable of undertaking. For example, an administrative officer of a growing private sports club who was hired when all tasks were done manually finds himself increasingly being asked to work with different data management software and he is not keen to learn how to use these applications. If he is unwilling to upgrade his skills to handle this new aspect of his job, he may have to be dismissed and replaced with someone who has the capability and aptitude required in this changed job role.

A third 'fair' reason for dismissal is redundancy because an employee's job no longer exists. This could be the case with the administrative officer in the example above, if the position itself was deemed to no longer exist (rather than just being redesigned). Redundancy occurs when positions are eliminated and resurrected in different forms (as could happen with a renaming of the administrative officer position), or are eliminated altogether because of downsizing. For example, a fitness club may dismiss one or more instructors if the classes they teach are discontinued.

We have focused on reasons for 'fair' dismissal, which presumes there can be 'unfair' dismissal. In most developed countries, the law prohibits employers from unreasonably, harshly or unfairly dismissing workers and sets out legal remedies should this occur. Specific potential reasons for claims of unfair dismissal are on grounds of gender or racial discrimination, joining a trade union, pregnancy or childbirth, taking or seeking parental leave, taking action to ensure health and safety standards are observed, retail employee refusing to work on Sundays, and taking lawful organized strike action (Lewis et al., 2003). Employees have recourse to claim compensation from the employer for unfair dismissal. Employers may also 'wrongfully' dismiss workers in which case an employee can sue for damages under common law as a civil remedy. The typical basis for a claim for wrongful dismissal is where an employer has improperly terminated a fixed-term contract. This circumstance is one that may apply to players contracted to professional sports clubs who are terminated before the expiry of the contract. If there is not a clause in the contract allowing this, or if the termination is not on contractually specified reasons, then the player may have grounds to claim 'wrongful dismissal.'

Resignation or retirement

Alternatively, an individual's employment may be terminated because of resignation or retirement, or voluntary departure. As noted earlier, volunteers may be dismissed from their role when their fixed term, such as on a board of directors, comes to an end. However, they are most likely to end their relationship with a sport organization because they choose to resign or retire from their position. Employee resignation or retirement may be due to age or health-related reasons, taking a job elsewhere, or following a spouse or partner to a different geographical location (Lewis et al., 2003). Resignation may also be due to breach of contract by the employer. Also known as 'constructive dismissal,' this form of resignation involves the employee terminating the contract (resigning) because of the employer's conduct with regard to changing the terms or conditions of employment without the employee's knowledge or consent (e.g., reduction in pay, change in position, work location or hours) (Lewis et al., 2003). If a sporting goods retailer decided to eliminate the sales staff's salary and put them on commission-only wages, they could claim constructive dismissal upon resigning from this less than desirable situation if they did not consent to the new pay structure. In the example of the administrative officer of the private sports club, if he decided to resign his position he could claim constructive dismissal as the basis for his resignation if he did not agree to the position changing to include different duties. Another grounds for constructive dismissal is harassment or abuse by the employer (Ontario Ministry of Labour, 2006).

Termination and severance pay

As a last gesture of the employee–management relationship, an organization may be required to provide termination pay, which is compensation in place of sufficient termination notice. Some employment standards laws exclude employees who are dismissed because of misconduct from receiving termination pay (e.g., Ontario Ministry of Labour, 2006). Termination pay is usually a 'lump sum payment equal to the regular wages for a regular work week that an employee would have earned during the notice period had notice been given' (Ontario Ministry of Labour, 2006: 5). In contrast, severance pay may be provided to employees to compensate them for loss of seniority and job-related benefits when their employment has been 'severed.' Employment is considered to be severed if the employee is dismissed, laid off for an extended period (e.g., at least 35 weeks in a 52 week period; Ontario Ministry of Labour, 2006), or laid off because the organization's business is permanently discontinued. Labour laws in different countries and regions dictate who qualifies for severance pay (e.g., minimum length of employment with an organization), and what organizations are obligated to provide such compensation (e.g., based on minimum payroll). To illustrate, a sales associate with a sporting goods store that is part of a national chain should receive termination pay if he or she is dismissed immediately without written notice. That same sales associate should also receive severance pay if he or she has been with the organization for a minimum period of time (e.g., 5 years; Ontario Ministry of Labour, 2006).

Exit interviews

When an employee resigns or a volunteer leaves, a sport organization may choose to undertake an exit interview or survey. The purpose is to try to understand, and identify patterns in, reasons for resignation. For example, are staff leaving because of pay levels, working conditions, the job or task itself (e.g., challenge, responsibility, boredom), the supervisor and his or her leadership style, relationships with colleagues, and so on. A sport organization may be inherently curious to know why an employee or volunteer chose to leave, with the understanding that it might try to do something to improve on particularly problematic areas. However, Torrington and Hall (1998) suggest that the data collected through exit interviews may not be very accurate. If an employee has already secured a new job, he may be not be able to clearly recall why he really left his original job; for example, if a coach is getting a higher salary at a new club, he may indicate that he left the last club because of low pay, when the primary reason was really because of lack of autonomy with respect to handling his team. Also, a former employee may still be hoping for reference letters from the organization, and so will be reluctant to say what she really thinks about the workplace. Nonetheless, the exit interview can provide the departing employee or volunteer with 'a chance to give some constructive feedback, and to leave on a positive note, with good relations and mutual respect' (Chapman, 2005: 1).

The exit interview may be conducted face-to-face, by phone, or as a survey which the departing employee or volunteer completes on-site or at home (either a pen and paper or online survey). The focus of an exit interview is typically on reasons for leaving, reflections on the positive and negative aspects of the organization, level of satisfaction with various aspects of the workplace (e.g., pay, workload, safety, training, promotion opportunities, leadership), the individual's job, and the organization in general. Table 9.3 provides a sample of questions from an exit survey that is conducted with former staff of a fitness club chain. Ideally, the individual would have an opportunity to elaborate on his or her answers, allowing that person to reflect on each aspect and providing the organization with more in-depth information. However, it can be a challenge to recruit departing employees and volunteers to take part in this voluntary process.

Table 9.3 Sample questions from an exit interview for departing staff of a fitness club (rating scale of 1 Unacceptable to 10 Perfect).
1. How would you rate the resources available to you to do your job?
2. How would you rate how well you were appreciated and thanked for your work?
3. How would you rate the skill development and training opportunities available to you?
4. How would you rate the level of teamwork, and people available to turn to for help?
5. How would you rate the flexibility of your work schedule, and/or work arrangements?
6. How would you rate the level of trust and respect you had for your manager?
7. How would you rate the career opportunities available to you?
8. How would you rate your salary or hourly wage?
9. How would you rate the commission and bonus portion of your pay?
10. How likely are you to recommend this club to your friends and/or family as a place to work?

Summary

Employee relations are defined as the activities and processes that maintain a productive workplace while satisfying the needs of employees. Employee–management relations are based on mutual obligations, which are reflected in the employee's psychological contract with the organization. Critical to positive employee relations is a sense of organizational justice. Staff and volunteers alike need to perceive that their working environment is characterized by distributive, procedural, and/or interactional justice. In general, the principles and practices associated with employee relations apply to volunteer relations with the organization as well.

Central to positive relations is the strategic process of employee and volunteer involvement. Effective communication and participation in decision making are two critical mechanisms for promoting employee involvement. Trade unions are another mechanism for employee involvement, as union members have a collective voice when negotiating or bargaining with the organization over working conditions such as pay, benefits, workload, and grievance procedures.

Formal grievance procedures in the union and non-union environment provide employees with the opportunity to seek recourse for what they perceive to be breach of contract or ill treatment. The grievance process must be well laid out and communicated to employees and volunteers, so that they know there is a fair and just mechanism in place for handling formal complaints.

A safe and healthy workplace must be provided to employees and volunteers. This means that the working environment must be relatively free from biological, chemical, ergonomic, physical, and psychosocial hazards. Controlling the risk of harm or adverse health affect due to hazards is the mutual responsibility of the organization and its employees and volunteers. Employee assistance and wellness programmes may be instituted to help staff deal with non-work personal problems that may affect their performance in the workplace.

The employee relationship will end with dismissal, resignation, or retirement. Grounds for employee dismissal may be the conclusion of a fixed-term contract, gross misconduct, lack of capability or qualifications, or redundancy. When an employee resigns, the organization may conduct an exit interview or survey to attempt to understand the reasons for the departure, as well as to gather any insight into the former employee's positive and negative experiences in the organization.

Discussion questions

1. Refer to an organization for which you have worked or volunteered. What efforts are there to promote employee or volunteer involvement, if any? (Consider communication, participation in decision making, or any other forms of involvement.) Is employee or volunteer involvement effective in that organization? How could it be improved?
2. Using the example of employees at a private golf club, design a plan to involve different types of staff in different types and levels of decisions. How much influence should they have (see Figure 9.1)?
3. Take a look at the CBA of one or more professional sport players' associations. Many are publicly available on the World Wide Web. What particular aspects of the CBA stand out for you? What is the strategic rationale behind the key features of each CBA?
4. Think of a sport organization with which you are most familiar. Describe various types of work hazards in that organization. What is the risk associated with each of those hazards (noting any variation by job type)? What does the organization do, if anything, to reduce the hazards and the risk of harm or adverse affect?
5. Look up the employment standards act in your state, province, or country. How is dismissal defined? What is the legal procedure for fair dismissal by an employer?
6. Design an exit interview or survey for volunteer coaches. What questions would you ask? What form would it take (personal or phone interview, pen and paper survey, online survey)? How would you encourage departing coaches to provide the desired information?

10 Succession and talent management

Chapter overview

Succession and talent management is a strategic and systematic process that focuses on ensuring the availability and sustainability of an adequate supply of capable employees and volunteers who are ready to assume key roles in the sport organization. In this chapter we discuss how succession and talent management provides a basis for ensuring that the right people are in the right place at the right time to achieve the organization's goals and deliver on its strategies. Issues such as the aging of the workforce, decreasing tenure within an organization as people change jobs and careers at an unprecedented rate, and effects of the downsizing and outsourcing of expertise, all challenge sport organizations to develop strategies to sustain performance and retain 'talented' performers and contributors.

As discussed in Chapter 3 on human resource (HR) planning, SHRM requires sport organizations to respond to the changing nature of work and anticipated roles of employees and volunteers into the future. Succession and talent management strategies aim to develop HR capability and enable organizations to respond to change. This is achieved via adopting an SHRM approach that targets the retention of talented and essential employees and volunteers, provides them with development opportunities and career paths, and responds to evolving leadership capability requirements (Taylor, Watt & Bennett, 2004). In succession management programmes individuals are evaluated and promoted for their contributions to the organization-wide effort in order to keep the individual in the organization, to minimize attrition of talent and to limit the organization's vulnerability to inevitable upheavals and change (Cohn, Khurana & Reeves, 2005).

Jacobs (2005) points to the 2003 Corporate Leadership Council's study on succession management as evidence of the benefits of effective succession management and highlights the strategic imperative for disciplined talent management. The Council's study found that organizations with top-tier leadership teams achieve shareholder return that is 10 percent higher than that of their industry peers. The use of succession and talent management provides a framework to build 'bench strength', that is, a healthy supply of employees and volunteers with needed capabilities, knowledge, and skills. It can reinforce organizational certainty and sustainability by providing talented and committed individuals with indicators of possible future advancement, a factor which has been identified as a key variable in the retention of individuals identified as having exceptional potential (Beeson, 2000).

What is succession management?

Succession management is a comprehensive set of assessment and development processes that support the attraction, development, reward, and retention of talented individuals, from entry level positions through to senior management. Effective talent optimization requires clear delineation of the organization's strategic priorities, leader success profiles, and capacity needs. Managing talent is located within a cycle of assessment, development, and talent deployment that includes identifying and developing internal talent as well as selecting new talent external to the organization (Bernthal & Wellins, 2006). Succession management incorporates a broad range of standardized performance evaluation methods and gathers information on employee and volunteer performance from multiple perspectives. It is designed to supplement subjective manager judgements of potential with independent objective assessment data related to key succession criteria (Taylor & McGraw, 2004).

Succession and talent management can be described using a professional baseball team analogy (Kesler, 2002: 1):

> The New York Yankees and the Atlanta Braves baseball teams have competed brilliantly in that American pastime on the basis of deep bench strength and the development of exceptional players in their minor-league organizations. While occasional championship teams buy their way in with newly acquired veteran teams, the Yankees and the Braves have demonstrated the power of relentless scouting, growing the most-talented farm teams and skilfully managing the movement of players through the system, with a constant eye on the depth of bench hitters and the pitching in the bullpens. They also occasionally acquire seasoned, star-quality players to fill specific gaps, but they do so as part of a larger strategy for building depth. From 1991 to 2001, the Braves won their division in all but one year, while winning four league championships and one World Series. The Yankees won four World Series in the six years between 1996 and 2001.

Many business leaders have similar ambitions about their organization's management teams but most 'can only dream about the kind of depth that the perennial champions of baseball' (Kesler, 2002: 1).

Succession management programmes can encompass employees and volunteers from the top of the organization, the CEO or Director of the Board, down through the ranks. Depending on the size of the organization or the position under consideration different approaches to succession and talent management and to the types of opportunities provided for employees and volunteers to gain particular skills, knowledge, and capabilities, may be taken. For example, a sport organization may target an individual role (volunteer board role), particular professional expertise

213

(merchandise and licensing manager) or more general classifications (programme coordinator).

Most organizations focus succession management efforts on senior leadership roles in the first instance, with a view to extending the process into other critical roles at lower classification levels in the future (Rioux & Bernthal, 1999; Bernthal & Wellins, 2006). These 'top end' processes are often aimed at CEO replacement, that is the 'transference of ultimate executive authority from one to another' (Santora, Clemens & Sarros, 1997: 109). The development for these senior leadership roles may focus on ensuring that candidates experience a wide range of challenging assignments to widely develop their capabilities and include work placements tailored to individual learning needs, along with training programmes and executive coaching.

Other organizations have identified critical roles first, such as ticketing technology specialists, statistical analysts, front-line operators. For these roles, the focus may be on multi-skilling a number of candidates to ensure that there are contingencies in place should a position become vacant. Succession management can also be targeted at professional roles, where expertise is not readily available outside the organization and is not likely to be a focus for development anywhere outside the organization (e.g., High Performance Logistics Manager). For these specialist roles, the focus may be on ongoing and rigorous development of professional expertise as well as broader development of management and leadership capabilities. Transferring highly specialized professional expertise to others within the organization through activities such as 'shadowing' is critical when there is no option to 'buy in' the expertise.

Developing entire cohorts of staff or volunteers through leadership and management development and other training initiatives, rather than focusing specifically on those with demonstrated leadership potential is another approach used. These broader succession and talent management programmes are, 'designed to ensure the continued effective performance of an organization, division, department or workgroup by making provision for the development and replacement of key people over time' (Rothwell, 1994: 5). A strategy of using general training rather than investing resources in accelerated leadership development may also be more appropriate for smaller sport organizations or those organizations with a minimal training budget. For example, an Athletics Federation could use internal re-assignment to develop skills for critical roles (at minimal cost to the organization); or a Triathalon Club's volunteer director could work with a business coach and access accelerated leadership development through an externally run training programme.

The outcomes should relate to the actions needed, with strategic focus, to produce the desired results. Strategic planning will inform the model chosen, as will future organizational needs, shifts in markets, individual potential and development, plus demographic, and social changes. Evaluation, monitoring, and measurement are required to ensure that the processes continue to produce a sustainable succession and talent management process. Evaluation methods for all aspects of HR are discussed in more detail in Chapter 12.

Succession Planning for Volunteers in Community Sport Clubs

It is normal for there are to be some turnover of jobs from year to year – and it's healthy too. But high turnover rates can be a real pain. Clubs can work towards retaining volunteers through good volunteer management practices. However, volunteers will still leave for various reasons and clubs need to be prepared for change. In many clubs, excessive loads are carried by one or two people and when they leave or step down, the quality and fortunes of the club can quickly decline. A succession plan is necessary to provide opportunities for potential leaders within a club to be identified and developed in readiness to move into leadership positions.

A succession plan refers to the process of building a long-term future for the club. It enables any new people to take on roles without having to start from scratch again. When someone leaves a club, a succession plan ensures that all the club information doesn't leave with them. Succession planning is identifying potential leaders within the club who are prepared to take on the leadership positions. Clubs who can plan towards smooth transitions of leadership positions are less likely to experience disruptions to their day-to-day operations and as a result are better positioned to replace volunteers who leave the club.

A good succession plan includes the following:

- *A business plan*: This does not have to be lengthy. It is a working document outlining the club's priorities, and should be consulted regularly throughout the year.
- *Job descriptions*: If you have a set of job descriptions, and a clear list of jobs required around the club, you are on the way to a good succession plan.
- *Policies and procedures manual*: This outlines the day-to-day tasks at the club, and who is responsible for carrying them out. It will also contain policies about selection processes, health and safety issues and volunteer management.
- *Reporting procedures*: These show the reporting lines back to the committee, either directly or through supervisors.
- *Education and development opportunities*: Not only do these increase job satisfaction, but they also broaden the range of skills of each volunteer. This means that if someone suddenly leaves, you are more likely to have someone else ready to step into the vacant job.

One way to encourage the use of a succession plan is to have a rolling committee in place. A rolling committee stipulates that members stand down after a set of period to allow for some fresh input from new members. This can work well as new people on a committee can renew enthusiasm. Losing committee members can mean that your club loses some experience. It's important to groom successors for certain positions, so that when the time for a changeover happens, it can be managed with a minimum of disruption and fuss. The ideal succession plan should allow the existing volunteers to walk away from the club without being missed.

For discussion:
There are many barriers to succession planning, how would you tackle these?

■ The 'gatekeeper' – a person who runs a system only he or she understands, and keeps the knowledge to him or herself?
■ Lack of young people in responsible jobs?
■ Long-time committee members approaching their use by date?

Source: Adapted from Australian Football League (2003) *Volunteer management for football clubs.*

Effective succession management

There are a number of key principles which contribute to effective succession management. Eastman (1995) provides the following list of commonly reported effective practices:

▓ receives visible support from the CEO and top management,
▓ is owned by line management and supported by staff,
▓ is simple and tailored to unique organizational needs,
▓ is flexible and linked with the strategic business plan,
▓ evolves from a thorough human resources review process,
▓ is based upon well-developed competencies and objective review of candidates,
▓ incorporates employee input,
▓ is part of the broader management development effort,
▓ includes plans for development job assignments,
▓ is integrated with other HR systems,
▓ emphasizes accountability and follow-up.

These fundamental components are supported by numerous studies that have found highly effective succession management systems are characterized by CEO involvement, support of senior management, line management identification of candidates, use of developmental assignments, and succession management processes linked to business strategies (Rioux & Bernthal, 1999). Conger and Fulmer (2003) complement this premise with five 'rules' for operationalizing succession management. Rule one, the fundamental rule on which the other four are built, is that succession management is a flexible system oriented toward developmental activities. Rule two is that the focus must encompass linchpin positions, jobs that are essential to the long-term health of the organization. Rule three is make succession management transparent, no secrecy. Rule four is regular measurement of progress. Rule five is to keep it flexible.

The other 'ground rule' which comes out emphatically from business consultants and academics alike is the need for the CEO to be clear about her or his position on the issues regarding the following (Kesler, 2002: 8):

- Expectations regarding the differentiation of talent.
- The role of line leaders in the development of people.
- Philosophy regarding the movement of people across businesses and functions.
- The role diversity will play in staffing strategy.
- Beliefs about hiring for potential vs. hiring for position.
- The role of HR leaders.

Succession and talent management should be an integral component of the organization's strategic and HR planning framework and aligned with current and evolving organizational needs. As outlined in Chapter 3, HR planning includes the analysis of demographic and trend data, forecasts of attrition rates and supply and demand for critical skill sets, availability of external labour. Succession and talent management programmes should be developed with these analyses in mind and linked to existing recruitment, performance management, training and development, leadership development, and career planning initiatives.

An approach to succession and talent management

As discussed above, a sport organization's approach to succession and talent management should be framed by its strategic goals, environmental context, and HR needs. Although every organization will have different requirements for its succession and talent management policies and processes there are a number of basic components to developing an appropriate process. As noted above accountability for any succession and talent management scheme starts with the CEO and is devolved to managers at all levels, without their support the plans are unlikely to succeed (Bernthal & Wellins, 2006). The six steps, listed and then outlined in more detail below, provide a framework for designing and implementing succession management (adapted from Australian Public Service Commission, 2003):

1. Designing the process.
2. Ensuring strategic integration.

3. Assessing the current situation.
4. Identifying and assessing talented individuals.
5. Implementation: planning and undertaking development.
6. Evaluation.

The first step is to *design the process*. In this initial phase the organization needs to first define a business case for succession management. The reasons for engaging in succession and talent management should be clearly outlined and the benefit it will bring to the organization should be assessed in relation to the organization's strategic goals. The other critical element is being confident that the process will be supported and championed by senior executives and supported down the line. As noted earlier in this chapter, a growing body of research clearly demonstrates the vital importance of executive backing (Carey & Ogden, 2000; Bernthal & Wellins, 2006).

Ensuring the process is transparent right from the start is vital (see Conger & Fulmer, 2003 rule three above). While transparency of the process is important, it is also critical that the confidentiality of individual details is maintained (Sambrook, 2005). Staff feedback systems should be built into the process and development of a communication strategy to inform people about the process in general terms is recommended (Poza, Alfred & Maheshwari, 1997), as well as feeding back specific information to individual employees as appropriate. The approach chosen should focus on the strategic development of capabilities, of which it will be necessary to measure outcomes over time (Rothwell, 2000).

The HR planning framework can be used to identify the roles critical to organization's success as well as those likely to emerge as critical over the medium to longer term. This moves us onto step two – *ensuring strategic integration*. This integration should be considered in light of the organization's demographics and implications of changing demographics on the supply of candidates for the critical organizational roles. Along with the HR planning process, the succession and talent management process should be integrated with training and development plans and the performance management system. For example, a Sport Centre Manager who will be involved in coaching staff may require training to develop her coaching skills by so that she can effectively coach the Service Manager. This training should be integrated into her job role and built around the strategic imperatives of the organization.

The ensuring strategic integration step also involves the identification of distinctive leadership capabilities that may provide a basis for the organization to be more effective than its competitors, now and into the future. This will take into account future organization needs, critical success factors, values, strategies, and expected challenges. For example, handling media enquiries and doing TV/radio interviews may be a minor component of the Executive Director's job at present, but if the sport organization is just about to launch a new style league competition then further training in this area, for the Executive Director and a small team of immediate reports, could strategically benefit the organization to fully capitalize on the potential increased media exposure. Initially, the succession and talent management process should be rolled out for those at least one to two levels below the target roles to build the required capability and provide depth.

In step three, *assessing the current situation*, a risk assessment of potential departures from existing critical roles is performed. This should draw on a demographic analysis flowing from the broader HR planning framework and project future requirements in critical roles, taking into account internal and external factors and identifying worst case scenarios. From this, the organization can determine the extent of any pending position shortage by projecting requirements, internal mobility, and attrition over the next 3–5 years.

For example, most western countries are confronting an aging workforce, this means a critical consideration for many sport organizations in the next decade will be the number of middle to senior managers and executives who will be retiring. Despite countless warnings about the impact of an aging workforce (Byham, Smith & Paese, 2000; Bernthal & Wellins, 2006) a recent study of 578 companies found that more than a quarter of US businesses are still not prepared for a major change in the nation's workforce as a record number of aging employees retire (Boston Business Journal, 2007).

Any gaps identified between current capability for key roles and future requirements could then be addressed through relevant succession and talent management strategies, including, internal capability development, external recruitment to target particular immediate skills gaps, or programmes to recruit and develop specialists.

Step four is *identifying and assessing potential*. This encompasses identifying critical roles within the organization and developing a clear understanding of the capabilities required for effectiveness in those roles. These would include positions that exert critical influence on the organization's activities. The essential skills and competencies identified are then mapped using consistent, objective criteria. These criteria are also used to identify and source high-performance and high-potential candidates with advancement potential. The organization will then define what talented or 'high potential' means, both within the organization and within the context of the identified critical organizational roles. For example, entrepreneurial skills, along with initiative and team player attributes may be necessary for high performance in a sales and marketing role in a professional sport franchise.

As part of this process the organization identifies people who could potentially fill and perform well in the targeted roles. The organization's values and required leadership competencies should also be taken into account along with each person's performance, along with their learning agility. It is important to understand strengths, potential, and drivers of those identified and how these individuals may meet future needs (Jacobs, 2005).

It is critical that accurate identification and assessment occurs. Subjectivity can be minimized by the use of multiple methods that are comprehensive and evidence based to assess potential and to identify employees who could potentially fill the identified roles. A good starting point for reviewing performance, potential, and development needs is existing performance management data, including the following:

- biographical data,
- current performance,
- observed behaviour,

- 360-degree feedback and formal appraisal outcomes,
- interviews to determine career preferences,
- assessment of likelihood of staying with the organization,
- behavioural interviews to determine past performance in challenging situations,
- feedback from a range of senior managers performance and the relative value of certain characteristics,
- external assessments such as assessment centres.

In most performance management systems the supervisor assesses their staff's performance. However, succession and talent is not always best dealt with by immediate supervisors. Assessment may be best done by an external or third party, or at senior levels in the organization. The organization may also consider providing individuals with opportunities to self-nominate and to express an interest in pursuing certain roles based on their personal preferences and objectives. A review meeting of senior staff should be held to discuss individual reports, to agree on the list of 'potentials' on and to compile the final list. Documentation of this process should include information for each employee, their potential, performance level, career interests and goals and retention risk.

Any issues of internal capacity will become apparent at this stage through forecasting potential shortages and surpluses of potential candidates. The analysis should not be done in isolation and should also draw on the HR analysis used in HR planning (see Chapter 3) and may include an evaluation of market factors of the availability of external skills, as well assessing where internal development resources should be focused.

Step five is *implementation* and involves planning and implementing the programme. The plan will outline the types of roles or experiences which may be offered as accelerated development opportunities, targeted against future organizational needs. Larger organizations may wish to consider whether to designate particular sets of duties as 'development roles' and use these as the developmental assignments for talented individuals. This step focuses on development of each individual's required capabilities through a programme of learning experiences that have clear performance objectives. The development plan should close any gaps and/or strengthen existing skills and competencies and goals should be aligned with the organization's strategic plan.

Development opportunities could include a targeted job assignment, managing a project, a formal training programme, or an external activity. Development may be accelerated to ensure a ready supply of staff for future role requirements, and/or undertaken as part of the organization's established performance management framework. Development plans incorporate factors such as individual capability requirements, anticipated role challenges, required organizational knowledge, and individual elements. Development plans usually include a programme that provides the individual with the following:

- Job rotation, special assignments, and cross-functional involvement that is challenging.
- Exposure to the strategic agenda and to senior levels of the organization.
- Self-development strategies.
- Access to executive level mentors.

It is important that opportunities for two-way feedback and regular review are built into the succession and talent management process. The organization should outline how often reviews are to occur and follow-up on development plans, noting whether reward structures are aligned with progress in meeting developmental goals. However, at the end of the day individuals are responsible for their own career development and are accountable for meeting developmental objectives and gaining and demonstrating new capabilities. The individual must take ultimate responsibility for meeting developmental goals and maintaining the quality of their performance.

The final step is *evaluation*, although it should be noted that evaluation as a process should be ongoing. The organization should establish clear timeframes for implementing and evaluating the approach and its outcomes. For the organization, evaluation of outcomes could be in terms of whether organizational risk has been reduced or minimized. For the individual, evaluation could include self-assessment about the degree of capability development and demonstrated changes in performance and behaviour in the workplace.

The overall succession and talent management process should be monitored. This may include periodic evaluation of progress on individual development plans, the degree of involvement of current leaders or senior executives and the proportion of internal to external appointments.

Succession Management in Action: The Case of Henrico County

Henrico County General Government borders the city of Richmond, Virginia and employs more than 3900 full-time employees working in more than 30 agencies. Henrico County implemented a succession management initiative to address two concerns: (1) the loss of intellectual capital in key positions as upper managers become eligible to retire in record numbers, and (2) the decreasing number of younger adults in the workforce available to develop the skills necessary to move into higher-level positions.

A goal of this initiative was to have a pool of internal candidates, organization wide, who would be competitive in an external recruitment process. In the 2 years leading up to the implementation of the succession management initiative, only two of seven upper manager positions were filled with internal candidates. During the first 2 years of this initiative, internal candidates filled all eight upper management position vacancies and there have been 15 of 16 appointments of internal candidates to upper management county positions since the initiative was introduced.

The programme consisted of two phases. Phase One taught supervisors how to guide employees through a professional development process using individualized learning plans. Phase Two provided information to upper managers on strategies for developing subordinate managers for the purpose of planning for succession. The five steps used were (1) clarify key positions for succession, (2) identify competencies needed, (3) develop employees, (4) assess employee's ability to do future work of key positions, and (5) evaluate the succession management programme.

1. The county manager determined during the early planning phases for this initiative that upper managers would be considered the initial 'key position holders', however; the intention from the start was that the initiative would be expanded to include lower-level management employees as well.
2. All upper managers identified the competencies needed to do their jobs at a highly productive level. Core competencies previously developed for Henrico County's leaders are available on the HR department's Web site and in the annual training catalogue distributed to each management employee. Henrico County's 20 core leadership competencies are listed below:

    1. Communication
    2. Conflict resolution
    3. Continuous improvement
    4. Critical thinking/decision making
    5. Customer orientation
    6. Employee development and coaching
    7. Financial and resource management
    8. Individual learning skills
    9. Interpersonal relations
    10. Organizational astuteness
    11. Orientation to the future
    12. Performance management
    13. Personal accountability
    14. Personal integrity
    15. Policy and procedure development and administration
    16. Strategic management
    17. Systems perspective
    18. Team leadership and empowerment
    19. Technological literacy
    20. Versatility

Leaders were encouraged to use the core competencies as a foundation for developing a comprehensive list of skills and abilities used in their jobs. Key position holders were held for meetings with their leadership teams, described the succession management initiative and distributed their competency list. The subordinate managers used this list to identify skills they needed to develop to be a viable candidate for a higher-level position. Managers not wanting upward development were guided through a process of determining ways they could develop and progress in their current positions.

3. Emphasis was placed on considering experiential learning opportunities, formal and informal learning and it was emphasized that development is ultimately an employee's responsibility. An 'Examples of Developmental Strategies for Leaders' handout listed managerial activities, the gap addressed, and sample learnings. For example:
   Gap to be addressed: Exposure to knowledge of a lateral manager in a different division
   Strategy: Cross-training
   Example: A recreation centre supervisor cross-trains with the special programme supervisor.

4. Managers assessed the progress and success of their employees' development. Assessment criteria include how well the employee has accomplished developmental objectives from both the employee's view and the incumbent manager's view, as well as feedback from peers, other managers, and even clients and customers. Objective assessments using 360-degree feedback instruments were encouraged. The individualized learning plan form is completed by the subordinate manager with guidance from the key position holder manager. It provides a place for describing how the success of each learning objective will be measured and for a notation that there is evidence that the objective was met.

5. The final step includes a process for completing a report that outlines the development activity that has occurred on a departmental level, and goals for future development. It also asks for information on any key position vacancies in each department, and reports any internal promotions that have occurred in the previous 6 months.

Source: Adapted from: Holinsworth, 2004

For discussion:

Compile a list of objective criteria that could be used to assess 3–5 of Henrico County's 20 core leadership competencies for the Sport Director of the Deep Run Recreation Centre position.

Issues in implementing succession management

As with any process there are a range of barriers and constraints to effective succession and talent management programmes. Jacobs (2005: 5) suggests that there are six common 'derailers' that cause succession and talent management outcomes to go off-track and she offers some ways to avoid these.

1. Inaccurate information and limited choices. Personal relationships and subjective experiences should be minimized in the identification and assessment of future leaders. Executives may rely too much on a small group of people, so limit the number of roles for which a person can be targeted. This forces thinking on the strength, breadth, and depth of the talent pipeline.
2. A focus on only one person for each specific role. If an individual selects their own replacement and only develops that single person into the role the prospects are limited. Focusing on a wider talent pool, and developing it, ensures flexibility and more options for all roles.
3. Poor experiential development. Although development activities are often part of training, they may be based on current needs and not future requirements. Development activities that expand skills, build expertise, test judgement, shape emotional intelligence, provide accountability, produce diversity awareness, and promote visibility should be used.
4. Misunderstanding what is needed for future success. Assessment of past and current performance capabilities assumes that the individual's strengths, style, and motivators will automatically carry them into success in a future role. Accurate personal insight, actionable feedback, and a clear perspective on capabilities and future requirements may be gained through a coach or mentor.
5. Failure to execute and follow through. Failing to see succession as an ongoing process may lead to its isolation from the day-to-day pressures of transactional business. To avoid this outcome, the development plan should be targeted and personalized, and actions should be integrated into other management systems and responsibilities.
6. Lack of accountability. Like any other critical human resource management strategy, strength in the talent pipeline needs discipline, focus, and commitment at all levels. To ensure its effectiveness, the senior executive group needs to be held accountable for the building of a talent pool as a key performance indicator, and be involved in mentoring and talent development across the organization.

Trends in succession and talent management

Analysing the results of a global benchmarking study of more than 4500 leaders from over 900 organizations, Bernthal and Wellins (2006) identified six trends in succession and talent management programmes:

1. Expand succession management to lower levels of the organization. Many organizations are now widening succession management to include assessment and development of individuals at lower levels in

the organization, reflecting the need for organizations to delve deeper into their ranks in preparation for future openings. This includes having a development plan that includes some type of assessment for long-term leadership potential. Those individuals with higher potential can be guided along predetermined career paths.

2. A complete success profile for assessing readiness.
   Organizations are identifying a pool of high potentials early in their careers and placing them in 'acceleration pool' to prepare them for a variety of positions. While it is time-consuming and expensive to offer every employee the opportunity for individual assessment and development planning, the organizations identifying and nurturing potential are likely to find a much larger pool of leaders in their future.

3. Assess the whole person for development purposes.
   The use of multiple assessment tools produces an in-depth evaluation of personal/motivational attributes, business management, leadership, and interpersonal skills for a role above the individual's current level. Use of talent identification and development programmes highlights employees who show potential. Bernthal and Wellins (2006) further suggest a full assessment of a leader against a success profile to address essential preparatory experiences (what one has done), organizational knowledge (what one knows), behaviourally defined competencies (what one is capable of), and personal attributes, which can include 'derailers' or constraints for senior-level leaders (who one is). Success profile requirements vary by level or position, job function or role, and by the particular organization's strategy and culture.

4. Select/deploy talent by leveraging an aging workforce.
   Selecting or deploying talent involves profiling leaders (individuals and teams) against specific strategic challenges to make effective placement and promotion decisions. Assessment and development of current employees and volunteers play a critical role in this process, but how organizations manage and deploy their talent may is shifting. As noted above, retirement of an aging workforce threatens to deplete the overall number of experienced individuals available for organizations. Many of these people will choose to remain active in the workforce, but at a reduced level of involvement. For sport organizations requiring volunteers this group may provide a growing target population to target and use to expand the volunteer pool.

5. Accelerate development through applied learning and mentoring networks.
   Development prepares individuals for future roles and challenges and therefore is central to talent optimization. Development experiences that link learning experiences to real life challenges through learning by doing have been found to be highly effective. To minimize risk involved in giving someone a turn in a higher-level role, a network of expert mentors can provide guidance and offer insight. Talent banks that list all employees and their areas of expertise and experience can be used to develop a network of experts to consult when faced with developmental challenges.

6. Focus/drive performance through measurement.

The widespread adoption of methods such as the balanced scorecard approach (Kaplan & Norton, 1996a) (this is discussed in more detail in Chapter 12) has placed increased attention on more holistic lead and lag measures of organizational progress. Some commonly used lead and lag measures (Bernthal & Wellins, 2006: 40) are given below:

Lead measures

1. Increased job satisfaction and engagement ratings.
2. Increased perception of growth opportunities.
3. Increased percentage of high potentials completing development plan.
4. Executive review board established with clear understanding of process and roles.
5. High potentials' perception of value regarding the succession process.
6. Percentage of participation in learning and development activities.
7. Percentage of leaders registered in the mentoring network.

Lag measures

1. Increased percentage of high potential leader retention.
2. Increased leadership diversity.
3. Increased performance relative to strategic goals.
4. Lower percentage of external hires for key positions.
5. Fewer key positions without ready successor.
6. Higher HR strategic value creation ratings (e.g., from executive team).
7. Positive return-on-investment from action learning projects.

Summary

This chapter has outlined how succession and talent management can be used by sport organizations to address issues of sustainability and competitive advantage in relation to employees and volunteers. Succession and talent management provides a process by which high potential and valuable staff are recruited, developed, rewarded, and retained by the sport organization. Succession and talent management programmes may focus on senior executive and leadership roles, critical roles, specialist jobs, or the entire workforce.

Effective succession management programmes are characterized by senior staff commitment to a process that is aligned with the organization's strategies and embedded in the HR activities of the organization. There are six key steps to a succession management programme: (1) designing the process; (2) ensuring strategic integration; (3) assessing the current situation; (4) identifying and assessing talented individuals; (5) implementation, planning and undertaking development; and (6) evaluation. Following these steps and avoiding and succession management 'derailers' will provide sport organization's with the basis for a sustainable and adequate supply of high-quality employees and volunteers.

Discussion questions

1. Identify the key principles for effectiveness in succession and talent management and discuss how these could be used in a sport organization where you have worked or volunteered.
2. Outline the six steps in a succession and talent management process and suggest some techniques that you could use to identify 'talented' staff or volunteers.
3. Discuss the implications of staff who are not included in an organization's talent management programme – that is those individuals not identified as 'having potential'.
4. Discuss how succession and talent management can contribute to SHRM in a sport organization you are familiar with. What might be some of the barriers/constraints to its implementation?

11 Sport organizations and diversity management

Learning objectives

After reading this chapter you will be able to:

- Define workplace diversity
- Explain factors contributing to workplace diversity
- Describe the potential positive and negative impact of diversity in the organization
- Discuss the strategic management of workplace diversity

Chapter overview

People differ in many ways and this has implications for workplace interactions. Diversity management refers to managing differences to capitalize on the benefits of diversity and to minimize its potentially negative consequences. This chapter will examine the nature and extent of diversity in the workplace, and identify various forces that contribute to that diversity. The challenges of a diverse organizational workforce and the potential for positive and negative impact are considered. This is followed by a discussion of strategies for managing diversity to ensure the fair treatment of all employees and volunteers, as well as to make the most of diversity in the workplace.

Diversity in the workplace

The nature of diversity

Diversity is defined as a variety, assortment, or mixture. Here we are interested in the nature and impact of a variety or mixture of personnel in sport organizations, and implications for strategic human resource management (SHRM). Cunningham (2007: 6) defines diversity in the workplace as '*the presence of differences among members of a social unit that lead to perceptions of such differences and that impact work outcomes*' (italics in original). A key element of this definition is that diversity is a perception and thus differences are in the 'eye of the beholder'. A group of male community sport club coaches may view themselves as very similar because they are all male, or very diverse because some are African-American and some are White, or some are parents of participants while others are not. According to Cunningham (2007: 5), 'it is the perceptions of being different, more so than the actual differences themselves, that impact subsequent outcomes.'

Perceptions of diversity may be based on demographic or surface level differences, and psychological or deep level differences (Harrison, Price & Bell, 1998). Surface level differences are found in personal attributes such as sex, age, race, or physical disability; characteristics which may be readily detectable by others. We may also include such personal demographics as sexual orientation, socioeconomic status, or religion in our description of surface level differences. They represent social categories that can be used to differentiate between people. These personal attributes contribute to individuals' perceptions that they are with others who are similar or different to themselves at least at a surface level.

Deep level differences are found in underlying psychological characteristics such as values, beliefs, and attitudes. Deep level differences may also be found in cognitive skills and abilities, including knowledge and experience (Jackson, May & Whitney, 1995; Milliken & Martins, 1996). These attributes are less readily observable and for the most part can be known only through extended interaction with others. Thus, diversity based on deep level differences may only become apparent after individuals or the workgroup have had some meaningful interaction.

We can expect deep level differences to have the greatest consequences for workplace outcomes, because they reflect diversity in the values and attitudes that inform people's decision making and behaviour (Adler, 1997). However, diversity based on surface level features may generate anxiety among staff and volunteers about possible differences among individuals, given the unknown, uncertainty, and even prejudice that may accompany the perception of diversity. These can have a considerable impact on workplace outcomes as well. Nonetheless, research indicates that, as people continue to interact with one another in the workplace, differences in surface level attributes become less important than deep level attitudinal diversity (Harrison et al., 1998).

Considering again the example of the community sport club coaches, they may appear on the surface to be a diverse group because of differences in race, or parental status, or both; or they may perceive themselves to be a homogeneous group because they are of the same sex. In fact, any diversity within the group may instead be a function of deep level differences in values regarding community level sport and how it is played. Some of the coaches may feel that it is most important for all kids to have a chance to play; others may feel it is most important for the team to experience success, perhaps at the cost of having lesser skilled players spend more time on the bench. This diversity in perspectives may be expected to be more critical to the coaches' effort and performance, and the outcomes of the organization as a whole, than any surface level differences such as race or parental status. Nevertheless, the example suggests a link between deep and surface characteristics; for example, it may be the parents who value all children playing. We can in fact expect a link between deep and surface level attributes (Doherty & Chelladurai, 1999; Cunningham, 2007). Individuals will possess any or all of the values, beliefs, and expectations, as well as the customs and behaviours, of various groups of others who have similar surface characteristics (e.g., parents) to the extent that they identify most closely with those various characteristics (e.g., a coach may identify most strongly as being a parent, a male, an African-American, and/or a Christian). However, we risk inaccurate and harmful stereotyping if we assume that someone with a given surface level characteristic possesses the underlying values and beliefs of that group (Johns & Saks, 2001). Only through interaction can we know an individual's deep level attributes and understand whether we are similar or different in that regard.

Several factors contribute to workplace diversity. Changing population demographics, legislation regarding hiring practices, proactive hiring to increase diversity in the organization in order to capitalize on potential benefits, changes in the nature of work that reflect a more team-oriented approach where interdependence and interaction is intensified, globalization, and changing attitudes in society and the workplace towards differences that lead to an increased awareness of diversity, all contribute to the increasing perception and reality of differences among staff and volunteers in sport organizations (Johns & Saks, 2001; Cunningham, 2007). We consider each of these factors further.

Changing population demographics

Changing population demographics has a direct influence on the makeup of the workforce in general, which translates to diversity in the workplace. Two population changes that are particularly notable with regard to the workforce or employment pool are aging and immigration. A report from the Population Division of the United Nations Secretariat (as cited in Australian Bureau of Statistics [ABS], 2004a) projects that, between 2005 and 2050, the proportion of the World population under 15 years of age will drop from 28.2 to 20.2 per cent, the proportion of what is defined as the working age (15–59 years) will drop from 61.4 to 58.1 per cent, and the proportion of the population aged 60 years and over will increase from 10.4 to 21.7 per cent. Table 11.1 provides details for several countries. With an aging population we can expect greater age diversity as organizations, including sport organizations, increasingly rely on older workers and volunteers to meet their needs.

Immigration makes a substantial contribution to population growth in many Western countries. This can have a major impact on the proportion of racial or visible minorities in the workforce, as well as increasing the ethnic, language, and religious diversity. For example, in Canada, visible minorities comprised 15.7 per cent of the population in 2006 (Belanger & Malenfant, 2005). This figure is expected to increase by one-third to 20.6 per cent in just a 10-year period. During that period, the largest proportion of immigrants is expected to continue to be from China and South Asia, however, the greatest increase will be among Arab, West Asian, and Korean immigrants. In Australia, the greatest proportions of visible minority immigrants are from China and India, constituting 13.4 per cent of all immigrants between 1995 and 2005 (Andrews, 2006). Immigration is expected to continue to make a substantial contribution to the projected 40 per cent increase in the population of Australia through to 2051, largely because of its 'non-discriminatory immigration policy' (Andrews, 2006: 1). Diversity in the workforce as a result of increasing immigration will

Table **11.1** Projected population figures (per cent) of selected countries (ABS, 2004a)

Country	2005			2050		
	Under 15 years	15–59 years	60 years and over	Under 15 years	15–59 years	60 years and over
Australia	19.6	62.6	17.8	15.1	53.2	31.7
Canada	17.6	64.5	17.9	15.7	52.4	31.8
China	21.4	67.7	10.9	15.7	53.3	31.0
Japan	14.0	59.7	26.3	13.4	44.9	41.7
New Zealand	21.3	61.9	16.7	16.0	53.9	30.0
United Kingdom	17.9	60.0	21.2	16.4	54.2	29.4
United States of America	20.8	62.5	16.7	17.3	56.3	26.4
World	28.2	61.4	10.4	20.2	58.1	21.7

continue to be manifested in sport organizations as well. The Coaching Association of Canada is one sport organization that is aware of changing population demographics with respect to immigration. It has commissioned a study on 'Engaging new Canadians in coaching', the purpose of which is to determine recent immigrants' motives and barriers to getting involved in coaching (Coaching Association of Canada, 2006).

Legislation

Diversity in the workplace may be attributed in large part to legislation protecting the rights of individuals in the recruitment and selection process. Sport organizations are held to local, regional, and federal government statutes that are in place to ensure equity and equality in hiring. Civil and human rights legislations and equal opportunity laws make it unacceptable and illegal to discriminate based on sex, age, race, disability, and so forth. The Australian Human Rights and Equal Opportunity Commission Act (1986), Disability Discrimination Act (1992), Sex Discrimination Act (1984), and Racial Discrimination Act (1975), the Canadian Charter of Rights and Freedoms (1982), and Human Rights Act (1985), the American Civil Rights Act (1991), and Americans with Disabilities Act (1990), and the United Kingdom's Disability Discrimination Act (1995) are some of the laws that protect prospective employees in these countries. The result is increasing diversity based on surface level characteristics that were a traditional basis for discrimination in hiring.

Title IX and Gender Diversity in Sport Leadership

Title IX of the Education Amendments Act (1972) in the US is a law that prohibits sex-based discrimination in educational programmes that receive federal government funding. While the legislation is not specific to sport, it likely impacts sport more than any other law (Cunningham, 2007). It requires that males and females be given equal opportunities to participate in federally funded activities, which includes athletics programmes in high schools, colleges, and universities.

Title IX has had a major impact on the growth of female participation in sport, particularly in high schools where girls comprised only 5 per cent of high school athletes in 1972 and 41 per cent in 2002 (Acosta & Carpenter, 2005). At the collegiate level, the average number of women's teams per institution rose from 2.5 in 1972 to 8.32 in 2004 (Acosta & Carpenter, 2005).

Despite, or perhaps because of, the increased support for girls' and women's athletic programmes as a result of Title IX, there has actually been a decrease in the proportion of women in coaching and administrative leadership. Ninety per cent of coaches of women's teams were women in 1972, which dropped to around 40 per cent by 2004 (Acosta & Carpenter, 2005). In 1972, 90 per cent of administrators of women's athletics were women, but that dropped to less than 20 per cent by 2004.

There are several explanations for this dramatic decline in the participation of women in sport leadership, including individual and structural factors that influence women's interest and opportunity to be involved. Another explanation is that leadership opportunities in well-supported and increasingly prestigious women's programmes are an attractive option for men, who are more likely to be hired in those positions than women (Cunningham, 2007).

In the end, this legislation, which has been successful in its mandate to ensure equal opportunities for male and female participation, has likely had a negative impact on the participation of women leaders in high school and collegiate sport organizations, and reduced the level of diversity there.

Affirmative action is government policy stemming largely from human rights legislation that actively seeks to redress past employment discrimination by increasing the representation of certain disadvantaged groups, particularly women and racial minorities. It is manifested in organizations through initiatives ranging from encouraging members of underrepresented groups to apply for jobs, to the establishment of quotas for the hiring of individuals from particularly disadvantaged groups. The intent of affirmative action is to correct the imbalance of underrepresented groups of employees in an organization that have historically faced employment discrimination. Yet, affirmative action is not without its critics, who claim that it is in fact reverse discrimination, contravening human rights legislation as it gives preferential treatment to one group over another. Consequently, affirmative action policies and programmes have generally evolved to include an 'all things being equal' clause, where an individual from a targeted group is selected if all bases for selection are considered equal among all candidates. Affirmative action is a factor affecting increased diversity in sport organizations. The following example illustrates the positive effect of affirmative action in sport organizations:

IOC Gender Diversity Targets

In order to increase the number of women occupying leadership and administrative positions in Olympic sport, in 1997 the

International Olympic Committee (IOC) set a target for National Olympic Committees (NOCs), International Sports Federations (IFs), and sports bodies belonging to the Olympic Movement to have at least 20 per cent of the positions in all their decision making structures held by women by the end of 2005 (IOC, 2006). At the close of 2004, approximately 30 per cent of the NOCs and 29 per cent of the IFs had achieved that target. By the end of 2005, women comprised 6.6 per cent of the IOC Executive Board, 13 per cent of IOC members (representatives to their home nations), and 15.3 per cent of IOC Commissions (task forces struck to examine various issues pertaining to the Olympic Movement); a state of affairs that may represent a 'marked increase' yet is undoubtedly a 'continuing challenge' (IOC, 2004a: 2). Nonetheless, a study of Women, Leadership, and the Olympic Movement (IOC, 2004b: 7) concluded that 'the target approach can be said to have had success in ... bringing talented women in to the Olympic family, and of improving Olympic governance.'

Beyond beginning to redress gender imbalance, further apparent benefits of the IOC's affirmative action initiative are consistent with the diversity strategy of proactive hiring, which is discussed shortly. We have also discussed this matter in other chapters of this book in relation to human resource (HR) planning, selection, orientation, training and development, and succession and talent management.

In our discussion of various forces that influence workplace diversity, we should take a moment to consider the degree of diversity in sport organizations:

How Diverse are Sport Organizations? A Sample of Human Resource Profiles

The Institute for Diversity and Ethics in Sport at the University of Central Florida published the 2005 Racial and Gender Report Card summarizing and giving a 'grade' based on the proportion of men, women, and racially diverse groups in sport leadership in professional and college sport in the US. The following are highlights from the report:

■ In Major League Baseball (MLB), 30 per cent of coaches were African-American or Latino, almost 40 per cent of players were Latino, African-American or Asian, 27 per cent of staff in MLB's central office were people of colour, and 18 per cent of senior administrators with MLB teams were women.

- In the National Basketball Association (NBA), almost 78 per cent of players were people of colour including 73 per cent of African-American descent, women held 41 per cent of professional positions in the NBA League Office, and 37 per cent of NBA head coaches were African-American.
- In the Women's National Basketball Association (WNBA), 19 per cent of the players were from overseas, and 70 per cent of league office employees were women.

The Institute released its 2007 National Collegiate Athletic Association (NCAA) Division 1A demographic study entitled 'Decisions from the top: Diversity among campus, conference leaders at Division IA institutions'. The report revealed that 85.7 per cent of the athletic directors were White, and specifically 80.7 per cent were White men. Only 5 per cent of the athletic directors were women and all were White. According to the report 'the leadership of Division 1A athletics [the highest level of intercollegiate sport] ... reached a new all-time record for athletics directors with 12 African-Americans, four Latinos, and a Native American ... for 14.3 per cent of the total' (Institute for Diversity and Ethics in Sport, 2007: 1). Only 5 (4.2 per cent) of the head football coaches were African-American (all men).

Across a number of countries, including Canada, Australia, and England, the profile of community sport volunteers is fairly narrow, suggesting a relatively homogeneous rather than diverse volunteer workforce with regard to certain surface level attributes. According to a report from Canada, the 'typical' community sport volunteer is male (64 per cent), 35–44 years of age (41 per cent), a college or university graduate (53 per cent), married (73 per cent) with dependents at home (62 per cent), employed full time (82 per cent), with a household income of $60–99,000 (Canadian) (43 per cent) (Doherty, 2005a). Coaches are an even more similar group, where 73 per cent are men (Doherty, 2005a). Data from Australia and England reveal similar profiles (Cuskelly, Hoye & Auld, 2006).

Discussion question

In your opinion, are sport organizations (as described here, and based on personal knowledge) diverse? Do they encourage diversity?

Proactive hiring

The preceding examples of increasing gender and racial diversity in sport organizations may be attributed to employment legislation, affirmative action, or both. It may also be the result of proactive hiring. The strategic objective of proactive hiring is to actively increase diversity in the organization in general, or with respect to a particular surface level attribute (e.g., gender, age, race, physical disability), with the intent of capitalizing on the potential benefits of a diverse workplace. These benefits include increased creativity and improved problem solving because of the diversity of values, perspectives, and attitudes that are presumed to be brought to the table by people who differ from each other. Another potential benefit of diversity is increased understanding of the marketplace, which allows the organization to better serve different customers, and to further develop services and marketing strategies targeted to a broader (more diverse) customer base. Proactive hiring may also benefit the organization's image as a socially responsible company (Weiner, 1997). Some of these benefits have been realized by the Olympic Movement as a result of the IOC's affirmative action initiative, although this was not necessarily its intent. Despite the potential benefits of proactive hiring and the resultant diversity in the workplace, it presents many human resource management (HRM) challenges as well. These are discussed shortly.

The following example illustrates a preliminary proactive hiring initiative to increase diversity in NASCAR (National Association for Stock Car Auto Racing, Inc.) organizations:

Diversity Internships at NASCAR

The National Association for Stock Car Auto Racing Inc. (NASCAR) Diversity Internship Program provides opportunities for qualified candidates to work with NASCAR's sanctioning body, NASCAR sponsors and licensees, NASCAR teams and track, and other motorsports-related companies.

The programme employs college/university students in a 10-week summer programme designed to introduce them to the world of NASCAR and the exciting career opportunities available throughout the motorsports industry. The programme is designed to support deserving students with an interest in the motorsports industry, who are of Alaskan Native, American Indian, Asian/Pacific Island, African-American, Hispanic, or other racial minority descent.

For more information about the NASCAR Diversity Internship Program visit www.diversityinternships.com.

The changing nature of work

As organizations structure their work around teams (Johns & Saks, 2001), employees work more interdependently and their interaction with others increases. It is not uncommon, for example, that a national sport organization will create committees to work on various initiatives, such as developing a coaching education programme. Such a committee may comprise individuals with surface and deep level differences. A 'team' of lifeguards at an aquatics facility may be established to improve communication, generate cohesion among the staff and commitment to the organization, and increase efficiency in scheduling. Given demographic changes in the workforce, and changing attitudes towards diversity in the workplace (see below), we may expect some degree of diversity in this workgroup. Through workgroup or team member interaction, surface and deep level differences become apparent, and are reinforced through continued interaction (Harrison et al., 1998).

Globalization in the sport industry and its impact on sport organizations may be reflected in the diversity it creates in the workplace. Examples of workplace diversity created through globalization include the composition of international sport governing bodies (e.g., IOC), the staffing of multinational sport corporations such as Nike with local employees, parent country nationals and third country nationals, and the international movement of athletes and coaches (e.g., players in North America's National Hockey League (NHL) come from 17 countries around the world. A global workforce requires employees and volunteers to interact with others from different national cultures and backgrounds.

Changing attitudes towards diversity

Changing population demographics, human rights and employment legislations, proactive hiring, and the changing nature of work have brought us face to face with people who are different from ourselves. The increasing level of diversity, but particularly its increasing acceptance in society and in the workplace, has heightened our awareness of differences. Employees and volunteers cannot be expected to completely set aside their values, lifestyle preferences, and even customs when they join an organization (Robbins, 1997). It has made us more aware that we are different in many ways. As noted earlier, diversity in the workplace is really a function of the perception of diversity; whether we see differences among ourselves or not. Therefore, diversity in sport organizations, as in all organizations, is also affected by our increasing awareness of differences (both surface and deep level). To the extent that diversity is beneficial in the organization, the organization will benefit from increasing awareness about differences among people.

The impact of diversity in the workplace

Diversity in the workplace is a critical concern for SHRM because of its potential impact on workplace outcomes. SHRM is concerned with aligning an organization's human resources with its strategic goals and initiatives. A diverse workforce creates certain challenges that can both threaten and enhance organizational effectiveness. We now discuss the potential positive and negative ramifications of diversity at work.

Benefits of diversity

In general, diversity is assumed to be beneficial to an organization because of the different values and perspectives it brings to the workplace. Most of the research on organizational diversity has focused on surface level differences, such as gender, race, and age. Thus, it is important to bear in mind that when we talk about the benefits, and challenges, of workplace diversity we are generally referring to surface level differences and the deep level diversity that implies.

As noted earlier, the benefits of diversity in the workplace include an enhanced reputation as a diversity employer (Weiner, 1997), improved recruiting when the organization's employee or volunteer profile matches the labour pool (Johns & Saks, 2001), and greater marketing insights that may be available from diverse employees (Chelladurai, 2005). These insights and different perspectives (deep level diversity), as a function of diverse backgrounds and experiences, are what contribute to increased creativity and innovation, a broader range of alternatives, and higher-quality ideas in a diverse workplace. Diverse individuals and groups may be expected to 'generate unique alternatives and challenge old ideas and standard ways of doing things' (Doherty & Chelladurai, 1999: 284). In this way, diversity can be a source of constructive conflict in the group or organization such that higher-quality decisions are the result.

The benefits of diversity depend on the extent to which individuals work on complex tasks where there is discretion in decision making and new ideas are expected and valued (Doherty & Chelladurai, 1999); for example, event planning, policy development, or marketing strategy. Benefits are also more likely to accrue when diverse individuals work interdependently with others on tasks that require interaction and collaboration (Doherty & Chelladurai, 1999). Thus, diversity will be more or less meaningful in different situations. It can be expected to be less beneficial, and less detrimental, where people work on simple, standardized tasks, or have little need or opportunity for interaction with others in the workplace, or both; for example, a parking lot attendant at a sports facility, ticket takers at a sports event, and even sales associates at a fitness club or sporting goods store, where the tasks are very standardized and scripted. In the latter case, however, a diverse staff who mirror the (current and potential) customer base may be very beneficial to the organization.

The potential benefits of diversity do not come without a cost. In addition to the challenges of workplace diversity, which we will discuss shortly, research indicates that a diverse group is likely to take longer than a more homogenous group to complete its problem-solving tasks (Cunningham, 2007). It takes time to overcome some of the challenges created by the interaction of diverse individuals. Nonetheless, the outcome of that interaction (idea generation, decision making) can be expected to be superior to that of groups of individuals who are similar to each other. Efficiency may be sacrificed for the effectiveness that comes from workplace diversity.

The following case provides an illustration to let us consider how workplace diversity can benefit a sport organization:

The Original Gus Macker 3-on-3 Basketball Tournament

Gus Macker 3-on-3 basketball has grown from a driveway game in Lowell, Michigan in 1974 to the Macker Tour which hosts indoor and outdoor tournaments in over 75 cities across the US (and one in Canada). More than 200,000 players and 1.7 million spectators take part in 3-on-3 competitions every year. Local hosts partner with the national organization to operate the tournaments. There are competition categories for men and women, boys and girls, catering to almost every age and ability level. Participants are very diverse; the only thing they may have in common is their love of street basketball!

The six basic objectives of Gus Macker are as follows:

1. A wholesome, family-oriented event.
2. A tournament designed by players for players.
3. A value to sponsors.
4. An outstanding fundraising event for the local community.
5. A major media sporting event.
6. Entertaining for the spectators.

The national organization is focused on the long range success and continued growth of the Gus Macker 3-on-3 Basketball Tournament.

With information from www.macker.com.

For discussion:

Consider (with specific examples) how surface and deep level diversity could help the national organization (and local hosts) meet these objectives and continue to grow.

Challenges of diversity

One of the basic challenges of a diverse workforce is the anxiety and even fear that it can generate among employees and volunteers who are faced with the unknown. When someone is different from us, in either surface or deep level characteristics, it creates some uncertainty about what to expect from that person. For example, if a woman joined the all male group of community level coaches described earlier in this chapter, her presence may create some anxiety on the part of the group because of the surface level perception of her being different from the other coaches, and thus an unknown entity with regard to coaching. Some members of the group may have concerns about her ability, interests, and intentions with regard to coaching. Uncertainty and anxiety may be heightened when one or more persons in the group is diverse from the others in several respects; for example, with regard to gender, age, sexual orientation, and race. Multiple differences may intensify the sense of the unknown and the associated discomfort. When members of the community level coaching group get to know the new female coach, through personal and group interactions, they will become aware of her deep level attributes (including her ability, interests and intentions with regard to coaching). This increased understanding may reduce, or further increase, perceptions of diversity and associated uncertainty.

Diversity can also create barriers to effective communication, such that the intended message is not received or is not understood by the intended recipient. Potential barriers to communication among a diverse workforce include language that is not understood well by the receiver (e.g., too sophisticated or technical, not the receiver's first language), and 'noise' in the communication channel caused by biases and prejudice on the part of the sender or receiver (McKenna & Beech, 2002). Communication is critical to carrying out the work of the organization. As noted in Chapter 9, it is also key to involving employees and volunteers in the organization and promoting positive employee relations. Diversity training, which is discussed later in this chapter, is aimed at reducing the biases that compromise communication by educating and enlightening employees and volunteers about the nature of differences in the workplace. English-as-a-second-language (ESL) training is another example of attempts to reduce barriers to effective communication among a diverse workgroup by promoting a common language in a country where the first language is English. Barriers to communication can, of course, intensify the unknown and uncertainty associated with diversity in the workplace, where different individuals are not hearing or understanding each other.

Prejudice is a key barrier to communication and workplace relations, and may be heightened where there is diversity. It is defined as an unfavourable attitude towards a group, and by extension anyone who is perceived to be a member of that group, by virtue of some characteristic that all members of the group possess. Prejudice is a negative bias that is often based on 'faulty and inflexible generalization' (Allport, 1954: 9). Discrimination is the further act of distinguishing or differentiating between people on the basis of some personal characteristics, such as age, sex, race, disability, religion, political beliefs, or sexual orientation. Discriminatory behaviour occurs when a potential or current employee or volunteer is treated less favourably because of some personal attribute, when compared to someone without that attribute. Discrimination can range from subtle favouritism (e.g., a supervisor selects someone more similar than different to himself for a preferred assignment) to overt antagonism (e.g., refusing to work with a colleague who is considered to be different on surface or deep level characteristics, or both), to harassment. Harassment is a behaviour 'that is unwanted by [an] individual that affects the dignity of any individual or group of individuals at work' (Lewis, Thornhill & Saunders, 2003: 414). Acts of harassment include not only unwanted physical, written, or verbal contact, but also social exclusion. Harassment in the workplace is consistent with bullying (Booth, Fosters, Robson & Welham, 2004). The likelihood of prejudice and discrimination in the workplace is increased when employees or volunteers can be distinguished or differentiated on some personal basis. Research suggests that discrimination is pervasive in sport organizations: women tend to face limited opportunities for advancement in intercollegiate athletics departments, women have more negative work experiences than men, racial minority coaches perceive fewer opportunities for advancement and receive fewer promotions, and gays and lesbians report prejudice and fewer opportunities for advancement in the workplace (Cunningham, 2007).

Diverse individuals who are in the minority in the organization or workgroup are likely to experience more stress in the workplace than others, and are at a disadvantage if their differences are not tolerated. They are less likely to be effective and succeed in the organization when attitudes and behaviour different from their own are expected and rewarded. Yet, diversity can also have a negative impact on those who are in the majority in terms of shared surface and deep level attributes. With diversity they may face contrasting and conflicting values and expectations, disrupted communication, and threats to their power and status in the workplace. Diversity comes with benefits and challenges.

The outcome of the diversity challenges may be reduced communication, misunderstanding, ambiguity or confusion, and destructive conflict where consensus is not possible and the conflict becomes more important than the task at hand (Doherty & Chelladurai, 1999). These outcomes can be expected to have a further impact on reduced effort and performance, absenteeism, and turnover.

Sport organizations can realize the potential benefits of diversity to the extent that there is diversity in the workplace, it is accepted there, and individuals and workgroups take advantage of differing perspectives that diversity may bring. However, the organization must effectively manage those differences and work to overcome the potential challenges of miscommunication, stereotyping and prejudice, and the uncertainty and anxiety that may cause for all in the organization, not just those who may be in the minority. We turn now to a discussion of strategies to effectively manage diversity.

Managing diversity

The focus of managing diversity is about both creating and optimizing on a diverse workforce. As noted earlier, diversity is likely inevitable in the organization, yet it should also be proactively cultivated. However, there are both benefits and challenges associated with a diverse workforce, with implications for SHRM. We begin by considering legal requirements related to managing diversity, then examine how an organization may capitalize on diversity through an organizational culture that values diversity. Finally, we examine diversity training as a mechanism for meeting an organization's legal requirements as well as developing and strengthening an organizational culture that values diversity.

Legal perspective

In many countries and regions, governments have enacted legislation to ensure the fair treatment of citizens, including employees and volunteers in the workplace. Many of the legal requirements that have led to an increasingly diverse workforce, and which were noted earlier (i.e., civil and human rights legislations), also serve to support and protect organizational employees from discrimination, inequity, and harassment. Thus, legislation also serves to manage diversity by protecting people who may be discriminated against on the basis of being different.

Many sport organizations and sport-governing bodies have also adopted their own policies that dictate fair and just practices with regard to the treatment of diverse employees. Canadian Interuniversity Sport (CIS), the governing body for interuniversity athletic competition in Canada, has an equity policy which states that it:

> accepts the principles of equity and equality and will ensure that these principles are adhered to in all its activities... Equity refers to treatment that is fair and just. This definition includes gender, race, ethnicity, language, disability, income and other diversities... Equality means that all persons enjoy the same status regardless of gender, race, ethnicity, language, disability, income, and other diversities. It means that all persons have equal conditions for realizing their full rights and potential and to benefit from the results. (CIS, 2006: 90–91)

All Canadian universities that are part of the CIS must abide by its policies, and demonstrate a commitment towards gender equity; for example, in hiring practices, coaching salaries, and support for professional development.

Organizational culture approach

The focus on managing diversity implies that the realization of potentially positive or negative consequences of diversity is a function of how that diversity is managed. We cannot just expect good things to come of differences in the workplace; there are many challenges and potentially negative consequences of diversity as well. Government legislation and organizational policies provide formal guidelines and requirements that help to deal with diversity and the potential challenges it creates. Doherty and Chelladurai (1999) provide a different perspective which is to consider organizational culture as a guiding force for managing diversity.

In Chapter 5, we introduced organizational culture as an underlying system of values, beliefs, and assumptions regarding what is important and how things are done in an organization. These values, beliefs, and assumptions are manifested in such organizational processes as communication patterns, decision making, performance appraisal, and rewards systems, which reflect what is valued and how things are done, and help to guide employee and volunteer behaviour. Thus, Doherty and Chelladurai (1999) argue that an organizational culture that values diversity provides a superior backdrop for the effective management of diversity, in comparison to an organizational culture that values similarity. As noted earlier, employees and volunteers cannot be expected to completely set aside their values, lifestyle preferences and even customs when they join an organization. These things contribute to diversity in the organization. Instead, the challenge to the organization is to accommodate differences and value the diversity they bring to the organization (Robbins, 1997).

An 'organizational culture of diversity' (Doherty & Chelladurai, 1999) is characterized by respect for differences, flexibility, risk acceptance, tolerance of ambiguity, conflict acceptance, and equifinality or achieving the same ends by different means. It is manifested in two-way, open communication, performance appraisal based on performance or outcomes rather than style, a flexible and equitable reward system, multilevel decision making, and open group membership. In contrast, an 'organizational culture of similarity' (Doherty & Chelladurai, 1999) is characterized by parochialism or ethnocentrism which assumes that there is one best way of doing things, rigidity, risk avoidance, intolerance of ambiguity, conflict avoidance, and a 'difference is deficit' perspective. It is manifested in one-way, closed communication, performance appraisal that focuses on style or how things are done rather than how well they are done, an inflexible reward and promotion system, unilateral decision making, and closed group membership.

Figure 11.1 presents a theoretical framework that makes several propositions regarding the interactive effect of workplace diversity (on a continuum of high to low) and an organizational culture that values diversity or similarity (Doherty & Chelladurai, 1999). It assumes a strong organizational culture where values and assumptions are widely understood and accepted, and guide member behaviour (McKenna & Beech, 2002; see Chapter 5). Cell 1 describes an organization characterized by high diversity and an organizational culture of similarity. In this situation, it is expected that few benefits of diversity may be realized and there is an increased likelihood of negative consequences. The challenges of diversity are heightened as differences are very present in the organization yet are not tolerated there. As a result, individuals

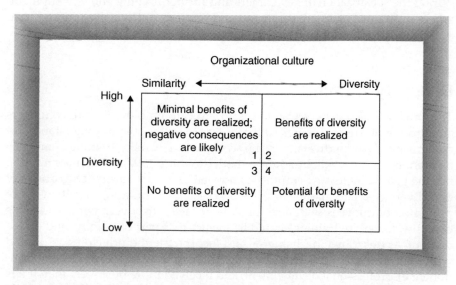

Figure 11.1 The impact of diversity as a function of organizational culture (*Source*: adapted from Doherty & Chelladurai, 1999: 290).

are likely to feel discriminated against; 'time is not taken to overcome the ambiguities associated with . . . diversity, and the opportunity for constructive conflict is avoided' (Doherty & Chelladurai, 1999: 290).

Cell 2 describes an organization characterized by high diversity and a culture that values diversity. The benefits of diversity can be realized as individuals feel accepted, and enhanced creativity and constructive conflict can result. In addition, organizations that are more aware and accepting of different points of view become more open to new ideas in general and can be more responsive to their environment than those that have closed and rigid approaches to problem solving (Milliken & Martins, 1996). Cell 3 describes an organization that has little diversity and values similarity. In this situation the potential benefits of diversity cannot be realized, although the challenges of diversity are also less likely to be experienced. Cell 4 describes an organization characterized by low diversity yet an organizational culture that values diversity. In this situation there is potential for the benefits of diversity to be realized if the organization was to become more diverse.

The framework has implications for the effective SHRM of diversity in terms of developing and strengthening an organizational culture that values diversity and increasing diversity in the organization to capitalize on the benefits that may be accrued in this environment. In Chapter 5, we discussed several ways to strengthen or change organizational culture. Briefly, the organization's leaders have an important influence on guiding the direction of organizational culture through what they pay attention to and modelling their own workplace behaviour. Organizational culture is influenced through recruitment and selection, where employees or volunteers with certain values and perspectives can help to reinforce or change culture in a desired direction. This is consistent with the notion of proactive hiring to increase diversity discussed earlier. Organizational culture can also be strengthened or changed during the socialization of newcomers and further training and development, where desirable values are presented and reinforced. Diversity training is an opportunity to develop and strengthen an organizational culture of diversity.

Diversity training

The purpose of diversity training is to educate employees and volunteers about diversity-related issues so that they are better able to understand and deal positively with diversity in the workplace. Diversity training comprises awareness training, skill-building, or both (Robbins, 1997). Awareness training has the goal of increasing employee knowledge of and sensitivity to diversity and diversity-related issues in the workplace. Skill building has the goal of providing employees with a set of skills to deal effectively with workplace diversity. Diversity training should be included as part of training and development, as described in Chapter 6, and incorporate the principles associated with that process. In this way, diversity training may be viewed as one component of professional development, and received more positively than if it is addressed as an obligation on the part of the organization and its staff to be 're-educated' to be more 'politically correct'.

There are many potential benefits of diversity training (e.g., increased attraction and retention of diverse employees who are bolstered by the organization's commitment to diversity, fostering understanding among diverse individuals and groups, curbing lawsuits) (Cunningham, 2007). However, there are also several barriers to its success: sensitive issues such as oppression, prejudice, discrimination, and sexual harassment are typically not discussed in open conversation; staff may resist the notion of re-education in political correctness or feel that they are being 'blamed' for any negative effects of diversity; and individuals may resist being 'helped' or singled out because they are different. These barriers to success can increase the negative effects of diversity (Cunningham, 2007).

Effective diversity training must be tailored to the particular organization, focusing on issues that are most salient there (e.g., discrimination against women or older workers, intolerance of different perspectives). A preliminary 'needs analysis' should be undertaken to identify the most salient diversity issues in the organization, as well as to confirm who will take part in the training, what information should be addressed, and in what form (Cunningham, 2007). Some of these considerations must take into account the 'training conditions', including trainees' readiness to learn and support for the training from managers and staff.

Diversity training methods may take a variety of forms, ranging from instructor-led information sessions, to cooperative group meetings, to mixed-gender or mixed-race role play sessions (Johns & Saks, 2001; Cunningham, 2007). Sessions usually begin by illustrating the value of diversity in the workplace, including the benefits that have been noted in this chapter, and increasing awareness of common stereotypes, including how they are formed and the implications of making (often false) generalizations. Diversity training is most effective when it provides an opportunity for individuals to reflect on their own differences, including how those differences may be assets to the organization, and to reflect on 'what it is like' or 'what it would be like' to be treated differently. This approach can enhance individuals' engagement in the training process. The next step is to develop skills to help individuals and workgroups deal effectively with workplace diversity. To be effective, diversity training must focus on the process of attitude change, and skills development that is relevant to the needs of the organization (Johns & Saks, 2001). This may include skills for resolving intercultural conflict, team building, or a second language. Finally, an effective diversity training programme should include a follow-up, to assess the content and form of the training itself (e.g., evaluate reactions, knowledge development, short-term behaviour), and promote transfer of learning (e.g., ensure a supportive environment for change, reinforce and reward for positive behaviour).

Summary

Workplace diversity can impact on work outcomes, both positively and negatively. Diversity is based on surface level or demographic differences, and deep level or psychological differences. Changing population demographics, especially an aging population and an increasing influx of immigrants to Western nations, has an impact on diversity in sport organizations. Other factors that contribute to workplace diversity include employment-related legislation and practices (e.g., affirmative action), proactive hiring to capitalize on the potential benefits of diversity, changes in the nature of work, and changing attitudes that lead to increased awareness of the diversity around us.

The benefits of diversity in the organization include creativity and better quality decisions as a result of different perspectives that challenge traditional ways of doing things. The organization may also benefit from an enhanced reputation as a diversity employer, improved recruiting when people in the workforce see people like themselves in the organization, and greater marketing insights into the needs and habits of diverse customers. Yet, workplace diversity also presents a number of SHRM challenges to the organization. Uncertainty, misunderstanding, ambiguity, confusion, anxiety, poor communication, stereotyping and prejudice, stress, and destructive conflict may result from the interaction of individuals who are different from each other. A further outcome may be reduced effort and performance, absenteeism, and turnover.

The potential challenges and benefits of workplace diversity depend on the effective management of that diversity. Legislation exists to protect workers from discrimination based on being different. Organizational culture may be viewed as a strategic mechanism for ensuring that diversity is valued in the workplace, and that supportive organizational processes are in place. The potential benefits of diversity can be expected to be optimized, and the challenges minimized, where an organization has workplace diversity and an 'organizational culture of diversity' which is supportive of and capitalizes on differences.

Diversity training is a strategic programme to educate employees and volunteers about diversity-related issues. The intent is to make the participants more aware of differences, including their own, and better prepared to deal with diversity issues in a positive way. Diversity training is one mechanism to develop or strengthen an organizational culture of diversity.

Discussion questions

1. Think of an organization where you have worked or volunteered, or with which you are very familiar. Describe the diversity in the organization's workforce (consider surface and deep level characteristics). How does that diversity (or lack of diversity, but rather, similarity) impact how work gets done, and how well it gets done (consider, for example, communication, conflict, creativity)?

2. In groups, discuss some general- and work-related stereotypes based on gender, race, and age. Next, discuss stereotypes in sport based on these characteristics. What other stereotypes are there in sport organizations?

3. What deep level differences might be associated with age? Consider the values, expectations, customs, and behaviours of different age groups.

What implications does this diversity have for the organization and all who work or volunteer there?

4. In groups, discuss affirmative action policies and programmes, using real or hypothetical examples. Are you, and your group, for or against affirmative action? Defend your position. Additionally, discuss affirmative action with regard to the parallel strategy of proactive hiring. Are you, and your group, for or against a joint programme of affirmative action and proactive hiring? Defend your position.

5. Refer back to the organization you described in Question 1. Based on the extent of diversity in the organization and your perception of the organizational culture there, where does it fit into the Doherty and Chelladurai (1999) framework in Figure 11.1? What can the organization do, if anything, to improve its management of diversity (e.g., increase diversity, develop or strengthen an organizational culture of diversity)? Discuss particular strategies for making that happen.

6. Identify an organization or type of organization (e.g., professional sports team, community recreation department) of your choice. Design a hypothetical diversity training programme for that organization. Consider how you would design a needs analysis, training conditions, content and form of training, and follow-up.

12 Evaluating and improving human resource management

Learning objectives

After reading this chapter you will be able to:

- Understand the approaches to evaluating human resource management (HRM) activities
- Describe how effective evaluation contributes to the strategic achievement of organizational goals
- Outline the steps and phases involved in benchmarking
- Outline the key components of a return-on-investment (ROI) evaluation

Chapter overview

Strategic human resource management (SHRM) is all about aligning human resources activities, planning, recruitment, selection, orientation, training, performance management, rewards, and motivation to meet a sport organization's goals. In this book we have suggested that well-planned and executed HR activities will make a significant contribution to the organization's performance and success. The implementation of HR policies and activities requires commitment and investment by the organization, and therefore it is logical to assume that there should be some assessment of the value of this investment. Commonly used measures of evaluation are presented in this chapter, together with discussion of considerations and issues in measuring HR effectiveness.

As HRM assumes a more strategic focus, understanding the relationship between HR activities and organizational performance becomes critical. The impact, benefit, or cost of HR activities should be assessed in some way (Cabrera & Cabrera, 2003). Evaluating the effectiveness of HR practices can provide the basis for making future decisions about how to manage the organization's human resources. The key questions in evaluating HR activities are: what is the relationship between the organization's human resources and can this relationship be measured? And, how does this measurement assist us to identify HR policies, processes, and programmes that will be able to positively contribute to the organization's success? While this may sound relatively straightforward, coming up with an effective way to measure the precise relationship between the contributions that HR makes to the organization and the 'bottom line' or the increasingly important 'triple bottom line'[1] has proven somewhat elusive. Many HR measures relate to outputs such as the efficiency of a specific HR activity as measured by turnover rates or performance ratings. These types of indicators, while useful, do not assess the impact HR has on organizational effectiveness and the delivery of the organization's strategic priorities.

Throughout this book we have discussed and presented 'good practice' in HR emphasising that sport organizations which engage in a strategic, people-centred approach to developing and implementing HR policies and practices can create a positive and productive work environment for employees and/or volunteers, and for the sport organization. Measuring this relationship with standard assessment procedures can be somewhat problematic as sport organizations will have a diverse range of goals relating to success, effectiveness, and efficiency. A community sport organization with a strategic goal of increased participation might set key performance indicators relating to the effective recruitment, training, and retention of volunteer coaches, managers, and board members. On the other hand a professional sport organization might

---

[1] A combination of economic, social, and environmental performance indicators.

determine that a key performance indicator relates to the training of staff to increase customer satisfaction ratings and expand market share. The measures selected to evaluate HR policies, processes, and activities should specifically address which HR dimensions have contributed to the attainment of the critical strategic objectives for the sport organization in question.

The importance of HRM measurement and evaluation

Measurement provides a basis for determining how HR adds value to the organization and improves its capacity to deliver its mission. This means that strategic and annual performance plans should assess progress on HR policies, processes, programmes, and success against key performance indicators. The evaluation will identify areas that have met or exceeded targets and highlight poorer performing dimensions for attention. Some of the more common evaluation measures include: performance relative to strategic goals, job satisfaction ratings, the level of participation in training and development activities, level of participation in mentoring programmes, percentage of employee/volunteer retention, and customer satisfaction surveys. In addition, surveys of workforce satisfaction or engagement are commonly used as forms of HR evaluation.

Organizational effectiveness measures are designed to link HR practices with outcome-related business performance measures and establish the HR–organization performance relationship (Becker, B., Huselid, M., & Ulrich, D, 2001). In one form or another, these approaches measure the HR outcomes and their impact on how well the organization performs. Some of the more commonly used HRM measurements such as the HR Audit, benchmarking, the balanced scorecard, and ROIs are presented in this chapter.

HR audit

An HR audit is used to assess effectiveness and efficiency and to ascertain how well HR polices, processes, and activities are aligned with the organization's strategic objectives. The audit may be carried out internally or might be outsourced to a specialist assessment agency. Audit methods include questionnaire surveys, interviews, focus groups, or document analysis. An HR audit includes aspects such as:

- The productivity per dollar of people costs (e.g., salary, benefits, training, etc.).
- Delivery on diversity, affirmative action, and/or equity criteria.

- The extent to which recruitment, selection, and retention processes meet the organization's targets in skill and knowledge areas.
- Effectiveness of the employee or volunteer orientation programme.
- The number of employees/volunteers completing required training programmes.
- Assessment of the extent to which the organization's development initiatives meet current and emerging organizational knowledge requirements.
- Success rate of specialized recruiting programmes in attracting qualified candidates.
- Success rate of talent identification and succession management programmes aimed to develop current employees for promotion.
- The number and nature and resolution of employee grievances.
- The 'people costs' incurred in order to generate a dollar of profit.
- The degree to which training has closed the gap between current competencies and needed future competencies.
- The percentage of 'poor' performers' improved performance as a result of HR initiatives.
- Employee satisfaction and engagement levels.

The importance of evaluating the success of HR policies is paramount. Merely documenting an HR policy is not a guarantee that there will be associated practices that successfully address the issue. For example, Moore, Parkhouse and Konrad's (2001) study of a range of sport organizations (in the USA) found that despite having substantive gender equality initiatives in place, the equality policies had no effect on increasing female manager representation in the sport organization. They concluded that the organizations' HR programmes were 'symbolic' rather than effective and that HR professionals need to better educate managers about the significant effects that discrimination has on the contemporary labour market in the sport industry.

Benchmarking

Benchmarking is a systematic process of measuring an organization's products, services, and practices against those of similar organizations, particularly those organizations that are deemed superior performers. This evaluation technique is used to identify the best ways to improve the HR function being evaluated and assure that it is aligned with the sport organization's strategic goals. Successful benchmarking assists with HR alignment through providing information for strategic HR planning, quality management, and employee/volunteer involvement. The development of efficiency and effectiveness ratios for measuring HR has provided the basis for benchmarking against other organizations (Fitz-enz, 1995). While benchmarking components will vary, some of the basic elements typically covered include the following:

- Employment and Deployment.
- Salaries and Remuneration.

- Staff Training and Development.
- Equal Employment Opportunity.
- Occupational Health Safety and Welfare.
- Employee Relations.

Camp (1989) developed a step-by-step model of benchmarking, identifying 10 steps in the process that encompasses four phases which are as follows:

Step 1: Identify the essential functions, products, or outputs to benchmark.	Phase 1: Planning
Step 2: Identify external organizations or functions within the organization with superior work practices for comparison.	Phase 2: Analysis
Step 3: Determine what data sources are to be used (e.g., HR systems, personnel records, surveys, interviews).	
Step 4: Determine the current level of performance. The baseline measurement will enable the gap in performance to be identified.	
Step 5: Develop a vision for improving future practice based on the benchmarking findings.	Phase 3: Integration
Step 6: Report progress to all stakeholders on an ongoing basis. Communication and feedback are crucial components of benchmarking.	
Step 7: Establish functional goals linked to the overall vision for the organization.	Phase 4: Action
Steps 8 & 9: Develop action plans and implement the best practice findings.	
Step 10: Update knowledge on current work practice to facilitate continuous quality improvement.	

The *Racial and Gender Report Card* (RGRC) is an example of a benchmarking exercise that is completed by an independent external organization. This is a generic evaluation and does not provide data against the organization's strategic goals, but rather it provides an industry specific overview of how well sport organizations are performing against specific equity criteria. The RGRC is an annual assessment by the Institute for Diversity and Ethics in Sport of hiring practices of women and people of colour in most of the leading professional and amateur sports and sporting organizations in the US.

It refers to players, coaches, and administrators in the National Basketball Association (NBA), National Football League (NFL), Major League Baseball (MLB), Major League Soccer (MLS), Women's National Basketball Association (WNBA), and collegiate athletics departments (NCAA). Grades given in each category for race are determined in relation to overall US demographics. As approximately 24 per cent of the US population is people of colour, if an organization has at least 24 per cent of employees classified as people of colour then the organization receives an employment grade of 'A' for race. For female employees a benchmark of 40 per cent results in an employment grade of 'A' in the gender category.

The *Report Card* is a useful benchmark to assist professional and college sport with its future HR policies, processes, and activities. In 2005, the NBA was rated as the best men's league performer for the 13th time, and earned its highest grade ever for race and its highest combined grade for race and gender (Lapchick, Martin, Kushner & Brenden, 2006). At the other end of the scale the practical application of the benchmarking data is evidenced in its use by the MLS which went from the industry's first-ever 'F' (i.e., poor rating) for gender in 2003 to score a 'B' for gender in 2004. After the MLS received the F grade in 2003, MLS league executives worked 'to dramatically alter their hiring guidelines and adopting several other initiatives aimed at improving diversity' (Lapchick et al., 2006: 15).

The benchmarking results for 2005 professional administration in college athletics detailed in Table 12.1 is an example of the *Report Card*. As indicated in the data presented in Table 12.1 women continue to be largely employed in academic advisor/counsellor positions, and in life skills coordinator positions. The NCAA has acknowledged this as a problem and in 2005 created a new position for a vice president for Diversity and Inclusion to address the issue (Lapchick et al., 2006).

Another example of benchmarking is the *Centre for Environmental and Recreation Management Performance Indicators (CERMPI®)*. This series of indicators provide a measure of financial accountability (efficiency) and customer service quality (effectiveness) for sport and leisure centres (Crilley, 2001). While CERMPI® is not an explicit evaluation of HRM activity, it does have implications for HR policy and practice. Based on total quality management (TQM) principles together with a programme evaluation approach the indicators used for benchmarking include finance, services, facilities, marketing, human resources, and risk management.

An annual report is produced for each participating organization and provides individual centre results on key performance indicators as well as medians for each of the indicators, providing the basis for comparison with similar sports and leisure centres' operating results and established industry benchmarks (Bell & Crilley, 2002). This information can be strategically used to target gaps in operational performance and devise HR strategies to address the problem areas (e.g., training programmes to improve low rating on customer service) or to reinforce a competitive advantage identified by the indicators (e.g., an organization's above industry standard results for highly knowledgeable and trained staff could be used in attracting highly qualified new staff). An example of how an Aquatic and Leisure Centre (owned

Table 12.1 Example of data from the RGRC

2005–2006	White		Black		Asian		Hispanic		Native American		Other Minority	
College professional administration by position *Division I*	Men (%)	Women (%)	Men (%)	Women (%)	Men (%)	Women (%)	Men (%)	Women (%)	Men (%)	Women (%)	Men (%)	Women (%)
Academic advisor/counsellor	24.50	49.10	13.50	10.00	0.00	0.10	1.20	1.00	0.00	0.00	0.30	0.30
Business manager	42.80	48.30	1.00	2.10	0.30	0.70	1.00	2.80	0.00	0.30	0.00	0.70
Compliance coordinator/officer	43.50	42.30	7.90	4.40	0.30	0.30	0.90	0.30	0.00	0.00	0.00	0.00
Equipment manager	75.40	9.90	7.00	1.60	1.90	0.00	2.40	1.10	0.50	0.00	0.00	0.30
Fundraiser/development manager	64.60	26.50	4.50	1.10	0.70	0.70	0.90	0.20	0.20	0.00	0.20	0.40
Facility manager	79.20	11.60	4.10	1.60	1.90	0.30	0.80	0.00	0.00	0.00	0.50	0.00
Life skills coordinator	17.80	57.20	10.60	9.60	0.50	0.00	1.40	1.90	0.50	0.00	0.00	0.50
Promotions/marketing manager	59.50	32.30	2.90	2.40	0.50	0.00	1.60	0.50	0.00	0.00	0.30	0.00
Sports information director	88.40	9.50	0.40	0.40	0.00	0.40	0.90	0.00	0.00	0.00	0.00	0.00
Assistant or associate SID	69.70	24.40	1.50	1.10	0.60	0.80	0.60	0.60	0.20	0.00	0.40	0.00
Strength coaches	75.20	9.90	10.30	1.20	0.80	0.20	0.80	0.40	0.60	0.20	0.00	0.20
Ticket manager	52.40	38.80	3.30	1.60	1.00	1.00	1.30	0.30	0.00	0.00	0.00	0.30

Note: Data provided by the NCAA. Historically Black Institutions excluded
Source: Lapchick et al. (2006).

by a local council and operated under lease by a management firm) interpreted its CERMPI® report is provided below.

Aquatic Leisure Centre – Annual CERM Performance Indicator Review[2]

Results

The target for overall satisfaction of patrons at the Centre has been exceeded. Our objective was to gain a level of satisfaction which exceeded 90 per cent of the industry mean. We achieved a rating of 3.51 per cent above the industry mean (5.9 compared to 5.7). This was extremely pleasing given the disruption at the Centre caused by the installation of the new UV filtration plant which would have undoubtedly influenced patron's perceptions.

Operational management

- Visits per square metre at the Aquatic Leisure Centre are above the CERMPI® Group 7 median (79 compared to 64). This is a significant improvement on last year and is 23 per cent above the industry mean. Growth in this area is expected to continue. The year saw 690,000 visitations to the Centre.
- An expense recovery result of 109 per cent represents excellent financial management in regard to expenditure vs. income. The Council is getting a higher than average financial return on every dollar that is invested into the Centre (industry standard recovery is 91 per cent). Overall expenses have been closely monitored and preventative maintenance regimes are now in place throughout the Centre, resulting in a reduction in overall maintenance costs. The marketing and focus of the Centre has assisted in the record 'expense recovery' results. The Centre has continually offered exciting and new courses and programmes while ensuring we actively promote to the greater community.

Customer service quality

- The Centre customers recorded an overall satisfaction mean above the CERMPI® mean (5.9 vs. 5.7), and well above the mean recorded in the previous survey (5.55).
- The percentage of customers who experienced a problem while attending the Centre (40 per cent) is still higher than the CERMPI® mean (38 per cent).

---

[2] Adapted from http://notesweb.hurstville.nsw.gov.au/ebpweb/buspapr2003.nsf/
399al99e8d373197ca256da9000fce25/04ac0b920aad7de3ca2571260016adaa?
Open Document retrieved 12 March 2007.

- The total percentage of respondents who would 'recommend' and 'strongly recommend' the centre to others is slightly below the CERMPI® mean (87 per cent vs. 92 per cent). This is a marginal improvement on last year.

Areas of strength

Based on customers' ratings of service quality, the Aquatic Leisure Centre's areas of strength include:

- Organization: This reflects the ongoing improvement and development of the Centre to meet the Annual Business Plan objectives and the changing needs of the community.
- Staff friendliness: Any facility is a reflection of its staff. An ingredient for repeat business is the way in which the customer is treated and made to feel and this attribute will contribute and assist in the goal for a record usage of the Centre. Staff friendliness provides an incentive to return.
- Staff experience/knowledge: Ensures that the patrons are well catered for and professionally and appropriately taught, guided, and supervised.
- Staff presentation: Ensures that the patrons can not only identify staff but also that they are presented to a high standard displaying the professionalism demanded.
- Instructors' experience and knowledge: Patrons are clearly comfortable that they are gaining the optimum instruction and direction when using the facility – be it in the swimming pool, gym, or stadium.

Areas for development

Areas for development from the previous year have all been addressed, showing a clear response to the feedback provided by patrons in the previous CERM customer survey.

Areas for ongoing monitoring

Based on customers' ratings of service quality, the areas for ongoing monitoring are as follows:

- Parking suitability: on occasions there is insufficient parking space for the numbers of patrons using the facility.
- Food and drink facilities: Review results indicated some dissatisfaction with the food and drinks offered at the Centre. Issues such as junk food and 'slow service' are highlighted. Additional catering staff will be engaged during peak periods and consideration will be given to the reconfiguration of the counter-area to help further promote the health food alternatives presently on offer.

Conclusion

Generally, the Aquatic Leisure Centre's results in the CERM Survey have proved to be a great improvement over last year's results and reflect the growing success of the Centre both in the areas of financial viability and service provision. Not only have successful financial results been achieved in comparison to the CERM medians, but the Centre has also achieved a record number of users.

Overall, the CERM survey results have confirmed the positive direction and focus that Centre Management has taken in the last few years. This CERM result has confirmed that the Aquatic Leisure Centre is meeting the needs of the greater community.

Discussion question

1. What aspects of the report relate directly or indirectly to HRM?

Another widely used measure of overall organizational progress is the *balanced scorecard approach* (Kaplan & Norton, 1996a, b). The balanced scorecard is a management and measurement system that provides a framework for translating an organization's vision and strategy into action. Feedback on both the internal business processes outputs and external outcomes are provided to continuously improve strategic performance. The balanced scorecard builds on concepts such as customer-defined quality, continuous improvement, employee empowerment using measurement-based management, and feedback. The scorecard is used to translate strategy into operational terms by measuring a full range of perspectives: financial, customer, internal business process, and learning and growth. A comprehensive set of measures or indicators for each perspective is articulated via metrics developed from the sport organization's strategic plan priorities. The outcome measures reflect the status of the sport organization at any given point in time and provide information to suggest improvements on a continuous basis. The analysis of data and the measures or indicators should also be evaluated regularly (Becker, Huselid & Ulrich, 2001).

The 'broader balanced' scorecard is complemented by the *HR Scorecard* which is an organizational level HR measure that describes and measures how people and HRM systems create value in organizations (Becker et al., 2001). *The HR Scorecard*[3] focuses on measures of five key HR-related elements, which are as follows:

1. Workforce success: The degree to which the workforce has accomplished the key strategic objectives for the business.
2. Right HR costs: Is the total investment in the workforce appropriate?

[3] See: http://www.markhuselid.com/hr.html

3. Right types of HR alignment: The extent to which there is alignment of HR practices with the business strategy and differentiated across positions, where appropriate.
4. Right HR practices: The degree to which the design and implementation of best HR management policies and practices is used throughout the organization.
5. Right HR professionals: The skills in HR needed to design and implement a world-class HR management system.

An example of an HR Scorecard and its components is presented in Figure 12.1.

The HR scorecard was developed to assist organizations manage human resources as strategic assets. The HR Scorecard explains and measures how human resources and the associated management systems create value in organizations, as well as serving the broader function of communicating the organization's objectives in this area.

An evaluation framework and return on investment (ROI)

Kirkpatrick's (1998) four-level model of categorizing evaluation data is a commonly used systemic approach to measuring training's impact. The four levels are as follows:

Level 1: Measures *reaction and the action planned* following training or learning initiatives.
Level 2: Measures *learning* and knowledge changes as it relates to successful programme implementation, using a range of methods such as self- or facilitator assessment or skill tests.
Level 3: Measures the extent to which trainees *apply* learned skill and knowledge to the job.
Level 4: Measures changes in *business results* related directly to the HR initiative, using a range of methods such as increased revenues, improved quality, reduced response times, and enhanced efficiency.

In addition, Phillips (1997) suggested a fifth level of HR evaluation to capture the financial impact of training programmes or return on investment (ROI). ROI is a traditional financial measure based on historic data and thus is a relatively static measure. The formula for ROI is:

$$(\text{Total benefit} - \text{Total costs})/\text{Total costs} = --- \times 100 = \text{ROI}$$

For example, to calculate the monetary ROI for a training programme used by a sport organization you would first identify the total financial benefit your organization draws the training programme and then subtract from that the total investment made to develop, produce, and deliver that programme. Measurement of all of the costs associated with the programme can be quite complex and it can be even more difficult to quarantine the financial benefits.

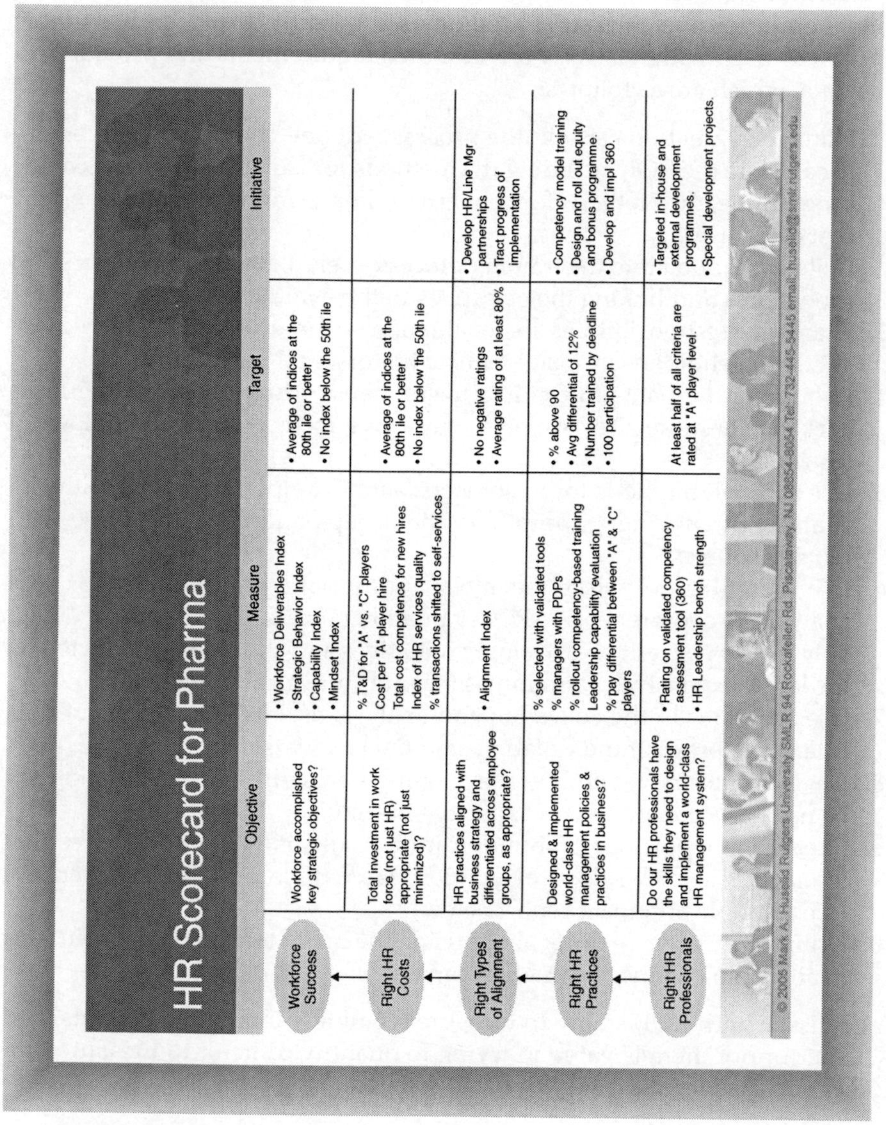
HR Scorecard for Pharma

	Objective	Measure	Target	Initiative
Workforce Success	Workforce accomplished key strategic objectives?	• Workforce Deliverables Index • Strategic Behavior Index • Capability Index • Mindset Index	• Average of indices at the 80th ile or better • No index below the 50th ile	
Right HR Costs	Total investment in work force (not just HR) appropriate (not just minimized)?	% T&D for "A" vs. "C" players Cost per "A" player hire Total cost competence for new hires Index of HR services quality % transactions shifted to self-services	• Average of indices at the 80th ile or better • No index below the 50th ile	
Right Types of Alignment	HR practices aligned with business strategy and differentiated across employee groups, as appropriate?	• Alignment Index	• No negative ratings • Average rating of at least 80%	• Develop HR/Line Mgr partnerships • Tract progress of implementation
Right HR Practices	Designed & implemented world-class HR management policies & practices in business?	% selected with validated tools % managers with PDPs % rollout competency-based training Leadership capability evaluation % pay differential between "A" & "C" players	• % above 90 • Avg differential of 12% • Number trained by deadline • 100 participation	• Competency model training • Design and roll out equity and bonus programme. • Develop and impl 360.
Right HR Professionals	Do our HR professionals have the skills they need to design and implement a world-class HR management system?	• Rating on validated competency assessment tool (360) • HR Leadership bench strength	At least half of all criteria are rated at "A" player level.	• Targeted in-house and external development programmes. • Special development projects.

© 2005 Mark A. Huselid Rutgers University SMLR 94 Rockafeller Rd. Piscataway, NJ 08854-8054 Tel: 732-445-5445 email: huselid@smlr.rutgers.edu

Figure 12.1

Benefits include costs saved by the organization, financial gains, and whatever else that adds directly or indirectly to the bottom line. Total costs might include development costs, programme materials, meals, facilities, cost of coordination, cost of job coverage during training, overhead of instructors, and any other cost incurred. Online course costs could include money spent for time on servers, graphics, web development, or CD-production costs.

As achieving a results-oriented evaluation focus can be time consuming and labour intensive, Burkett (2005a) devised a list of 10 approaches to ROI that can be used with relatively few resource requirements and provide reliable data, which are as follows:

1. Plan for evaluation early in the process – define components necessary to calculate the ROI, including the methods for isolating the effects of the programme, the methods for converting data to monetary value, and the cost categories.
2. Build evaluation into the training process – select evaluation policies and procedures and linking the objectives to the evaluation targets.
3. Share the responsibilities for evaluation – these would include managers, stakeholders, instructional facilitators, and participants.
4. Require participants to conduct major steps – through providing feedback via questionnaires, surveys, interviews, focus groups, and follow-up sessions.
5. Use shortcut methods for major steps – for example, save time with gap analysis by making assumptions about gaps and checking these with reliable sources.
6. Use sampling to select the most appropriate programmes for ROI analysis – a comprehensive ROI evaluation process is recommended with only 5 to 10 per cent of all training initiatives and should be conducted on the large, expensive programmes that are strategically important.
7. Use estimates in the collection and analysis of data – cuts costs of data collection, programme isolation, and data conversion.
8. Develop internal capability – developing staff skill-sets in evaluation can be used as a component of capacity building.
9. Streamline reporting – communicating results is vital and ensures that management views ROI evaluation as credible and business critical (see example of impact report below)
10. Utilize technology – think about using the many technological solutions available to enhance evaluation capabilities.

A key issue with ROI is how to measure seemingly intangible benefits, and whether or not there is value in trying to quantify difficult to measure outcomes such as increased employee satisfaction.

Calculating ROI

Let us look first at an example of how to use estimates for isolation and data conversion. In the first instance, participant estimates are obtained by asking a series of questions, usually in a post-programme questionnaire. Question-naire items include the following:

- As a result of this programme, what specific actions will you apply based upon what you have learned?
- How often will you apply this behaviour and under what conditions?
- What specific unit of measure will change as a result of your actions?
- As a result of these anticipated changes, please estimate the monetary benefits to your department over a 1-month period.
- What is the basis for your estimate?
- What level of confidence, expressed as a percentage, do you place on the above estimate? (100 per cent ¼ certainty and 0 per cent ¼ no confidence).
- What percent of this improvement can be attributed to the application of skills/techniques/knowledge gained in the training programme?
- What other factors, besides training, may contribute to benefits associated with process improvements changes?

Participant 1	Annual improvement value (A)	Basis of estimate	Isolation factor (B)	Confidence level (C)	Adjusted value (D)
	$36,000	Improvement in project efficiency. Time saved problem solving ($3k mth × 12)	50%	85%	$15,300

In this case the participant allocates 50 per cent of the improvement to training but is only 85 per cent confident about this estimate. The confidence percentage is then multiplied by the estimate to develop a cost–benefit value, as follows:

$$\text{Improvement value (A)} = \$36,000 \times \text{Percent of improvement isolated to training}$$

$$= 50\% \times \text{Confidence level (C)}$$

$$= \text{Cost–benefit improvement value (D) } \$15,300$$

The adjusted values (D) for all participant estimates are then totalled as cost–benefit data for the final ROI calculation, in which monetary programme benefits are compared to fully loaded programme costs. To calculate ROI, the programme costs are subtracted from the total benefits to produce the net benefits, which are then divided by the costs:

$$\text{ROI} = (\text{Total benefits} - \text{Programme costs}) \times 100$$

After considering additional factors, such as technology, procedures, and process changes, which could have contributed to reengineering improvements, senior management applied an additional subjective factor, in this case 50 per cent, to represent the ROI results that should be attributed to the training programme. The 50 per cent factor was developed in a meeting with top managers and therefore had the benefit of group ownership.

Example of impact study report

Programme Title: Continuous Improvement Program in Customer Relationship Management.

Target Audience: Pilot groups of cross-functional team members

Duration: 6 weeks (36 hours).

Technique to Isolate Effects: Participant estimation, trend analysis

Technique to Convert Data to Monetary Value: Historical costs, internal experts, labour cost per unit, units per person per hour (formula).

Fully Loaded Programme Costs: $53,000.

Reaction results	Learning results	Application results	Business impact results	ROI	Intangible benefits
4.8 out of 5 achieved on overall satisfaction 4.8 out of 5 achieved on recommending programme to others Rating of 4.5 on relevance of programme to daily job 94% reported intention to apply learnings to team project plan within 30 days of the workshop	Participants demonstrated ability with select continuous improvement skills during action learning scenarios (i.e., root cause analysis exercises; values added flow analysis demonstration) Participants completed qualification assessment with 100% accuracy	94% applied continuous improvement skills to a defined project within 30 days of workshop 86% report significant productivity increase in daily work as a result of applied continuous improvement skills	Monetary benefits from increased units per person per hour $79,550 value (based upon average CRM life cycle of 21.5 weeks) Monetary benefits from increased labour efficiencies: $70,058	ROI (%) = Net programme benefits/ Cost $149,608 – 53,000/ 53,000 = 1.82 × 100 = 182%	Increased systems view Increased problem-solving skills Improved cross-functional collaboration Improved decision making Improved process understanding Better picture of the cost associated with CRM

Source: Adapted from Burkett, 2005b.

Cost–benefit analysis is another decision making technique that involves explicitly considering the position outcomes (benefits) as well as the negative outcomes (costs) of different decision alternatives (Boudreau, 1990). It is used to make decisions re-consistently, systematically, and correctly and to communicate decisions. Cost-benefit analysis calculates the financial return of investing in human resources. This includes costing staffing systems, training programmes, volunteer management programmes, and HR systems. In addition to considerations of ROI the cost-benefit analysis will provide the information to answer the key question, 'Is it worth investing resources in this policy/practice to improve the quality of our human resources?'

Summary

Sport organizations should evaluate their HRM policies and practices to ensure achievement of strategic goals. Evaluation assists the organization to assess financial costs and benefits of HR plans and polices; with ensuring that accountabilities for HR do not fall off managers' agenda; identifying which practices need to be updated or removed; and 'marketing' and communicating about the importance of HR.

There are a range of evaluation measures that a sport organization can use to determine the success of its HR activity. The size of the sport organization and the resources it has at its disposal for evaluation will undoubtedly shape the analytical methods employed by the organization. Evaluation can be internally or externally focused and may be carried out by organizational staff, external agencies contracted to undertake evaluations, or by independent bodies. Each form of evaluation provides the organization feedback on which to assess how its HR contributes strategically to organizational effectiveness.

Discussion questions

1. Choose a sport organization that you have worked for or one that you are familiar with – list a range of evaluation techniques that you could use to measure the effectiveness of their HR policies and practices.
2. Devise a list of criteria and associated key performance indicators for evaluating a sport organization's employee/volunteer induction programme. What costs and benefits might you include if you were calculating an ROI for the induction programme?
3. The Aquatic Leisure Centre Review in this chapter is a report to the local council. How would you advise the council uses this evaluation in its future HR planning for the centre?

13 Managing change and future challenges in sport organizations

Learning objectives

After reading this chapter you will be able to:

- Explain factors driving change in sport organizations
- Describe the human resource (HR) implications of change in the workplace
- Understand how to strategically manage change with respect to HR
- Outline challenges to sport organizations in the future and understand the implications for strategic human resource management (SHRM)

Chapter overview

This chapter describes the key factors to consider with regard to SHRM when introducing or dealing with change in the sport organization. Planned change is a critical part of an organization's corporate strategy. The strategic corporate issue is the nature of change, while the SHRM issue is the implementation of that change and factors that influence the success of the change initiatives. The nature of change cannot be properly understood without acknowledging the acceptance of or resistance to the change among personnel who have to make it work. Effective human resource management (HRM) is an important part of the successful implementation of strategic organizational change.

There are many factors that drive change in sport and these can come from pressures from the external environment (e.g., changes to government policy, introduction of competitors into the marketplace, changing patterns of sport participation, aging population) or the internal environment (e.g., decline in membership numbers, financial challenges to overcome, organizational inefficiencies, training needs). Forces that drive different types of change in sport organizations are presented in this chapter. The organizational change process involves the stimulus to take action, identification of the problem and selection of a solution, and finally the implementation of that solution or change initiative which takes the organization from point A to point B. Organizational change is often resisted when employees and volunteers do not share the organization's view about the particular change, or about change in general. Humans are creatures of habit and dislike the uncertainty that accompanies any change process. There are several positive strategies that may be used to try to overcome resistance to change and to help people cope with the change in the organization. Key sources of resistance to organizational change and strategies for overcoming that resistance are presented here.

Sport organizations will face many challenges in the next 5–10 years, challenges which will have a major impact on the way HR is managed and will require organizations to manage the accompanying changes to survive. We outline some of these key challenges in this chapter.

Change in sport organizations

It is important to understand the concept of organizational change because (1) change is inevitable for survival, (2) change is paradoxical in that it is necessary and inevitable, yet stability and predictability are inherently preferred states for organizations and individuals, and (3) successful management of change is essential for organizational effectiveness (Slack & Parent, 2006). The focus of this chapter is on planned change that is systematically developed and implemented vs. day-to-day fluctuations in the organization. Organizational development is a form of planned change and is included within our conceptualization of change.

Types of change

Change may be in the form of products or services that the sport organization offers, production technology, organizational structure and systems (e.g., HR, rewards), or people (Slack & Parent, 2006). Changes to what the organization offers in terms of products or services may be the most common form of change, and may precipitate change in other areas of the organization. For example, when Nike bought the Bauer Sports Apparel Company, it added ice hockey skates to its well-established line of running and basketball shoes. This acquisition and change to its product line had further ramifications for the manufacturing, marketing, and retail systems of Nike Corporation, and resulted in changes to the organization's structure and personnel. On a smaller scale, when a fitness club updates its programmes (e.g., eliminating step classes and introducing spin classes), this is likely to have implications for personnel in the club, whether it is no longer employing staff who are not qualified to offer the new programmes or providing existing staff with retraining.

Changes in organizational technology are exemplified by the dramatic rise of the World Wide Web. If sport organizations are not on board with Internet technology (e.g., organization website, electronic retailing, online registration system) they may be considered behind the times and missing a critical mechanism for communicating with staff, volunteers, participants, and consumers. Other technological changes include updated production processes, and skills and methods to deliver services. Video replay in sporting contests, computerized scoring in judged sports, and athlete drug testing are a few examples of technological changes realized in sport.

Changes to organizational structure and systems include modifications to the division of labour or the hierarchy of authority in a sport organization. As a new sport consulting firm grows it may create differentiated units to attend to various aspects of the business; for example, event management, athlete representation, finance, and HR departments. Change to an organizational system can be illustrated by the partial or complete revision of a sporting goods retailer's pay structure; for example, with the introduction, or elimination, of a commission-based compensation system (see Chapter 8 for a discussion of rewards systems).

Finally, people changes refer to movement among and modifications within staff and volunteer ranks. People changes may involve hiring, promotion, transfer, and dismissal, as personnel come and go, or move elsewhere in the organization. Changes within people in the organization may involve at a personal level the development of new skills, values, and attitudes in the workplace as a result of training and professional development.

Forces for change

Both internal and external pressures can lead to change in the organization. Internal pressure for change may come from such things as financial challenges or opportunities, operational inefficiencies, or disgruntled employees. In order to overcome financial challenges; for example, a sporting goods retailer may eliminate staff, change its pricing structure, or sell off part of its stock. In contrast, in order to pursue financial growth opportunities, a community recreation centre may add programmes, hire additional staff, and even consider building or acquiring new sports facility space.

Pressures for change can also be exerted by external stakeholders of the organization and forces in the general environment. Pressure to keep up with competitors, and to better meet the needs of current and prospective customers, maintaining accountability to funding bodies (e.g., government, sponsors), changes in government policy, and sport legislative bodies can provide the impetus for strategic organizational change. Sports organizations also face external pressures from the general environment that affect all organizations; for example, changing population demographics, the economy, and legislation regarding free trade and human rights. The source, nature, and strength of internal and external pressures for organizational change may impact staff and volunteers' reaction to and acceptance of change. For example, a large influx of older adults into the region may require the local swimming centre to shift its focus from running learn-to-swim classes for children to offering aqua aerobics and senior's keep-fit sessions. This type of change is gradual and non-threatening. However, a swimming centre that changes from being a local government operated venture, offering programmes at low cost staffed by instructors with a community service orientation, to a commercial business only running programmes with high profit margins with an expectation that staff would engage in sales type activities might expect some resistance to change from its staff given the significant cultural shift required.

The organizational change process

As the above examples suggest, change involves moving from one state of affairs to another, based on various degrees of modification or complete replacement of existing conditions (products, services, technology, structures, systems, people), or the introduction of new conditions. Lewin's (1951) force field model suggests that, before embarking on planned change, an organization is in a state of equilibrium between forces that drive and restrain change. In order to effect change, the driving forces must be strengthened and the restraining forces weakened, so that the organization may 'unfreeze' from its current values, attitudes, and ways of doing things, 'change' towards the desired condition, and then 'refreeze' the values, attitudes, and practices that support the new condition.

Greiner (1967) elaborates on several stages that an organization goes through in the process of moving from one existing condition to another modified or new condition. A stages model of organizational change helps in recognizing the various pressures and actions throughout the process, and identifying where a breakdown in that process may have occurred. Figure 13.1 presents a simplified illustration of Greiner's stages of organizational change.

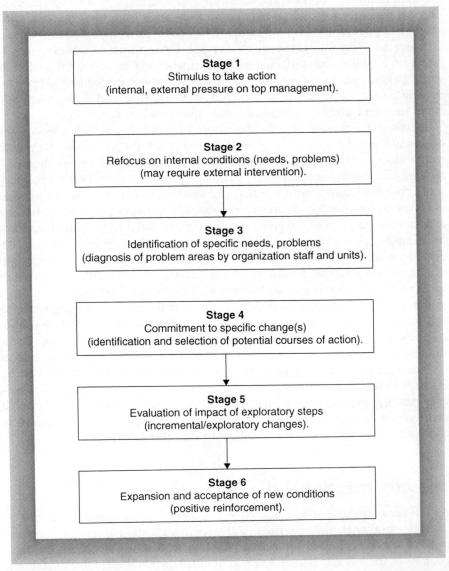

Figure 13.1 Stages of action (and factors influencing that action) in the organizational change process (Greiner, 1967).

Each stage describes the action taken by the organization and (in parentheses) the factors influencing or prompting that action. The role and influence of management and staff is indicated throughout Greiner's (1967) stages model. Top management is prompted to take action by sufficient internal or external pressure, or both (stage 1). Refocusing on what are acknowledged as internal problems or needs (stage 2) is followed by diagnosis of problem areas by individual staff and workgroups or units resulting in the identification of specific problem areas (stage 3). Here the 'problem' is used broadly to refer to a dilemma or challenge faced by the organization. Successful organizational change involves staff in the diagnosis and identification of problem areas as it sends the message that their input is valued by the top management (Greiner, 1967). This is also the case at the next stage where potential solutions are identified and a preferred course of action is selected (stage 4); again, the involvement of staff can enhance the creativity and practicality of alternative solutions (as they are the ones adopting the change) and increase their commitment to the change process. The final stages 5 and 6 involve evaluating the impact of small, incremental modifications as the specific organizational change(s) is introduced on a small scale at first, then expanded until the change is implemented in its entirety and, presumably, accepted.

Greiner's (1967) model is not perfect as it assumes a smooth, sequential process that does not account for incomplete or partial change (Slack & Parent, 2006). However, it is useful for understanding key steps in the change process, and the potential role and influence of staff at various stages. The importance of involving staff in the change process is consistent with the notion of creating positive employee relations presented in Chapter 9. It is also consistent with managing resistance to change that is manifested when people's views about change differ from the organization's and, at a basic level, when people prefer stability and predictability over the disruption and uncertainty that is inherent in organizational change. Resistance (restraining forces) must be overcome if the organization is to successfully unfreeze from its current conditions, change to its desired conditions, and refreeze into a state of equilibrium (Lewin, 1951). We turn now to a discussion of resistance to change, and managing that resistance.

Resistance to change

Organizational change is a critical SHRM issue in large part because of the expected internal resistance to change. Change may be resisted by external stakeholders as well; however, our discussion focuses on the internal workplace. As a restraining force (Lewin, 1951), resistance can affect how efficiently, and completely, the planned change has been implemented. Humans are creatures of habit and so we inherently prefer stability and certainty (Robbins, 1997; McKenna & Beech, 2002). As such, change can be uncomfortable because it challenges established routines and practices. Individuals with a particularly low tolerance for change may oppose change even though they recognize the benefits to the organization (McKenna & Beech, 2002). Of course, people will also resist change if they do not agree with the need, form, or consequences of the planned change. Slack and Parent (2006) identify four major sources of resistance to change (consider these with respect to some of the types of changes noted earlier):

- *Self-interest*: People are focused on their own self-interests in the organization. As a result, change may be resisted if; for example, it threatens one's power or influence and expertise in the organization, if it results in reduced resources allocated to one's programme or department, it compromises future job security and income, or challenges an individual's values and beliefs.
- *Lack of trust*: The uncertainty associated with change may breed mistrust between management and staff, or between staff who do and do not support the change. This mistrust is likely to cause resistance to change. If there is already a certain level of mistrust in the organization, change may heighten that situation and add to the resistance.
- *Differing perceptions of outcomes*: Individuals may not value or give much weight to the purported need for change and the anticipated benefits, or they may not feel that the anticipated benefits will be realized at all. As a result, they will resist change as a needless effort that will only create uncertainty and anxiety in the organization.
- *Cost of change*: Change may be resisted because of the anticipated costs, in terms of time, money, and effort, to implement the change, particularly if it is felt that the costs outweigh the benefits.

The expression of resistance to change may be overt or implicit, and it may be immediate or deferred (Robbins, 1997). Resistance is expressed immediately in direct response to the announcement (or rumour) of change. Deferred resistance may be played out over time and continue, or be postponed, to be well after the change has been implemented. Overt reactions include voicing complaints, writing letters, engaging in a work slowdown, or even threatening to strike. Implicit resistance is more subtle and may be difficult to link to the proposed change; for example, loss of motivation, absenteeism, poor performance, or reduced loyalty.

Managing resistance to change

Coping with change

Assuming that individuals prefer stability and certainty, and dislike the anxiety and stress caused by resistance to organizational change, we may expect that they will make every effort to cope with change. Coping is defined as a conscious effort to use one's resources to deal positively with a stressful circumstance(s) (Ashford, 1988). Understanding the psychological coping process can help organizations to support their workforce in dealing with change. Later in this chapter, we consider several strategies for helping personnel to overcome any resistance they may feel and to cope with the new organizational conditions.

According to Carnall (1990), employees and volunteers will go through a 'cycle of coping' with change; one that can have important implications for their self-esteem, motivation, and performance. In general, when first presented with a proposal for change, individuals may experience *denial* that any change is necessary. Through this denial they may feel a heightened sense of self-esteem as they reflect on their attachment to the current way of doing things. Subsequently, individuals may experience *defence* as preliminary discussions take place about the nature and form of the change. This resistance can manifest itself in lowered self-esteem, motivation, and performance as individuals feel threatened by the impending change. This resistance may continue as more concrete plans take shape and are presented in the organization.

The next stage in the coping cycle involves, eventually, *discarding* old attitudes and ways of doing things as individuals realize that the planned change is necessary and inevitable. This stage is consistent with 'unfreezing' the organization from its existing state (Lewin, 1951), and coincides with some improvement in self-esteem as individuals let go of 'the old way' and prepare to move on. Motivation and performance may continue to be suppressed as individuals experience uncertainty regarding what is expected in the transition from old to new. Next, individuals will experience *adaptation* by coming to terms with the new way(s) of doing things. This is consistent with the 'change' phase of Lewin's model. While individuals' self-esteem and motivation can be expected to increase with their greater understanding of and comfort with new conditions, performance may still lag behind, particularly where new skills are required. The final stage in the coping cycle is *internalization*, where the change is well understood and accepted, and the organization 'refreezes' to a state of equilibrium (Lewin, 1951). Increased self-esteem, motivation, and performance can be expected as individuals have adopted the new conditions and acquired the knowledge and skills to perform in the new environment.

Strategies

There are several ways to overcome resistance in the organization (Robbins, 1997; McKenna & Beech, 2002; Slack & Parent, 2006). These strategies are intended to address the various types of resistance noted above.

1. *Communication and education*: Resistance to change can result from a lack of information or misinformation about the need for change, nature of the change, and anticipated consequences. Effective communication of thorough, accurate, and timely information about the change process is

necessary for managing resistance to change. Information can be shared through various methods of communication, depending on the volume and complexity of the information, and whether feedback is desired; for example, memos or reports, individual, workgroup, departmental- or organization-wide staff meetings, or workshops. Communication and education is an effective strategy for reducing resistance to change, assuming that inadequate information is the cause of resistance, and there is mutual trust and credibility in the management–employee relationship.

2. *Participation*: Consistent with the employee relations approach advocated in Chapter 9, direct involvement in the change process, particularly in decision making, can be an effective way to generate commitment to the change, as well as taking advantage of the knowledge and creativity of the personnel who will be directly associated with that change. Staff and volunteer participation in the change process, from the early planning stages (Greiner, 1967), is particularly important for those individuals who are or may be expected to be the most vocal opponents of the (or any) change. The trade-off of reduced resistance, increased commitment, and greater quality decisions is the potentially heavy time cost to individuals and the organization of the meaningful involvement of staff and volunteers in the change process.

3. *Change teams*: Groups formed specifically to facilitate communication, education, and participation of staff and volunteers in the change process can be very effective mechanisms for managing resistance in the organization. A change team (or multiple teams) may be, for example, a task force, transition team, or an interdepartmental committee of employee representatives. Change teams are charged with participating in the change process on behalf of their colleagues, communicating with those colleagues about what is happening along the way (providing their perspective, or formal information from management, or both), assisting with any training that is required as a result of the change, and providing counselling to staff and volunteers as requested. The participation of change teams is likely more efficient than the involvement of the full organizational workforce, and may be more effective in terms of compiling the information and bringing it to their peers.

4. *Idea champions*: Individuals who are very committed to the notion of change in general, and the proposed organizational change in particular, are effective idea champions. They must be knowledgeable and well respected in the organization in order to play a key role in getting people involved in the change process, and helping to counter any resistance. Idea champions may be identified by the organization and co-opted to serve that role, or they may emerge informally based on their commitment and knowledge of the change. Either way, they may be 'one of the most effective weapons in the battle for change' (Daft, 1992: 273, in Slack & Parent, 2006).

5. *Facilitation and support*: Change teams, and the organization itself, can provide support to help staff and volunteers cope with the change process. A supportive atmosphere can help individuals deal with the

anxiety and stress resulting from the uncertainty associated with change, which may lead to resistance. Employee counselling or therapy, skills training, and even a short-paid leave of absence may facilitate the adjustment process, although there is no guarantee that these potentially costly efforts will lower resistance to change. They are most likely to be effective with personnel who need some help moving on to the 'discarding' and 'adaptation' stages of the coping cycle (Carnall, 1990).

6. *Negotiation*: Another, perhaps last resort, strategy for overcoming resistance to change is through exchanging something of value in return for compliance with the planned change. This negotiation or bargaining tactic may be necessary when resistance comes from a powerful individual or group in the organization. For example, when several Canadian national sport organizations relocated from Ottawa (the capital of the country) to Toronto, Ontario (the *corporate* capital of the country), senior staff members were offered a pay increase and housing allowance to encourage them to accept the change.

Several of these strategies for managing resistance to change may be used in combination as the organization deems appropriate and necessary. The more traditional practices of manipulation (e.g., distorting or providing false information about change that makes it seem more attractive to employees, splitting, and therefore weakening dissenting groups, or covertly influencing powerful resistors), and coercion (e.g., threatening demotion, transfer, or dismissal) for managing resistance by completing bypassing it are not consistent with the SHRM approach (McKenna & Beech, 2002).

Our discussion to this point has identified change as a strategic corporate issue that has critical implications for effective HRM to ensure its successful implementation in the organization. We turn now to a discussion of several challenges that will present internal and external pressures for change in sport organizations in the near future.

Challenges for HRM

The sport organization of today and the future faces challenges related to globalization, technology and telecommunication advances, deregulation, diversity and other workforce trends, demographic changes, a shift towards a service society, as well as trends in the nature of work (Dessler, 2000). Issues will emerge over the next 10 years that we cannot even contemplate today. Some of the challenges that currently face sport organizations are outlined below.

Globalization and change

Globalization is 'commerce without borders, along with the interdependence of business operations in different locations' (Cascio, 2003: 404). While sport may still be delivered in local markets its reach and context is increasingly global. Regional vision is being replaced by a new global economic perspective and strategic vision, which means sport organizations are increasingly moving to thinking globally and acting locally. Markets are no longer locally restricted and global trends impact local demand and organizational requirements.

The globalizing of a sport organization is reflected in a range of indicators such as the amount of foreign investment in the sport (e.g., the number of non-UK owned football teams in the English Premier League), and the growing presence of multinational companies (e.g., Dorna Sports in Spain, UK & Japan). Satellite dishes in world's most remote areas bring the sport product to audiences anywhere and anytime, and there is intense competition to buy the media rights to broadcast sport in and beyond national boundaries. Global telecommunication has opened up sports markets (e.g., the use of EBay for match tickets and all types of sporting merchandize means that you can purchase by phone and speaking with someone in another province, state, or even country). These changes have significant implications for workers and organizations (Cascio, 2003).

Sport organizations that move or expand production overseas to reduce costs or to develop synergies with local and regional market requirements will need to ensure that their HRM policies and practices are appropriate to these other localities. This may necessitate adjusting job specifications and requirements, employment contracts, reward structures, and performance management systems to meet local conditions. When moving into developing countries there may also be a need to increase the amount of training and development offered to staff. For example, the implementation of the anticipated National Basketball Association (NBA) sponsored and branded league in China will require the further development of sport business skills and knowledge in the local workforce.

Multinationals may put greater emphasis on creating job opportunities for knowledge workers to deal with the expanding service sector and capitalize on more advanced and skilled workforces. It is also anticipated that with global expansion there will be an increasing number of people who will be working for an organization, but who will not be working in the organization. This, accompanied by the decreasing number of people with 'permanent' contracts of employment, and the proliferation of other types of work arrangements such as part-time and temporary work will challenge traditional industrial relations approaches to accommodate different types of employment contracts, and different types of pay systems to reward performance and skills. This requires flexible, adaptive HRM policies, and practices that can be responsive to change and transformation and capture creativity and innovation in the search for better processes, and improved products and services across borders.

Globalization of the workforce also relates to sport volunteers. It was reported that the Athens Olympic Games organizers recruited Games time volunteers from 201 countries, including 10 per cent Greeks abroad and 23 per cent of non-Greek origin, and they processed some 41,500 applications from overseas (Atkinson, 2004). Similarly, the 2008 Beijing Olympic

Organizing Committee aims to recruit significant numbers of volunteers from outside China to assist with the delivery of the Games.

Increasing diversity in the workplace

Effectively managing a diverse body of talent can bring innovative ideas, perspectives, and views to the sport organization. The challenge is to capitalize on the potential of workplace diversity as a strategic organizational asset and to value diversity as an opportunity. As the organizational workforce becomes increasingly diverse an environment that does not support diversity broadly risks losing talent to competitors. As more and more organizations become global in their market expansions, either physically or virtually, there is a necessity to employ diverse talents to understand the various niches of the market.

As discussed in previous chapters in this book, one critical demographic issue is the ability to deal with the challenge of an aging workforce. Senior positions in many sport organizations are held by older persons who will retire in the next 5–10 years. The success of future recruitment of younger persons into the organization and the organization's ability to retain key personnel will be of increasing importance. The projections of an aging population and the associated retirements will create potential gaps and result in a loss of critical expertise, both for employees and managers. In dealing with this issue it is also paramount to address negative attitudes towards older workers to ensure that there is no age discrimination in HRM practices. This includes tackling the main barrier, which is people's perceptions and attitudes about the worth of older workers; exploring new recruitment options, and developing a reputation as an active recruiter and a good employer of older workers; utilizing older workers as trainers/mentors, allowing for transfer of knowledge and corporate memory; and bringing in flexible working arrangements to facilitate the retention of experienced workers such as allowing phased in retirement, long-term care insurance, pre-retirement planning, health and wellness programmes, and comprehensive medical coverage.

Information requirements and different ways of delivering the sport product

Work performed in sport organizations is being increasingly tied to providing information and knowledge production and capitalizing on new technologies. Increasing compliance requirements and the thirst for information means that sport organizations are constantly collecting and providing data on their participants, customers, and sponsors. The introduction of customer relationship marketing systems and information-based marketing and communication initiatives has changed the nature of business for many sport organizations. Additionally, the sport product is being complemented by online delivery modes, via pod casts, and discussed on blogs and played in virtual situations. We need to become accustomed to dealing with mental, creative, and innovative work. This shift is shaping the skill, knowledge and mindsets for future sport organization workers and will also lead to different work practices and reward structures for employees.

Work life issues and ways of organizing work

Quality of life encompasses good salaries and benefits, adequately defined tasks, a healthy organizational environment, supportive and efficient leadership, high motivation, and continuous feedback. It means providing rewards for productive contributions such as psychological effort, communication and interaction, and creates the psychological state necessary for the employee to produce quality work for the organization in return. This involves looking to non-traditional ways to better meet their professional and personal needs, and finding a balance between work and life commitments by providing flexible working arrangements. Initiatives may include; guaranteed part-time work for employees aged 55 years and over, lifestyle leave and flexible leave, career breaks to pursue personal development or family commitments, job sharing, telecommuting, and flexible work child care policies.

As noted in relation to globalization, traditionally structured jobs and work practices are being replaced by new work practices such as high-performance and virtual teams, telecommuting, flexible work patterns, and more diverse and integrated work. Work is moving from being done during a standard 8-hour day to being completed at anytime, and at any place, to the extent that workers are becoming suppliers for various activities and even different companies at the same time. The notion of a single job for life, exclusive and full time, is being redefined in the digital age. New forms of reward structures focus on how the employee delivers on strategy and results, and on being innovative and creative. These will all impact on HR issues such as motivation, leadership, training, and development of high-performance cohesive work teams.

Customer service orientation

The focus of sport organizations has traditionally been the sport product or service. However, recent shifts indicate that the customer to whom this product or service is targeted has become increasingly critical. Internally focused strategies on how to best deliver sport are being replaced by an external focus on the customer of the product or service. This means moving from concentrating on the products and services that sport organizations offer to looking after the customer's needs. At the organizational level, research suggests that managers need to consider the importance of emphasizing the organizational cues that help to build a service orientation climate and that HRM should be more market oriented (Saura, Contri, Taulet & Velázquez, 2005). In particular, provision of service rewards and service training has been found to support better service orientation (Berthon, Hulbert & Pitt, 1999). Furthermore, Brown, Mowen and Donovan (2002) suggest personality traits such as emotional stability, agreeability, and the need for activity account for most of the variance in the customer orientation of employees. HR managers might consider how to develop their own performance measures for customer orientation and key indicators of specific service behaviours which can be built into selection procedures, training programmes, reward structures, and performance evaluations.

Volunteer and paid staff relationships

A working relationship between volunteers and paid staff continues to evolve in non-profit voluntary sport organizations (see Figure 1.1 in Chapter 1). While sport organizations in other sectors may also rely on volunteers to carry out their activities, volunteer participation is a defining feature of voluntary sport organizations (Cuskelly, Hoye & Auld, 2006). Community, provincial or state, and national level amateur sport organizations are the most common examples of voluntary sport organizations. While these organizations are governed and primarily run by volunteer personnel (e.g., board of directors, committee members, coaches), there is a continuing incidence of hiring paid staff to help deal with the increasing complexity and sophistication of organized sport (Cuskelly et al., 2006). The so-called 'professionalization' of amateur sport is a function of hiring paid 'professional' staff, as well as the adoption of more sophisticated management practices to increase organizational effectiveness.

While a voluntary sport organization can undoubtedly benefit from the assistance provided by paid staff, this depends on an effective working relationship between the paid staff and volunteers. This relationship is particularly critical at the management level. Typically, staff are hired and supervised by a volunteer management committee or board of directors, and have a non-voting role with that group. The board sets policy and the staff implement it. However, the working relationship may be challenged by the high levels of organizational knowledge held by staff, which can create a shift in board power because of its dependence on staff for information (Pearce, 1993). Amis, Slack and Berrett (1995) suggest that voluntary sport organizations are more susceptible to internal conflict because of the combination of volunteer leadership and professional staff expertise which must involve sharing of responsibility for the work of the organization. The likelihood of conflict may be increased because of different orientations to work and expectations of the two groups. Further to this, the relationship is inherently constrained by the regular turnover of committee and board members as a result of the organization's constitutional election and appointments process (Cuskelly et al., 2006). With the increasing complexity of the environment and operations of voluntary sport organizations (e.g., Nichols, Taylor, James, King, Holmes & Garrett, 2003), continuing professionalization of voluntary sport organizations, including the involvement of paid staff, is an SHRM challenge.

SHRM into the future

As HRM assumes a more strategic role in sport organizations it will be increasingly critical to the organization. While not all sport organizations recognize this yet, those that have moved in this direction emphasize the collaborative links between line managers, employees, volunteers, customers, strategic partners, and members of community organizations in order to be more effective in managing the organization's human resources. The ways in which effective SHRM can be achieved have been discussed in this book in some detail.

The HR function involves a partnership of HR professionals, line managers, employees, and volunteers. We have discussed how HRM was traditionally concerned with the short-term, operational aspects of personnel management. Now, human resources are much more broadly conceptualized and thus are increasingly involved in the longer-term, strategic directions of the organization.

SHRM involves understanding the strategic direction of the sport organization, including understanding the product or service, its customers, and how it is positioned competitively in the marketplace. The process of linking human resources to the broader, long-term needs of organizations is the essence of SHRM (Jackson & Schuler, 2000; Storey, 2001). The management of human resources should be considered in both formulation and implementation of strategy (Thompson & Strickland, 1998). Strategy and its objectives serve as the basis for activities that are specifically associated with HRM (Pfeffer, 1998a).

SHRM also requires innovative approaches and solutions to improve productivity and the quality of work life while complying with government and legislative requirements in an environment of high uncertainty and change, and intense global competition. Managing human resources through strategy implementation is often about change. The responsibility of managing the change process, both at the individual and the organizational level is a significant HRM role.

As sport organizations grapple with new technologies, structures, processes, and cultures, HRM will accordingly facilitate organizational change and ensure flexibility and adaptability. This means being aware of anticipated changes to the external environment, and working to ensure that the right skills and competencies are available at the appropriate time.

While large sport organizations will employ HR specialists and generalists, many sport organizations will not have individuals with special expertise in human resources; that is people with specialized and technical knowledge of HR issues, laws, policies, and practices. In these cases the responsibilities of HR will fall to the employees and managers to deal with. Sport organizations will choose to allocate responsibility for HR activities in many different ways; however, whatever the approach, good HR management will link HR activities to strategy and help the sport organization achieve competitive advantage, effective operations, motivated and satisfied employees, and volunteers, and improved quality of work life.

Summary

Organizational change is inevitable, paradoxical because of our innate desire for stability, and a critical issue for SHRM. There are innumerable examples of planned organizational change in the ever-changing sport industry. Sport organizations face internal (e.g., financial challenges, inefficiencies, training needs) and external forces (e.g., government policy, consumers, competitors, sport governing bodies) that pressure them to make changes for growth and for survival. In simple terms, the process of organizational change involves 'unfreezing' current conditions, moving to the desired state, and 'refreezing' those new conditions. However, the process may be hindered by too strong restraining forces in the form of staff and volunteer resistance to that change. Resistance occurs because of the perceived threat of change to one's own self-interests in the organization (e.g., one's power, expertise, resource allocations, job security), mistrust of management and others who support the change, differing perceptions about the expected outcomes of the change, and the cost in terms of time, money, and effort to implement the change. To overcome resistance and help people cope with change in the organization, strategies are directed towards educating staff and volunteers about change, involving them in the change process, and providing additional support through change teams, idea champions, and various organizational measures such as counselling, therapy, and retraining. Negotiating or bargaining for compliance on the part of resistors may not have the lasting effect that is desired.

Discussion questions

1. Building on information provided in the chapter, describe other examples of product or service changes, technology changes, structure and system changes, and people changes in sport organizations. Discuss what prompted each of these changes.

2. Think of an organizational change initiative with which you are most familiar. What type of change was it? What prompted the change (what internal and/or external pressures influenced the organization)? Describe any internal (employee, volunteer) resistance to the change, and how the organization managed that resistance. Was the change process successful? If not, where did the breakdown occur (consider Greiner's stages of organizational change in Figure 13.1)?

3. Building on information provided in the chapter, discuss further the potential advantages and disadvantages of each of the strategies for managing resistance to change.

4. Consider each of the SHRM challenges introduced in this chapter. Elaborate, where you can, on examples of each in sport in general, or in a particular sport organization with which you are most familiar (e.g., What else do you know about volunteer–staff relationships in sport?).

What are some of the key SHRM issues associated with each challenge? As a manager, how would you deal with these issues? (Reflect back on relevant chapters in the text to frame your answer.) *Suggestion to instructors: Students could form groups and each group addresses one of the challenges listed here.*

5. What do you think is the greatest SHRM challenge for sport organizations in the future, and why? Describe how this challenge may lead to change in the organization. What is the nature of that change? What are the implications of that change for HRM?

Book summary

HRM is becoming increasingly involved with strategic planning and the development of means by which people can work proactively towards the achievement of organizational objectives. Employees and volunteers are no longer just an organizational resource; they provide the basis for competitive advantage and organizational sustainability. It is people who shape such intangibles as the organization's image or reputation, organizational culture, customer service, creativity and innovation, competitiveness, and the basis for dealing with the changing sport landscape over the next 5–10 years. Recognition of this shift is found in the changing nomenclature of HR departments to titles such as: 'people and culture', 'performance and people', and 'people capital and breakout'. This is a change from a function-oriented to a process-oriented culture, from an organization that offers services to a concern for the organization's intellectual capital and its ultimate productivity.

Employees and volunteers are integral to the development and execution of the organization's values, policies, and goals. Therefore, they need to be engaged through a range of participative programmes, assisted to achieve their needs and aspirations, and receive appropriate rewards and recognition. Achievement of organizational objectives occurs through the contributions of the people directly linked with the final results. Recruitment and selection processes should validly identify and attract people with the requisite characteristics and talents. Training and development processes should generate results for the organization and the employee or volunteer. Reward systems should be capable of motivating and supporting efforts to achieve desired goals, results, and related issues.

Good SHRM addresses the need for competitiveness in a changing global marketplace and the importance of employee and volunteer contributions of internal partners to attract clients and achieve results. The SHRM approaches, practices, and trends identified in this book reflect the capacity people have for developing and creating value and how to develop and support that capacity for the success of the organization. An organization's competitiveness based on its employees and volunteers is what SHRM is all about.

References

Abney, R. (1991). Recruiting and mentoring sport leaders. *Journal of Physical Education, Recreation and Dance*, **62**(3), 48–51.

Acosta, R.V. & Carpenter, L.J. (2005) *Title IX*. Champaign, IL: Human Kinetics.

Adams, J.S. (1965). Inequity in social exchange. In *Advances in Experimental Psychology*, Vol. 2, pp. 267–299 (Berkowitz, L., ed.). New York: Academic Press.

Adkins, G. & Caldwell, D. (2004). Firm or subgroup culture: Where does fitting in matter most. *Journal of Organizational Behavior*, **25**(8), 969–978.

Adler, N.J. (1997). *International Dimensions of Organizational Behaviour*, 3rd edn. Cincinatti, OH: South-Western College Publishing.

Allen, D.G. (2006). Do organizational socialization tactics influence newcomer embeddedness and turnover? *Journal of Management*, **32**(2), 237–246.

Allport, G.W. (1954). *The Nature of Prejudice*. Cambridge, MA: Addison-Wesley.

Amis, J., Slack, T. & Berrett, T. (1995). The structural antecedents of conflict in voluntary sport organizations. *Leisure Studies*, **14**(1), 1–16.

Amis, J., Pant, N. & Slack, T. (1997). Achieving a sustainable competitive advantage: A resource-based view of sport sponsorship. *Journal of Sport Management*, **11**, 80–96.

Andrews, K. (2006). Australia's cultural diversity set to remain. Retrieved 9 May 2007, from http://www.minister.immi.gov.au/media/media-releases/2006/v06017.htm.

Armstrong, M. (2006). *A Handbook of Human Resource Management Practice*, 10th edn. London: Kogan Page.

Armstrong, M. & Baron, A. (1998). *Performance Management: The New Realities*. London: Institute of Personnel and Development.

References

Arthur, W., Bennett, W., Edens, P.S. & Bell, S.T. (2003). Effectiveness of training in organizations: A meta-analysis of design and evaluation features. *Journal of Applied Psychology*, **88**(2), 234–245.

Ashford, S.J. (1988). Individual strategies for coping with stress during organizational transitions. *Journal of Applied Behavioural Science*, **24**(1), 19–36.

Ashford, S.J. & Black, J.S. (1996). Proactivity during organizational entry: The role of desire for control. *Journal of Applied Psychology*, **81**(2), 199–214.

Ashforth, B.E. & Saks, A.M. (1996). Socialization tactics: Longitudinal effects on newcomer adjustment. *Academy of Management Journal*, **39**(1), 149–178.

Atkinson, M. (2004). Travel notes for parliament. Adelaide: South Australia Parliament.

Auld, C.J. (1997). Professionalisation of Australian sport administration: The effects on organisational decision making. *European Journal for Sport Management*, **4**(2), 17–39.

Australian Bureau of Statistics (ABS). (2004a). Population projections, Australia, 2004 to 2101. Cat. No. 3222.0. Canberra: Australian Bureau of Statistics.

Australian Bureau of Statistics (ABS). (2004b). Trade union membership, Australian labour market statistics. Cat. No. 6105.0. Canberra: Australian Bureau of Statistics.

Australian Bureau of Statistics. (2007, April). Employee earnings, benefits and trade union membership in Australia – August 2006. Cat. No. 6310.0. Canberra: Australian Bureau of Statistics.

Australian Public Service Commission. (2003). *Managing Succession*. Canberra: Commonwealth of Australia.

Australian Sports Commission. Recruitment and retention checklist for clubs. Retrieved 24 April 2007, from http://www.ausport.gov.au/coachofficial/tools/retaining/checklist_recruitment&retention.pdf

Australian Sports Commission. (2000). Volunteer management program retaining volunteers: Retrieved 13 March 2007, from http://ausport.gov.au/clubs/documents/vols_recruiting.pdf

Barney, J. (1991). Firms resources and sustained competitive advantage. *Journal of Management*, **17**(1), 99–120.

Barr, C.A., McDonald, M.A. & Sutton, W.A. (2000). Collegiate sport marketers: Job responsibilities and compensation structure. *International Sports Journal*, **4**(2), 64–77.

Barrick, M.R. & Mount, M.K. (1991). The big five personality dimensions and job performance: A meta-analysis. *Personnel Psychology*, **44**(1), 1–26.

Baruch, Y., Wheeler, K. & Zhao, X. (2004). Performance-related pay in Chinese professional sports. *International Journal of Human Resource Management*, **15**(1), 245–259.

Baumgarten, K. (1995). *International Human Resource Management*, pp. 205–228 (Harzing, A.W. & Van Ruysseveldt, J., eds). London: Sage.

Becker, B.E. & Huselid, M.A. (1992). The incentive effects of tournament compensation systems. *Administrative Science Quarterly*, **37**(2), 336–350.

Becker, B.E., Huselid, M. & Ulrich, D. (2001). *The HR Scorecard: Linking People Strategy, and Performance*. Boston, MA: Harvard Business School Press.

Beer, M. & Eisenstat, R. (2000). The silent killers of strategy implementation and learning. *Sloan Management Review*, **41**(4), 29–40.

Beer, M., Spector, B., Lawrence, P., Walton, R. & Mills, D. (1984). *Managing Human Resource Assets*. New York: Free Press.

Beer, M., Spector, B., Lawrence, P., Quinn, M.D. & Walton, R. (1985). *Human Resource Management: A General Manager's Perspective*. Glencoe, IL: Free Press.

Beeson, J. (2000). Succession planning. *Across the Board*, **37**(2), 38.

Belanger, A. & Malenfant, E.C. (2005). Population projections of visible minority groups, Canada, provinces and regions, 2001–2017. Cat. No. 91-541-XIE. Ottawa, ON: Statistics Canada.

Bell, B. & Crilley, G. (2002). An application of the CERM performance indicators program to benchmarking in the Australian caravan and tourist park sector. *Journal of Hospitality and Tourism Management*, **9**(2), 83–93.

Bernthal, P. & Wellins, R. (2006). Trends in leader development and succession HR. *Human Resource Planning*, **29**(2), 31–41.

Berthon, P., Hulbert, J.M. & Pitt, L.F. (1999). To serve or create? Strategic orientations toward customers and innovation. *California Management Review*, **42**(1), 37–58.

Beyer, J.M. & Hannah, D.R. (2002). Building on the past: Enacting established personal identities in a new work setting. *Organization Science*, **13**(6), 636–652.

Black, J.A. & Boal, K.B. (1994). Strategic resources: Traits, configurations and paths to sustainable competitive advantage. *Strategic Management Journal*, **15**, 131–148.

Booth, N., Fosters, S., Robson, C. & Welham, J. (2004). *Managing a Diverse Workforce*. London: LexisNexis.

Boselie, P., Paauwe, J. & Jansen, P. (2001). Human resource management and performance: Lessons from the Netherlands. *International Journal of Human Resource*, **12**(7), 1107–1125.

Boston Business Journal. (2007). U.S. Businesses not prepared for aging workforce. Retrieved 13 March 2007, from http://boston.bizjournals.com/boston/stories/2007/03/12/daily13.html

Boudreau, J. (1990). 'Cost-benefit' Analysis applied to personnel human resource management decisions: Answers to common questions, and a case-study application (Working Paper # 90-18 Center for Advanced Human Resource Studies (CAHRS) CAHRS Working Paper Series). Ithaca, NY: Cornell University.

Boyatzis, R. (1999). The financial impact of competencies in leadership and management of consulting firms (Working Paper). Cleveland, OH: Department of Organizational Behavior, Case Western Reserve University.

Brannen, P. (1983). *Authority and Participation in Industry*. London: Batsford Academic.

Bratton, J. & Gold, J. (2003). *Human Resource Management – Theory and Practice*, 3 edn. Basingstoke: Palgrave Macmillan.

Brown, T.J., Mowen, J.C. & Donovan, D.T. (2002). The customer orientation of service workers: Personally trait effects on self and supervisor performance ratings. *Journal of Marketing Research*, **39**(1), 110–119.

Burkett, H. (2005a). ROI on a shoe-string: Strategies for resource-constrained environments, Part 1. *Industrial and Commercial Training*, **37**(1), 10–17.

Burkett, H. (2005b). ROI on a shoe-string: Strategies for resource-constrained environments, Part 2. *Industrial and Commercial Training*, **37**(2), 97–105.

Buswell, J. (2004). Sport and leisure service encounter. In *Sport and Leisure Operations Management* (McMahon-Beattie, U. & Yeoman, I., eds). Oxon: CABI Publishing.

Byham, W.C. (2001). *Targeted Selection*. Pittsburgh, PA: Development Dimensions International Inc.

Byham, W.C., Smith A.B. & Paese, M.J. (2000). *Grow Your Own Leaders – Acceleration Pools: A New Method of Succession Management*. USA: DDI Press.

Cable, D.M. & Parsons, C.K. (2001). Socialization tactics and person-organization fit. *Personnel Psychology*, **54**(1), 1–23.

Cabrera, E.F. & Cabrera, A. (2003). Strategic human resource evaluation. *Human Resource Planning*, **26**(1), 41–50.

Camp, R.C. (1989). *Benchmarking: The Search for Industry Best Practice That Leads to Superior Performance*. Milwaukee, WI: ASQC Quality Press.

Campion, M.A. (1988). Interdisciplinary approaches to job design: A constructive replication with extensions. *Journal of Applied Psychology*, **73**(3), 467–481.

Campion, M.A. (1989). Ability requirement implications of job design: An interdisciplinary perspective. *Personnel Psychology*, **42**(1), 1–24.

Campion, M.A. & Berger, C. (1990). Conceptual integration and empirical test of job design and compensation relationships. *Personnel Psychology*, **43**(3), 525–553.

Campion, M.A., Mumford, T., Morgeson, F. & Nahrgang, J. (2005). Work redesign: Eight obstacles and opportunities. *Human Resource Management Review*, **44**(4), 367–390.

Canadian Interuniversity Sport (CIS). (2006) Policies and procedures: 90 – conduct and enforcement. Retrieved 10 May 2007 from http://www.cisport.ca/e/pol_proc/documents/09_90_Conduc_Enforcement.pdf#ee.

Carey, D.C. & Ogden, D. (2000). *CEO Succession: A Window on How Boards Can Get it Right When Choosing a New Chief Executive*. New York: Oxford University Press.

Carey, H.A. (1999). *Communication in Extension: A Teaching and Learning Guide*. Rome: FAO.

Carmeli, A. & Tishler, A. (2004). The relationships between intangible organizational elements and performance. *Strategic Management Journal*, **25**(13), 1257–1278.

Carnall, C. (1990). *Managing Change in Organizations*. Hemel Hemstead: Prentice-Hall.

Carr, J.C., Pearson, A.W., Vest, M.J. & Boyer, S.L. (2006). Prior occupational experience, anticipatory socialization, and employee retention. *Journal of Management*, **32**(3), 343–359.

Cascio, W. (1996). Managing for maximum performance. *HR Monthly*, September, 10–13.

Cascio, W.F. (2003). Changes in workers, work, and organizations. In *Handbook of Psychology* (Borman, W.C., Ilgen, D.R. & Klimoski, R.J., eds). Hoboken, NJ: John Wiley and Sons.

CCOHS. (1998). Job hazard analysis. Retrieved 3 April 2007, from http://www.ccohs.ca/ohsanwers/hsprograms/job-haz.html

CCOHS. (2005). Hazard and risk. Retrieved 3 April 2007, from http://www.ccohs.ca/ohsanswers/hsprograms/hazard_risk.html

CCOHS. (2006). Hazard control. Retrieved 3 April 2007, from http://www.ccohs.ca/ohsanswers/hsprograms/hazard_control.html

Chao, G., Walz, P. & Gardner, P. (1992). Formal and informal mentorships: A comparison on mentoring functions and contrast with nonmentored counterparts. *Personnel Psychology*, **45**(3), 619–636.

Chapman, A. (2005). Exit interviews. Retrieved 10 April 2007, from http://www.businessballs.com/exitinterviews.htm

Chass, M. (1994). As trade unions struggle, their sport unions thrive. *The New York Times*, 5 September, 1, 26.

Chelladurai, P. (2005). *Managing Organizations for Sport and Physical Activity: A Systems Perspective*, 2nd edn. Scottsdale, AZ: Holcomb Hathaway.

Chelladurai, P. (2006). *Human Resource Management in Sport and Recreation*, 2nd edn. Champaign, IL: Human Kinetics.

Chelladurai, P. & Madella, A. (2006). *Human Resource Management in Olympic Sport Organizations*. Champaign, IL: Human Kinetics.

Chermack, T.J. (2004). The opportunities for HRD in scenario planning. *Human Resource Development International*, **7**(1), 117–121.

Cleave, S. (1993). A test of the job characteristics model with administrative positions in physical education and sport. *Journal of Sport Management*, **7**(3), 228–242.

Coaching Association of Canada. (2006). Request for proposal: Engaging new Canadians in coaching and the National Coaching Certification Program (NCCP). Retrieved 9 May 2007, from http://www.coach.ca/eng/links/documents/RFPNCCPJune06.pdf

Cohn, J., Khurana, R. & Reeves, L. (2005). Growing talent as if your business depended on it. *Harvard Business Review*, **83**(10), 62–70.

Conger, J. & Fulmer, R. (2003). Developing your leadership pipeline. *Harvard Business Review*, **81**(12), 76–90.

Covell, D., Walker, S., Siciliano, J. & Hess, P.W. (2003). *Managing Sport Organizations: Responsibility for Performance*. Mason, OH: Thomson Learning.

Crilley, G. (2001). CERM PI® operational management (efficiency) indicators of public sport and leisure centres. Adelaide, SA: University of South Australia.

Cropanzano, R. & Greenberg, J. (2001). Progress in organizational justice: Tunnelling through the maze. In *Organizational Psychology and Development*, pp. 243–298 (Cooper, C.L. & Robertson, I.T., eds). Chichester: Wiley.

Cunningham, G. (2007). *Diversity in Sport Organizations*. Scottsdale, AZ: Holcomb Hathaway.

Cuskelly, G. & Hoye, R. (2004). *Problems and Issues in the Recruitment and Retention of Sports Officials*. Brisbane: Griffith Business School.

Cuskelly, G., Hoye, R. & Auld, C. (2006). *Working with Volunteers in Sport: Theory and Practice*. London: Routledge.

Cuskelly, G., Taylor, T., Hoye, R. & Darcy, S. (2006). Volunteer management practices and volunteer retention: A human resource management approach. *Sports Management Review*, **9**(2), 141–163.

Daft, R.L. (1992). *Organization Theory and Design*, 4th edn. St. Paul: West.

Das, B. (1999). Development of a comprehensive industrial work design model. *Human Factors and Ergonomics in Manufacturing*, **9**(4), 393–411.

De Cieri, H. & Kramar, R. (2003). *Human Resource Management in Australia*. Sydney: McGraw-Hill.

De Cieri, H., Kramar, R., Noe, R., Hollenbeck, J., Gerhart, B. & Wright, P. (2005). *Human Resource Management in Australia. Strategy-People-Performance*, 2nd edn. Sydney: McGraw-Hill.

De Knop, P., Van Hoecke, J. & De Bosscher, V. (2004). Quality management in sports clubs. *Sport Management Review*, **7**(1), 57–78.

Dessler, G. (2000). *Human Resource Management*, 8th edn. Englewood Cliffs, NJ: Prentice-Hall.

Doherty, A. (2003). *A Study of the Volunteers of the 2001 Alliance London Jeux du Canada Games*. London, ON: University of Western Ontario.

Doherty, A. (2005a). *A Profile of Community Sport Volunteers*. Toronto: Parks and Recreation Ontario and the Sport Alliance of Ontario.

Doherty, A. (2005b). *Volunteer Management in Community Sport Clubs: A Study of Volunteers' Perceptions*. Toronto: Parks and Recreation Ontario and the Sport Alliance of Ontario.

Doherty, A. & Chelladurai, P. (1999). Managing cultural diversity in sport organizations: A theoretical perspective. *Journal of Sport Management*, **13**(4), 280–297.

Dorsch, K., Riemer, H., Sluth, V., Paskevich, D. & Chelladurai, P. (2002). *What Affects a Volunteer's Commitment?* Toronto: Canadian Centre for Philanthropy.

Driscoll, M.P. (1994). *Psychology of Learning for Instruction*. Needham Heights, MA: Allyn and Bacon.

Drucker, P.F. (1995). *Managing in a Time of Great Change*. New York: Truman Valley.

Eastman, L. (1995). *Succession Planning: An Annotated Bibliography and Summary of Commonly Reported Organizational Practices*. Greensboro, NC: Centre for Creative Leadership.

Eddy, E., D'Abate, C, Tannenbaum, S., Givens-Skeaton, S. & Robinson, G. (2006). Key characteristics of effective and ineffective developmental interactions. *Human Resource Development Quarterly*, **17**(1), 59–84.

EOWA. Retrieved 19 April 2007, from http://www.eowa.gov.au/EOWA_Employer_Of_Choice_For_Women.asp

ESPN.com. Retrieved 15 March 2007.

Feldman, D.C. (1976). A contingency theory of socialization. *Administrative Science Quarterly*, **21**(3), 433–452.

Finlayson, J. (2007). Patterns of union density in the United States [Electronic Version]. *Industrial Relations Bulletin*, 39. Retrieved 2 April 2007, from http://www.bcbc.com/publications/industrial_relations.asp

Fiol, C.M. & Lyles, M.A. (1985). Organisational learning. *Academy of Management Review*, **10**(4), 803–813.

Fitz-enz, J. (1995). *How to Measure Human Resources Management*. New York: McGraw-Hill.

Folger, R. & Cropanzano, R. (1998). *Organizational Justice and Human Resource Management*. Thousand Oaks, CA: Sage.

Fombrum, C., Tichy, N. & Devanna, M.A. (1984). *Strategic Human Resource Management*. New York: Wiley.

Fortune Magazine. (2007) The 100 best companies to work for. Retrieved 22 January 2007, from http://money.cnn.com/magazines/fortune

Gagne, R. & Driscoll, M. (1988). *Essentials of Learning for Instruction*, 2nd edn. Englewood Cliffs, NJ: Prentice-Hall.

Gallant, H., Remick, L.Z. & Resnick, B.M. (2005). Labor relations in professional sports. In *The Management of Sport: Its Foundation and Application*, 4th edn., pp. 301–332 (Parkhouse, B.L., ed.). New York: McGraw-Hill.

Gallo, J. (2006). Byears shows new-look mystics what a difference a player makes mystics. *Washington Post Sunday*. Retrieved 28 May 2006, from http://www.washingtonpost.com/wp-dyn/content/article/2006/05/27/AR2006052700911.html

Gerrard, B. (2005). A resource-utilization model of organizational efficiency in professional sports teams. *Journal of Sport Management*, **19**, 143–169.

Gladden, J.M., McDonald, M.A. & Barr, C.A. (1998). Event management. In *Principals and Practice of Sport Management*, pp. 328–355 (Masteralexis, L.P., Barr, C.A. & Hums, M.A., eds). Gaithersburg, MD: Aspen Publishers.

Goldstein, I. & Ford, J. (2002). *Training in Organizations: Needs Assessment, Development and Evaluation*, 4th edn. Belmont, CA: Wadsworth.

Goleman, D. (1998). *Working with Emotional Intelligence*. New York: Bantam.

Gratton, L. & Truss, C. (2003). The three-dimensional people strategy: Putting human resources policies into action. *Academy of Management Executive*, **17**(3), 74–86.

Greenberg, J. (1987). A taxonomy of organizational justice theories. *Academy of Management Review*, **12**(1), 9–22.

Greiner, L.E. (1967). Patterns of organization change. *Harvard Business Review*, **45**(3), 119–130.

Griffeth, R.W. & Horn, P.W. (2001). *Retaining Valued Employees*. Thousand Oaks, CA: Sage.

Guest, D. (1987). Human resource management and industrial relations. *Journal of Management Studies*, **24**(5), 503–521.

Guest, D. & Conway, N. (1999). Peering into the black hole: The downside of the new employment relationship in the UK. *British Journal of Industrial Relations*, **37**(3), 367–389.

Guest, D. & Conway, N. (2002). Communication the psychological contract: An employer perspective. *Human Resource Management Journal*, **12**(2), 22–38.

Hackman, J.R. & Oldham, G.R. (1980). *Work Design*. Reading, MA: Addison-Wesley.

Hall, D.T. (1976). *Careers in Organizations*. Pacific Palisades, CA: Goodyear.

Hargrove, R. (2002). *Masterful Coaching: Extraordinary Results by Impacting People and the Way They Think and Work Together*. San Francisco, CA: Jossey-Bass.

Harrison, D.A., Price, K.H. & Bell, M.P. (1998). Beyond relational demography: Time and the effects of surface- and deep-level diversity on work group cohesion. *Academy of Management Journal*, **41**(1), 96–107.

Hatch, M.J. & Schultz, M. (1997). Relations between organizational culture, identity and image. *European Journal of Marketing*, **31**(5/6), 356–365.

References

Herzberg, F. (1968). One more time: How do you motivate people? *Harvard Business Review*, **46**(1), 53–62.

Hewitt and Associates. (2007). The best employers in Australian and New Zealand, from http://was7.hewitt.com/bestemployers/anz/2006-07list.htm

Higgins, M.C. & Kram, K.E. (2001). Reconceptualizing mentoring at work: A developmental network perspective. *Academy of Management Review*, **26**(2), 264–288.

Hofacre, S. & Branvold, S. (1995). Baseball front office careers: Expectations and realities. *Journal of Sport Management*, **9**(2), 173–181.

Holinsworth, S. (2004). Case study: Henrico County, Virginia: Succession management: A developmental approach. *Public Personnel Management*, **33**(4), 475–487.

Honold, L. (1991). The power of learning at Johnsonville foods. *Training*, **28**(4), 55–58.

Hoye, R., Smith, A., Westerbeek, H., Stewart, B. & Nicholson, M. (2005). *Sport Management: Principles and Application*. Oxford: Elsevier.

Hurstville City Council. Aquatic leisure centre – annual CERM performance indicator review. Retrieved 12 March 2007, from http://notesweb.hurstville.nsw.gov.au/ebpweb/buspapr2003.nsf/399al99e8d373197ca256da9000fce25/04ac0b920aad7de3ca2571260016adaa?OpenDocument

Huselid, M.A. (1995). The impact of human resource management practices on turnover, productivity and corporate financial performance. *Academy of Management Journal*, **38**(3), 635–672.

Huselid, M., Becker, B. & Ulrich, D. (2001). *The HR Scorecard*. Boston: Harvard Business School Press.

Institute for Diversity and Ethics in Sport. (2007). Decisions from the top: Diversity among campus, conference leaders at Division LA institutions. Retrieved 9 May 2007, from http://www.bus.ucf.edu/sport/public/downloads/2007 Division LA Demographics Study.pdf.

International Olympic Committee. (2004a, February). *Olympic Review*. Retrieved 9 May 2007, from http://multimedia.olympic.org/pdf/en_report_792.pdf

International Olympic Committee. (2004b). Women, leadership and the Olympic movement. Retrieved 9 May 2007, from http://multimedia.olympic.org/pdf/en_report_994.pdf

International Olympic Committee. (2006, February). Women in sport leadership: Evaluation of the 10–20 per cent objectives (women representation in the IOC). Retrieved 9 May 2007 from http://multimedia.olympic.org/pdf/en_report_98.pdf

Jackson, S.E. & Schuler, R.S. (1999). Understanding human resource management in the context of organizations and their environments. In *Strategic Human Resource Management*, pp. 4–28 (Jackson, S.E. & Schuler, R.S., eds). Oxford: Blackwell Business.

Jackson, S.E. & Schuler, R.E. (2000). *Managing Human Resources: A Partnership Perspective*, 7th edn. Cincinnati, OH: South-Western College Publishing.

Jackson, S.E., May, K.E. & Whitney, K. (1995). Understanding the dynamics of diversity in decision-making teams. In *Team Decision-Making Effectiveness in Organizations*, pp. 204–261 (Guzzo, R.A. & Salas, E., eds). San Francisco, CA: Jossey-Bass.

Jacobs, D. (2005). In search of future leaders: Managing the global talent pipeline [Electronic Version]. *Ivey Business Journal Online*, March/April.

Jaques, E. (1961). *Equitable Payment*. New York: John Wiley and Sons.

Johns, G. & Saks, A.M. (2001). *Understanding and Managing Life at Work: Organizational Behaviour*, 5th edn. Toronto, ON: Addison-Wesley Longman.

Judge, T. & Cable. DM. (1997). Applicant personality, organizational culture and organization attraction. *Personnel Psychology*, **50**(2), 359–394.

Kabanoff, B. (1991). Equity, equality, power and conflict. *Academy of Management Review*, **16**(2), 416–441.

Kammeyer-Mueller, J.D. & Wanberg, C.R. (2003). Unwrapping the organizational entry process: Disentangling multiple antecedents and their pathways to adjustment. *Journal of Applied Psychology*, **88**(5), 779–794.

Kane, R. (1997). Human resource planning and career development. In *Human Resource Management in Australia*, 3rd edn, pp. 210–256 (Kramar, R., McGraw, P. & Schuler, R., eds). Sydney: Longman.

Kaplan, R.S. & Norton, D.P. (1996a). *The Balanced Scorecard: Translating Strategy into Action*. Boston, MA: Harvard Business School Press.

Kaplan, R.S. & Norton, D.P. (1996b). Using the balanced scorecard as a strategic management system. *Harvard Business Review*, **74**(1), 75–85.

Kelly, M. (2004). A biographical interpretation of women's journeys through athletic leadership: Pre and post title ix legislation. Unpublished Ph.D. Dissertation, University of Maryland.

Kesler, G. (2002). Why the leadership bench never gets deeper: Ten insights about executive talent development. *HR Planning Society Journal*, **25**(1), 1–28.

Kikulis, L.M. (2000). Continuity and change in governance and decision making in national sport organizations: Institutional explanations. *Journal of Sport Management*, **14**(4), 293–320.

Kim, M., Chelladurai, P. & Trail, G.T. (2007) A model of volunteer retention in youth sport. *Journal of Sport Management*, **21**, 151–171.

Kirkpatrick, D.L. (1976). Evaluation of training. In *Training and Development Handbook*, pp. 294–312 (Craig, R.L., ed.). New York: McGraw-Hill.

Kirkpatrick, D.L. (1998). *Evaluating Training Programs*. San Francisco, CA: Berrett-Koehler.

Knowles, M.S., Holton III, E.F. & Swanson, R.A. (1998). *The Adult Learner*. Houston, TX: Gulf Publishing.

Koustelios, A. (2001). Burnout among Greek sport centre employees. *Sport Management Review*, **4**(2), 151–163.

Kovach, K.A., Hamilton, N.G. & Meserole, M. (1997). Leveling the playing field. *Business and Economic Review*, **44**(1), 12–18.

Karmar, R., McGraw, P. & Schuler, R. (1997). Human resource management in Australia. In *Human Resource Planning and Career Development*, pp. 210–256 (Kane, R., ed.). Sydney: Longman.

Lado, A. & Wilson, M.C. (1994). Human resource systems and sustained competitive advantage: A competency-based perspective. *Academy of Management Review*, **19**(4), 699–727.

Lapchick, R.E., Martin, S., Kushner, D. & Brenden, J. (2006). *2005 Racial and Gender Report Card*. University of Central Florida, Orlando: Institute for Diversity and Ethics in Sport.

League, A.F. (2003). *Volunteer Management for Football Clubs*. East Melbourne, Vic: Australian Football League.

Lee, S.K.J. & Yu, K. (2004). Corporate culture and organizational performance. *Journal of Managerial Psychology*, **19**(4), 340–359.

Legge, K. (1995). *Human Resource Management: Rhetorics and Realities*. London: Macmillan.

Levinthal, D.A. (1991). Organizational adaptation and environmental selection-interrelated processes of change. *Organization Science*, **2**(1), 140–145.

Lewin, K. (1951). *Field Theory in Social Science*. New York: Harper and Row.

Lewis, M. (2003). *Moneyball: The Art of Winning an Unfair Game*. New York: W.W. Norton.

Lewis, P., Thornhill, A. & Saunders, M. (2003). *Employee Relations: Understanding the Employment Relationship*. London: Prentice-Hall.

Lock, D., Taylor, T. & Darcy, S. (2007). Fan identity formation in a new football club and a revamped league: The a-league (Australia). *Sport Marketing Europe*, **1**, 30–35.

Lok, P. & Crawford, J. (1999). The relationship between commitment and organizational culture, subculture, leadership style and job satisfaction in organizational change and development. *Leadership and Organization Development*, **20**(7), 365–376.

London, M. (2003). *Job Feedback Giving, Seeking, and Using Feedback for Performance Improvement*, 2nd edn. Mahwah, NJ: Lawrence Erlbaum Associates.

Lough, N. (1998). Promotion of sports for girls and women: The necessity and the strategy. *Journal of Physical Education, Recreation and Dance*, **69**(5), 25–27.

MacDuffie, J.P. (1995). Human resource bundles and manufacturing performance: Organisational logic and flexible production systems in the world of the auto industry. *Industrial and Labour Relations Review*, **48**(2), 197–221.

MacIntosh, E. & Doherty, A. (2005). Leader intentions and employee perceptions of organizational culture in a private fitness corporation. *European Sport Management Quarterly*, **5**(1), 1–22.

MacIntosh, E. & Doherty, A. (2007a). Inside the Canadian fitness industry: Development of a conceptual framework of organizational culture (Working paper). London, Ontario: The University of Western Ontario.

MacIntosh, E. & Doherty, A. (2007b). Extending the scope of organizational culture: The external perception of an internal phenomenon. *Sport Management Review*, **10**(1), 45–64.

MacLean, J. (2001). *Performance Appraisal for Sport and Recreation Managers*. Champaign, IL: Human Kinetics.

MacLean, J. & Chelladurai, P. (1995). Dimensions of coaching performance: Development of a scale. *Journal of Sport Management*, **9**(2), 194–207.

Makover, B. (2003). Examining the employee–customer chain in the fitness industry. Unpublished Ph.D. Dissertation, Florida State University.

Martin, J.J. (1992). *Cultures in Organizations: Three Perspectives*. New York: Oxford University Press.

Maslow, A.H. (1943). A theory of human motivation. *Psychological Review*, **50**, 370–396.

Maslow, A.H. (1954). *Motivation and Personality*. New York: Harper.

May Kim, M.S. (2004). Influence of individual difference factors on volunteer willingness to be trained. Unpublished Ph.D. Dissertation, The Ohio State University.

Mayer, R.E. (1982). Learning. In *Encyclopedia of Educational Research*, pp. 1040–1058 (Mitzel, H.E., ed.). New York: Free Press.

McClelland, D. (1961). *The Achieving Society*. Princeton, NJ: Van Nostrand.

McDaniel, M.A., Whetzel, D.L., Schmidt, F.L. & Maurer, S.D. (1994). The validity of employment interviews: A comprehensive review and meta analysis. *Journal of Applied Psychology*, **79**(4), 599–616.

McGill, M.E. & Slocum, J.W. (1994). *The Smarter Organisation: How to Build a Business That Learns and Adapts to Marketplace Needs*. New York: Wiley.

McGillivray, D. (2006). Facilitating change in the educational experiences of professional footballers: The case of Scottish football. *Managing Leisure*, **11**(1), 22–38.

McGraw, P. (2002). The HR function in local and overseas firms: Evidence from the Pricewaterhouse Coopers-Cranfield HR Project (1999). *Asia Pacific Journal of Human Resources*, **40**(2), 1–24.

McGregor, D. (1957). An uneasy look at performance appraisal. *Harvard Business Review*, **35**(3), 89–94.

McKenna, E. & Beech, N. (2002). *Human Resource Management: A Concise Analysis*. London: Prentice-Hall.

McShane, S.L. (1995). *Canadian Organizational Behaviour*, 2nd edn. Toronto: Irwin.

Meglino, B.M. & Ravlin, E.C. (1998). Individual values in organizations: Concepts, controversies, and research. *Journal of Management*, **24**(3), 351–390.

Meyer, H.H., Kay, E. & French, J.R.P. (1965). Split roles in performance appraisal. *Harvard Business Review*, **43**(1), 123–129.

Meyer, J.P., Allen, N.J. & Smith, C.A. (1993). Commitment to organizations and occupations: Extension and test of a three-component conceptualization. *Journal of Applied Psychology*, **78**(4), 538–551.

Milkovich, G.T. & Newman, J.M. (1990). *Compensation*, 3rd edn. Homewood, IL: Irwin.

Milliken, F.J. & Martins, L.L. (1996). Searching for common threads: Understanding the multiple effects of diversity in organizational groups. *Academy of Management Review*, **21**(2), 402–433.

Mintzberg, H. (1990). The design school: Reconsidering the basic premises of strategic management. *Strategic Management Journal*, **11**(3), 171–195.

Mitchell, T.R. & Daniels, D. (2003). Motivation. In *Handbook of Psychology*, Vol. 12, *Industrial and Organizational Psychology* (Borman, W.C., Ilgen, D.R. & Klimoski, R.J., eds). Hoboken, NJ: John Wiley and Sons.

MLPBA. (2007). Basic agreement. Retrieved 2 April 2007, from http://mlbplayers.mlb.com/pa/info/cba.jsp.

Moore, M., Parkhouse, B. & Konrad, A. (2001). Women in sport management: Advancing the representation through HRM structures. *Women in Management Review*, **16**(2), 51–61.

Morisette, R., Schellenberg, G. & Johnson, A. (2005, April). Diverging trends in unionization. Cat. No. 75-001-XIE. Ottawa, ON: Statistics Canada.

Mowday, R.T. (1999). Reflections on the study and relevance of organizational commitment. *Human Resource Management Review*, 8(4), 387–401.

Mullins, L. (1996). *Management and Organizational Behaviour*, 4th edn. London: Pitman Publishing.

NBPA. (2005). Collective bargaining agreement. Retrieved 3 April 2007, from http://www.nbpa.com/cba.php

New South Wales Department of Sport and Recreation. Retrieved 8 April 2007, from http://www.dsr.nsw.gov.au/industry/index.asp

NFLPA. (2006). Collective bargaining agreement. Retrieved 3 April 2007, from http://www.nflpa.org/cba/cba.aspx

NHLPA. (2005). Collective bargaining agreement. Retrieved 3 April 2007, from http://www.nhlpa.com/cba/index.asp

Nichols, G., Taylor, P., James, M., King, L., Holmes, K. & Garrett, R. (2003). Pressures on sports volunteers arising from partnerships with the central government. *Loisir et Societe/Society and Leisure*, 26(2), 419–430.

Noe, R. (1988). An investigation of the determinants of successful assigned mentoring relationships. *Personnel Psychology*, 41(3), 457–479.

Nonaka, I. & Takeuchi, H. (1995). *The Knowledge Creating Company: How Japanese Companies Create the Dynamics of Innovation*. New York: University Press.

O'Nell, S., Larson, S., Hewitt, A. & Sauer, J. (2001). RJP [realistic job preview] overview. Retrieved 16 March 2007, from http://rtc.umn.edu/docs/rjp.pdf

Ontario Ministry of Labour. (2006). Termination of employment and severance pay. Retrieved 4 April 2007, from www.labour.gov.on.ca/english/es/factsheets/fs_termination.html

Ormrod, J.E. (1999). *Human Learning*, 3rd edn. Sydney, NSW: Prentice-Hall Australia Pty Ltd.

Ostroff, C. & Kozlowski, S.W.J. (1992). Organizational socialization as a learning process: The role of information acquisition. *Personnel Psychology*, 45(4), 849–874.

Papadimitriou, D. & Taylor, P. (2000). Organisational effectiveness of Hellenic national sports organisations: A multiple constituency approach. *Sport Management Review*, 3(1), 23–46.

Parks, J. & Parra, L. (1994). Job satisfaction of sport management alumnae/i. *Journal of Sport Management*, 8(1), 49–56.

Patterson, M.G., West, M.A., et al. (1997). *Impact of People Management Practices on Business Performance*. London: Institute of Personnel and Development.

Pearce, J.L. (1993). *Volunteers: The Organizational Behaviour of Unpaid Workers*. London: Routledge.

Pfeffer, J. (1998a). *The Human Equation: Building Profits by Putting People First*. Boston: Harvard Business School Press.

Pfeffer, J. (1998b). Six dangerous myths about pay. *Harvard Business Review*, 76(3), 109–119.

Phillips, J.J. (1997). *Return on Investment in Training and Performance Improvement Programs*. Houston, TX: Gulf Publishing.

Porter, M.E. (1979). How competitive forces shape strategy. *Harvard Business Review*, **57**(2), 137–145.

Porter, M.E. (1980). *Competitive Strategy*. New York: Free Press.

Poza, E., Alfred, T. & Maheshwari, A. (1997). Stakeholder perceptions of culture and management practices in family and family firms – a preliminary report. *Family Business Review*, **10**(2), 135–155.

Prahalad, C.K. & Hamel, G. (1990). The core competence of the corporation. *Harvard Business Review*, **68**(3), 79–91.

Pulakos, E. & Schmitt. N. (1995). Experience-based and situational questions: Studies of validity. *Personnel Psychology*, **48**(2), 289–309.

Rimeslåtten, A.K. (2004). Equality, democracy and participation in Norwegian sports – equal opportunities or gender difference? A study of female employees and elected representatives in the Norwegian Olympic committee and confederation of sports. Unpublished M.Sc. research report in Social Psychology, London School of Economics and Political Science.

Rioux, S. & Bernthal, P. (1999). *Succession Management Practices Survey Report*. Pittsburgh, PA: Development Dimensions International.

Robbins, S.P. (1997). *Organizational Behaviour: Concepts, Controversies, and Applications*, 6th edn. Englewood Cliffs, NJ: Prentice-Hall.

Robbins, S.P. & Langdon, N. (2003). *Organizational Behaviour: Concepts, Controversies, and Applications*, 3rd Canadian edition. Toronto: Prentice-Hall.

Rodgers, R. & Hunter, J. (1991). Impact of management by objectives on organizational productivity. *Journal of Applied Psychology*, **76**(2), 322–326.

Rothwell, W. (1994). *Effective Succession Planning: Ensuring Leadership Continuity and Building Talent from within*. New York: Amacom.

Rothwell, W. (2000). *Effective Succession Planning: Ensuring Leadership Continuity and Building Talent from within*, 2nd edn. New York: Amacom.

Rousseau, D.M. (2001). Schema, promise and mutuality: The building blocks of the psychological contract. *Journal of Occupational and Organizational Psychology*, **74**(4), 511–541.

Royal Yachting Association. Onboard development officer job. Retrieved 29 April 2007, from http://www.rya.org.Uk/AboutRYA/jobvacancies/onboarddevelopmentofficer.htm

Running Room. (2007a). About John Stanton. Retrieved 13 April 2007, from http://www.runningroom.com/hm/inside.php?id = 3035

Running Room. (2007b). History. Retrieved 13 April 2007, from http://www.runningroom.com/hm/inside.php?id = 3036

Sackmann, S. (2001). Cultural complexity in organizations: The value and limitations of qualitative methodology and approaches. In *International Handbook of Organizational Culture and Climate*, pp. 143–163 (Cooper, C.L., Cartwright, S. & Earley, P.C., eds). New York: John Wiley and Sons.

Saks, A.M. & Ashforth, B.E. (1997). Organizational socialization: Making sense of the past and present as a prologue for the future. *Journal of Vocational Behaviour*, **51**(2), 234–279.

Sambrook, S. (2005). Exploring succession planning in small, growing firms. *Journal of Small Business and Enterprise Development*, **12**(4), 579–594.

Santora, J., Clemens, R. & Sarros, J. (1997). Views from the top: Foundation CEOs look at leadership succession. *Leadership and Organization Development Journal*, **18**(2), 108–115.

Saura, I., Contri, G., Taulet, A. & Velázquez , B. (2005). Relationships among customer orientation, service orientation and job satisfaction in financial services. *International Journal of Service Industry Management*, **16**(5), 497–525.

Schein, E.H. (1985). *Organizational Culture and Leadership*. San Francisco, CA: Jossey Bass.

Schmidt, F.L. & Hunter, J.E. (1983). Individual differences in productivity: An empirical test of estimates derived from studies of selection procedure utility. *Journal of Applied Psychology*, **68**(3), 407–414.

Seippel, Ø. (2002). Volunteers and professionals in Norwegian sport organizations. *Voluntas: International Journal of Voluntary and Nonprofit Organizations*, **13**(3), 253–269.

Senge, P. (1990). *The Dance of Change: The Challenges of Sustaining Momentum in Learning Organizations*. New York: Doubleday.

Shea, G.F. (1999). *Making the Most of Being Mentored: How to Grow from a Mentoring Relationship*. Menlo Park, CA: Crisp Publications.

Sheridan, J.E. (1992). Organizational culture and employee retention. *Academy of Management Journal*, **35**(5), 1036–1056.

Silverthorne, C. (2004). The impact of organizational culture and person-organization fit on organizational commitment and job satisfaction in Taiwan. *Leadership and Organization Development Journal*, **25**(7/8), 592–599.

Sisley, B.L. (1990). A time to network – how to assist yourself and others. *Journal of Physical Education, Recreation and Dance*, **61**(3), 61–65.

Slack, T. & Parent, M.M. (2006). *Understanding Sport Organizations: The Application of Organization Theory*, 2nd edn. Champaign, IL: Human Kinetics.

Smart, D.L. & Wolfe, R.A. (2000). Examining sustainable competitive advantage in intercollegiate athletics: A resource-based view. *Journal of Sport Management*, **14**, 133–153.

Smith, A. & Shilbury, D. (2004). Mapping cultural dimensions in Australian sporting organizations. *Sport Management Review*, **7**(2), 133–165.

Smucker, M.K. & Kent, A. (2004a). The influence of referent selection on pay, promotion, supervision, work, and co-worker satisfaction across three distinct sport industry segments. *International Sports Journal*, **8**(1), 27–43.

Smucker, M.K. & Kent, A. (2004b). Job satisfaction and referent comparisons in the sport industry. *International Journal of Sport Management and Marketing*, **5**(3), 262–280.

Steel, R. & Ovalle, N. (1984). Self-appraisal based on supervisor feedback. *Personnel Psychology*, **37**(4), 667–685.

Storey, J. (2001). *Human Resource Management: A Critical Text*, 2nd edn. London: Thomson Learning.

Suffield, L. (2005). *Labour Relations*. Toronto: Pearson Education Canada.

Taylor, T. & Ho, C. (2005). Global human resource management influences on local sport organisations. *International Journal of Sport Management and Marketing*, **1**(1/2), 110–126.

Taylor, T. & McGraw, P. (2004). Succession management practices in Australian organisations. *International Journal of Manpower*, **25**(8), 741–758.

Taylor, T. & McGraw, P. (2006). Exploring human resource management practices in non-profit sport organisations. *Sport Management Review*, **9**(3), 229–251.

Taylor, T., Watt, B. & Bennett, A. (2004). Strategic development of organisational talent: The use of succession management approaches. In *Australian Master Human Resources Guide*, 2nd edn., pp. 1099–1120. Sydney: CCH.

Taylor, T., Darcy, S., Hoye, R. & Cuskelly, G. (2006). Using psychological contract theory to explore issues in effective volunteer management. *European Sport Management Quarterly*, **6**(2), 123–148.

Thomas, D. & Dyall, L. (1999). Culture, ethnicity and sport management: A New Zealand perspective. *Sport Management Review*, **2**(2), 115–132.

Thompson, A.A.J. & Strickland, A.J.I. (1998). *Strategic Management: Concepts and Cases*, 10th edn. Boston: Irwin McGraw-Hill.

Tichy, N., Fombrum, C. & Devanna, M.A. (1982). Strategic human resource management. *Sloan Management Review*, **23**(2), 47–61.

Torrington, D. (1989). Human resource management and the personnel function. In *New Perspectives on Human Resource Management*, pp. 56–66 (Storey, J., ed.). London: Routledge.

Torrington, D. & Hall, L. (1998). *Human Resource Management*, 4th edn. London: Prentice-Hall.

Tosi, H.L., Mero, N.P. & Rizzo, J.R. (2000). *Managing Organizational Behaviour*, 4th edn. Maiden, MA: Blackwell Publishers Inc.

Van Maanen, J. (1976). Breaking in: Socialization to work. In *Handbook of Work, Organization, and Society*, pp. 67–130 (Dubin, R., ed.). Chicago, IL: Rand-McNally.

Van Maanen, J. & Schein, E. (1979). Towards a theory of organizational socialization. In *Research in Organizational Behavior*, pp. 209–264 (Staw, B.M., ed.). Greenwich, CT: JAI Press.

Veale, D.J. & Wachtel, J.M. (1996). Mentoring and coaching as part of a human resource development strategy: An example at coca-cola foods. *Management Development Review*, **9**(6), 19–24.

Volunteer Canada. (2006). The Canadian code for volunteer involvement. Ottawa: Volunteer Canada.

Volunteering Australia. (2003). Volunteer rights and volunteer checklist. Retrieved 6 April 2007, from http://www.volunteeringaustralia.org/files/VMJRV6JZMW/Volunteer%20Rights%20and%20Checklist.pdf

Vroom, V.H. (1964). *Work and Motivation*. New York: Wiley.

Wanous, J.P. & Colella, A. (1989). Organizational entry research: Current status and future directions. In *Research in Personnel and Human Resources Management*, Vol. 7, pp. 59–120 (Ferris, G.R. & Rowlands, K.M., eds). Greenwich, CT: JAI Press.

Ward, D. (1996). Workforce demand forecasting techniques. *Human Resource Planning*, **19**(1), 54–55.

Ward, D., Bechet, T.P. & Trip, R. (1994). *Human Resource Forecasting and Modeling*. New York: Human Resource Planning Society.

References

Watson, T. (1977). *The Personnel Managers: A Study in the Sociology of Work and Industry*. London: Routledge and Keegan Paul.

Watt, B., Bennett, A. & Taylor, T. (2004). Career planning and development. In *Human Resources Guide*, pp. 371–384 (Redden, J. & Martin, G., eds). Sydney: CCH Australia Ltd.

Weaver, M. & Chelladurai, P. (2002). Mentoring in intercollegiate athletic administration. *Journal of Sport Management*, **16**(2), 96–116.

Weiner, N. (1997). *Making Cultural Diversity Work*. Scarborough, ON: Carswell, Thompson Professional Publishing.

Whitmore, J. (2004). *Coaching for Performance: Growing People, Performance, and Purpose*, 3rd edn. London: Nicholas Brealey Publishing.

Wolfe, R., Wright, P.M. & Smart, D.L. (2006). Radical HRM innovation and competitive advantage: The moneyball story. *Human Resource Management Journal*, **45**(1), 111–145.

Wright, A.D. (2000). Scenario planning: A continuous improvement approach to strategy. *Total Quality Management*, **11**(4–6), 433–438.

Wright, P.M. & McMahon, G.C. (1992). Theoretical perspective for strategic human resource management. *Journal of Management*, **18**(2), 295–320.

Subject index

Author index

Author index